WOMEN OF THE RIGHT

EDITED BY **KATHLEEN M. BLEE AND SANDRA McGEE DEUTSCH**

WOMEN OF THE RIGHT

Comparisons and Interplay Across Borders

The Pennsylvania State University Press
University Park, Pennsylvania

Part 2 pg 132

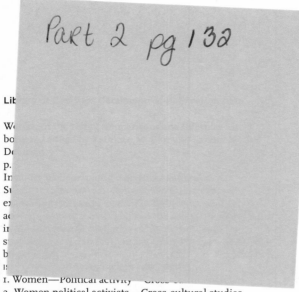

Lib

W
bo
De
p.
In
Su
ex
ac
in
s
b
i

1. Women—Political activity— Cross-cu
2. Women political activists—Cross-cultural studies.
3. Women conservatives—Cross-cultural studies.
I. Blee, Kathleen M.
II. Deutsch, Sandra McGee, 1950– .

HQ1236.W63855   2012
320.52082—dc23
2011031329

CONTENTS

ACKNOWLEDGMENTS

The editors thank Kelsy Burke, Amy McDowell, and Marie Skoczylas of the University of Pittsburgh for assistance in the preparation of the manuscript and Ashley Currier of Texas A&M University and Julia Schiavone Camacho of the University of Texas at El Paso for comments on an earlier draft of the introductory essay. We also thank William Durrer for his suggestions and computer expertise. Finally, we express our appreciation to the Dr. and Mrs. W. H. Timmons Professorship of Borderlands History at the University of Texas at El Paso for providing funds for translation.

ABBREVIATIONS

ACVV	Afrikaanse Christelike Vroue Vereniging
AIB	Brazilian Integralist Action
AMAC	Association of Women of Catholic Action
AQI	Al-Qaeda in Iraq
BJP	Indian People's Party
BPW	Business and Professional Women
CAMDE	Brazilian Women's Campaign for Democracy
CBLPI	Clare Boothe Luce Policy Institute
CD	Centrum Democrats
CEDAW	Committee on the Elimination of Discrimination Against Women
CGT	General Confederation of Workers
CPUSA	Communist Party of the United States
CRC	Civil Rights Congress
CSW	Commission on the Status of Women
CWA	Concerned Women for America
DAR	Daughters of the American Revolution
DWM	December Women's Movement
ECOSOC	Economic and Social Council
ERA	Equal Rights Amendment
FBI	Federal Bureau of Investigation
FMF	Feminist Majority Foundation
FN	Front National
FNSL	Front National Second Life
GJM	global jihadi movement
HT	Hizb ut-Tahrir
HUAC	House Committee on Un-American Activities
ICTY	International Criminal Tribunal of the Former Yugoslavia
IWF	Independent Women's Forum
IYC	International Year of the Child
JBS	John Birch Society
JI	Jamaah Islamiyah
JUL	Yugoslav United Left
KKK	Ku Klux Klan

LT	Lashkar-i-Tayyabia
MRND	Mouvement Républicain National pour la Démocratie et le Développement
NAACP	National Association for the Advancement of Colored People
NAOWS	National Association Opposed to Woman Suffrage
NASW	National Association of Social Workers
NB	Netherlands Blok
NCBW	National Congress of Black Women
NeW	Network of enlightened Women
NFRW	National Federation of Republican Women
NOW	National Organization for Women
NP	National Party
NSDAP	Nationalsozialistische Deutsche Arbeiterpartei
NVP	Nasionale Vroue Party
NVU	Dutch People's Union
NWPC	National Women's Political Caucus
OEF	Overseas Education Fund
OFS	Orange Free State
PAC	political action committee
PNDC	Provisional National Defense Council
PTA	Parent Teacher Association
RSS	Rashtriya Svayamsak Sangh
SDS	Serbian Democratic Party
SK-PJ	League of Communists—Movement for Yugoslavia
SL	Second Life
SPS	Socialist Party of Serbia
SRS	Serbian Radical Party
TAN	transnational advocacy network
UFCM	Unión Femenina Católica Mexicana
UOT	Textile Worker Union
VHP	World Hindu Council
VNP	Vroue Nasionale Party
VTVPA	Victims of Trafficking and Violence Protection Act
WIN	Women's Information Network
WJCC	Women's Joint Congressional Committee
WKKK	Women of the Ku Klux Klan
WPCND	Women's Patriotic Conference on National Defense
WPPC	Woman Patriot Publishing Company

Kathleen M. Blee and Sandra McGee Deutsch

This book grew out of a workshop we facilitated at the 2008 Berkshire Conference on the History of Women to stimulate dialogue among scholars working on women's right-wing activism in a variety of times and places and from different disciplinary perspectives. It certainly did so. Scholars writing in a number of locations on diverse topics found that they were wrestling with similar questions and problems. This volume builds on the intellectual energy of the Berkshire Conference, bringing together revised and expanded papers from workshop participants with research by other scholars across the globe who are exploring the tensions, contradictions, and implications of gender on the political right.

We open this volume by situating these essays in the recent history of scholarship on right-wing women. It was only twenty-five years ago that research on the right almost exclusively focused on men, as ideas of gender dualism established men as the only political actors. Right-wing women were simply overlooked or considered unimportant; certainly, they were not considered active agents in the construction of right-wing ideology or the mobilization of right-wing movements or parties. This has now changed. A booming literature on right-wing women has proven conclusively that rightist activism has almost never been the sole province of men.

The first wave of work in this field, including our own research on women in the United States and Latin America, respectively, addressed basic issues such as how and where women participated in the right. This scholarship showed that women were involved in a variety of right-wing groups and efforts, including those that favored racism, fascism, right-wing terrorism, religious conservatism, and the suppression of labor militancy.[1] It also made clear that right-wing politics were gendered beyond the mere fact of women's participation. Early studies found that many right-wing efforts were deeply committed to a hierarchical, gendered division of social life. Women who participated in rightist politics were often relegated to tasks and roles that their male counterparts regarded as minor or distinctly feminine, such as socializing children into right-wing ideas or providing food for rightist events.

This volume also builds on a series of edited collections that introduced a more comparative wave of scholarship. Some of these compendia examined women who were situated in different sectors of the right, while others juxtaposed essays on rightist and leftist women. All plumbed the relationships between different shades of right and feminism, demonstrating that women's organizing does not necessarily take a feminist form, even though rightists and feminists have occasionally worked together for specific causes. A number of these works also expanded the geographical scope of studies of right-wing women beyond the Americas and Western Europe.[2]

An influential volume that appeared in 2002 featured studies of women on the right throughout the world. Despite the quite heterogeneous forms of right-wing politics represented in the articles, the book's editors, Paola Bacchetta and Margaret Power, pointed to certain commonalities. One was that women are agents in a variety of movements in India, Africa, the Middle East, and Australia, suggesting that such activism is broader than the global North or West. Second, the disparate cases in Bacchetta and Power's compendium suggest gender essentialism and a dualistic sense of public and private spheres on the right. The authors associate women in rightist movements with private, less visible, and often subordinated aspects of daily life and politics, while identifying the public, visible, and dominant aspects as reserved for men. Right-wing politics, Bacchetta and Power noted, often advance traditional arrangements of women's subordination and men's authority, even though women may pursue these goals in public, assertive, and aggressive ways that are antithetical to notions of women's proper place. Finally, Bacchetta and Power observed that rightist women differ in their relationship to feminism. Some support women's empowerment as a means to other goals, such as white supremacism or state power. Others vehemently oppose any moves toward social equity, including women's rights.[3]

The scholars in our volume take another step toward a global understanding of right-wing women by addressing three interrelated issues about political boundaries. The focus of part 1, "Transnational and Comparative Studies," is how right-wing ideas circulate among women across boundaries of space. Building on the knowledge that women's right-wing activism is vital in many areas across the globe, these essays bring to light issues that go unnoticed in studies of a single place. Some emphasize comparison, looking at similarities and differences among women rightists within nations and across the borders of nations and continents. Others focus on transnational flows, exploring how rightist discourse and practices travel back and forth across spatial boundaries.[4]

The second focus of this volume is the intricacies of the boundary between public and private that earlier scholars identified as a significant dimension of right-wing politics. Rather than assuming that this binary is a constant in women's right-wing politics, the essays in part 2, "Privatizing the Public, Politicizing the Private," probe the origins and permeability of the line between the two. They show that right-wing women can transgress, even erase, such borders as well as uphold them.

The volume's final focus is the boundaries of ideology. The essays in part 3, "Countering the Left," explore how women's right-wing politics interact with leftist and feminist ideas and practices. Although scholars have often understood the right as a counterforce, characterized more by what it opposes than what it advocates, the relationship between the right and other ideological tendencies is not straightforward, monolithic, or timeless. This is also true for right-wing women's politics. These essays address this complexity by looking in detail at how women along the rightist spectrum position themselves vis-à-vis progressive movements in different times and places around the world, thus complicating the binary and boundaries of left and right.

The articles gathered in this volume demonstrate the new reach of scholarship on right-wing women. More than half address the period from 1945 to the present, the rest focusing on the earlier twentieth century. As we discuss below, these chapters introduce themes, directions, and questions that will carry scholarship into the next decade and beyond. Each part is organized chronologically to highlight changes over time in women's participation on the right. From a variety of scholarly disciplines and with differing geographic concentrations, the authors create a global perspective that shows how women matter in the national and transnational "connections and interactions" of rightist politics.[5]

In the remainder of this section, we introduce the themes of the three parts. The overview of each part is prefaced with a personal reflection, situating our earlier studies of U.S. racist and South American radical right women in the evolving scholarship of right-wing women to highlight the significant changes of emphases and frameworks in this body of research. As we present the essays in each part, we also suggest parallels to cases in other parts to underscore comparisons and interplay that occur throughout the volume's studies of right-wing women's activism in different local and national settings and times.

Part 1: Transnational and Comparative Studies

Kathleen M. Blee:
I did not fully realize the importance of international dimensions of women's rightist activism when I began to study women in U.S. racist movements, including those in the massive Ku Klux Klan (KKK) of the 1920s and the modern neo-

Nazi, white power skinhead, KKK, and white supremacist groups.[6] When I started this research in the mid-1980s, feminist studies had made it possible to understand racist women as more than political nonentities or auxiliaries to men's political movements. Indeed, the half-million or more white, native-born, Protestant women who poured into the Women of the Ku Klux Klan (WKKK) in the early 1920s were significant actors in that decade's massive crusade of racial and religious bigotry. These Klanswomen not only embraced white supremacism, anti-Semitism, and anti-Catholicism like Klansmen but challenged their male counterparts for control over Klan money, ideas, and organizations. A feminist lens also allowed me to ask whether women might organize racial and religious bigotry differently than did men. Again, in the 1920s they certainly did. WKKK members argued that supremacist ideas were essential to guarantee the rights of (white, native-born, Protestant) women against the exploitative and predatory behavior of African American, Jewish, and Catholic men.

Despite a feminist perspective that facilitated an understanding of women as political actors, U.S. sociological scholarship in the 1980s was largely American-centric, and mine was no exception. Lacking a global perspective in which to situate U.S. racist movements, I focused my studies of racist women exclusively within that nation. I did not explore the circulation of white supremacist or anti-Semitic ideas across borders or oceans, nor did I work to uncover practices and organizations in other countries that might have shaped how racist movements developed in the United States. This myopic focus was also consistent with the way that racist activists in the United States portrayed themselves, at least until the turn of the twenty-first century. The KKK of the 1920s was fiercely nationalistic, declaring that it was "100 percent American" in its aims and its membership. Racist groups in the 1980s and early 1990s were likewise intensely nationalistic, seeking to build their membership through xenophobic attacks on immigrants and foreigners.

In retrospect, an analytic framework so tightly focused on the United States seems parochial and limited. Global perspectives that situate the United States within a broader context—in the flow rather than necessarily at the center of the transnational movement of ideas, people, and institutions—can open new ways of looking at the right in a single country. The ideas of nationalism, racism, and even women's rights that the Klan seized on in the 1920s were not locally born. Rather, the vast migrations of people across oceans and within continents in the early decades of the twentieth century created a transnational circulation of ideas that influenced even the Klan's "100 percent American" racism.

A global lens is now even more pressing for understanding the modern racist movement, which is linked internationally through new technologies of communication. Among U.S. racists, ideologies of nationalism have declined significantly. Many racist activists now seek to form pan-Aryan alliances against Jews and persons of color across the globe. Forging such international coalitions is difficult for the far right, which has traditionally shunned them, as several chapters in this volume show. Yet, clearly, the future direction of organized U.S. racism is global.

Scholarship by those committed to understanding, and stopping, racist movements must be similarly global.

This volume opens with three chapters that focus specifically on the transnational aspects of women's right-wing activism, taking up the challenge to understand the "connections and interactions" of such movements. Each examines the flow of right-wing ideas and the connections across national borders in a different setting and raises provocative new issues about the role of women in transnational rightist efforts.

In a study of anticommunist women in Brazil, Chile, and the United States in the 1960s and 1970s, Margaret Power notes that the ideas and strategies of the right do not only flow across borders in one direction, from the global North to the South, as commonly assumed in research on the transnational diffusion of social movements. Rather, as she shows in the chapter "Transnational Connections Among Right-Wing Women," rightist ideologies and information also traveled from Brazil to Chile and from Latin America to the United States. Anticommunist women activists in Chile looked to their counterparts in Brazil for inspiration and ideas as they worked to overthrow the democratic leftist government of Salvador Allende. Similarly, anticommunist women in the United States sought counsel from Latin American women rightists in their own struggle against what they saw as communist influences in the government and society. Until recently, scholars have not looked for evidence of such transnational cooperation, not only because it involved women but also because it went against the assumption that conservatives and antileftists are insular and uninterested in advice from or contacts with activists abroad. Power's study as well as later essays by Nancy Aguirre and Karla Cunningham show that this was not necessarily the case. Having experienced the Mexican Revolution firsthand, women contributors to the right-wing newspaper *La Prensa* in Texas sought to convince readers across the border to oppose it. Similarly, Islamist ideas that circulate within the Muslim world have politicized women.

Jill A. Irvine's study of the Concerned Women for America (CWA) in "Exporting the Culture Wars" points out that transnationalism exists on many levels, but right-wing activists may not seek to operate on every level. Organized in 1979, the CWA participates in global campaigns such as those against international trafficking in women and girls, but it is still somewhat reluctant to build alliances with similar groups in other nations. Since right-wing movements like the CWA generally support nationalism and are suspicious of internationalism, it is difficult for them to form the global networks that would make a worldwide rightist movement possible. Indeed, this may be a general weakness for rightist movements that seek to act on a global stage, as seen also in a later chapter by Kathleen Blee and Annette Linden on the xenophobic, extreme right movements of Europe and the United States.

Yet, as Power finds, transnational influence can shape nationalist movements, even when they do not formally link themselves to nationalists in
other countries. Transnationalism, these works and others in this volume
suggest, operates through global institutions and mass media as well as personal networks.

The circulation of ideas within and among religious-based transnational
networks—in Irvine's case, the anti-trafficking campaigns supported by the
CWA, Catholics, and Muslims—is not unique. The Catholic Church itself
is a transnational network. In the early twentieth century, Catholic notions
of women's domesticity circulated among the faithful in many countries,
including Argentina, as Mariela Rubinzal shows later in this volume. Writers
and activists adapted and spread such ideas in pursuit of right-wing goals in
Argentina and elsewhere.

Moreover, transnationalism does not even require geographic movement,
as Randolph Hollingsworth reminds us in "Memoirs of an Avatar." In the
twenty-first century, people move across borders, oceans, nations, and time
in the virtual worlds of the Internet such as Second Life, forming connections and interacting with others in a rapid and fluid way. They can do so to
relax and satisfy a curiosity. But they can also experiment with rightist ideas
and ways of being that they would otherwise never experience. The avatars of
Second Life can take any form, thereby striking at the stable identities of race,
ethnicity, and gender that are key to mobilizing women into the right, as
shown, for example, in the later chapter by Kathleen Fallon and Julie Moreau
on women's involvement in ethnic violence in Rwanda. Fascist and racist
sites in this virtual world allow people to try on new rightist identities and
"perform" in ways that transcend their fixed earthly identities. Fantasy and
image easily blur with ideology and message in right-wing virtual life. In the
evolving world of computer-mediated communications, what we know about
right-wing women's activism in the "real," embodied world may be upended.
It may be that women are not mobilized into the right by leaders and groups
but are provided a space in which to enact a political self that is otherwise
unavailable or stigmatized.

The next three chapters in part 1 explore women's right-wing activism in
a comparative framework by examining differences and similarities among
rightist activists, ideas, and campaigns across countries. Such comparisons
bring to light aspects of women's rightist politics that are difficult to perceive
in single-nation studies. Among these are varying styles of mobilization and
problems of categorization.

In their comparative study of women's activism in sub-Saharan Africa in
the 1980s and 1990s, "Righting Africa?," Kathleen Fallon and Julie Moreau
argue that dualisms of left and right are imprecise in some contexts, as the
very concept of "right-wing" may be tied to political structures that do not
exist cross-nationally. They maintain that the notion of a political right assumes a society with contending political parties, a stable state, and a demo-

cratic process, none of which are firmly in place in the countries they examine. In Ghana, Nigeria, Kenya, Malawi, and other nations in sub-Saharan Africa, they observe, dictators create state-run women's organizations to generate support for their ruling regimes. Women's participation in these organizations does not fit the traditional Western model of political rightism, but, as in the Brazilian and Chilean women's groups studied by Power, it serves to bolster military and authoritarian governance. As also observed in subsequent chapters, some women's activism in sub-Saharan Africa takes the form of setting boundaries between groups, a process that involves the effort of "Othering" those who are different. Cataclysmic violence can result from Othering, as Fallon and Moreau show in their depiction of the key players in Rwanda. Even this process, they argue, takes place against the background of military dictatorships, which give women little choice but to participate in order to survive.

Karla Cunningham's multinational comparison of Muslim women's movements in "Gender, Islam, and Conservative Politics" highlights the wide diversity of ideas and tactics that have operated within conservative Islam in the last several decades and how these travel across and within nations. Arising as a defense against Western secular influence and a response to authoritarian states, conservative Islamic groups created an alternative public space for women as well as men. Despite the strictures that some Islamic movements have placed on women, Cunningham shows that the movements have also provided opportunities for women from highly traditional families to be politically active in public life. Contrary to the common assumption that the right wing embraces religion and the left wing does not, this essay shows that religious ideas and practices cut across ideological lines in Muslim societies. Echoing Fallon and Moreau's conclusion about sub-Saharan Africa, Cunningham notes that it is impossible to clearly categorize Islamist movements as completely left or right in orientation.

By comparing Dutch and U.S. women in the far right from the 1990s to the present, Kathleen Blee and Annette Linden show that women enter and experience right-wing activism differently depending on whether they affiliate with a rightist political party or a less structured right-wing group. In "Women in Extreme Right Parties and Movements," Blee and Linden report on their life history interviews with women in the far right in both the Netherlands and the United States, a method that allows them to capture the point of view of the activists themselves. Women in Dutch parties talk of coming into extreme right politics through a personal tie to a party member, generally a man. Women in U.S. racist movements, in contrast, talk about sliding into these movements and groups on their own, a process that resembles the casual flirtation with far-right ideas in the virtual world of Second Life that Hollingsworth describes. In each case, women express a lack of planned intent in their transition to the radical right.

Part 2: Privatizing the Public, Politicizing the Private

Sandra McGee Deutsch:

In 1977, when I began to study South American radical right-wing groups, I was surprised to find that women had been active in them. Few works had appeared on rightist women anywhere in the world. I found that rightist ideologues, who constructed their movements as masculine, drew rigid distinctions between the domestic and public arenas and assigned women to the former. Given these ideas, why did they recruit women, and how did they justify the intrusion of women in the masculine public realm? The answers lay in their views of family. "The family was the tiny fatherland; the fatherland was the large family," proclaimed a Brazilian rightist leader in 1920.[7] The strength of the nation relied on the strength of the family, which in turn depended on women. It was precisely their roles in the home that made women's involvement in rightist movements vital.

With hindsight I see that the notion of the family as a microcosm of society called into question the boundaries between the two, between private and public. So did cases of rightist women who stepped outside their usual sphere and of right-wing men who accepted their trespasses. According to many rightists, women's duties in their groups did not defy domesticity but rather extended it, because they resembled the tasks that women fulfilled in households, schools, and churches. Yet women in the Brazilian fascist Ação Integralista Brasileira (Brazilian Integralist Action) in the 1930s wore military-style uniforms, marched in the streets, and occasionally appeared at scenes of bloodshed. Were they stretching the private sphere to its limits or entering the public sphere of political activism and violence? Or was it permissible for women to assume these traits and actions under extreme circumstances, as long as they shed them when the crisis ended and did not threaten male control?[8]

Extreme rightists believed that women had to enter politics precisely to protect the family from leftism and other nefarious forces; if they did not do so, the family could vanish, and with it women's treasured roles and affective relationships. Just as the Bolsheviks had carried out the revolution of the proletariat, Integralists intended to carry out the revolution of the family, thereby restoring, strengthening, and elevating it. Thus, Brazilian fascists blurred the lines between family and politics, private and public. The separate spheres were, in fact, inseparable.

The chapters in part 2 further develop these ideas, particularly by demonstrating women's agency. Describing the onslaughts on individuality and leisure time in fascist regimes, Robert Paxton observed that the fascist redrawing of boundaries between private and public virtually erased the former.[9] He implied that men were responsible, yet as this section shows, rightist women have also redrawn such borders. Some have made private concerns public by using particular views of family and femininity to advance a political agenda. Others have sought to influence government control over intimate lives. Many have favored violence and political militancy in public spaces to main-

tain the bourgeois family model. And rightist women have not always adhered to the domestic-style activities of helpmate, teacher, and charity giver;
as Blee and Linden's study of neo-Nazi women in the Netherlands and the
United States shows, some have assumed the male public duties of formulat-
ing and spreading ideology and participating in paramilitary actions.

In "Maternalism Goes to War," Kate Hallgren describes a number of well-
off U.S. women who promoted conscription during World War I. Disseminating their views through magazine articles and letters to politicians and
newspapers, these Spartan mothers explained their support for the military
draft in terms of their relationships with their sons, making public what is
usually private. This linkage of intimate matters with political goals, seen
also in the Better Life Program of Nigeria's dictatorial government that Fallon and Moreau detail, broke down the barriers between the two spheres.
Hallgren shows how women, acting as ideologues and publicists, helped construct and performed "patriotic motherhood." The aim of spreading the casualties beyond privileged white youths was the underlying reason for why
these women favored the draft. The desire to safeguard their class against
perceived threats from immigrants, and the conservative implications of patriotic motherhood, contributed to the nativism, anticommunist hysteria,
and decline of women's reformism of the postwar era that Kirsten Delegard
describes later in the volume.

The supporters of conscription were not the only women in this book who
deployed motherhood and domesticity to justify war, racism, or ethnocen-
trism. Focusing on the 1920s, Louise Vincent notes in "From Suffrage to
Silence" that Afrikaner nationalists in South Africa politicized the private by
recognizing the political significance of women's roles in reproducing the
community, a process also found in the Islamist movements that Cunningham studies. They envisioned women as mothers of the emerging Afrikaner
nation as well as of the family. Indeed, the nation was the home writ large;
there was no separation between public and private. Yet men justified wom-
en's involvement by claiming that it was not political; instead, its goal was to
realize the divinely ordained project of Afrikaner nationhood. One factor that
threatened this objective was the concern that impoverished Afrikaners might
mix with blacks. Afrikaner nationalist women addressed this perceived problem by aiding the poor and working to integrate them into the Afrikaner
community.

As Vincent shows, policing borders between one's ethnic group and the
racialized Other has been an important activity for rightist women. Various
authors in this volume discuss how these women have reinforced the lines
between white and black in South Africa and the United States; aristocrats
and immigrants in the United States; Jews and non-Jews in Germany and
Argentina; Hutus and Tutsis in Rwanda; and non-Muslims and Muslims in
the former Yugoslavia, India, and the Netherlands. This policing has taken
place in the public arena of party politics, internecine conflict, and published

writings. It has also occurred in the more intimate spaces of households, neighborhoods, and women's groups. Thus, it too blurs public and private.

Rather than exclude the Other, some rightist women themselves were the Other. In "Porfirista Femininity in Exile," Nancy Aguirre explains how the *ricas* (rich women) of San Antonio, Texas, in the early twentieth century defended their status in the face of discrimination. As supporters of President Porfirio Díaz (1876–1911), they and their families left Mexico when the Revolution—which they bitterly opposed—removed him from power. In Mexico they belonged to the upper class; in the United States they enjoyed prestige in the barrio but experienced prejudice outside it. Their page in *La Prensa* exalted Catholicism, Parisian couture, domesticity, and whiteness. Few Mexican American women, however, could dress elegantly, afford a leisurely life at home, or claim European culture and appearance. Over time the page embraced modernity and some local customs by voicing approval of flappers and women's suffrage. Support for women's education indicated the ricas' vision for uplifting women in their beleaguered community; advertisements for skin bleach suggested its limits. Still, the ricas claimed spaces for their less privileged compatriots. "Porfirian femininity" in the United States expressed a rightist class agenda and politicized the private sphere, yet it also represented resistance to marginalization.

Daniella Sarnoff explains in "Domesticating Fascism" how the French fascist leagues in the 1920s and 1930s placed women and the family squarely in the center of their concerns, not at the margins as some scholars have claimed was true for fascism as a whole. Echoing contemporaries in the United States, South Africa, and Argentina, as described by Mariela Rubinzal in part 3, they considered the private to be of utmost significance and therefore politicized it. Fascist gender ideology did not mean keeping women in the home, leaving men as the sole occupiers of the public arena. In fact, women marched in the name of maternalism and domesticity; advocating the private within the public sphere brought the two together. The attention paid to cooking, fashion, and other household matters in the women's sections of fascist newspapers reflected the "domestication" or privatization of fascism. Was there a separation between the peaceful private domain of fascist women and the sometimes brutal masculine public face? The "domestic was political," and fascists had to protect it, through combat if necessary. By at least implicitly accepting this stance, women shared responsibility for violence and normalized it within the context of familial life.

Working with the racialist National Socialist regime, and sometimes even surpassing it in zeal, German Aryan housewives normalized repression more blatantly than French fascist women. As housekeepers of the home and society, they rid their abodes of dirt and their neighborhoods of perceived enemies of Nazism. As Vandana Joshi shows in "The Volksgemeinschaft and Its Female Denouncers in the Third Reich," women complained to the Gestapo about the people closest to them, denouncing their husbands as sexually diseased and subversive and their in-laws and neighbors as Jews. The government may have redrawn the boundaries between public and private to the benefit of the former; driven by vindictiveness and class resentment, however, women further chipped away at the latter. They politicized the private sphere by inviting government intrusion into the family and making one's "private life public," in Hallgren's words—putting domestic problems on public view and labeling private behavior treasonous. They also privatized the public sphere by using the regime to avenge themselves on their spouses and neighbors. The blurring of private and public affected men as well as women. Silenced by the regime in public spaces, men criticized it at home. The state and its women allies, however, extended the tentacles of hatred into domestic space, which could no longer serve as a refuge.

In part 3, Kirsten Delegard shows how free-market conservative U.S. women in the 1920s contrasted sharply with the Nazi housewives. Opposed to official health and welfare programs, these activists argued that women and children should rely on men for support instead of the government. They sought to exclude rather than invite government involvement in the private sphere.

Despite the passage of time, many rightist women continue to politicize maternity. Hindu nationalist women in recent years have cast themselves as mothers of a nation supposedly threatened by Muslims. Thus, as Meera Sehgal demonstrates in "Mothering the Nation," motherhood stretches across the public/private divide. Samiti ideologues portray Hindu women as strong figures through their identification with Mother India, an image that contrasts with male views of Hindu women as possible targets of Muslim men. They have also reinvented Hindu "tradition" to justify women's participation in the public sphere. Despite their subordinate status within a male-dominated movement, these activists have expanded the boundaries of behavior considered acceptable for women. They travel long distances by themselves, engage in physical exercise, express anger in public (against Muslims), and even perform paramilitary duties. These Spartan mothers have encouraged their sons to attack Muslims; like Serbian rightist women in the 1990s, discussed by Carol Lilly and Jill Irvine in part 3, they praise such behavior as truly masculine. Indeed, they have privatized the public ideology by normalizing hatred of the ethnic/religious Other in their homes and women's circles.

Part 3: Countering the Left

Sandra McGee Deutsch:
Argentine, Brazilian, and Chilean rightist organizations of the years 1890 to 1939 contested the left in the shape of unions, communism, socialism, anarchism, and feminism. Men did so by attacking union and leftist militants, as well as con-

structing and expressing ideas that favored class conciliation over class conflict and nationalism over Marxist and anarchist internationalism. The question I sought to answer was how women in these groups countered the left. Did their practices differ markedly from those of men?

As I saw it at the time, there was a gender-based division of duties. Women in the Liga Patriótica Argentina (Argentine Patriotic League, which arose in 1919 and still exists) disseminated piety, obedience, the work ethic, and loyalty to the nation, the given order, and the bourgeois family—all explicitly antileftist—in social programs and schools they created for immigrant working-class women and children. While their male cohorts fought laborers, women tried to attract them by showing them that they could improve their lives in small yet tangible ways under capitalism.[10]

Twenty-odd years later in Brazil, Integralist women countered leftists and reformers in ways that resembled yet also differed from those of their precursors. They, too, participated in philanthropic endeavors to model a future society that, they claimed, would genuinely help the poor and end class warfare. Opposing the libertine sexuality and the destruction of familial bonds supposedly fostered by communism, Integralists worked to strengthen the Christian patriotic family. Now that literate women exercised suffrage, Integralist women taught members to read so they could vote for the movement's candidates, who included a few women. They also reworked feminist ideas, insisting that they stood for a "rational feminism" that was truly Christian and Brazilian. Not restricted to philanthropy, women served as ideologues, candidates, and occasionally combatants, roles resembling those of men. I now can see that what I had regarded as a dual gendered strategy against the left—suppressive and co-optative—was becoming a single intertwined one. These findings suggest the complex patterns of rightist engagement with leftism, whose definition has evolved according to the context.

As the chapters in part 3 demonstrate, countering the left has meant appropriating, reshaping, and subtly entangling with elements of the rival doctrines, as well as confronting them. U.S. rightist white women denounced welfare legislation in the 1920s and feminism in 2008, while Argentine Nationalists and Catholics in the 1930s criticized women's leftist militancy and participation in the labor force. A few African American women openly resisted civil rights in the 1950s to 1960s. In these cases, rightist women lambasted communism, progressive movements, and social change, although some of them obscured the differences between their views and those they opposed. After the Cold War, the lines between communism and the right blurred even further in the former Yugoslavia.

U.S. suffragists had thought that by acquiring the vote, women would be able to push through wide-ranging social welfare legislation. Instead, Kirsten Delegard shows in "'It Takes Women to Fight Women'" that conservative women, including opponents of women's suffrage, utilized their newfound political power to prevent such reforms in the 1920s. The Daughters of the

American Revolution (DAR) and other groups argued that proposed government aid to women and children constituted "state socialism" and tied it to the communist threat. These initiatives, they claimed, would sever women economically from their husbands, weaken parental authority, and in general destroy the family. Such efforts echoed Bolshevism, which rightist women insisted had promoted "free love" and "nationalized" women and children, just as it had nationalized private enterprises. State control of the family meant state control of property, and conservative women opposed both. They stymied welfare reforms by wielding electoral clout, drawing on women's networks, lobbying Congress, and spreading the politics of fear through their writings.

Their discourse strongly resembled that of the Argentines described by Mariela Rubinzal in "Women's Work in Argentina's Nationalist Lexicon, 1930–1943." In the 1930s, this country witnessed the accelerated entry of women into the industrial labor force, particularly into textile factories, where Communist unions were gaining strength. Radical rightist concerns about women working outside the home intertwined with their fears of leftism. As had U.S. conservative women in the 1920s, Nationalists and their Catholic allies conflated the decline of the patriarchal family with communism, further associating these perceived threats with Jews. Libertine Communists, in their view, were bent on demolishing the traditional family by implementing divorce, "free love," and women's legal equality with men. Men and women authors countered the left by extolling male rule in the household, decrying women's exploitation in the workplace and the double day, and condemning class warfare. Yet some rightists understood the need to create women's labor unions, carefully stripped of leftist ideology, to prevent women from joining those dominated by Communists or Socialists.

Rhetoric similar to that of the DAR and Argentine Nationalists permeated subsequent groups. Rightist women in Chile and Brazil in the 1960s prided themselves on rescuing the family from communism, notes Power, and their allies in the United States applauded them. Irvine explains how the Christian CWA criticized the United Nations and other international organizations for promoting "radical" efforts to undermine the family. After the Cold War, however, the CWA increasingly utilized global forums to spread its rigid gender notions, including opposition to feminism and sexual and reproductive freedom.

It was in the context of the Cold War that an African American undercover FBI informant, Julia Brown, publicly denounced the Communist Party, to which she had once belonged. In " 'To Tell All My People,' " Veronica A. Wilson shows that Brown had joined the party and the Civil Rights Congress, composed of liberals and Communists, believing that they stood for an integrated and racially just society. However, she eventually became convinced that these groups fomented dissatisfaction among blacks to serve their own ends and discriminated against them. After testifying against the party in

Congress in 1962, she became a spokesperson for the extreme rightist John Birch Society, in the process turning against civil rights. In numerous speeches, Brown denounced Martin Luther King Jr. and the movement as part of a communist conspiracy to weaken the nation. Denying police brutality against blacks, she instead claimed that African American radicals and even King were responsible for violence. Furthermore, she thought that the civil rights laws and War on Poverty of the 1960s promoted communism.

The women writers and activists of Mexican origin in San Antonio were another case of minority women who opposed the left, in the form of the Mexican Revolution. Yet these women, as Aguirre describes them, were hardly as extreme as Brown. Moreover, they favored a genuine lifting of minority status, unlike this Communist-turned-John-Bircher in her later years. In contrast, and more typical of the right, Hallgren's "patriotic mothers" during World War I were privileged white women who countered what they saw as an immigrant and proletarian threat to their class.

Extreme right-wing women leaders in the former Yugoslavia in the 1990s bore a more complex relationship to the left than the movements discussed thus far, as Carol Lilly and Jill A. Irvine demonstrate in "Leading the Nation." They sought to cleanse Serbian lands of the Muslim presence through violent words and deeds, thus overturning Communist policies that had aimed at uniting the various ethnic groups. The chief standard-bearer of chauvinistic nationalism, the ruling Socialist Party of Serbia (SPS), however, had Communist roots, as did one of the three women leaders described in this chapter. The SPS and other rightist parties, and especially their prominent women members, continued to embrace such leftist notions as gender equality. This stance opened spaces for women and enabled some of them to assume positions of power, although it did not lead to broad improvements for women. Partly owing to this rhetorical support for gender equality, Serbian nationalist women felt little need to display feminine softness in urging war on Muslims. Rightists also used their gender beliefs as a tool to distinguish their "modernity" from Muslim "backwardness." In some ways, then, they represented an insidious intertwining of left and right.

The line between left and right has also blurred elsewhere in recent decades, as Cunningham notes of Islamic movements. The same has been true for Africa, according to Fallon and Moreau. Hutu minister Pauline Nyiramasuhuko, an architect of genocide in Rwanda, fought the Tutsis because of their economic and social domination, which the Belgians had promoted. As radical ethnic chauvinists, Nyiramasuhuko and other Hutus opposed leftist notions of tolerance, yet an arguably leftist resistance to inequality and colonialism underlay their sentiments.

Rightists had little reason to fear Communists after the Berlin Wall fell in 1989, but, as seen in Irvine's chapter, other progressives took their place. Ronnee Schreiber, in "Dilemmas of Representation," explains how conservative women seized on Sarah Palin's vice presidential candidacy on the Republican Party ticket in 2008 as a means of countering feminism. Once unsure whether to promote the election of women to office, women rightists used their backing for Palin to claim that they, unlike "radical" and "elitist" feminists, truly represented ordinary women. They insisted that feminists were hypocritical and sexist because they opposed a viable woman candidate. Conservative women not only contested but also appropriated the mantle of feminism, trying to reshape it by incorporating individualist and free-market ideas. Although feminists claimed that conservatives sought to confine women to the home, the latter rejoined that homemakers' views should be represented in politics and that women's political activity was permissible if their families backed it. Epitomizing these notions and aided by her family, Palin was a "true feminist," asserted her women supporters. Conservative women also utilized Palin's candidacy to spread their restrictive notions on sexuality, which opposed those of feminists and resembled those of the DAR, Argentine Nationalists, and CWA.

Comparisons and Future Study

The comparisons among the studies in this collection demonstrate both that right-wing women's actions and ideologies can diverge in surprising ways and that they can share unexpected similarities. This tension between comparability and differences suggests that scholars of right-wing women need to attend to the local context of rightist mobilization and, at the same time, be attuned to how local contexts are shaped by transborder influences. We find three areas in which such local-global comparisons could be productive.

One is the change over time in global right-wing women's activism. As the above discussion shows, there has been a remarkable continuity in the themes of women's rightist activity through the years. Yet a comparison of the essays in this volume also suggests some important historical turning points. World War I ushered in waves of nationalism throughout the world and movements of patriotic motherhood in warring nations. Fascist regimes implemented gender policies long cherished by rightists, sometimes with results the latter had not imagined. The Cold War nurtured right-wing movements based on anticommunism and ended with heightened nationalism in many countries, along with new scapegoats and perceived enemies. The process of decolonization was accompanied by nationalist movements in Asia and Africa, some of which fueled militaristic governments that tilted to the right. The expansion of the Internet and mass communications has made possible new forms of transnational contact among rightists. Future scholars should tease out more carefully the implications of these turning points for the fate of right-wing women's movements in various settings and the transnational spread of right-wing ideas and practices among women.

This volume also points to the importance of ethnicity and to its complexity. While rightist women in many contexts have tightened the lines between their ethnic group and those they despise, the pioneering studies in this volume show that women from ethnic minorities have also participated in the right. Minority women, as this volume demonstrates, can both challenge and seemingly bolster the boundaries of ethnic separation. Future scholarship should pay more attention to the generally invisible role that ethnic or racial minority women have played on the right and the extent to which there are transnational exchanges among them.

Finally, future scholars need to push the geographic scope of studies of right-wing women even further. The inclusion of comparative studies of women across regions of sub-Saharan Africa and the Muslim world helps set this volume apart. Not only does such research fill a long-standing void in the English-language scholarship on the right, but it also raises profound questions about the definition and nature of rightist politics in governance systems quite different from those of the better-studied nations of the West and global North. We need to know more about women in these regions, as well as their counterparts in East Asia, where warfare, decolonization, communism, economic development, and gender norms may have interacted to produce a distinct dynamic. Understanding how to conceptualize women's involvement on the right in theocratic governments and military dictatorships and analyzing their participation in East Asia are important next steps toward a global scholarship of right-wing women.

Interplay and Complexity

In their approaches to the study of rightist women, the essays in this volume undermine the boundaries separating nation from nation, private from public, and left from right. They highlight the interplay between activists in different countries, between the domestic and public spheres, and between ideas and practices along the political spectrum. Their authors thereby challenge easy explanations of women's involvement in the right.

The following chapters show that rightist women—like all human beings—are complex. As nationalists, they have distrusted global ties even as some have constructed them. Their hostility toward the foreign and the left has not prevented them from accepting imported ideas and reshaping progressive notions. Nor has loyalty to the upper classes kept some from seeking working-class converts. Despite their reverence for the past, rightist women have often adopted new technologies and habits. Love of the home has not imprisoned them within it, nor has their maternalism obscured the violent prejudices some have held. In fact, women on the right have simultaneously embraced customary gender notions while tearing them down. The complicated images of rightist women that emerge in this volume will fascinate and haunt us long after we put it aside.

NOTES

1. Several groundbreaking books include Jill Stephenson, *Women in Nazi Society* (New York: Barnes and Noble, 1975); María Teresa Gallego Méndez, *Mujer, Falange y Franquismo* (Madrid: Taurus, 1983); Rebecca E. Klatch, *Women of the New Right* (Philadelphia: Temple University Press, 1987); Claudia Koonz, *Mothers in the Fatherland: Women, the Family, and Nazi Politics* (New York: St. Martin's Press, 1987); Victoria de Grazia, *How Fascism Ruled Women: Italy, 1922–1945* (Berkeley: University of California Press, 1992); Glen Jeansonne, *Women of the Far Right: The Mother's Movement and World War II* (Chicago: University of Chicago Press, 1996). Reviews of the literature on several countries can be found in Julie V. Gottlieb, ed., "Right-Wing Women in Women's History: A Global Perspective," *Journal of Women's History* 16, no. 3 (2004): 106–86.

2. Kathleen M. Blee, ed., *No Middle Ground: Women and Radical Protest* (New York: New York University Press, 1997); Victoria González and Karen Kampwirth, eds., *Radical Women in Latin America: Left and Right* (University Park: Pennsylvania State University Press, 2001); Paola Bacchetta and Margaret Power, eds., *Right-Wing Women: From Conservatives to Extremists Around the World* (New York: Routledge, 2002); Kevin Passmore, ed., *Women, Gender, and Fascism in Europe, 1919–1945* (New Brunswick: Rutgers University Press, 2003).

3. Bacchetta and Power, *Right-Wing Women.*

4. On how such "flows" have influenced feminism, see Jayati Lal et al., "Recasting Global Feminisms: Toward a Comparative Historical Approach to Women's Activism and Feminist Scholarship," *Feminist Studies* 36, no. 1 (Spring 2010): 13–39.

5. Bonnie G. Smith, "Women's History: A Retrospective from the United States," *Signs: Journal of Women in Culture and Society* 35, no. 3 (Spring 2010): 723–46.

6. Kathleen M. Blee, *Women of the Klan: Racism and Gender in the 1920s* (Berkeley: University of California Press, 1991) and *Inside Organized Racism: Women in the Hate Movement* (Berkeley: University of California Press, 2002).

7. Quoted in Sandra McGee Deutsch, *Las Derechas: The Extreme Right in Argentina, Brazil, and Chile, 1890–1939* (Stanford: Stanford University Press, 1999), 117.

8. Margaret Power, *Right-Wing Women in Chile: Feminine Power and the Struggle Against Allende, 1964–1973* (University Park: Pennsylvania State University Press, 2002), 178–80.

9. Robert O. Paxton, *The Anatomy of Fascism* (New York: Vintage, 2004), 144.

10. Sandra F. McGee, "The Visible and Invisible Liga Patriótica Argentina, 1919–1928: Gender Roles and the Right Wing," *Hispanic American Historical Review* 64, no. 2 (May 1984): 233–58; Sandra McGee Deutsch, *Counterrevolution in Argentina, 1900–1932: The Argentine Patriotic League* (Lincoln: University of Nebraska Press, 1986).

PART 1

Transnational and Comparative Studies

1

Transnational Connections Among Right-Wing Women:
Brazil, Chile, and the United States

Margaret Power

Brazil offers an outstanding example of how women can save a nation from Communist take-over. . . . It is primarily the women who deserve the credit for the overthrow of the Communist Allende in Chile. . . . Anything that Brazilian and Chilean women can do, positive American women can do.

—Phyllis Schlafly, *The Power of the Positive Woman*

I first read these words written by Phyllis Schlafly, the head of the Eagle Fo-rum and the conservative activist who led the successful campaign to defeat the Equal Rights Amendment, just before I went to Chile in 1993 to conduct research for my dissertation on right-wing women in that country.[1] Intrigued by Schlafly's reference to the very women whom I planned to study, I con-tacted the Eagle Forum to see if it had any suggestions as to how I could get in touch with these women. The organization sent me the name of a North American priest who lived in Chile and had been very supportive of the mili-tary regime headed by General Augusto Pinochet that had ruled Chile from 1973 to 1990. At the time, I mainly thought of connections between right-wing activists in the United States and Chile as unidirectional—traveling from north to south. However, I now realize that the relationship between right-wing women in Brazil, Chile, and the United States is multidirectional, also flowing from the south to the north, and the south to the south. This chapter looks at the transnational flow of information and ideas about anti-communism and movement building from conservative women in Brazil and Chile to right-wing women in the United States in order to develop a new and more complete perspective on the relationship between right-wing women in the United States and Latin America.[2]

The literature on right-wing women in the United States has largely ignored their connections to women in Latin America. Instead, it analyzes U.S. women in terms of the national context, in isolation from the global world of which they are a part. For example, Lisa McGirr's excellent study on the right in Southern California does not consider the possible influence that contemporaneous anticommunist women from Brazil or Chile, either as symbols or as political actors, might have had on it.[3] Equally, Donald Critchlow's informed study of Phyllis Schlafly does not mention that Schlafly was aware of the successes of conservative women in Brazil or Chile, nor that she presented them as role models for women in the United States to emulate.[4] Nor does Marjorie J. Spruill's discussion of how gender issues and the conflict over the 1977 International Women's Year Conference contributed to the emergence of socially conservative activists consider the impact that conservative Brazilian and Chilean women may have had on these women's goals.[5]

In this chapter, I will explore multiple instances in which conservative Brazilian and Chilean women shared their political experiences and victories with U.S. women, who were in turn inspired by them. In the late 1950s and early 1960s, at the height of the Cold War, the U.S. right worked to overcome the electoral defeats it suffered nationally and locally and to build a movement that could both challenge what it defined as the "Red Menace" and return conservatives to political power. Lisa McGirr's study of the "suburban warrior" in Orange County, California, during this period analyzes the successful organization of conservative forces at the grassroots level as well as their ties to and impact on the right at the national level. Like their counterparts across the country, they were "obsess[ed] with communism" and scared by what they believed to be the "spread of communism since World War II." The victory of the Cuban Revolution in 1959 and the triumph of pro-Soviet national liberation struggles in Asia and Africa heightened their fears and intensified their commitment to organize against the Communists.[6]

It was in this context that conservative forces in the United States welcomed the successes of the anticommunist women of Brazil and Chile. How gratifying to counter the victory of pro-socialist forces in Cuba and around the world by trumpeting the triumph of anticommunist Brazilian and Chilean women! These women, many of whom were housewives, not politicians, were of symbolic and practical importance to conservative women in the United States. First, they represented the ability of the "everyday" woman to organize a successful movement and offered U.S. women role models whom they might emulate in order to accomplish their own goal of defeating communism, both domestically and internationally. Second, since these women had been successful in defeating the elected presidencies of João Goulart (1961–64) in Brazil and Salvador Allende (1970–73) in Chile, they served as a beacon of hope at a time when conservative forces felt "bereft of power and influence."[7]

Although the Brazilian, Chilean, and U.S. women discussed in this chapter lived in distinct nations located far from one another, they shared a common hatred and fear of communism. They also shared the belief that women had the power and responsibility to articulate and act upon their opposition to what they perceived to be communism, whether it be in the form of the reformism of João Goulart in Brazil, the socialism of Salvador Allende in Chile, or liberalism and the growing left in the United States. These women were devout Cold War warriors; they saw themselves as defenders of the nation, democracy, the free-market system, religion, and liberty—what the military regimes that later ruled Chile and Brazil referred to as "Western, Christian civilization" in response to the assaults launched against them by the (so-called) godless, totalitarian Communists.

In 1961 João Goulart, a reformist and nationalist, became president of Brazil and attempted to implement programs that would improve the economic situation of the large number of Brazilians living in impoverished conditions. For example, he worked to achieve land reform for the poor peasants in northeastern Brazil. Unfortunately, his positions in favor of Brazilian development incurred the wrath of U.S. corporations and the U.S. government, which labeled him a Communist. In Brazil, conservative women mobilized against the Goulart government because they claimed, inaccurately, that it threatened to "impos[e] a totalitarian system in Brazil."[8] Equally erroneously, they asserted that the Brazilian president was an atheist who threatened the Catholic Church and their freedom to practice religion. To protest the Goulart government, they wrote letters opposing his policies, spoke on the radio to explain their dislike for his programs, and organized marches to generate an anti-Goulart mass movement. After Goulart criticized some of these conservative women for using religion to further their own political ends, opposition forces called for a March to Make Amends to the Rosary, then changed the name to the March of the Family with God for Liberty so as to include non-Catholic Brazilians. Responding to this call, roughly five hundred thousand people, the majority of them women, demonstrated against Goulart in São Paulo on March 19, 1964, about two weeks before the military overthrew his government on March 31.[9] Despite the military's illegal seizure of power and use of repressive methods, the conservative women praised the coup and lauded their own role in the demise of the democratically elected government of João Goulart.

During the 1960s and early 1970s, anticommunist Chilean women looked to Brazilian women for inspiration and ideas for their own struggle against Salvador Allende, and Brazilian women were happy to share their stories with them.[10] Allende was democratically elected president in September 1970 on a program that envisioned far-reaching changes to the Chilean economy, including the nationalization of U.S. economic holdings, the redistribution of land held by the large landowners, and a redistribution of wealth in favor of the poor through increased wages and social services. Just as in Brazil, anticommunist Chilean women worked assiduously and boldly to organize other women to oppose the government, mobilize a public movement against it, and encourage the armed forces to overthrow it. Like their counterparts in Brazil, anti-Allende Chilean women employed a multitude of tactics ranging from leafleting, paid announcements in the newspapers, talks on the radio, protests, and marches to generate sentiment against Allende and foster a climate favoring the military's seizure of power. The military deposed Allende on September 11, 1973, declared a state of siege, and instituted brutal measures such as torture, murder, and exile to eliminate opposition, terrorize the population, and ensure its own rule. Throughout its seventeen years in power, the military praised the actions of these women and promoted them as heroines who had saved the nation from communism. The anti-Allende women reveled in this image and used it to project themselves as courageous women who had risked their lives to save their families, their way of life, and freedom in the face of what they claimed were the dire threats posed by the Allende government.[11]

U.S. Media Coverage of Conservative Brazilian Women

A central question regarding the transnational connections among these women is how they came to be aware of one another. When I put the question to Phyllis Schlafly, she responded, "I don't remember how I learned about Brazilian and Chilean women—I kept up on all the news about Communism in those days."[12] Although she could not recall specifically how she found out about these women, her reply makes it clear that their successes were known in the United States, at least among those sectors of the population most eager to relish the defeat of what they labeled communist governments. Indeed, what is notable is the extent to which news about these Brazilian and Chilean women, conveyed both in the media and through visits and tours, was available to the U.S. public.

One key source for information about these women was the print media in the United States, from the *New York Times,* to *Reader's Digest,* to *Time* and *Newsweek,* to small-town newspapers published throughout the country. When I first conducted research on these women, I read *Reader's Digest,* which had a special feature on Brazil that included the role that women played in building a movement against the Goulart government. I also examined major U.S. newspapers such as the *New York Times,* the *Washington Post,* and the *LA Times.* I subsequently realized that my exclusive focus on these newspapers privileged the urban, well-educated, metropolitan sector of the U.S. population and ignored the smaller cities, towns, villages, and rural areas where a large number of Americans lived and which have been fertile territory for right-wing organizing and ideology. When I looked for coverage of these conservative Brazilian and Chilean women outside the big cities, I was astounded to find that a large number of small-town newspapers reported on them and their role in building anticommunist movements in their respective countries. News about these women was published in syndicated articles or columns written by U.S. reporters based in Brazil or Chile, by U.S.-based anticommunist reporters such as John Chamberlain, or by conservative figures such as Phyllis Schlafly. In all of these cases, the stories clearly communicated the basic idea that women were central to the defeat of "communism" in Brazil and Chile. They also either implied or said outright that women in the United States should follow the lead of the valiant women of Brazil and Chile.

John Chamberlain started his career as a reporter for the *New York Times,* then moved to the right and came to admire such ideological luminaries of the conservative movement as Friedrich von Hayek, Ludwig von Mises, and William F. Buckley.[13] He wrote book reviews in Buckley's *National Review*[14] and was a syndicated columnist with King Features Syndicate, which was owned by William Randolph Hearst.[15] Through the King Features Syndicate, he wrote numerous articles that were distributed throughout the United States, extolling the actions of the Brazilian women who opposed Goulart and Chilean women who opposed Allende. One of these articles appeared in the *Light* (San Antonio, Texas) on April 10, 1964, a little over a week after the Brazilian military ousted Goulart.[16] In the article, Chamberlain wrote that when Brazilians learned that the Goulart government had issued instructions to "embassies and consulates to give visas to Communists who wished to come to Rio de Janeiro for a leftist congress," those who opposed their arrival launched a protest. Chamberlain noted, "In the business of hounding the leftist visitors from town to town, *Brazilian women played a dominating role.*"[17] A number of U.S. newspapers published roughly the same article, albeit on different dates, with different titles, and with some minor variation in the text.[18]

Pacific Stars and Stripes, the "authorized publication of the U.S. Armed Forces," also published one of Chamberlain's articles on Brazil. Titled "Brazilians Upset Castro's Applecart," the article boasted that "the Brazilian generals who toppled the leftist-leaning government of Joao Goulart has [*sic*] done more, so one may reasonably surmise, to check the march of communism than anything that has happened in the Western world since President Harry Truman decided to put his foot down in Korea." As in his other articles, Chamberlain praised women's role in the demise of the Goulart government. Referring to the action mentioned above, Chamberlain wrote, "The women of the city of Belo Horizonte led a demonstration that sent the leftist visitors scurrying to Goulart's own capital of Brasilia in search of a forum. Whereupon the women of Brasilia, in their own turn, formed what was the direct antithesis of a welcoming committee. The women's performance recalled that strong women all over the world are called Amazons, after Brazil's own great river."[19]

It should be noted that John Chamberlain was not the only journalist who wrote about the anti-Goulart women. Edgar Miller worked for the Associated

Press in Brazil in the 1960s and 1970s and likewise wrote about what Brazilian women did to encourage the "revolution."[20] In one article, he chronicled the rise of the anti-Goulart women's movement, concluding, "The women's crowning blow [against Goulart] was a mass protest march in Sao Paulo which mobilized some 500,000 persons shortly after Goulart's rally drew 200,000."[21]

In another article published in multiple newspapers, John Chamberlain drew an explicit link between Brazil and Chile and women's role in opposing Goulart and Allende. His message was that Brazilian women had defeated Goulart and Chilean women should do the same with Allende. In 1964 the U.S. government was very concerned that Salvador Allende, a leader of the Socialist Party, would defeat Christian Democrat Eduardo Frei, whom Washington supported, in the upcoming presidential elections. In the article "Chilean Hope Led by Women," Chamberlain wrote that "Brazilian women nipped an incipient Communist takeover" and claimed that the political shift against "communism" that he believed was taking place in Chile in the days preceding the vote was due to "the women [who] have taken the lead in forcing it."[22]

However, the U.S. publication that reached the largest number of people and was clearly calculated to have the greatest impact on the American people was the November 1964 issue of *Reader's Digest*.[23] Second only to *TV Guide* in circulation, the magazine educated Americans about the world, their place in it, and their relationship to it. As Joanne Sharp notes in her study of *Reader's Digest*, the magazine "illustrates why readers should care about global politics and what relevance distant events might have in their lives. Inevitably, the *Digest* explains why vigilance and action are required of individual readers in order that any threat to the United States can be stopped before it takes hold and challenges them and their families directly."[24]

Clearly convinced that the role Brazilians played in the overthrow of Goulart was important to Americans, Clarence W. Hall, a senior editor of *Reader's Digest*, wrote "The Country That Saved Itself," which lays out his (conservative) perspective on what happened there. Hall applauds the actions of "the embattled amateurs working against hardened communist revolutionaries" and lauds the "feminine but formidable" women, especially the "housewives [who] threw themselves into the struggle and, more than any other force, alerted the country."[25] He concluded that their story offers "a blueprint for every nation similarly threatened," since the ouster of Goulart "is invigorating proof that communism *can* be stopped cold, when people are sufficiently aroused and determined."[26]

The article highlights Amelia Bastos, a leader of the Rio de Janeiro–based Brazilian Women's Campaign for Democracy (CAMDE), one of the anticommunist women's groups. Hall describes her as "a diminutive, 90-pound package of feminine energy" and the "sparkplug and driving force of the Rio de Janeiro women's uprising." In 1962 she listened to "her husband and other anti-Red leaders discussing the looming threat" posed by Goulart. At that point, Bastos "suddenly decided . . . that politics had become too important to be left entirely to the men." She called on her friends, some "30 embattled housewives," to take action. Realizing that thirty women were not enough, "Dona Amelia and her fledging group rounded up 500."[27]

In Amelia Bastos, Hall found a symbol embodying the anticommunist drive that he admired and hoped women in the United States would emulate. He clearly intended the message that "concerned citizens" could successfully defeat communism to be read and understood by people across the United States and around the world. A page at the end of the article titled "How You Can Use This Article to Best Effect" urges readers to engage actively in sharing the "useful information" they have just read, since the "heartening" story "deserves the widest possible dissemination." It emphasizes, "The message is this: with determination and intelligent planning, an aroused citizenry can rid itself of even a deeply entrenched communist threat." The *Digest* then lists three things that readers can do: mail the article to a friend, obtain reprints to send abroad, and take copies along with them when they travel abroad.[28]

Brazilian Women Bring Their Message to the United States

In addition to reading what U.S. journalists wrote about anticommunist Brazilian women, Americans also heard from these women directly. In October and November 1964, the U.S. Department of State's Bureau of Educational and Cultural Exchange gave Leader Grants for a "two months' study tour in the United States" to fourteen Brazilian women who were "leaders of women's anti-Communist volunteer political movements."[29] The women came so that they could "observe the United States elections on Nov. 3."[30] (How ironic that they came to learn about U.S. elections shortly after they had agitated successfully for the military overthrow of Brazilian democracy!) The women participated in a seminar from October 19 to 30 at the Brookings Institution that was organized by the Overseas Education Fund (OEF) of the League of Women Voters.[31] While in Washington, D.C., they also attended the Thirty-Second National Convention of Catholic Women from November 11 to 14, which was organized by the conservative and anticommunist National Council of Catholic Women and had about three thousand women in attendance.[32] The women then went to Wellesley College, and from there they traveled to Ohio, Tennessee, Arizona, and the West Coast. The tour ended in New York City.[33]

While in Washington, D.C., three of the "Brazilian housewives" gave a press conference sponsored by *Reader's Digest* at the Pan American Room of the Statler Hotel. Journalist Elizabeth Shelton attended the press conference, and her story about the women was published in newspapers across the country. The Brazilian women stated that they wanted to tell people in the United States "how they helped counter a Communist takeover of their country by massing to march and distribute propaganda." Amelia Bastos, the leader of CAMDE and one of the fourteen Brazilian women touring the United States, ended the question-and-answer period by assuring Americans that after the coup Brazilians were "very friendly toward the American people in spite of the Communists' work."[34]

In addition to telling readers what the women had done to oppose Goulart, Shelton's story emphasized that the anticommunist women had donated their gold wedding rings (in exchange for iron ones) and other jewelry to raise three million dollars to aid "the cause of democracy in Brazil after the communists had been driven from the country, taking most of the national treasury with them." In admiration, and as a testament to these women's strength, an article on the "Woman's Page" of the *Beckley Post-Herald* noted that "in modern Brazil, women's wills match their wedding rings. Both are made of iron."[35] A very similar article appeared in the *Daily Northwestern,* except that this one featured Amelia Bastos. While visiting the United States, the article pointed out, Bastos "has given some Americans engaged in action similar to theirs iron wedding rings to be worn as friendship rings, symbolic of the fight for freedom in Brazil. Should you see such a ring on an American woman you will know she has been recognized as one continually aware of the necessity to preserve freedom through action."[36] Another article on the woman's page of a California newspaper compared "love" in Red China, Russia, and Brazil. The article ridiculed the communist women's organization in China because it counseled prospective brides not to be tempted by "worldly things" and urged them to concentrate on "political factors" in their search for a future husband. The U.S. columnist clearly approved of the Brazilian women who "turned over $3 million worth of wedding rings and other jewelry to their government after the pro-Communists were thrown out," repeating the story told by the indefatigable Amelia Bastos, who "is in the United States now telling of the work of Brazilian women."[37]

The Brazilian women had a message that they wanted to communicate to their audience in the United States: women were important in the fight against communism. To illustrate this point, they brought "photographs with them showing how more than 1,000,000 women massed in Rio and São Paulo last spring to demand and give thanks for the delivery of their country from an imminent Communist takeover."[38] Amelia Bastos wanted women in the United States to know that "women are even better at infiltration than Communists." Her message to U.S. women was "that though Brazilian women feel they are 'out front' in the free world, they know they have only won one battle against Communists. 'We women of Brazil have discovered our power. We're now going to work to preserve the democracy we helped to save,' she declared." When Bastos was in New York City, she "was honored by the Reader's Digest, which this month tells [her] story in an article: 'The Country That Saved Itself.' "[39]

Brazilian women were not the only ones who recounted their successful efforts to defeat "communism." Mrs. George Colman helped found the first Young Women's Christian Association in Rio de Janeiro. She and her husband, Dr. Colman, who worked for the U.S. State Department in Rio de Janeiro, lived in Brazil for twenty-five years. Dr. Colman later served as an American consul in Punta Arenas, Chile, before they both returned to the United States. Mrs. Colman had previously taught at Greeley High School in Colorado. During the same time that the Brazilian women were touring the United States, she addressed the Greeley Women's Club on the topic of "Brazilian women and the role they took in the April 1 revolution against Communism."[40]

Chilean Women: Symbols of the Anticommunist Struggle

Throughout the rest of the 1960s, references to conservative Brazilian or Chilean women appeared sporadically, at best, in the U.S. media. However, with the 1970 election of Salvador Allende, conservative Chilean women once again captured the attention of the U.S. media and, as we shall see below, of anticommunists like Phyllis Schlafly. For much of the first year of the Allende government, two stories dominated the U.S. media's coverage of Chilean women: their reluctance to wear hot pants (their husbands disapproved!) and their obsession with *Simplemente María,* a soap opera that "90 percent of all Chilean women [with a TV] watch" every night.[41] Yet, on December 1, 1971, only one week after the latter story was printed in U.S. newspapers, thousands of Chilean women marched through Santiago, waving empty pots and chanting anti-Allende slogans. Although a few articles appeared that portrayed Allende's relationship with women in a positive light, the image of thousands of women parading through the streets of Santiago captured the attention of the U.S. media and was published in newspapers and magazines across the nation. Catapulting women to the center stage of Chilean politics (forget the hot pants and the soap opera!), the *New York Times* coverage of the protest led the way with its sensationalist first sentence: "The rhythmic pounding of empty pots and pans by thousands of Chilean women last week had the sound of war drums." It characterized the march as "the most violent since President Salvador Allende Gossens took office 13 months ago."[42]

Other newspapers also focused on the role of Chilean women, the violent response to their action on the part of Allende's supporters, and the spirit of the women who carried out the march. The articles bore titles such as "Leftists Attack Chilean Women During Protest," drawing on gendered ideas of femininity and masculinity to simultaneously portray the women as heroic victims and the (male) supporters of the Allende government as unchivalrous brutes.[43] *Time* magazine's two-page article on the march echoed this same theme.[44] The picture of Chilean women waving pots and pans in protest against the government while the leftists attacked them became fixed in the U.S. media. In October 1972, at the height of the antigovernment truckers' strike, U.S. newspapers again carried pictures of exuberant anti-Allende women carrying the Chilean flag, holding empty pots aloft, smiling, and looking triumphant.[45] Several newspapers repeated the title "Leftists Attack Chilean Women" (or variations of it) in subsequent articles, just in case the reader missed the earlier suggestion that leftist Chilean men had assaulted conservative Chilean women.[46]

After the military overthrew the Allende government on September 11, 1973, a number of articles appeared in the U.S. media that highlighted women's influence in the coup. David Belnap's article in the *Los Angeles Times* trumpeted that "organized women's groups opposed to Allende played a decisive role in the events that led to Allende's downfall."[47] Other articles reported on the military dictatorship's plans (which never came to fruition) to build a monument "to the women of Chile for their role in the overthrow of the left-wing government of President Salvador Allende one year ago." These articles, which characterized the women as "spunky," contributed to the dissemination of awareness that anticommunist women had played an important part in the defeat of Allende and were getting a well-deserved reward for their work.[48]

As was true in the case of the pro-military Brazilian women, anticommunist Chilean women spoke directly to the U.S. public about their support for the military regime and their role in the ouster. However, by 1973 the public climate was much more critical of U.S. foreign policy in general and of the U.S. government's role in the overthrow of Allende and the establishment of the military dictatorship in particular. Additionally, not only did leading members of the U.S. Congress (such as Edward Kennedy) condemn the coup, but a vibrant solidarity movement emerged that challenged conservative interpretations of the Allende government, strongly censured the U.S. role in the coup, voiced opposition to the repressive policies of the dictatorship, and welcomed Chilean political refugees into the United States.[49] Increasingly, the testimonies of anti-Pinochet women were heard while the voices of anti-Allende and pro-military speakers were muted and listened to primarily by conservative forces in the United States. One exception occurred in Madison, Wisconsin (of all places!), which held a two-day symposium on Chile in October 1974. The featured speaker at the event was Carmen Puelma, a Chilean journalist who had written scathing articles against the Allende government and in support of the anticommunist women who opposed it. After the coup, she served as the cultural and press attaché in the Chilean embassy in Washington, D.C. When asked about the political prisoners in Chile, she remarked, "I do not talk about the numbers any more because I am tired of it." She was much more comfortable talking about the women who opposed Allende. Puelma noted that they had "staged a series of 'pots-and-pans marches'" and that "'an incredible number' of women had protested Allende's economic policies." Further, she attributed the "heightened political conscious-ness of women to the fact that they were 'in the streets almost 24 hours a day' looking for the goods that Allende had made nearly impossible to obtain."[50]

Yet some articles in support of the anticommunist women and the mili-tary dictatorship did appear in the U.S. media. Eda Bolla and her husband, a retired Shell Oil executive, spent three months in Chile in 1980. In an inter-view in the *Alton Telegraph,* a newspaper from Phyllis Schlafly's hometown, Bolla pointed out that women in Chile did not need the Equal Rights Amend-ment (ERA) because "of all the women in the world, they're as emancipated as you can find." She supported the military dictatorship of General Augusto Pinochet that then ruled in Chile and attributed much of the coup's success "to a group of women journalists who published pamphlets and posters and started demonstrations." These women "got the people of Santiago . . . to bang on empty pots for thirty minutes" every day to signal their dislike of the Allende government. Because of them, "the communist [*sic*] government knew it was through."[51]

As noted above, one important figure on the U.S. right who drew on the example of the anticommunist Brazilian and Chilean women was Phyllis Schlafly. In his study of Schlafly, Donald Critchlow argued that she was a powerful and effective leader of the postwar Republican right because of "her ability to translate conservative ideas to grassroots activists and motivate them to achieve political goals."[52] One central method she employed to do this was study groups. In personal correspondence to me, Schlafly wrote that in 1958 or 1959 "I developed a study program of 10 sessions, each based on a congressional report or hearing about Communism. I repackaged the pro-gram for three organizations to which I belonged: the Cardinal Mindszenty Foundation (Catholic, anti-Communist), the Illinois Federation of Republi-can Women, and the Daughters of the American Revolution. At one time we bragged that we had 5,000 local Study Groups."[53] The Study Groups, which included both women and men, consisted of ten sessions, in which the par-ticipants read documents published by the U.S. Congress or the Cardinal Mindszenty Foundation.[54] Schlafly explained, "I promoted knowledge of those [Brazilian and Chilean] women to get Americans to believe we could be successful. The people who attended study groups would have known and admired the South American women and have looked to them for encouragement."[55]

Phyllis Schlafly also wrote about these women in *The Phyllis Schlafly Re-port.* In 1977, when worldwide repudiation of the Pinochet regime was wide-spread, Schlafly praised the military government's success in exchanging the imprisoned leader of the Communist Party of Chile, Luis Corvalan, for dis-sident Vladimir Bukovsky from the Soviet Union. In the same article, she excoriated the Allende government as a "disaster," praised the military re-gime for piloting Chile's "recovery," and extolled the "women who initiated the overthrow of Allende. "On December 3, 1973 [the march took place on

December 1, 1971]," Schlafly wrote, "they staged an impressive demonstration called the March of the Empty Pots. Thousands of women marched through the streets of Santiago beating with spoons on their empty pots and pans."[56]

Conclusion

In order to examine the influence of these women on people in the United States, I shifted my attention from the big-city newspapers of record, which I had automatically turned to in the past, to the scores of newspapers read by people outside the metropolitan centers. I examined what those who lived in the small towns, cities, and rural areas read, publications that I had earlier ignored or dismissed as possible sources. I admit, I was surprised to discover the widespread coverage of conservative Brazilian and Chilean women in these newspapers, and it made me realize how limited my previous research had been.

In addition to exploring a new range of sources, this chapter moves beyond the idea that the United States played the sole tutelary role regarding anticommunism in the Americas. Instead, it illustrates that anticommunist activity and thinking among and between women in the Americas has also traveled from the south to the north, not just from the north to the south, as has generally been assumed. Brazilian women led the way, through their mobilization against the reformist presidency of João Goulart. They offered anticommunist women throughout the continent a stirring example of women successfully organizing and demonstrating to rid their country of a democratically elected president and supporting the installation of a repressive military dictatorship. Chilean women who opposed Allende drew on this example and their own history of anticommunist activity to forge a conservative women's movement that called on the armed forces to overthrow Allende and impose a military dictatorship.

These women's work and successes were publicized in the United States through the writings of U.S. journalists stationed in South America, U.S.-based syndicated columnists, and conservative organizers such as Phyllis Schlafly. In addition, conservative Brazilian and Chilean women spoke directly to people in the United States through, in the case of the former, a tour sponsored by the U.S. State Department and, in the case of the latter, as part of the efforts of the Chilean military government to counter the worldwide protests launched against it for its vile violation of human rights.

This chapter illustrates that the nationalist discourses and identities that define the right in Brazil, Chile, and the United States (and elsewhere) do not preclude its simultaneous embrace of transnationalist influences, contacts, and resources. Instead of analyzing the right as exclusively immersed in its national context, this chapter should encourage scholars to examine it in relation to and as part of the transnational currents from which it draws ideas and support.[57] This approach, I believe, allows us to obtain a deeper understanding of the multiple methods, diverse tactics, and varied strategies that the right employs to organize, often successfully, for the implementation of its conservative agenda and its ascension to power.

NOTES

1. Phyllis Schlafly, *The Power of the Positive Woman* (New York: Jove Publications, 1987), 221–23; Margaret Power, *Right-Wing Women in Chile: Feminine Power and the Struggle Against Allende, 1964–1973* (University Park: Pennsylvania State University Press, 2002).

2. This chapter's focus on the contributions that Brazilian and Chilean women made to the development of anticommunist thinking and activism in the United States is not meant to deny or minimize the central role that multiple official U.S. actors and institutions have played in fomenting anticommunism in the Americas.

3. Lisa McGirr, *Suburban Warriors: The Origins of the New American Right* (Princeton: Princeton University Press, 2001). She does discuss Fred Schwartz and the Christian Anti-Communism Crusade but not its implications for transnational connections between conservatives in Southern California and in other countries. Similarly, Kim Phillips-Fein's outstanding book on the conservative movement in the United States focuses on the contributions made by businessmen to its growth, not on the ties it had to any non-U.S.-based forces. Kim Phillips-Fein, *Invisible Hands: The Making of the Conservative Movement from the New Deal to Reagan* (New York: W.W. Norton, 2009).

4. Donald T. Critchlow, *Phyllis Schlafly and Grassroots Conservatism: A Woman's Crusade* (Princeton: Princeton University Press, 2005).

5. Marjorie J. Spruill, "Gender and America's Right Turn," in *Rightward Bound: Making America Conservative in the 1970s*, ed. Bruce J. Schulman and Julian E. Zelizer (Cambridge, Mass.: Harvard University Press, 2008).

6. McGirr, *Suburban Warriors*, 69–70.

7. Ibid., 66.

8. "Manifesto," *O Diário de Pernambuco*, March 8, 1964.

9. John F. W. Dulles, *Unrest in Brazil: Political-Military Crisis, 1955–1964* (Austin: University of Texas Press, 1970), 275. March 19 is the day of Saint Joseph, the patron saint of the family.

10. Solange de Deus Simões, *Deus, pátria e família* (Petrópolis: Editora Vozes, 1985), 134.

11. For a broader discussion of these women, see Power, *Right-Wing Women in Chile*.

12. Phyllis Schlafly, e-mail message, October 27, 2009.

13. Linda Bridges and John R. Coyne, *Strictly Right: William F. Buckley and the American Conservative Movement* (Hoboken, N.J.: John Wiley and Sons, 2007), 26–27.

14. Ibid., 40.

15. See "The Birth of King Features Syndicate," King Features, http://www.kingfeatures.com/history/historyeIntro.htm.

16. The *Light* was a Hearst-owned newspaper. In 1945 "the circulation was approximately 70,000," and it grew to 122,292 in 1972. See Frances Donecker, "San Antonio Light," *Handbook of Texas Online*, http://www.tshaonline.org/handbook/online/articles/SS/ees5.html.

17. John Chamberlain, "Brazilian Nutcrackers," *Light*, April 10, 1964. Emphasis added.

18. See, for example, "Brazilian Generals Who Upset Goulart Threw Block in Advance of Communists," *Muscatine Journal* (Iowa), April 10, 1964; "Brazil's Boom," *Daily Messenger* (Canandaigua, New York), April 15, 1964.

19. John Chamberlain, "Brazilians Upset Castro's Applecart," *Pacific Stars and Stripes*, April 15, 1964.

20. Edgar Miller, personal communication, November 16, 2009.

21. Edgar Miller, "Brazilian Women Spurred Revolution," *Alton Telegraph*, June 21, 1964. Alton, Illinois, was the hometown of Phyllis Schlafly. Like the article by John Chamberlain, variations of Miller's article appeared in different newspapers across the United States. See, for example, articles in *Cedar Rapids*, June 28, 1964; *Garden City Telegram* (Kansas), July 8, 1964; *Progress* (Clearfield, Curwensville, and Philipsburg, Pennsylvania), July 11, 1964; *Port Angeles Evening News* (Washington), August 6, 1964. See also "Brazilian Ladies Helped for Freedom," *Victoria Advocate* (Texas), July 5, 1964; "Brazilian Women Spurred Revolution," *Ada Evening News* (Oklahoma), June 19, 1964.

22. John Chamberlain, "Women May Save Chile from Commies," *Chronicle-Telegram* (Ohio), August 21, 1964. This article was published under different titles on the same date, as "Chilean Hope Led by Women," *Oneonta Daily Star* (New York); "Chilean Women," *New Castle News* (Pennsylvania); "The Women May Yet Save Chile," *Daily Courier* (Connellsville, Pennsylvania); "Voting in Chile," *Daily Messenger* (Canandaigua, New York); "Chilean Politics and OAS Sanctions," *Cumberland News* (Maryland); "Chilean Left Defeat Seen," *Gazette* (Emporia, Kansas); "These Days," *Columbus Daily Telegram* (Nebraska), August 25, 1964.

23. The reading audience for the magazine's story went beyond *Reader's Digest*. Newspapers referred to it in their articles on the Brazilian women, thus multiplying the impact of the issue. See, for example, "Brazilian Women Sacrifice Golden Rings for Freedom" under the heading "The Woman's Page" in *Beckley Post-Herald* (West Virginia), November 24, 1964, and "Another Opportunity to Defuse the Reds: Pray Our Leaders Use It," written by the Cardinal Mindszenty Foundation, in *Sunday News and Tribune* (Jefferson City, Missouri), November 15, 1964.

24. Joanne P. Sharp, *Condensing the Cold War: "Reader's Digest" and American Identity* (Minneapolis: University of Minnesota Press, 2000), x.

25. Clarence W. Hall, "The Country That Saved Itself," *Reader's Digest*, November 1964, 137 and 143.

26. Ibid., 137.

27. Ibid., 143–44.

28. Ibid., 159.

29. Lydia Van Zandt, "Brazilian Women Fight Communism," *Christian Science Monitor*, November 27, 1964.

30. Mary Hornaday, "Brazil's Women Hit Their Stride," *Christian Science Monitor*, November 20, 1964.

31. Lydia Van Zandt, "South Americas Take a Long Look," *Christian Science Monitor*, October 13, 1964.

32. Elizabeth Shelton, "They're Wedded to the Freedom of Brazil," *Washington Post*, November 11, 1964, sec. E1 ("For and About Women"); "Catholic Women Attend Meeting in Wakeman," *Sandusky Register* (Ohio), October 13, 1964; "LCBA Told of National Get-Together," *Leader Times* (Sandusky, Ohio), January 15, 1965. For a discussion of the National Council of Catholic Women, see Mary Jo Weaver, *New Catholic Women: A Contemporary Challenge to Traditional Religious Authority* (Bloomington: Indiana University Press, 1995), 119–23.

33. Van Zandt, "Brazilian Women Fight Communism."

34. Shelton, "They're Wedded to the Freedom of Brazil."

35. "Brazilian Women Sacrifice Golden Rings for Freedom," *Beckley Post-Herald* (West Virginia), November 4, 1964.

36. "Wills, Rings of Iron," *Daily Northwestern* (Oshkosh, Wisconsin), November 23, 1964.

37. Lucie Lowery, "Communists Take Varied Look at Love," *Independent* (Pasadena, California), November 17, 1964.

38. Hornaday, "Brazil's Women Hit Their Stride."

39. Ibid.

40. "Greeley Woman's Club Slates International Day," *Greeley Tribune* (Colorado), November 6, 1964.

41. See, for example, "Soap Opera Brings Calm to Nightlife in Chile," *Anniston Star* (Alabama), November 25, 1971; Luis Martínez, "Hot Pants Rejected," *Lima News* (Ohio), August 10, 1971.

42. Juan de Onis, "The Ominous Pounding of Pots," *New York Times,* December 5, 1971.

43. For one example, see "Leftists Attack Chilean Women During Protest," *Lawton Constitution* (Oklahoma), December 2, 1971.

44. "Chile: Empty Pots and Yankee Plots," *Time,* December 13, 1971.

45. See "Chilean Women Demonstrate Against Allende," *Daily Republic* (Mitchell, South Dakota), October 11, 1972.

46. Steven H. Yolen, "Leftists Attack Chilean Women," *Bucks County Courier Times* (Pennsylvania), September 6, 1973. This article appeared a week before the military coup; after the military seized power, it not only attacked women but murdered them as well.

47. David Belnap, "'Corn Pie Plot,' Chile's Women—Power Behind Allende's Fall," *Los Angeles Times,* January 31, 1974. This syndicated article was reprinted in newspapers throughout the United States.

48. Charles E. Padilla, "They Led Fight Against Marxism," *Salinas Journal* (Kansas), October 3, 1974. For similar articles, see "Spunky Chilean Women Honored: Heart of 'Machismo' Country," *Daily Review* (Haywood, California), September 29, 1974.

49. Margaret Power, "The U.S. Movement in Solidarity with Chile in the 1970s," *Latin American Perspectives* 6, no. 6 (November 2009): 46–66.

50. Lew Sword, "Chile's Problem: A 'Human' Question," *Daily News Record* (Harrisonburg, Virginia), October 18, 1974.

51. Dali Hoover, "In Santiago, Chile, Equal Rights Is a Past Issue for Educated Women," *Alton Telegraph* (Illinois), May 5, 1980.

52. Critchlow, *Phyllis Schlafly and Grassroots Conservatism,* 6.

53. Phyllis Schlafly, e-mail message, October 27, 2009. In 1958 Phyllis Schlafly, her husband, Fred, and her daughter Eleanor created the Cardinal Mindszenty Foundation, "named for an imprisoned Hungarian priest, to educate American Catholics about the persecution of priests and Christians in Communist countries." See Donald T. Critchlow, *The Conservative Ascendancy: How the GOP Right Made Political History* (Cambridge, Mass.: Harvard University Press, 2007), 36.

54. *The Cardinal Mindszenty Foundation Invites You to Combat Communism with Knowledge and Facts,* brochure (Cardinal Mindszenty Foundation, 1973).

55. Phyllis Schlafly, e-mail message, October 22, 2009.

56. *The Phyllis Schlafly Report,* vol. 10, no. 10, sec. 1, p. 4.

57. See Martin Durham and Margaret Power, eds., *New Perspectives on the Transnational Right* (New York: Palgrave Macmillan, 2010).

2

Exporting the Culture Wars: Concerned Women for America in the Global Arena

Jill A. Irvine

In her testimony to Congress in 2006 concerning the adoption of UN Security Council Resolution 1325, Janice Crouse, chief political analyst of Concerned Women for America's Beverly LaHaye Institute and architect of its global activism policies, stated, "We emphatically support the human rights of women and girls." In further testimony, however, she made it clear that human rights as they pertained to women were not to be confused with the women's rights movement or the "gender mainstreaming" effort, which had "policy implications far beyond human rights concerns."[1] Crouse explained why Concerned Women for America (CWA), the largest conservative women's organization in the United States, has rejected most of the gains of the global women's movement in the past two decades. Feminists, she argued, seek to create new human rights and impose their extreme ideology on the rest of the world's women, while CWA provides an alternative vision that represents women's true interests.

Women's global activism has become emblematic of the potential of the global human rights campaign, but the past decade has also seen challenges to this campaign mounted by conservative religious organizations, including CWA.[2] CWA has challenged what it considers to be the hegemony of elitist feminists who claim to speak for women internationally. Paradoxes abound in this organization, whose constituency is focused primarily on domestic concerns but which has led the way in challenging the views and activities of

I would like to thank Andrew Halterman for his research assistance on this chapter. Thanks also to Carol Mason, Sandy Holguin, Carol Lilly, and two anonymous reviewers for their input on earlier drafts of the chapter.

many Northern feminist organizations operating globally. Initially hostile to the very existence and purpose of the United Nations, CWA has become increasingly adept at and committed to participating in the processes of UN conferences, meetings, and deliberations. Composed of American women, CWA claims to represent the vulnerable women of the global South as it vigorously promotes an alternative vision of women's rights at the UN and other international venues.

This chapter examines CWA's global activity concerning women's rights. While a great deal has been written on feminist global activism, CWA's international activities remain relatively understudied. Building on several fine studies of the Christian right, I examine CWA's efforts to represent women around the globe.[3] Such a study can shed light on the extent to which women's conservative and religious organizations may offer a serious challenge to feminist global activism. The first part of the chapter examines the development of CWA's global agenda concerning women's rights and its increasing activity at the UN. The second part of the chapter treats CWA's efforts in the international arena to combat human trafficking. I argue that while the CWA has become increasingly active globally, it has failed to build transnational alliances of conservative women around such issues of importance to it as sex trafficking. Ambivalence about the project of organizing internationally and recruiting potential partners as well as mobilizing its own constituency on behalf of international women's issues has hindered its challenge to global feminist activism.

CWA and Global Activism

CWA was established in 1979 during the second wave of the women's movement as an alternative conservative women's voice. According to founder Beverly LaHaye, wife of prominent evangelist and later author of the Left Behind series Tim LaHaye, she and other women were deeply disturbed by the platform of the 1977 National Women's Convention in Houston, which endorsed the Equal Rights Amendment (ERA).[4] Not long after that, a group of women met in LaHaye's home in San Diego to brainstorm about how they might best respond, which resulted, ultimately, in the formation of CWA in January 1979. CWA's founding purpose was to oppose the ERA and other goals of the liberal women's movement and, in general, to represent conservative women in the emerging "culture wars." The small group of twenty-four founding members grew steadily over the next several years. CWA currently claims to be the "largest public policy women's organization" in the United States, with more than five hundred thousand members.[5]

CWA's purpose may have been to restore the United States to "moral sanity," but the focus of its first sustained campaign was, in fact, aimed at exposing the dangers of the UN and convincing the American government to withdraw from membership in it. Revealing both the focus on international activism and the deep distrust of international institutions and movements that were to characterize CWA for the next two decades, CWA's campaign against the International Year of the Child warned of the dangers of "radical organizations pushing for the internationalization of our children" and of the dark forces at work at the UN.[6] LaHaye argued that global forces at the UN were implacably opposed to the family as the basic unit of society and intent on laying the groundwork for the right to abortion on demand.[7] CWA members were exhorted to inform themselves about this "worldwide threat" and take steps to counteract it, "awaken" the rest of America, and offer "stiff resistance to the United Nations as well as those radical organizations" pushing for the "internationalization" of children.[8]

During the first fifteen years of its existence, CWA's attention to international issues was rooted firmly in the context of the Cold War fight against communism and other dangerous international forces that might encroach upon American sovereignty and threaten traditional, religious values. With the end of the Cold War, the organization's focus underwent a fundamental shift. Concurrent with the emergence of global feminist activism, particularly at the UN, CWA's international focus shifted from protecting American women and families against the forces of darkness from abroad to protecting international women from the forces of darkness emanating from the United States and other Western countries.

This shift in its global orientation was aided by three further developments. First, in the mid-1990s, the Christian right in the United States turned its attention to international human rights issues as they related to the persecution of religious minorities, and it came together politically with other faith-based and secular organizations and activists to pass the International Religious Freedom Act in 1998.[9] Second, the political environment shifted crucially with the entrance of the Vatican and faith-based organizations into the international discussion about women's human rights. Exerting its power as a "global moral authority," the Vatican offered stiff resistance to global feminism through its new "discursive strategy of claiming to speak for the real needs of the world's women. CWA and other Christian right groups adopted this strategy with more or less modification."[10] Finally, CWA encountered new political opportunities with the election of George W. Bush in 2000. The Bush administration shared the orientation of conservative religious groups toward human rights and rewarded CWA by appointing its leaders to delegations at the UN and inviting them to consult with the White House on human trafficking and other matters.

CWA responded to this new situation by establishing an affiliated think tank in 1999, the Beverly LaHaye Institute: A Center for Studies in Women's Issues, whose mission was international as well as national in its focus. This more formal organizational attention to international issues and activism was reinforced by the choice of Janice Crouse as the institute's founding director. A former speechwriter for the Bush Sr. administration, Crouse had been working for the Institute on Religion and Democracy, where she focused on, among other issues, human trafficking. During the previous three years, she had worked on preparing conservative delegates to attend the Fourth UN World Conference on Women at Beijing as well as organizing annual conferences for evangelical women to raise awareness about important international developments. With her combative and polemical style and her international orientation, Crouse quickly raised CWA's profile in international meetings and institutions, foremost among them the UN.

CWA and the United Nations

CWA began its work as an organization implacably opposed to the UN and the "one world order" it embodied. Just as the UN conferences and committees provided the political opportunity structure for feminist activists, CWA also found its activities in the global arena inevitably structured by the UN.[11] Paradoxically, for an organization opposed to the very existence of the UN, CWA became increasingly active there in order to exert its influence over UN documents, resolutions, and treaties. Thus, while CWA attention toward the UN may have initially been directed at bringing American involvement in this international body to an end, CWA became increasingly invested in UN processes as it sought to influence global norms concerning women's rights.[12]

Its foremost goal at the UN was to counteract what it perceived as the "elitist feminist perspective" on women's rights that predominated there. Fighting feminism was a cause to which CWA had been devoted since its formation, and this struggle proved relatively easy to transfer to the UN. CWA had long argued that it represented the vast majority of women from "Main Street" in the American context and that feminists were an extremist, vocal minority.[13] Similarly, it argued that global feminism was the invention of a tiny group of "privileged women" from "decadent western nations," whose positions did not reflect the values and views of most women in their own societies, let alone the developing world."[14] As a religious organization based on the protection of traditional values, CWA claimed to better represent the majority of the world's women and pledged to give these women a "real voice" at the UN.[15]

CWA's increasing engagement at the UN followed the general trajectory of the Vatican-led Christian right, which was first mobilized in response to the 1994 Population Conference in Cairo and the 1995 World Conference on Women in Beijing. CWA sent a delegation of five activists to Beijing, headed by CWA president LaHaye, where they represented conservative women's voices and positions. LaHaye, whose daily radio broadcast from the conference reached up to half a million listeners, brought international women's issues and the role of conservative women on the international stage to CWA's constituents for perhaps the first time. In appealing for donations from her listeners to finance the delegation's trip, LaHaye warned of the conference's "radical feminist agenda" and the need for conservative women to fight against it.[16] In Beijing, CWA delegates handed out leaflets and presented conservative views on abortion and other issues in an effort "to influence the thinking of other delegates, particularly those from developing countries."[17]

During the months after the Beijing conference, CWA played an important role in an emerging "countermovement" of conservative, "pro-family" religious organizations determined to resist and reframe UN documents concerning women's rights.[18] According to Louise Chappell, a transnational advocacy network (TAN) emerged at Beijing among Christian and Muslim states and organizations, spearheaded by the Vatican and dedicated to presenting an alternative view on women's rights from the one reflected in the Platform for Action.[19] This pro-family TAN promoted "a pro-life, pro-family and pro-marriage" agenda, which it argued would provide much better protection for women, especially in the developing world, than the "anti-life, anti-family, anti-marriage" agenda purportedly pushed by feminists.[20] Over the next several years, CWA became a pivotal force in the regional and international conferences organized by the "pro-family" forces. The World Congress of Families II, held in Geneva in 1999 in anticipation of the Cairo + 5 and Beijing + 5 meetings taking place at the UN, produced the Geneva Declaration, which was based on three major ideas: (1) differences between the sexes are natural and God-given, (2) gender roles within the family and society should reflect these differences, and (3) the family, as the basic social unit, should be protected by the state.[21] CWA used this declaration as the basis for its subsequent lobbying efforts at the UN and other international bodies.[22]

CWA stepped up its activity at the UN in anticipation of the Cairo + 5 and Beijing + 5 meetings. In 1998 it applied for consultative status at the UN in order to have better institutional access and a more effective voice in these and other processes. This same year, CWA attended the UN's annual meeting of the Commission on the Status of Women (CSW) for the first time. It was awarded Economic and Social Council (ECOSOC) Special Consultative Status in 2001. Meanwhile, CWA activists joined with other conservative religious activists to "make a stand" at Cairo + 5 and Beijing + 5 for an alternative vision for women's rights and human rights.[23] Joining with the NGO Caucus for Stable Families, CWA's pro-family delegates pushed to make sure that language in the preparatory documents reflected their concerns. Although CWA and its pro-family allies did not succeed in significantly revising the Platform for Action adopted at Beijing, CWA did express satisfaction that at Beijing + 5, "with the help of CWA, the Third World countries stood strong and successfully resisted the radical feminist agenda."[24]

When CWA leaders Janice Crouse and Wendy Wright were appointed by the Bush administration to the official delegation to the CSW in 2003 and 2004, CWA's visibility at the UN increased. In her capacity as official delegate to the CSW, Crouse argued forcefully for CWA's views on a host of issues, including its strong opposition to "the hegemony of global feminists" and the creation of any "new human rights," such as "the right to abortion."

At the 2005 meeting of the CSW, which reviewed the Platform for Action in anticipation of the Beijing + 10 meeting to be held later that summer, the U.S. delegation expressed strong opposition to the reproductive rights included in the platform. The U.S. delegation, headed by Ellen Saubrey, who shared CWA's views on women's rights, threatened to boycott the CSW meeting unless the document included wording that explicitly repudiated the creation of any new human rights, such as the right to abortion.[25] By 2006 CWA claimed to be "directing" the efforts of the pro-family lobby at the CSW.[26]

As CWA lobbyists assumed a higher profile at the UN, Crouse began to sound a different note about the UN and CWA's role there. Not all members were happy with this increased focus on the UN, nor was the leadership of the CWA unified in its position on this subject. CWA leaders had previously warned only of the dangers of the UN, and CWA president Wendy Wright continued to reflect this view. In contrast, although expressing reservations about the "corrupt" institution of the UN, Crouse now argued that it was essential for the CWA to have a presence there. The negotiations and debates of UN commissions and conferences were "serious business," Crouse wrote, and "they have a major impact around the world."[27] As such, they could not be ignored, only counteracted. "The United Nations is worth fixing," she told her readers, "because there are thousands of [conservative] women around the world who need to know they are not alone."[28]

In its lobbying efforts, CWA soon secured its allies and identified its enemies. As part of the pro-family coalition, it could count on support from the Vatican and other conservative, religious NGOs such as C-FAM, which had a permanent presence at the UN. Catholic states such as Poland, Nicaragua, Costa Rica, and other countries in Latin America also became close allies. Most interestingly, especially given the sometimes anti-Muslim tone of religious conservatives, CWA also closely cooperated with Muslim organizations and countries from the Organization of the Islamic Conference. Such close cooperation did not extend to liberal Christian women's groups. Religious feminists, found among such groups as United Methodist Women, were labeled the biggest enemies of true equal rights for the world's women.[29]

In lobbying its friends and denouncing its enemies at the UN, CWA effectively utilized the organizational resources at its disposal on behalf of its global agenda. Elisabeth Friedman has argued that as women's rights advocates became more sophisticated and successful in promoting their agenda, they "taught" their opposition how to respond to them.[30] While this is undoubtedly true, CWA possesses additional resources as a religious group that its leaders could bring to bear on its transnational activism. CWA adheres to theological views that support the need for global action. The eschatological beliefs of evangelicals, even those profoundly inward-looking in their orientation, require a knowledge and acceptance of God's work on a global scale. It is here that the forces of good and evil contend, and for many Christians it is essential that they understand and even participate in this "unfolding of

God's plan." Although CWA generally avoids the use of such language and concepts at the UN and in much of its work, the idea of a cosmic struggle is important to the organization's members and never far from the structure of their thinking.

CWA's belief that it is part of a cosmic moral struggle allows it to clearly identify allies and enemies as good and evil. CWA may use religious language strategically, avoiding it at the UN, but it is not shy about identifying and denouncing its enemies in unequivocal terms. CWA is also able to draw upon the religious fervor and commitment of its members and leaders. The organization relies less on membership dues (there are none) and far more on the willingness of its constituents to take action and devote time on behalf of "God's worthy cause." Moreover, CWA is part of a larger social movement of the Christian right, whose financial and other resources it is able to tap. CWA's budget was $14 million for 2008, far more than its secular feminist rivals.[31] Finally, CWA is able to draw upon "the power of prayer" to bring issues far from home into the homes of its constituents. Asking members to pray for Asian victims of human trafficking or potential victims of cloning legislation in India is a powerful tool for raising interest and awareness about global women's issues.

CWA and the Campaign Against Sex Trafficking

The campaign to reduce violence against women has been a centerpiece of global feminist organizing for the past fifteen years and is often considered one of its biggest successes. According to Keck and Sikkink, this struggle against violence toward women generated the most successful transnational advocacy network in the recent history of global organizing.[32] Reducing violence against women has also been central to CWA's mission as a women's organization. Thus, it provides a useful case study to evaluate whether and how CWA presents an alternative approach to feminist global activism.

In their study of global activism, Keck and Sikkink identify several factors that account for the success of the global campaign against violence toward women. First, feminist activists were successful in framing the issue in such a way that it not only spoke to the concerns of women from different regions of the world but also linked forms of violence that had previously been regarded as unconnected to each other—for example, "private" domestic violence and "public" state-directed violence against women. Second, they were able to organize to present these issues at UN conferences and committees in terms that mobilized public outrage and ultimately support for international action. Third, activists adopted a networking strategy that allowed them to forge alliances across borders, mobilize multiple domestic constituencies, and exchange beliefs and information. Such networks allowed women from "far-flung places" to define and redefine the concept of violence against women as well as the "action repertoires" the network would undertake.[33] In short, framing the issue and networking across borders led to the successful outcome of influencing international deliberations, documents, and norms.

CWA also became increasingly active in the international campaign to reduce violence against women during this period, but it chose to focus specifically on the issue of human trafficking. Keck and Sikkink argue that those issues that involve clear bodily harm are most likely to lead to a successful transnational advocacy effort. CWA has met this criterion by focusing on sex trafficking and the victimization of women and girls. It frames the problem in terms of the demand for sex that it believes is driving this trade, arguing that Third World women and girls are the most likely victims of men from the developed North. For CWA, the struggle against prostitution cannot be separated from the struggle against trafficking; outlawing prostitution, then, becomes a major goal of transnational efforts to stop sex trafficking. Thus, the victims as well as the guilty are clearly defined and coupled with a strong sense of moral outrage. As Crouse writes, all good people must engage in the struggle against trafficking "to ensure the triumph of the righteous over those who would engage in evil purposes against those who are desperate and at the mercy of people to whom much has been given."[34]

In its efforts to frame the issue of human trafficking, CWA has set itself in opposition to feminists, who, it claims, fail to defend the real interests of women on this issue. In her study of conservative Christian women, Schreiber points out that when CWA became involved in issues related to violence against women in the United States in the 1980s, this terrain had already been "staked out" by feminists.[35] CWA did not wish to ignore this issue of foremost importance to women, but neither did it wish to join forces with feminists. Its response was to reframe the issue of violence against women as one focused on pornography, which it claimed was a chief cause of violence directed toward women. Since feminists were divided over the impact of and best response to pornography, the terrain was clear for CWA, which, in any case, found that its emphasis on pornography corresponded well with its moral agenda.

CWA has pursued a strategy similar to its treatment of violence against women in the international realm in its opposition to human trafficking. Just as CWA has focused on pornography as a major cause of violence against women in the domestic context, it has focused on prostitution as a major cause of trafficking in its international efforts. This focus on demand, and especially on the degrading nature of prostitution in all cases, resonates well with CWA's moral concerns. It also puts the organization at odds with some women's activists who support legalized prostitution and the regulation of the sex trade industry. Indeed, just as feminists fought over the issue of pornography in the 1980s in the United States, they have disagreed over the issue of prostitution and its relation to the sex trade. Efforts by global women's activists to come together around this issue in the campaign against violence toward women failed as a result of deep disagreements about the best approach.[36] This left room for CWA to claim and frame this issue in the international sphere.

According to CWA, feminists do not represent the true interests of women when it comes to the struggle against human trafficking. Reducing the considerable disagreements and debates among feminists to one position, CWA charges that feminists are more interested in pushing sexual and reproductive freedom than they are in stopping this terrible form of violence against women.[37] CWA denounces feminists' alleged support for prostitution as a legitimate career choice in no uncertain terms. "How any one can argue that prostitution is NOT inherently harmful to women is beyond me," Crouse wrote.[38] Indeed, CWA actions at the UN are often as much about denouncing feminist support for prostitution as about denouncing the evils of sex trafficking. CWA has also denounced the Committee on the Elimination of Discrimination Against Women (CEDAW) process for refusing to sanction countries for human trafficking and prostitution. CWA accuses CEDAW of preferring to uphold women's right to choose their profession, in this case prostitution, over women's right to remain free of the violence engendered by pornography and prostitution.[39]

This approach to trafficking and its emphasis on prostitution frustrates some women's rights activists, who object to the way in which it reinforces traditional gender roles. "It's very interesting to think about how this is being used by many people to fit in with traditional notions of femininity and sexuality," said Ann Jordan, director of the Anti-Trafficking Initiative of the International Human Rights Law Group, based in Washington, D.C. At issue here for many feminist global activists is agency. For them, the best solution to the problem of human trafficking is to regulate prostitution and to support a movement for sex workers' rights. CWA's approach reduces the possibility for women to act and choose their work. According to Jordan, "The idea of the pure, simple, naïve, innocent who needs to be rescued by the Good Samaritan deprives adults of any kind of agency."[40] Nevertheless, CWA's approach corresponds closely with the position of many global women's activists and feminists who agree that demand for sex is what drives the problem and that prostitution is inherently exploitative of women.

CWA has invested considerable effort in combating human trafficking, but it has remained aloof from two other major international issues concerning violence against women: domestic violence and gender-based violence in civil conflict. Both of these issues pose difficulties for CWA, although for different reasons. Domestic violence is a topic on which CWA has remained largely silent in the national as well as the international context, probably because it raises questions about the safety of the family for women. CWA argues that women can best achieve their human rights within the context of the family and opposes what it claims are feminist depictions of the family "as a place of violence."[41] Moreover, CWA vigorously opposes the notion that domestic or international law should be extended into the private sphere, a fundamental tenet of women's human rights campaigns. Similarly, supporting the international campaign to reduce violence against women in conflict settings, which has centered on prosecuting perpetrators through international tribunals and courts, would force CWA to endorse a positive role for these institutions; it has adamantly refused to do this on the grounds that such international bodies would violate national sovereignty.[42]

Thus, CWA has focused on human trafficking in its international efforts against violence toward women, which it has framed in terms of clear physical and emotional harm to women and girls. It has clearly identified the cause of the problem as a demand for sex. In its emphasis on the harmfulness of prostitution, CWA attempts to mobilize support to stop the brutal victimization of a vulnerable population and avoids more complex, and perhaps to the public more confusing, discussions about women's agency. This would seem to give it a framing advantage in its efforts to garner public and international support for this cause. To what extent has CWA been able to draw on support from women's activists and organizations, especially in the developing South, to create a successful transnational campaign against trafficking? Has its global agenda translated to "written traces" in the documents produced by the UN? Finally, has CWA succeeded in linking its own constituency to its global campaign against trafficking?

CWA began its activism concerning human trafficking in the American context, at least in part as an outgrowth of its participation in a coalition to pass the International Religious Freedom Act in 1998. Shortly thereafter, faith-based groups turned their attention to the task of passing legislation designed to curb human trafficking in the United States and abroad. CWA focused on the need to tackle the source of this problem: prostitution and other forms of commercial sex trade. Its opposition to prostitution in any form was eventually incorporated into the language of the Victims of Trafficking and Violence Protection Act (VTVPA) passed in 2000 and, under the Bush administration, was given real teeth.[43] During the next several years, CWA continued to agitate for the Bush administration's policy of withdrawing VTVPA funding from any domestic or international organization that provided support for legal prostitution or services to prostitutes.[44]

In addition to addressing human trafficking through U.S. foreign policy, CWA expanded its efforts in the international arena, especially at the UN. CWA drew attention to human trafficking and the need to tackle the problem of demand for commercial sex at the Beijing + 5 meetings in 2000, condemning attempts by the European Union and other Western countries to distinguish between the situation of children and that of women with regard to victimization by pornography, prostitution, and sex trafficking.[45] CWA took an even stronger stance at the CSW meeting in 2003, where violence against women and girls was a major theme. As a member of the official delegation to the CSW meeting, Crouse was in a better position to have a concrete impact on its outcome. CWA delegates condemned the failure of CSW documents to mention pornography in the media and praised efforts by countries such as Israel, Iran, Egypt, and Pakistan to emphasize pornography and prostitution as major causes of violence against women.[46] After hard-fought sessions over document wording, the CSW meeting ended without consensus for the first time when it could not agree with the U.S. position that prostitution is inherently harmful to women.[47] As Crouse described gleefully, "[w]e fought the radicals to a standstill." A further victory came for CWA at the CSW meeting in 2005, when the United States introduced a UN resolution "addressing how demand, particularly for commercial sexual exploitation, fuels human trafficking." The resolution was adopted by consensus with more than fifty co-sponsors.[48] Thus, in conjunction with its pro-family allies and with the support of the Bush administration, CWA was able to impact the discussion about human trafficking at the UN.

This impact, however, has not translated into greater cooperation with UN initiatives concerning the fight against human trafficking. In 2007 the UN launched the UN.GIFT, a multiyear program to combat human trafficking. In its voluminous writings on trafficking and various domestic campaigns against it, CWA has completely ignored the UN campaign. No information about it was presented on the CWA website, where the Beverly LaHaye Institute tracks and reports on issues related to trafficking. Thus, while CWA works to publicize its approach to this issue at the UN, it appears unwilling to participate in its international efforts. Rather, CWA appears, at least at this point, to see its role at the UN as a primarily negative one of putting the brakes on or providing a critical voice against the "hegemonic ideas" of feminists in this venue. In keeping with its skepticism toward and ambivalence about the UN in general, CWA has preferred to concentrate its efforts on shaping American foreign policy on this issue.

In addition to eschewing cooperation with the UN campaign against human trafficking, CWA has failed to establish networks among women's advocacy groups elsewhere in the world that might bolster its claims to represent the majority of the world's women. Transnational advocacy networks involve "vibrant alliances" encompassing grassroots advocates, regional women's organizations and movements, NGOs, policy networks, academics, elected officials, and other actors such as diplomats or foundations.[49] CWA has directed one cross-border anti-trafficking project, funded by the U.S. State Department, in conjunction with local "pro-family" NGOs in Mexico.[50] This represented a serious effort at cross-border cooperation between government officials and civil society actors to curb the sex trafficking of Mexican women and children. However, it did not involve the exchange of views and information among regional women's organizations and movements, grassroots advocates, and NGOs that might constitute a "vibrant alliance." Such cross-border cooperation among women from the United States and Latin America might

form the nucleus of a TAN dedicated to fighting human trafficking and demand for commercial sex, but it has not emerged as yet. Nor has CWA invested
its organizational energy in this direction. Whereas CWA has cooperated with
a robust coalition of forces to pass legislation on trafficking in the United
States, it has shied away from building such alliances in the international
sphere. Rather, CWA's international activity concerning trafficking remains
largely confined to influencing discussion and counteracting "elitist feminist's
support for prostitution" at the UN.

CWA may have shied away, thus far, from building an effective TAN
around a campaign against sex trafficking and the commercial sex trade, but
it has invested a great deal of energy in mobilizing its own constituency
around this cause. To what extent has CWA linked its campaign against trafficking in the United States to a larger awareness of global issues and global
women among its own members? As Sara Diamond pointed out in her 1998
study of CWA, the group's organizational structure provides an extremely
effective way to bring the concerns of the leadership in Washington, in this
case concerns about sex trafficking, to the rank and file.[51] CWA is organized
through prayer chains (what might be described as a cell structure). In each
state, seven people form a prayer group that meets at least once a month and
oftentimes more frequently; seven prayer groups are organized into chapters,
whose leaders are directed by the heads of the state CWA. Each month, prayer
concerns are sent from Washington to the state directors, who then pass
them along to the chapter leaders. Putting international prayer concerns
such as sex trafficking on the agenda can provide a useful mobilizing tool.[52]
Evangelical women not only hear about global women's issues but are encouraged to become personally engaged in them "by putting feet to their
prayers" and taking action.[53]

Nevertheless, thinking globally is sometimes a hard sell to a constituency
that is wary of internationalism and international bodies, and it is not clear
just how successful CWA has been in getting its members to turn their attention to the global aspects of sex trafficking, let alone to appreciate the work
that CWA is performing at the UN. In part, this may reflect the ambivalence
of CWA's leadership in communicating the importance of global issues and
the organization's work in this arena. CWA's monthly magazine, Family
Voice, for example, rarely devotes any articles to international topics. Indeed,
from 1995 to 2008, the magazine featured only one article on a topic related
to global issues. Similarly, Beverly LaHaye's popular radio show has remained
focused on domestic concerns. The prayer requests issued to state leaders
devote far less attention to international issues than domestic ones, and the
link between the two is rarely made clear. Moreover, state directors do have
some say over which issues they will choose to highlight, and some of these
leaders choose not to focus on international developments, which are of less
concern to their members.[54] According to one state director, CWA members

are not really aware of the international dimensions of the problem of human trafficking.[55] Rather, they see it largely in terms of domestic demand that should be addressed by the American government. Moreover, they view their relationship to women in other countries largely as one of "benefactor," rescuing those in harm's way and rehabilitating them in the United States when possible. Thus, although CWA has raised awareness about human trafficking among its members and they, in turn, are having an impact in raising awareness in their communities, this issue is rarely linked with more global concerns about women's rights or human rights.

Conclusion

In 1979 CWA was established as a conservative women's organization implacably opposed to the UN and its purported intent to internationalize the world's children. Less than three decades later, CWA was an accredited NGO at the UN, and its leaders were arguing that participation there was necessary to represent the views of and "provide hope to" the majority of the world's women. As we have seen, this shift in attitude toward the UN has caused CWA to become increasingly involved in the very international institutions it initially opposed, with allies it does not entirely trust. In offering an alternative vision of women's rights, CWA has often claimed to represent the "common and indigenous" women of the world, especially in the global South. To what extent has it reached out to form alliances with these women over important issues such as human trafficking? Although a full answer to this question must await further study of conservative women's global activism, a preliminary examination does not find evidence of such linkages. CWA has cooperated directly with pro-family NGOs in Mexico, but it has displayed little interest in cultivating ties with women's organizations or organizing anything close to a conservative women's countermovement in the global arena. Ironically, while CWA denounces the UN as the "playground" of elitist feminist forces, it is there that it conducts the vast majority of its international activism. Unlike feminist organizations, which have been instrumental in forging close, though sometimes contentious, ties between Northern and Southern activists, CWA has confined its activism and its claims to speak for the world's women to the halls of the UN.

NOTES

1. Janice Crouse, "The United States and U.N. Security Resolution 1325," *Townhall,* May 21, 2008, http://townhall.com/columnists/JaniceShawCrouse/2008/05/21/the_united_states_and_un_security_resolution_1325.

2. Elisabeth Friedman, "Gendering the Agenda: The Impact of the Transnational Women's Rights Movement at the UN Conferences of the 1990s," *Women's Studies International Forum* 26, no. 4 (2003): 313–31.

3. Didi Herman, "Globalism's 'Siren Song': The United Nations and International Law in Christian Right Thought and Prophecy," *Sociological Review* 49, no. 1 (2001): 56–77; Friedman, "Gendering the Agenda"; Doris Buss and Didi Herman, *Globalizing Family Values: The Christian Right in International Politics* (Minneapolis: University of Minnesota Press, 2003); Allen Hertzke, *Freeing God's Children: The Unlikely Alliance for Global Human Rights* (Lanham, Md.: Rowman and Littlefield, 2004).

4. Beverly LaHaye, *Who but a Woman?* (New York: Thomas Nelson, 1984), 27.

5. See http://www.cwfa.org/joincwa.asp; Steven Gardiner, "Concerned Women for America: A Case Study," Feminism and Women's Studies, http://feminism.eserver.org/cw-of-a.txt. Gardiner asserts that "membership estimates vary widely, from 350,000 to 750,000." For comparison, the National Organization for Women (NOW) claims to be "the largest organization of feminist activists in the US," with 500,000 contributing members (regular dues are $35 per year).

6. LaHaye, *Who but a Woman?* 9.

7. Ibid., 36–40.

8. Ibid., 33. By "internationalization of our children," LaHaye was presumably warning against the dangers of communist and other undesirable influences propagated by international forces like the UN.

9. Hertzke, *Freeing God's Children*.

10. Buss and Herman, *Globalizing Family Values*.

11. Friedman, "Gendering the Agenda."

12. Buss and Herman, *Globalizing Family Values*.

13. Ronnee Schreiber, *Righting Feminism: Conservative Women and American Politics* (New York: Oxford University Press, 2008).

14. Janice Crouse, "A Contest of Wills," March 1, 2004, http://www.cwfa.org.

15. Wendy Wright, "Countries Call for Revamping Commission on the Status of Women," March 8, 2004, http://www.cwfa.org.

16. Mike Fiala, "Religious Right Challenges 'Anti-Family' Beijing Agenda," *Chicago Sun-Times*, September 10, 1995.

17. Ibid.

18. Friedman, "Gendering the Agenda."

19. Louise Chappell, "Contesting Women's Rights: The Influence of Religious Forces at the United Nations" (paper presented at the Australasian Political Studies Association Conference, University of Adelaide, 2004), http://www.adelaide.edu.au/apsa/docs_papers/Others/Chappell.pdf; Jennifer Butler, *Born Again: The Christian Right Globalized* (London: Pluto Press, 2006).

20. Buss and Herman, *Globalizing Family Values*.

21. "Geneva 1999: The Geneva Declaration," World Congress of Families II, http://www.worldcongress.org/WCF2/wcf2_declaration.htm.

22. Jennifer Butler, "The Religious Right at the Beijing + 5 PrepCom," *Global Policy Forum Newsletter*, April 25, 2000, http://www.globalpolicy.org/component/content/article/177-un/31728.html; Buss and Herman, *Globalizing Family Values*.

23. Friedman, "Gendering the Agenda," 326; Butler, "Religious Right at the Beijing + 5 PrepCom"; Buss and Herman, *Globalizing Family Values*; Luke Jalsevac, "Small Pro-family Contingent Had Big Impact on Beijing + 5," *Life Site News*, June 13, 2000, http://www.lifesitenews.com/resources/small-pro-family-contingent-had-big-impact-on-beijing5; Anick Druelle, *Right-Wing Anti-feminist Groups at the United Nations*, report from the Institut de Recherches et d'Études Féministes, Université du Québec à Montréal (Quebec: IQAM Press, 2000), http://www.newyorkeagleforum.org/eagle_articles/Anti-Feminist%20Groups-USLetter.pdf; Sandhya Nankani, "Right-Wing Forces Mobilize to Challenge Beijing Platform," *Women's Wire*, www.womenswire.net/right-wing.htm; Butler, *Born Again*.

24. "History Ends and 'Herstory' Begins," June 6, 2000, http://www.cwfa.org; Butler, *Born Again*.

25. Butler, *Born Again*, 52–55.

26. Janice Crouse, "Those Wacky, Leftist Women," March 3, 2006, http://www.cwfa.org; Wendy Wright, "The Breathtaking Arrogance of the CEDAW Committee," September 23, 2002, http://www.cwfa.org.

27. Janice Crouse, "The U.N.: Is It Worth Fixing?" March 5, 2007, http://www.cwfa.org.

28. Ibid.

29. Janice Crouse, "Three Predictable Problems at the Commission on the Status of Women," March 8, 2007, http://www.cwfa.org; Janice Crouse, "Is the Commission on the Status of Women Passé?" March 7, 2007, http://www.cwfa.org.

30. Friedman, "Gendering the Agenda," 327.

31. Although aligned with the evangelical movement, CWA is an independent organization with 501c3 and 501c4 operations. The organization stresses that the vast majority of its donations, averaging less than $30, come from individual contributors. From 2007 to 2009, five hundred thousand individuals purportedly either donated or acted on a CWA issue. The decentralized chapter-based structure of NOW, in which local chapters raise their own revenues, makes comparison difficult. In FY 2007 the national office of NOW spent $4,057,347 and the NOW Foundation spent $894,645. In that same year, the California chapter of NOW spent $880,913.

32. Margaret E. Keck and Kathryn Sikkink, *Activists Beyond Borders: Advocacy Networks in International Politics* (Ithaca: Cornell University Press, 1998).

33. Friedman, "Gendering the Agenda."

34. "Crouse: A Block to Human Trafficking," *Washington Times*, December 16, 2008, http://www.washingtontimes.com/news/2008/dec/16/a-block-to-human-trafficking/.

35. Schreiber, *Righting Feminism*.

36. Keck and Sikkink, *Activists Beyond Borders*.

37. "Beijing + 5—Anti-family NGOs and Delegates Deliver Conflicting Messages," June 7, 2000, http://www.cwfa.org.

38. Angie Vineyard, "Are Women More Vulnerable to Violence?" 2003, http://www.cwfa.org.

39. Crouse, "United States and U.N. Security Resolution 1325."

40. Quoted in Jennifer Block, "Sex Trafficking: Why the Faith Trade Is Interested in the Sex Trade," *Catholics for Choice*, Summer/Autumn 2004, http://www.catholicsforchoice.org/conscience/archives/c2004sum_sextrafficking.asp.

41. "Mother's Day Under Attack?" podcast interview with Wendy Wright, May 8, 2009, http://www.cwfa.org.

42. Crouse, "United States and U.N. Security Resolution 1325."

43. Victims of Trafficking and Violence Protection Act, Pub. L. No. 106–386 (2000), http://www.state.gov/documents/organization/10492.pdf.

44. Janice Crouse, "Ending Modern-Day Slavery: Some Solutions to Sex Trafficking," September 23, 2004, http://www.cwfa.org.

45. "Beijing + 5—Anti-family NGOs and Delegates Deliver Conflicting Messages."

46. "UN Delegates: Let's Talk About Porn," March 11, 2003, http://www.cwfa.org.

47. Janice Crouse, "Beijing and Abortion, Leftists Are Asking," March 2, 2005, http://www.cwfa.org.

48. Ellen Sauerbrey, "Promoting Strong Families as a Foreign Policy Goal" (speech delivered at the World Congress of Families IV, Warsaw, Poland, May 11, 2007), http://www.worldcongress.org/wcf4.spkrs/wcf4.sauerbrey.pdf.

49. Mary Hawkesworth, *Globalization and Feminist Activism* (Lanham, Md.: Rowman and Littlefield, 2006), 109.

50. Brenda Zurita, "Christians Shine the Light on Sex Trafficking," *Family Voice*, July/August 2005; Janice Crouse, "CWA's 'Bridge Project' Made Huge Strides in the Battle Against Sex Trafficking," *Family Voice*, March/April 2007.

51. Sara Diamond, *Not by Politics Alone: The Enduring Influence of the Christian Right* (London: Guilford Press, 1998). See also Sara Diamond, *Spiritual Warfare: The Politics of the Christian Right* (Boston: South End Press, 1989).

52. Diamond, *Not by Politics Alone;* Gardiner, "Concerned Women for America."

53. "Crouse: A Block to Human Trafficking"; Zurita, "Christians Shine the Light on Sex Trafficking."

54. Linda Casswell, Oklahoma state director of CWA, interview by Jill Irvine, July 2009.

55. Ibid.

3

Memoirs of an Avatar: A Feminist Exploration of
Right-Wing Worlds in SecondLife.com

Randolph Hollingsworth

Since the early days of computerized communications, "wired" women have
found new platforms for social and political power—and even intense pleasure.[1] What are the implications for right-wing activism among women? On
the one hand, geographical distance, nationality, ethnicity, and gender roles
may be less important in digital communities than outside, thereby undermining the rigid categories of right-wing thinking. On the other hand, the
racist, sexist, and homophobic expressions of right-wing hate groups across
the globe are increasingly accessible to everyone. Online communities are
easily connected, and women can readily interact and transmit images and
audio files across traditional barriers of race, ethnicity, or class. Women who
might be inhibited offline by the vagaries of real life can experiment and connect with people, like right-wing extremists, whom they might not otherwise
have met.

This essay is an abridged and adapted version of a web log ("blog") that I
constructed during the process of exploring the virtual world of SecondLife
.com and searching for evidence of right-wing activities by women. The blog's
authorship was tied to my Second Life (SL) avatar's name, and any communications with other residents of SL flowed through the related e-mail addresses
based on my avatar's name and crafted just for the use of the blog. Through
the inherently unstable nature of digital text, a blog allowed me to interact
with individuals connected to communities centered on hate. By using one of
the more popular blog platforms, my entries pulled in new viewers, including some who used the blog's comment box to leave behind slogans of praise
for their political party. Originally, I had begun using the blog's tag feature
(i.e., I would choose terms that best characterized a particular posting) as an

organizational strategy for my writings. Sorting my posts by the use of tags such as "neo-Nazi" or "racist skinhead" gave me a better sense of the ground covered up to a certain point in my journey—giving me an overall sense of what types of right-wing hate groups I was finding. The tags also pulled in viewers seeking information on these topics as they used popular search engines. Few of the general viewers left comments, but there seemed to be regular upticks in viewing statistics with each new entry. If I felt uneasy or threatened by a reader's comment, I could just alter or delete the comment or the whole blog itself.

This transcript of a real experience in a digital world attempts to capture how right-wing sites contest the meanings of woman, power, and identity in the twenty-first century. By definition, the digital online world is global, but political and economic factors often determine women's levels of access to the online global community. Even while the Internet grows exponentially, local and national forces of discrimination often disadvantage women. This is a human rights issue in today's information age. Women's voices in the most contested spaces—time or geographic locale—can resound powerfully across the Internet in ways that other communication channels may not allow. Women's expressions of their personal and political experiences via the World Wide Web create greater transnational exigencies than ever before.

A Blog

Hello World!
March 15, 2008
Tags: Second Life, avatar
Welcome to my new blog, a chronicle of my exploration in the virtual world of Second Life (SL). SL is an online intentional environment, not unlike the social networking platforms of Facebook or MySpace, in which there are many and various ways to create alternate identities in order to share interests with an international community. As in other virtual worlds, a "resident" or account holder is embodied primarily as avatar: an alter ego of the computer user.[2] SL attracts an unusual set of virtual world users because everything in it has been created by the users for their own purposes and it provides near unlimited freedom in creativity.[3]

Being a Troll—Will It Work?
March 16, 2008
Tags: Racist skinhead, cyberself, avatar
It took some time to decide what form my avatar would take to interact with those of right-wing sensibilities. I thought about what might pass easily in a crowd, and I chose a finely toned shade of white skin with freckles and blonde hair. Serious gray eyes and braids. I wanted her to look more like a little sister

than a potential sexual partner. In an effort to seem even less intimidating, I chose the lowest possible setting for female avatar height.

My new avatar joined as many conservative groups as she could find in the search engine and began her cyberlife as a "troll." Judith S. Donath described trolling as identity deception in online chat rooms and games.[4] It is the presentation of a false self that "is played without the consent of most of the players . . . [and] attempts to pass as a legitimate participant, sharing the group's common interests and concerns."[5] Not truly believing in the political ideologies or cultures inherent in these groups, how could my new avatar do anything but deceive others who approach her as a comrade? Donath warned that trolls can be costly to online communities: disrupting the discussion, disseminating bad advice, and, especially, damaging the feeling of trust in the online community. Since right-wing groups are likely to be skittish and suspicious when nonmembers interact with them online,[6] this does not bode well. I began my new exploration of SL as a troll with some trepidation.

Body as Cyber-Performance
March 17, 2008
Tags: cyberself, avatar, Judith Butler
In thinking about how to cross a boundary that is so clear in the minds of members of racist groups—how to soften the visual effect of being one of those on "the outside"—I tried to imagine what would be least threatening, maybe even a bit comforting. Chris Atton asserts that a website of right-wing groups such as the British National Party "constructs white identity as Othered (that is, as repressed and in need of defence), yet perceives that identity as under threat by cultures which themselves are subject to Othering."[7] Where best to find my clothes and more cultivated white "skin" (images that could slightly hone my avatar's shape and body to include more lifelike attributes such as a blush, a pleasant smile, or gentle brow) but in an area where whiteness is assumed and even celebrated? I found a sim (a virtual neighborhood or island) that perpetuates the stereotypical white, middle-class 1950s, and I bought more clothes there.

Judith Butler's theory of performativity[8] is illustrated by my decisions about my new avatar's body shape, color, hair, clothing, and movements. SL easily allows for multiple manifestations of self. I am struggling to craft a gender performance that will be both recognizable and comforting to my intended audience.

Anti-immigrant, nationalist parties in Europe now recruit women heavily, especially into their "so-called comrade groups—small, informed unions of far-right sympathizers."[9] In the United States, women help make neo-Nazi and skinhead groups more acceptable to new recruits from the mainstream. Kathleen Blee wrote that women activists in U.S. organized hate groups may find empowerment but also find that racist activism does not contribute much to them personally: "For women, becoming a racial activist requires adopting a racist self that is fraught with complications, a self that many ultimately find unsatisfactory."[10] Will this hold true for women in SL?

Blonde, petite, and pretty in an old-fashioned kind of way, I go looking for other representations of women in SL who are associated with white power, neo-Nazis, or racist Confederate flag–loving southerners.

Stormfront and SL

March 18, 2008

Tags: neo-Nazi, fascist, Front National, Stormfront

The December 2006 stories in the *Second Life Herald* about Front National (FN), a French nationalist party, opening a recruiting office in SL during the French presidential elections attracted my curiosity.[11] I was certain I would find women in its cleanly designed and beautifully arranged garden site. Several visits to the FN sim proved that Le Pen was interested in recruiting young people. Posters at the sim showed a kind of ideal young female: nubile, her skin a soft golden-brown color, airbrushed to the kind of perfect sexlessness of a young woman brushing her teeth in a TV commercial for toothpaste. I agree with Kim Nielsen that we should carefully avoid "'exoticizing' women of the right as a bizarre and titillating Other"[12] and not assume that women's identities are as static as these posters. I still have not yet found anyone there when I visit the sim. Perhaps I'm not there at the right time of the day (or night). Or perhaps this empty environs—despite its lovely graphics and open plaza-like design—has not really captured the necessary essence for a regular gathering spot in order to recruit activists in SL.

So, I continue to sift through the Stormfront.org discussion forums. I find a good lead: on November 24, 2007, one of the organizers of the SL sim for another extreme right youth political organization wrote an invitation on Stormfront.org, the largest right-wing discussion forum online. A white supremacist discussion forum often cited as the earliest and longest continually published hate site,[13] Stormfront was founded in the mid-1990s by former Ku Klux Klan member Don Black to create and maintain communities among extremists. So it seemed natural for the Stormfront member to use that platform to post pictures of the new sim he was building for the Renouveau Français, a French far-right political organization. It took but a moment for me to find the sim and the SL resident who had built it. His profile picture, taken in front of a poster for a military boot camp for young white men, portrays a hypermasculinized militancy. The few images of women were of Joan of Arc, who served as a champion for French sovereignty against oppression from the English, and the winged Nike—medieval and classical images of woman meant to rally military-minded men to duty for family and nation. This focused, self-conscious, and organized racism demarcates the ultraconservative from the mainstream. It is what Blee defined as a "social milieu in which venomous ideas . . . take shape."[14] Here is direct evidence of the crossover capabilities of the Internet for right-wing groups.

Is It Just the Sexy Uniform?

March 19, 2008

Tags: neo-Nazi, Auschwitz, intolerance, Katja Eisenberg

In reading the *Second Life Herald* articles on past activities by right-wing activists, I found a couple of intriguing interviews with a woman avatar, Katja Eisenberg.[15] She had by then been banned eight separate times for creating and promoting Nazi titles and imagery, thus violating the community standards of tolerance.[16] One of her last acts in SL was to build a Nazi concentration camp that looked like Auschwitz with images of Jews in prison garb and followers in SS uniforms. When the reporter asked her why she was interested in the SS, she replied, "They had the sexiest Uniforms. I love the uniform. Doesn't mean I love Nazis." Later, she explained that she admired "the Strength. Brotherhood. Family of a Military that is strong. The Uniforms just make it all the funner. Not even the symbols on the Uniforms. A Plain black SS Uniform with nothing on it—to me would be sexiest of all."[17] Her passion for the timelessness of the uniform of an autocratic power, even without a particular insignia, raises for me the question of women's participation in sadomasochistic performances of right-wing groups in SL. Does she want to be taken by the violent man in the uniform? Is she crafting and creating experiences of masked terror for her own personal pleasure, or is this a behavior, a speech pattern, expected of her in order to gain and maintain acceptance in certain groups? Gender and sexuality are major signifiers for political ideologies in SL where maleness is celebrated.

Searching for Donna Haraway's Cyborgs

March 20, 2008

Tags: cyberself, cyborg, feminist

In thinking more carefully about what I'm trying to do, I realize that there will be only rare instances of right-wing group activity in SL. The very nature of this virtual world provides a daunting openness about it—a freedom to be and do whatever you want—that both attracts and repels ultraconservative activists. When Alan Scholl introduced SL in January 2007 to his readers of The John Birch Society website,[18] he described it as a fascinating place "free from government interference" but also cautioned that a "new danger" has emerged in the virtual world—government regulation, taxation, and control.

I am looking for physical/virtual beings—cyborgs. I don't mean the kind of cyborg described in Star Trek. Instead, I reference Donna Haraway's idea of a combined, new self. Haraway wrote that we need to be aware of and interact with the "cybernetic organism, a hybrid of machine and organism, a creature of social reality as well as a creature of fiction."[19] In an online world, the self is connected physically as well as electronically. An avatar is an embodiment of a right-wing activist, but the activist is changed by the experiences of the avatar. "The cyborg is a kind of disassembled and reassembled, postmodern collective and personal self." And so "the machine is us, our processes, an aspect of our embodiment."[20]

I need to keep in mind that by searching for evidence of the KKK, neo-Nazis, racist skinheads, and homophobic/misogynist Christians in SL, I become connected to them. Haraway wrote, "Cyborg imagery can suggest a way out of the maze of dualisms in which we have explained our bodies and our tools to ourselves. . . . It means both building and destroying machines, identities, categories, relationships."[21] That which we might call disembodied communication patterns of the Internet are physically unbound in a computer-generated world. There is a "new interactivity with symbolic structures. . . . The observer is no longer merely an observer, but rather becomes a participant."[22] Where will I find the courage to interact so directly with hate?

The Great Libertarian Hordes
March 24, 2008
Tags: libertarian, Lillie Yifu, Christian identity
In searching for conservative elements in SL, I found a few groups by using the SL search engine. In conversation with a human rights activist avatar, Lillie Yifu, who called the right-wing element of SL "the great libertarian hordes," I realized an important difference between those who play with conservative ideology and those who live according to organized racism/homophobia/xenophobia. The Internet allows access to a variety of communication channels and encourages those who may be more passive in real life to experiment with new identities and behaviors. The collaborative nature of virtual worlds enhances the use of multiple media, and those who might fear repercussions from controversial statements in real life can play out their fantasies in a variety of ways. It is not always easy to see immediately the difference between someone play-acting a new role and someone expressing their real-life ideologies in the virtual world. However, with close attention over time, observers can distinguish between an actual right-wing presence and a role-play.

Christian anti-abortion sites are an example. They have lovely sims with a coffee house, a community center complete with a swimming pool and slide, and a modern church where visitors can have their avatar baptized by a minister. The space reserved for women is described but not visible until a visitor is accepted as a member of the women's prayer group. Visitors can access recordings of the church meetings conducted live by the avatars in SL for one another. I listen to a few—the body of woman is reduced to a uterus in many of the sermons. Sometimes I am joined by a church member who is alerted by my visit to the island by a visitor counter. Everyone is handsome, very polite, and welcoming. However, I do not have the heart to attend the Bible study and woman's prayer session to which I have been kindly and gently, repeatedly invited.

A Tremor in the Spiderweb

March 27, 2008

Tags: neo-Nazi, Second Life, cyberself, Second Life profile

I see my journey not only as one of trepidation into the darker parts of an online world but also as a journey through my knowledge and belief structures as a feminist scholar. I enter with some unwillingness the nonlinear structure of SL. I watch myself walking in the virtual world as an avatar, knowing it is really just me playing a part. At the same time, I struggle with how to perform as an intellectual, moving between theory and practice in a very real way. I bought a shirt with a Confederate flag and felt better about my avatar's appearance, but I couldn't shake my personal inhibitions about having constructed an identity whose primary purpose is to be recruited by a hate group.

As I get up the nerve to approach a conservative activist to ask for an interview, I search for members of conservative groups so I can send someone a request via an instant message. Searching on the term "nazi," I found the Bosatsu Royal Family group, founded by Odin Bosatsu (a name no longer in SL's archives, so he must have been perma-banned). The group charter states, "We are neo-Nazi and Proud of it. Seig [sic] heil!" There is one member still active in the group. I send the avatar a message asking if I could talk about the Bosatsu Royal Family and its role in neo-Nazi activities in SL. The response from the server is quick: this avatar is not online and my message is archived for viewing on next login. I spend another hour or so exploring further leads and trying on different hairstyles, but I didn't want to reach out to someone else before I heard back. Eventually, I logged off.

Conservative Coalition

March 30, 2008

Tags: libertarian, conservative, Selwyn Duke

I received a group posting from the Conservative Coalition today: "Want to be inspired by Conservative Thought? Then read 'Conservatism is Dead; Long Live Conservatism?' a brief article by Selwyn Duke. In it he laments the defensive nature of Conservatism and the offensive nature of the Left which merely has to wait on a series of compromises with the Right to achieve its goals." In other groups in SL, when a post comes across the group chat, there are some members who will contribute to the group conversation. Sometimes they joke, and sometimes it becomes a conversation. No conversations ensued as a result of this directive. The communication is one-way here for this group.

Stand Strong America

April 4, 2008

Tags: anti-immigrant, conservative, nationalist, Stand Strong America

Advertised as a new organization on Stormfront.org, Stand Strong America started up in SL on March 23, 2008. I joined the group and got a group message right away:

Group Notice

Greetings
I would like to thank you for joining.

This group is part of the new conservative grassroot movement Stand Strong America. Our website located at http://standstrongamerica .novahost.org contains our mission statement and other information. I would like to take this opportunity to lay down a few recruitment regulations:

1. we accept any american citizen

2. as you recruit members, please make sure to have them check our mission statement on our site and register on our site.

3. Even though Stand Strong America is conservative oriented, we welcome democrats and/or independants [sic] to join us. The only thing needed is for them to believe in our mission statement and other documents found on our site

Soon thereafter, I contacted an avatar who had announced via Stormfront.org that he was a member of Stand Strong America. Unlike other members of Stormfront.org who announced they were in SL, this one showed his SL name on a discussion forum posting. He seemed friendly enough but clearly was distracted, and we did not get a chance to meet in-world.

Women and Neo-Confederates
April 10, 2008
Tags: KKK, Second Life, slavery, Museum of the Confederacy, neo-Confederates
Looking for gathering places for white supremacists, I found a Museum of the Confederacy—a big Georgian mansion with a campsite of neatly arrayed tents and campfire nearby. No one is here, but I find images on the walls and around the building that revise history to show the South winning the War of Northern Aggression, the Confederate term for the U.S. Civil War. I looked up the female names associated with the museum. One is the founder of a group whose logo features battle flags of the Confederate States of America. When I contacted her to ask about the group, she was offline. Later, she answered and we arranged to meet the next morning. When I logged on and sent her a message, she replied right away that she was concentrating on building something. I looked again at her profile as the founder of a group dedicated to the memory of the Confederacy and the Old South. Her portrait shows her in an elegant dress from the nineteenth century. Creative graphic designers find the SL platform easy to manipulate, and it is likely that she had crafted the museum—a Georgian mansion on the outside and open galleries on the inside—within a few hours. There is money to be made by an entrepreneur who sells clothing or settings to members of groups wanting realistic role-playing environments. After a while, she went offline again, and we

never got a chance to talk. A few days later when I returned to the site for the museum, it was gone. The impermanence of these buildings gives informality to the whole endeavor but also allows for flexibility and rapid response to the needs of a group or individual leader switching tactics.

Virtual Tribal Identity of White Masculinity
April 10, 2008
Tags: Ku Klux Klan, masculinity, tribal identity, white power
Virtual communities like Stormfront.org allow connections among individuals or groups dedicated to promoting racist ideologies, although their anonymity and informal, hidden nature make it difficult to create sustained political actions in real life. On the other hand, an individual whose avatar gains affiliation with a hate group learns a fixed identity with a specific, virtual ethnicity. Denise Bostdorff describes efforts of hate groups like the Ku Klux Klan to promote nostalgia for an imagined past, that is, aiming for "the creation of a virtual tribal identity of white masculinity."[23]

In SL, the relationships that are formed during virtual role-play like Civil War reenactments can strengthen right-wing groups. SL Community Affairs Director Daniel (Linden) Huebner[24] described how social networking environments can bind together ever more expanding groupings based on an individual's level of trust. For example, if one member of a group mutes a harasser or bans an offensive avatar from a sim, this action could be shared with others in the group, thus allowing like-minded individuals or groups to include this action in their mute or banned lists. This sharing component inherent to a social network is what makes it a much more powerful medium of communication than the typical use of the Internet for a static website or broadcast email. Similarly, Brian Levin found that when legal actions broke up organized hate groups, the Internet became a crucial support for right-wing activists engaged in "leaderless resistance."[25] The very nature of social media makes possible a collective approach to the construction of something that becomes common knowledge; the shape of these collective intelligences shifts rapidly.

Conservative Groups in SL
April 13, 2008
Tags: conservative, Second Life
In a world that is increasingly dependent on the Internet as a method of communication, it seems natural for ultraconservatives to use this as a platform. Searches in groups in SL on words like "conservative," "Nazi," "skinhead," and "fascist" yielded several interesting leads:

- Conservatives and Patriots: "To advance conservative principals [*sic*], help define and identify the flaws of liberalism to the unenlightened and contribute to the rescue of our nation from the tyrany [*sic*] of the left."

- Second Life Conservatives: "We're the Second Life Conservatives. . . . We don't need to be ashamed of being conservative."
- Conservative Coalition: "AMERICANS WORKING TO PROMOTE CONSERVATIVE IDEAS. To become part of the coalition: 1. Must be a Patriotic American 2. Must be a Conservative 3. Must Promote Conservative Ideas."
- Division Germania: "This group is for all the Skinheads and Nationalists all over the world ;) We must secure the existence of our people and a future for White children."
- Rush Limbaugh Fans: "We will try to meet at regular intervals to discuss the issues going on in our country and to learn from the master of 'Advanced Conservative Studies' . . . Mister Rush Limbaugh."
- Fascist Furs: "Nazi Furs (name changed to 'Fascist Furs' by SL's Linden Censors) is founded to establish a community for members of the furry fandom who harbor an interest in WWII era Germany for historical, militaristic, strategic, sociopolitical, or fetish reasons. We are not a hate group, nor do we support hate groups of any kind, rather we seek to further the understanding of Hitler's Germany through study and understanding."
- SL Fascist Party: "A group devoted to spreading the word of Fascism, and exposing the lies of Communists and the Left. Silence the Leftists, at whom's [sic] hands easily over 100 million people were mercilessly massacred. That includes Stalin, Lenin, and Mao. DISCLAIMER: Fascism isn't strictly anti-Semitism or racism. Speak to Griffith Benelli before complaining."
- Stand Strong America: "Stand Strong America is a grassroots movement which promotes conservative principles and values by educating the electorate, supporting solid candidates (at all levels of government) and working through the Republican party to effect transformational change and conservative policies for our nation."
- Midian City's Skinheads: "Somewhat more than a gang, but not even close to family. Kids, adults, people who are sick of the disgusting streets of Midian [a role-play sim]. People who are afraid of walking down the street without getting jumped, beaten, harassed just because of being human, or the way they dress. The skinheads stick together, have loud, obnoxious mouths, and love to pick fights. As they united, there [sic] fear of walking in their own neighbor [sic] has resided, now they walk the streets, proud and full of pride."

Exploring Headquarters for Renouveau Français
April 14, 2008
Tags: anti-abortion, Christian, Front National, homophobia, Renouveau Français, xenophobia, neo-Nazi
Finding the new headquarters for the French right-wing activists in SL wasn't hard. A search in places in SL yielded Renouveau Français (French Renewal)

at a sim called Ghloogums. Teleporting in, I saw a large meeting space with a few benches with pose balls for seating. The benches faced a podium with large pictures behind it emphasizing the classical ideals of French conservative thought—including the warrior Joan of Arc.[26] According to the note card welcoming visitors, "Our organization defines itself politically as nationalist, catholic and anti-revolutionary (meaning hostile to the false dogmas and false principles of the 1789 revolution). . . . We will set the record straight and propose a counter-information against the downpour of lies and omissions perpetuated continuously by the servile mass media." There is no doubt that this virtual meeting space is trying to recruit followers with a message of cultural purity. The welcome note goes on to declare that "besides the broadcast of our analysis and proposals to the greater number of French possible, we are working on training politically, philosophically, and humanly a new generation of executives which will be essential tomorrow in any attempt to redress our nation. We will particularly focus our efforts toward youth as its generosity and enthusiasm allows us to hope in the future. Help us to make possible a rebirth of France!"

The posters along the back of the meeting space included one that used homophobic humor to poke fun at the members of the Communist Party of Second Life, a group dedicated to working against fascist activism in SL. On another wall, I found a poster calling for the youth of France to join their revolution and one describing the purpose of the European National Front. Among its many goals, this organization exists to defend "our culture, our traditions and our Christian identity against the cultural globalization, the uncontrolled in migration . . . [and in] defense of life and traditional family against the crime of abortion, gay marriages and the adoptions by homosexual pairs." The poster gives brief biographies of two post–World War I fascist leaders: Corneliu Zelea Codreanu (1899–1938, founder of the fascist Iron Guard in Romania) and José Antonio Primo de Rivera (1903–1936, founder of the nationalist party Falange Española, or Spanish Phalanx). But they really don't need to refer to nationalist history of decades ago—there are many ultranationalist movements taking place throughout Europe today, and their messages are bolstered through the use of the Internet.

Antifa Reactions Still Smoldering
April 15, 2008
Tags: antifa, fascist, nationalist, neo-Nazi
The antifa (antifascist) responses to Renouveau Français and to Le Pen's Front National (FN) are not as militant or eventful as last year in SL,[27] but the signs and group slogans remain. A week later, the poster referring to the FN as a neo-Nazi organization was gone. Likely, it was protested by members of the FN and deemed by SL director Linden as going too far in its depiction of this party's ideology as Nazism.

Satire in SL
April 27, 2008
Tags: American Nazi Party, Conservative Heaven, Gen. JC Christian, satire, neo-Nazi, Second Life
Is it safe to be satirical about conservatives in SL?

Early in my wanderings I found General JC Christian, builder of the Wellstone Cafe and Conservative Heaven. He encouraged me to talk to a few of his friends and told me about the discussion forums at Stormfront.org as a resource. He said that other than a few "griefers" (that is, avatars out to just harass or irritate others) who took offense when he made fun of conservative ideology, he had not encountered any references to extreme right-wing politics. Today, I see in his blog that his luck has changed. His site is littered with boxes marked with swastikas.[28]

A New Sim for Front National Second Life (FNSL)
April 29, 2008
Tags: nationalist, Front National, Le Pen, xenophobia
There is a bright new spot in SL, the platform of the right-wing French FN. It's easily found in the SL search engine, and when teleporting in, you find yourself on a long rectangular platform high in the air. It is a lovely open space filled with bushes and flowers in the carefully constructed green areas and bounded with white walls. The glowing white podium area includes seats in a round for a sizeable meeting space with posters and flags well displayed around the edges. At the center of the main walkway to the meeting area, I found a donation box ready for avatars to contribute funds for the cause. Nearby, a lighted cone is scripted to count visiting avatars and record their names. It glows with a floating text that shows visitors that their presence is being noted and archived.

I found a group of avatars gathering for a meeting. Although kind enough to try and communicate with me in English, they were not particularly interested in speaking with me. So I wandered off to take pictures. Beside a map that portrayed immigrant populations as overwhelming France, I find posters. One, featuring a young woman of color, attracted my attention first. I try to read it with my rusty college French. It offers the FN as the solution to the "broken" ideas of the French parties of the political left and the political right. A downward thrust of a beautiful girl's thumb is used to suggest that mainstream French concepts of nationality, assimilation, a social ladder, and secularism are wrong. Rather, the party promotes "traditional" values, especially removing women from the workforce and "sending back" immigrants and their children.

At the far end of the platform, visitors find a series of posters with reprinted news articles and internal communications from the leaders of the party. The images of Le Pen are beatific and could easily convince the casual observer that his message is wholesome and good. One poster, dated today, complains about the latest media attack on Jean-Marie Le Pen's remarks on World War II, suggesting that such attacks bring discord to France. It suggests that FN is the victim of the mainstream press, and it is not their fault that "more than 80% of the French people consider us dangerous."

Protesting FNSL
April 30, 2008
Tags: nationalist, neo-Nazi, anti-Semitic, antifascist, furry, Front National, protest
I journeyed once again to the FN platform to see if I could get a conversation going with members of the party. No big questions to ask. Just wander in with my blonde-haired, petite white avatar dressed as an American cowgirl—and then wait. I wondered if any members of this right-wing group might be interested in recruiting me.

This time, there was some action. A group gathered together at the back of the platform huddled together while being harassed by a protester. A bear standing upright (I'll call her Elle) was dancing around in the center of the group holding a big poster that denounced fascism and a flag of German antifascism. She wore a Roman toga over long trousers and had sneakers on her feet. The contrast of the slender two-legged bear with a busty dominatrix in a red miniskirt, black stockings, and a whip highlighted for me how different women can be portrayed in SL. As I stood there watching, I was responding via instant message to one of the FN members who may have been attracted to the list of conservative groups in my profile . . . and Elle chatted in English and in French as she continued to dance and wave her flag.

In between private instant message texts with the FN avatar (I'll call him René), I watched the text chat scroll by as the group continued to converse in French, despite the protester's interruptions. René began interacting with me in a friendly and inquisitive way, asking if I was a National Socialist. Instead of replying in IM, I asked in the open chat window what Elle was doing. René responded, "Bad, bad," but Elle replied in English, "Just protesting," before she shrieked (via text) and danced around even more frantically. Then she started writing in French about her antifascist poster, pestering the group, who had now resorted to silence—likely using text messaging within the FN group list. Elle taunted them, asking why they would be concerned about the antifa poster if the FN is not fascist. She directed her next statement likely to me, though it was still in French: all the activists here are racists. At that, René privately texted to me that Elle is "jewish" and "lol"—laughed out loud.

This is not much of a protest compared to the real-life antifascist extremist groups in Germany or England,[29] but the bear's protest could be annoying to users for whom the visual medium is important and a sense of proprietary ownership of space is strong. However, the group didn't seem to mind her all that much and continued interacting via text chat and voice throughout the time I was there. As I watched, the chat text between the dominatrix and the bear moved into a discussion about the Jewish and Islamic versions of creation, with the dominatrix talking about how all Jews, Arabs, and blacks should be annihilated. I started examining her profile. I saw that one of the groups to which she belonged emphasized the role of sexual politics in avatar behavior: placing the strong-willed woman within constraints to assure control, or otherwise her lustful passions would rule society unchecked and destroy it. A world turned upside down.

I realize now that I may have been looking in the wrong places in SL for ultraconservative women. I might not find them only in right-wing sites. They may use SL to explore the edges of their own power and the strength of their convictions in other sites as well. As role-players they could spend time exploring their sexual roles and political ideas throughout SL.

Reflection on My Journey
May 1, 2008
Tags: Second Life, cyberself
And so my journey ends. The freedom that is offered in SL allows for a wealth of experiences, and the opportunities are endless. I am constantly modulating who I am—when I am alone in an empty sim, when I shift my conversation from observer/Other to comrade, when I see a place to shop for a better pair of boots. The creativity involved in the design of an avatar and strategies for communications tend to overwhelm my senses even though I'm sitting safe at home in front of my computer. Although I might have started out thinking that online anyone can be anybody or anything, gender, race, class, age, and heterosexuality remain important in SL. Jumping between the 3-D world of SL, photo editor software, web pages, scholarly books, and my notes is exhausting. My cyborg self, blending human and nonhuman, seems clumsy and stupid in the fast world spinning around me. Might this also be true for women in right-wing groups in SL?

My journey into virtual right-wing activities has only skimmed across the surface of many groups (large and small) that are experimenting with this new form of online branding, communication, and place. Groups like the FN or Stand Strong America use the Internet to solidify and fix right-wing identities, not to explore the multiplicity of possible identity formations. For these organizations, SL is not a place for role-playing and simulation; it is for real. Yet some right-wing women racists also try out new identities in the virtual world, using the plasticity of a virtual world to take on other "skins" and sexual powers.

Elusive and secretive as they elude the mainstream populations that are often bound by national borders or language barriers, right-wing women avatars in SL have found an easy way to meet online, role-play tactics, and strategize with like-minded individuals. At the same time, they play out sexualized fantasies of how women might act, look, and communicate. Whether dressed in a pseudo-Nazi uniform, a Southern belle's dress, or as a skingirl, women in the virtual world have easy access to right-wing groups, especially those who are skilled in graphic design or programming scripts that help construct the simulated environments. Languages and geographical distance are no barriers in this arena.

Gender plays a major role in the virtual world of SL. Whether or not women are behind the right-wing female avatars, virtual hate groups present themselves as decidedly patriarchal. In a "digital borderland"[30] of virtual technologies, they deploy powerful imaginings of women's bodies and female participation in right-wing groups that transcend boundaries of place and time. At the same time, the "Internet is a place where race happens."[31] Geographical distance and national boundaries fade as obstacles to an online community of like-minded individuals dedicated to honing their racist expressions of hate. In this three-dimensional cultural media, hate groups rise above national identities to find and use common iconic costumes of power or to gather and practice strategies that need few verbal translations. Women in virtual worlds can articulate and participate in new forms of ultraconservative social interactions that are powerful and disturbing.

NOTES

1. Lynn Cherny and Elizabeth Reba Weise, eds., *Wired Women: Gender and New Realities in Cyberspace* (Washington: Seal Press, 1996). For an alternative view—that the Internet has not wrought a greater intimacy but instead leads to passive spectator behavior—see Richard DeGrandpre, *Digitopia: The Look of the New Digital You* (New York: AtRandom, 2001).

2. See Celia Pearce, *Communities of Play: Emergent Cultures in Multiplayer Games and Virtual Worlds* (Cambridge: MIT Press, 2009), among other sources.

3. Paul Carr and Graham Pond, *The Unofficial Tourists' Guide to Second Life* (New York: St. Martin's Griffin, 2007).

4. Judith S. Donath, "Identity and Deception in the Virtual Community," in *Communities in Cyberspace*, ed. Marc A. Smith and Peter Kollock (London: Routledge, 1999), 29–59.

5. Ibid., 45.

6. Brian Levin, "Cyberhate: A Legal and Historical Analysis of Extremists' Use of Computer Networks in America," *American Behavioral Scientist* 45, no. 6 (February 2002): 958–89; Chris Atton, "Far-Right Media on the Internet: Culture, Discourse, and Power," *New Media and Society* 8, no. 4 (August 2006): 573–87.

7. Atton, "Far-Right Media," 578.

8. Judith Butler, *Gender Trouble: Feminism and the Subversion of Identity* (New York: Routledge, 1999).

9. Ursula Sautter, "The Mothers' Land," *Time Europe*, May 7, 2001, 27. Sautter estimates that there are 51,000 far-right sympathizers in Germany today and that at least 1,000 are female. She quotes Rüdiger Hesse, from Lower Saxony's Office for the Protection of the Constitution, who notes that "the right wing is emancipating itself" and reaching out for women to join in its activities.

10. Kathleen M. Blee, *Inside Organized Racism: Women in the Hate Movement* (Berkeley: University of California Press, 2002), 53.

11. "Another SL First? French Extreme Right Political Party Opens Office in Second Life," *Second Life Herald*, December 9, 2006, http://www.secondlifeherald.com/slh/2006/12/another_sl_firs.html (accessed March 8, 2008); "A Visit to Le Pen's Headquarters in SL," *Second Life Herald*, December 10, 2006, http://www.secondlifeherald.com/slh/2006/12/a_visit_to_le_ep.html (accessed March 8, 2008); Wagner James Au, "Fighting the Front," *New World Notes* (blog), January 15, 2007, http://nwn.blogs.com/nwn/2007/01/stronger_than_h.html (accessed March 8, 2008).

12. Kim E. Nielsen, "Doing the 'Right' Right," *Journal of Women's History* 16, no. 3 (2004): 168–72.

13. Denise M. Bostdorff, "The Internet Rhetoric of the Ku Klux Klan: A Case Study in Website Community Building Run Amok," *Communication Studies* 55, no. 2 (Summer 2004): 340–61.

14. Blee, *Inside Organized Racism*, 3.

15. Neal Stewart, "Controversial German Designer Returns from Her 8th Suspension—Interview 1/2," *Second Life Herald*, February 24, 2005, http://www.secondlifeherald.com/slh/2005/02/controversial_g.html (accessed March 9, 2008).

16. The SL Terms of Service (4.1) assert that users shall not "take any action or upload, post, e-mail or otherwise transmit Content as determined by Linden Lab at its sole discretion that is harmful, threatening, abusive, harassing, causes tort, defamatory, vulgar, obscene, libelous, invasive of another's privacy, hateful, or racially, ethnically or otherwise objectionable." http://secondlife.com/cororate/tos.php (accessed October 23, 2009).

17. Neal Stewart, "Controversial German Designer Returns from Her 8th Suspension—Interview 2/2," *Second Life Herald*, February 27, 2005, http://www.secondlifeherald.com/slh/2005/02/controversial_g_1.html (accessed March 9, 2008).

18. Alan Scholl, "Escaping to the Matrix," The John Birch Society, http://www.jbs.org/node/2456 (accessed March 20, 2008).

19. Donna J. Haraway, *Simians, Cyborgs, and Women: The Reinvention of Nature* (New York: Routledge, 1991), 149.

20. Ibid., 163, 180.

21. Ibid., 181.

22. Ingeborg Reichle, "Remaking Eden," in *Cyberfeminism: Next Protocols*, ed. Claudia Reiche and Verena Kuni (New York: Autonomedia, 2004), 252.

23. Bostdorff, "Internet Rhetoric of the Ku Klux Klan," 352.

24. His lecture is part of the seventy-seven-minute workshop archived at http://video.google.com/videoplay?docid=2642394922604088000#.

25. Levin, "Cyberhate: A Legal and Historical Analysis," 958–88.

26. For a history of the use of imagery and rhetoric on Le Pen's website, see L. Clare Bratten, "Online Zealotry: La France du peuple virtuel," *New Media Society* 7 (2005): 517–32.

27. See http://www.youtube.com/watch?v=XqVnAW_IJ3g.

28. General JC Christian, "Thinking Liberally This Week," *Thinking Liberally: The General's Second Life* (blog), April 27, 2008, http://thinkingliberally.blogspot.com/2008/04/thinking-liberally-this-week.html (accessed April 28, 2008).

29. Anna Key et al., *Beating Fascism: Anarchist Anti-fascism in Theory and Practice*, Anarchist Sources 6 (London: Kate Sharpley Library, 2006); Martin Lux, *Antifascist* (London: Phoenix Press, 2006); David Renton, "'A Day to Make History'? The 2004 Elections and the British National Party," *Patterns of Prejudice* 39, no. 1 (2005): 25–45.

30. Johan Fornäs et al., eds., *Digital Borderlands: Cultural Studies of Identity and Interactivity on the Internet* (New York: Peter Lang, 2002).

31. Lisa Nakamura, introduction to *Cybertypes: Race, Ethnicity, and Identity on the Internet* (New York: Routledge, 2002), xi.

4

Righting Africa? Contextualizing Notions of Women's
Right-Wing Activism in Sub-Saharan Africa

Kathleen M. Fallon and Julie Moreau

Despite the growing body of scholarship on right-wing women cross-nation-ally, there are still no studies of right-wing women in black sub-Saharan Africa.[1] Do right-wing women's movements exist in this region? In this chapter we explore why it is challenging to categorize women's activism as right-wing in sub-Saharan Africa, where a left-right political continuum has been con-founded by the legacy of late colonialism and a history of political instability. We begin by drawing from existing comparative works to define right-wing activism as a process of Othering that creates boundaries between social groups based on difference. This process often manifests itself in nationalist discourses, which view the state as an instrument for enforcing social order, often through violence, as well as traditional gender roles. Using this defini-tion as our base, we then examine state-sponsored women's organizations across sub-Saharan African nations before turning our attention to Pauline Nyiramasuhuko and her role in the Rwandan genocide. We conclude by re-visiting the notion of "right-wing" and whether this term can be appropri-ately used to describe women's activity in sub-Saharan Africa.

Background

Much of the research on right-wing women's activism in developing coun-tries relies on political party affiliation to classify their activity. In Chile, rightist women mobilized against Allende and the leftist Popular Unity gov-

We appreciate the comments and feedback from Kathleen Blee and Sandra Deutsch.

ernment under the pretext of conserving family values.[2] The Brazilian fascist movement of the 1930s, Brazilian Integralist Action (AIB), had a strong following of women, as it claimed to protect marriage, motherhood, and Catholicism, which, according to AIB, were threatened by leftist parties.[3] In India, women in the 1990s supported a coalition of rightist parties linked to Hinduism. They argued that the notion of secularism, tied to the Indian state and introduced through colonization, threatened indigenous religion and culture.[4] In South Africa, Dutch Afrikaner women supported the National Party by weaving a narrative that combined Christian morals, family traditions, nationalist ideology, and racial purity to create a boundary between themselves and the Other (whether black South Africans or white British South Africans).[5]

In many sub-Saharan African countries, however, a history of colonization and political instability has generally not led to the development of political parties along a left-right continuum. Under colonization, Europeans often attempted to gain control of African countries by placing ethnic groups in opposition to one another.[6] These colonization practices emphasized differences between groups. When independence was gained and political parties were formed, most were created along ethnic lines. Political instability occurred often since exaggerated notions of difference could be used to justify military coups or, in more extreme cases, genocidal campaigns. Left or right ideological affiliations were subsumed by ethnic difference.

From the 1960s to the 1980s, international interference tied to the Cold War acted as an additional factor confounding left versus right political agendas in many countries of sub-Saharan Africa.[7] The United States and the Soviet Union provided money and resources to various factions within African countries for the purpose of gaining allies on the side of free trade or communism. However, the ideological divide between the superpowers did not necessarily transfer to their African proxies. In North American and European contexts, to be on the political right means advocating both a minimal degree of state involvement in the economy and certain positions on social issues such as immigration or abortion, while the political left is associated with economic redistribution by the state and opposite positions on the same social issues.[8] Many military rulers in Africa came to power with the intention of acquiring resources and not of toeing leftist or rightist party lines, as understood in Western contexts. On the one hand, leftist dictatorships, often supported by the Soviet Union, tended to use state resources to provide wealth and opportunities to relatives and members of their ethnic group and to repress ethnic and political rivals, while espousing rhetoric of equality for all. Such contradictory actions were found in Ghana, Zambia, Tanzania, and Sierra Leone, among other countries. On the other hand, dictators allied with the United States were not necessarily right-leaning. For example, in Malawi, a country supported by the United States, Kamuzu Banda focused on increasing women's rights and status through education and community development. The Cold War therefore contributed to political instability through the material support of dictatorships whose ideologies did not map neatly onto a left-right political divide.

Because there is often no stable system of competing political parties, let alone a tradition of right-wing politics, analysis of right-wing women in Africa should take into account the frequent absence of a clear left-right divide. Bacchetta and Power's work on right-wing women provides some suggestions for looking at this form of mobilization in diverse contexts.[9] First, they argue that right-wing women, cross-nationally, rely on the notion of difference to create boundaries between themselves and others. Although difference may be emphasized through political party platforms, it may also be captured through boundaries created between right-wing women and the Other, represented by race, nation, ethnicity, religion, or similar characteristics.[10] These boundaries are particularly evident in the nationalist rhetoric used by right-wing women. Second, this notion of difference is combined with anti-Other discourse that creates a sensation of fear, inciting mobilization of the right around its cause. Right-wing movements can be characterized by their focus on ethnicity in combination with the promotion of violence as a tactic or goal.[11] The Other may also be gendered. Othered men are viewed as threats to the rightist community and to women's sexuality, and Othered women are viewed as breeders of the enemy or asexual and unsupportive of their men.[12] The third and final commonality of right-wing women's organizations involves the exaltation of motherhood and the heteronormative family.[13] Women's power is seen as tied to women's role within the family, and motherhood thus becomes an object of emphasis.[14] Heterosexuality allows for the reproduction of the right and reasserts the importance of women's role in the family, while simultaneously establishing the family itself as in need of protection from outside forces—whether these be related to Othered men's sexuality, homosexuality, racial or religious miscegenation, or similar possible encroachments.

The definition of "right-wing" provided above, with its emphasis on the process of Othering, offers the possibility of examining right-wing women in black sub-Saharan Africa. The definition moves beyond the left-right political party divide as a determining factor and rather facilitates the exploration of the right wing as a component of ethnic Othering, particularly expressed in nationalist discourses. This allows us to take into account the historical specificities of sub-Saharan Africa that relate to the roles of colonization and the Cold War. We may thus consider some women to be right-wing because of their contributions to the process of Othering certain social groups, their advocacy of and participation in ethnic violence, and their exaltation of heteronormative notions of motherhood.

Using this definition as our base, we begin by discussing the presence of national state-run women's organizations that are operated and supported by authoritarian regimes. Many regimes created state-run women's organizations to co-opt women and strengthen their own rule. Those who did not support the ruling parties, both men and women, were often presented as a threat to the nation and its development. We start with this example because it shows women supporting oppressive political rulers and contributing to the construction of an Other. We then investigate the role of Pauline Nyiramasuhuko, the former minister of family and women's development in Rwanda and one of the key players in the Rwandan genocide in 1994. Rwanda's history of colonization and political instability shaped Nyiramasuhuko's actions of ethnic Othering, which in turn contributed to political campaigns of mass violence. Although both of these examples contain elements of women's right-wing activism, they also reveal the difficulties of identifying right-wing women in sub-Saharan Africa.

State-Run Women's Organizations

Across sub-Saharan Africa, dictators and their governments often came to power through violence. In order to remain in power, rulers needed to ally themselves with other elites, as well as with segments of the larger population. One method of gaining support was through the creation of state-run women's organizations, which existed and continue to exist across Africa; these include Umoja wa Wanawake wa Tanzania, the Women's League of Sierra Leone, the United National Independence Party's Women's League in Zambia, the National Union of Malian Women, the 31st December Women's Movement in Ghana, the Better Life Program in Nigeria, and Maendeleo ya Wanawake in Kenya. These organizations were/are created by ruling regimes, often run by the wives of heads of state, and formed with the professed intent of supporting women economically.

The creation of large state-run women's organizations reinforces existing authoritarian regime ideology, but with particular reference to women. As resources are often scarce under authoritarian regimes, offering economic incentives to women who support state-run women's organizations often generates support for those in power.[15] Women's groups therefore face the choice of either receiving resources from the ruling party by becoming participants in large state-run women's organizations or quietly operating separately with limited resources. The ultimate goal of state-run women's organizations is to diffuse any opposition to the state, as well as to foster nationalist sentiment and allegiance to ruling parties.[16] Due to the tyrannical nature of authoritarian regimes and the success of these women's organizations, military regimes often succeed in garnering support and preventing oppositional mobilization.[17]

In Ghana, Flight Lieutenant Jerry John Rawlings started the 31st December Women's Movement (DWM) in 1982, and his wife, Nana Konadu Agyeman Rawlings, became president of the organization in 1985. The ostensible purpose of the organization was to encourage women to become involved in

the state economically, socially, and politically; however, it acted as an apparatus to mobilize women under Provisional National Defense Council
(PNDC) rule.[18] Specifically, the 31st DWM would entice women to join by
offering existing women's groups seed money to start income-generating activities. Of course, groups that did not wish to join the organization would
not receive financial support. Many women who could gain access to resources
through their affiliation with the 31st DWM embraced the opportunity. This
allowed the 31st DWM to co-opt women's organizations, engendering support
for the party and ultimately for the PNDC state.[19] The 31st DWM had branches
throughout Ghana, which provided resources to women and also held festivi-
ties for women that celebrated the organization and the ruling regime. Members were often given cloth to be worn as skirts; on the cloth were pictures of
Rawlings and symbols of the 31st DWM and the PNDC. At rallies for the 31st
DWM and for the PNDC, women dressed in attire demonstrating their allegiance to the government, and this brought further attention to the regime
within their local communities. Thus, through their actions, women showed
support for Rawlings and PNDC rule.

In Malawi, Kamuzu Banda appropriated the "mbumba culture" to gain
political support from women when he created the Women's League in 1958.[20]
Among the Chewa, an ethnic group in Malawi, *mbumba* refers to the relationships among a group of women in a community. This group of women may
have a male guardian, typically a brother or uncle, called a *nkhoswe*. Banda
deemed himself the primary nkhoswe in Malawi, making him the guardian
of all mbumba women across the country—even among ethnic groups where
mbumba had not previously existed. He thus became a benefactor to the
women of Malawi. Similar to the 31st DWM in Ghana, women who participated in Malawi's Women's League received benefits from doing so. The
league's emphasis was on economic development, but those who were dedicated to the mbumba culture and to Banda were also accorded status through
positions within the organization, were flown abroad for events, and received
recognition within their respective communities. As part of their commitment, women were required to wear uniforms embellished with Banda's portrait, and for any political events, they sang songs of praise and danced for
Banda and his ruling regime.[21] Women's performances became symbolic of
the Malawian nationalism that Banda had created.

In Nigeria, the Better Life Program was established in 1987 under then
dictator Major General Ibrahim Badamasi Babangida by his wife, Maryam
Babangida. The purpose of the program was to provide women in rural areas
with economic support through the creation of economic cooperatives, literacy programs, and technical training in areas such as farming.[22] Women who
worked for the Better Life Program, inclusive of elite women, gained status
through their participation in international conferences, as well as within the
country.[23] The program's primary intent, aside from earning Maryam Babangida public attention for running it, was to bolster support for the military

regime among rural and urban women across Nigeria. Thus, as in Ghana and Malawi, women contributed to Nigerian nationalism and supported the ruling regime in return for economic incentives.

In the cases described above, military rulers created programs that co-opted women to support their agendas. In exchange for economic incentives, which came directly from the government, many women openly supported state-run women's organizations and the ruling regimes. In doing so, they simultaneously contributed to the nationalism that the military rulers attempted to enforce. In spite of the violence that brought the military leaders to power and the repression that continued under their command, women in several countries chose to praise and support their oppressive rule. Women sang, danced, and wore clothing in recognition of the regimes.

State-Run Women's Organizations as Right-Wing

Despite the unclear demarcations of a political right in many sub-Saharan African countries, state-run women's organizations did engage in a process of Othering those who did not support the ruling regime. Since ruling regimes created the state-run women's organizations with the intent of gaining support from women, many women found themselves openly supporting repressive dictatorships and contributing to the sense of nationalism that the military regimes sought to enforce. Women were also encouraged to generate support among other women within their communities through their outward praise of existing rulers. Women's role was to "spread the benevolence" of these governments and, in doing so, contribute to the construction of the Other by discouraging any dissenters. Military dictatorships also attempted to create fear of the Other by intimating that the Other would contribute to increased political instability and economic ruin. Those who opposed the government often suffered consequences, ranging from restricted access to resources to intimidation tactics and sometimes death. Female supporters of the government thus received benefits while also reinforcing the nationalist stance of the political rulers.

Of course, women's participation was much more complicated than simply supporting repressive military rulers. Although some women may have done so solely out of commitment to ruling parties, others gave their support for two additional reasons. First, some recognized that if they did not, they could be viewed suspiciously by the regime; thus, they chose the safest path. Second, providing support to the regime allowed women access to resources they would not otherwise have had. Often confronting poverty, women would use whatever resources were available to them to improve their economic situations. They frequently saw state-run women's organizations as an opportunity to improve their circumstances. Therefore, although some women no doubt truly exalted military rulers, others participated because of what they gained by providing support to the regime—safety and resources.

Women who participated and continue to participate in large state-run women's organizations display elements of right-wing organizing since they contribute to the process of Othering. However, defining these women as right-wing is complicated by their circumstances. Most often, women are not actively creating and defining an Other, an activity that is done by the state, but are instead receiving goods in exchange for their political participation. They are also not directly threatening those who are Othered and instead may themselves feel threatened by the state. Women's precarious socioeconomic status and personal safety complicate identification of women's right-wing activism. More research needs to be done to determine whether the apparent political pragmatism of some women, or their support of a particular regime in exchange for material or political benefits, is sufficient to consider them right-wing actors in the sub-Saharan African context.

We now turn to the case of Pauline Nyiramasuhuko, who more closely exhibits right-wing political behavior because of her active role in the process of violent ethnic Othering carried out in Rwanda.

Pauline Nyiramasuhuko

Pauline Nyiramasuhuko, a Hutu, was the minister of family and women's development at the time of the mass genocide in Rwanda, where 500,000 to 1 million Rwandans, primarily Tutsis, were murdered within a four-month time span, from April to July 1994. In 1999 the International Criminal Tribunal for Rwanda indicted Nyiramasuhuko for conspiracy to commit genocide, genocide, rape, and crimes against humanity. Although she continues to deny her involvement, many eyewitnesses have placed her at the scene of massacres, where she gave the orders. She was also named as one of five members of the inner circle created by the former prime minister Jean Kambanda for the purpose of crafting and later executing the genocide plan.

Nyiramasuhuko grew up as the daughter of subsistence farmers in a community just outside of Butare, a city with a large Tutsi population, and she was considered a success story. In high school, she befriended Agathe Kanzige, who would later become the wife of President Juvenal Habyarimana. After high school, Nyiramasuhuko began working as a social worker within the Ministry of Social Affairs, where she focused on women's empowerment, the prevention of HIV, and child care.[24] Due to her government connections, she quickly moved up the ranks. She was loyal to President Habyarimana's party, the Mouvement Républicain National pour la Démocratie et le Développement (MRND), which emphasized economic development for all.[25] Although the MRND did not have a strong following in Butare, Nyiramasuhuko attempted to create a presence there by holding political rallies and institut-ing roadblocks through town, which targeted Tutsis.[26] She became the local MRND boss, curried favor with the MRND government, and in 1992 was appointed the minister of family and women's development.

When the genocide began in 1994, Nyiramasuhuko played a central role in planning and executing the murders and rapes within Butare, a city that had once posed a challenge to the MRND ruling party. It was home to the National University and was the intellectual hub of the country; moreover, it was considered to be a place where Hutus and Tutsis intermingled without consequence. Many Tutsis fled to Butare during the genocide, believing it to be the one location in which they could find refuge. Nyiramasuhuko preyed on this belief by traveling the roads in a car saddled with megaphones, announcing that there was refuge at a nearby stadium where the Red Cross was providing sanctuary and food to Tutsis. Thousands of Tutsis gathered there hoping to find safety. Instead, they were massacred. Nyiramasuhuko arrived with Hutu Interahamwe[27] to attack the Tutsis, ordering that the women should first be raped before being killed. The remaining refugees were attacked with machine-gun fire from all sides, and grenades were showered down upon them; any survivors were killed with machetes.[28]

The ultimate goal of the genocide was to eradicate the Tutsi and maintain a pure Hutu ethnic group. For this reason, Nyiramasuhuko encouraged the use of rape as a weapon of war to destroy the purity of the Tutsi. Women represented the reproduction of the Tutsi line and were therefore targeted not just for killing but also for rape and more extreme torture, such as rape with machetes, leading to death. According to testimonies, Nyiramasuhuko used her title as minister to authorize the rape and killing of girls and women, and she used rape as an incentive for Hutu soldiers. She allegedly referred to Tutsi women as "cockroaches" and "dirt," encouraging soldiers to keep young girls as sex slaves and to kill old women. Even before the genocide, former employees of the ministry indicated that Nyiramasuhuko openly derided Tutsis and would complain about any interactions she was forced to have with them.

Since the Tutsi minority controlled the government in the 1950s, there was residual fear among the Hutu that the Tutsi would regain that power. Thus, when General Habyarimana seized power in 1973, he created government structures that limited Tutsi influence.[29] The Tutsi were simultaneously demonized and presented as untrustworthy by the regime. This environment helped increase the number of Hutu supporters and spurred the genocide in 1994. The MRND government under Prime Minister Jean Kambanda orchestrated the genocide to rid Rwanda of any Tutsi influence and ensure Hutu purity. In accordance with government orders, Hutus slaughtered Tutsi men, women, and children. Members of the government released HIV-positive men from hospitals for the sole purpose of unleashing an HIV epidemic among Tutsi women. Tutsi women were targeted both because they were seen as propagating the Tutsi ethnic group and because they were presented by the MRND government and newspapers as seductive temptresses to the Hutu.[30] These women were defined as a deviant Other that needed to be destroyed, allowing for the desecration of Tutsi women and the purification of Hutu women. Nyiramasuhuko played a central role in spreading this message and in the mass rapes, torture, and genocide that were carried out.

Nyiramasuhuko as Right-Wing

Nyiramasuhuko's actions suggest that she represents a right-wing woman in sub-Saharan Africa. Like those participating in ethnic cleansing in Nazi Germany and in the former Yugoslavia, Nyiramasuhuko believed in eradicating one ethnic group to maintain the power, presence, and sanctity of another group, in this case the Hutu. She worked for, and virulently supported, a government that touted ethnic purity and disparaged those who threatened it. She held political rallies that targeted Tutsis as the enemy, while also setting up roadblocks to harass Tutsis in Butare. She contributed to the fear that the Tutsi could regain political control—a fear incited by the MRND government.[31] Along with the government, she constructed Tutsi women as an Other that was sexually deviant, impure, and intent on seducing Hutu men. These women threatened the loyalty of Hutu men, the lineage of the Hutu, and the roles of Hutu women as wives and mothers. Because of Tutsi women's ability to endanger Hutu rule, dominance, and family, Nyiramasuhuko advocated their rape and murder. Her aim was to tarnish the Tutsi lineage and, in line with the objectives of the ruling regime, to ultimately eradicate Tutsis from Rwanda altogether. With the support of the MRND government, Nyiramasuhuko created the Tutsi Other, contributed to fear among the Hutu, and characterized the Tutsi as not worthy of life. According to the multiple representations of the Tutsi provided by Nyiramasuhuko and the MRND government, the Tutsi could destroy the Hutu both politically and socially, and this set the stage for the planned genocide.

To understand what "right-wing" might mean in this context, it is necessary to gain a better understanding of the role of colonization in the genocide—particularly as it affects conflicts between Hutus and Tutsis.[32] Before the arrival of the Germans and then the Belgians, the Hutu and the Tutsi had coexisted for years. They spoke the same language, had the same religion, lived among each other relatively peacefully, and intermingled. The primary differences between them were based on the work that they did. The Tutsis were generally herders, and the Hutus, farmers. Despite these differences, both Hutus and Tutsis intermarried, and their ethnic status could change depending on their resources and activities. When the Belgians took over the colony, they created racial identity cards and categorized the Hutu and Tutsi according to the resources they had and their phenotypical features. Approximately 15 percent of the Rwandan population was categorized as Tutsi, while approximately 85 percent was categorized as Hutu. The Belgians then deemed the Tutsi a superior race and organized Rwanda according to these divisions. The Hutu participated in hard labor while the Tutsi supervised. The Tutsi were also allowed access to education and encouraged to enter into governmental positions, while the Hutu did not gain the same access to such resources. Colonialism thus exacerbated any existing divisions between the Tutsi and the Hutu, and it contributed to rising resentment among Hutus toward the Tutsi.

In the late 1950s, after independence, the Hutu gained political power. However, the injustices and inequalities created under Belgian rule had already solidified, as the Tutsi maintained their higher social and economic status within Rwanda. They had higher educational levels, their economic status was significantly greater, they owned and operated many businesses, and they were considered to be among the intellectual elite. The political dominance of the Hutu, therefore, did not erase other divisions between the Hutu and Tutsi that had been embedded over time. The resentment among the Hutu continued, and fear of the Tutsis' return to political dominance, in addition to social and economic dominance, was reflected by the actions of the Hutu government. The regime's goal was to end this fear of Tutsi domination through mass genocide. Thus, although the rhetoric was based in rightist formulations of racial purity, these notions were created and solidified through colonization.[33] Differences between the Hutu and the Tutsi were first emphasized by the Belgians and later reasserted through the MRND. The construction of the Other began only when the divide between privileged and underprivileged was linked to ethnicity and made salient.

Nyiramasuhuko's right-wing activity emerges in the context of this colonial history. She was raised as a Hutu in a Tutsi-dominated community. She experienced firsthand the inequalities that resulted from Belgian racial categorization. Although she and others within the MRND constructed the Tutsi Other in terms of ethnic threat, this fear was grounded in the stark inequalities created under colonialism, which allowed resentment to grow among the population. The structural inequalities that led to one of the greatest genocides in sub-Saharan Africa were, in part, generated by colonizers racializing and exacerbating existing ethnic tensions among the Hutu and the Tutsi through economic, social, and political discrimination. Thus, the right-wing ideologies and actions of Nyiramasuhuko are tied directly to the consequences of colonialism as well as practices implemented under colonization.[34]

Conclusion

Do right-wing women exist in black sub-Saharan Africa? Conventional definitions of right-wing women, which focus on party affiliation, overlook the activism discussed here. Because of the history of colonization, which encouraged the Othering of different ethnic groups, and the political instability exacerbated by the Cold War, political ideologies do not tend to fall along the conventional left-right divide. Moreover, the circumstances surrounding women's mobilization render it difficult to know whether some women in sub-Saharan Africa are ideologically inclined to right-wing policies or are simply acting and reacting to their economic, political, and social-structural situations. Nevertheless, in the processes of mobilization described here, some women do demonstrate elements of right-wing activism, particularly in relation to the practice of Othering, as it is tied to ethnicity and nationalism.

Large state-run women's organizations have led many women to laud repressive military dictators and contribute to the notion of the Other. However, women's choices to participate in state-run women's organizations that support military regimes are not clear-cut. Socioeconomically, women need access to resources for themselves and their families, particularly during times of hardship, and many will do whatever it takes to improve their socioeconomic situation—including participating in state-run women's organizations. Women under military dictatorships in sub-Saharan Africa often do not enjoy political and civil liberties, especially if they do not support the ruling regime. Many women may therefore participate in state-run women's organizations simply to avoid repression. Thus, while women's participation contributes to the construction of the Other and nationalism, it may not reflect women's political will.

As for Nyiramasuhuko, her participation in the genocide falls in line with current definitions of right-wing activism. Nyiramasuhuko, along with the MRND government, relied on highlighting differences between Hutus and Tutsis in order to Other the Tutsi in Rwanda. Nyiramasuhuko and those close to her contributed to the anti-Other fear through the use of political rallies, roadblocks, and media representations. In addition, she gendered the Tutsi Other by suggesting that Tutsi women were threats to the Hutu family and lineage. The rhetoric and behavior of Nyiramasuhuko and the MRND were directly tied to ethnic difference, which was exacerbated through structural inequalities created by Belgian colonials. Belgian colonials instilled notions of racial purity and difference in Rwanda that, over time, became ingrained in Rwandan society.

The role of colonial history combined with political instability across the continent limits the applicability of current understandings of women's right-wing activism to black sub-Saharan Africa. A focus on the process of Othering provides a theoretical guideline for ongoing explorations of women's political behavior. Nonetheless, it does not provide a straightforward method for categorizing African women as right-wing. We should continue to examine the use of the term "right-wing" in discussions of women in sub-Saharan Africa, as well as their mobilization in the context of their specific historical experiences.

NOTES

1. For the remainder of the chapter, when we reference sub-Saharan Africa, we are referring to black sub-Saharan Africa. This includes all countries south of the Sahara. It excludes all white South Africans and other nonblack citizens of African countries.

2. Margaret Power, *Right-Wing Women in Chile: Feminine Power and the Struggle Against Allende, 1964–1973* (University Park: Pennsylvania State University Press, 2002).

3. Sandra McGee Deutsch, "Christians, Homemakers, and Transgressors," *Journal of Women's History* 16, no. 3 (2004): 124–37.

4. Tanika Sarkar and Urvashi Butalia, *Women and Right-Wing Movements: Indian Experiences* (New Jersey: Zed Books, 1995).

5. Marijke Du Toit, "The Domesticity of Afrikaner Nationalism: Volksmoeders and the ACVV, 1904–1929," *Journal of Southern African Studies* 29, no. 1 (2003): 155–76.

6. Mahmood Mamdani, *Citizen and Subject: Contemporary Africa and the Legacy of Late Colonialism* (Princeton: Princeton University Press, 1996); Bruce Berman, "Ethnicity, Patronage, and the African State: The Politics of Uncivil Nationalism," *African Affairs* 97, no. 388 (1998): 305–41.

7. Christopher O'Sullivan, "The United Nations, Decolonization, and Self-Determination in Cold War Sub-Saharan Africa, 1960–1994," *Journal of Third World Studies* 22, no. 2 (2005): 103–20; John Kent, "United States Reactions to Empire, Colonialism, and Cold War in Black Africa, 1949–57," *Journal of Imperial and Commonwealth History* 33, no. 2 (2005): 195–220; Jesse Lutabingwa, "Cultural Pluralism, the Cold War, and Africa's Integration in the World Economy," *International Journal on World Peace* 15, no. 2 (1998): 3–9.

8. Jens Rydgren, "The Sociology of the Radical Right," *Annual Review of Sociology* 33 (2007): 241–62.

9. Paola Bacchetta and Margaret Power, introduction to *Right-Wing Women: From Conservatives to Extremists Around the World*, ed. P. Bacchetta and M. Power (New York: Routledge, 2002), 1–18.

10. Ibid., 7–8.

11. Kathleen M. Blee and Kimberly A. Creasap, "Conservative and Right-Wing Movements," *Annual Review of Sociology* 36 (2010): 269–86.

12. Sara Diamond, *Roads to Dominion: Right-Wing Movements and Political Power in the United States* (New York: Guilford Press, 1995), 8.

13. Ibid.

14. Raffael Scheck, *Mothers of the Nation: Right-Wing Women in Weimar Germany* (Oxford: Berg, 2004).

15. Takyiwaa Manuh, "Women, the State, and Society Under the PNDC," in *Ghana Under PNDC Rule*, ed. E. Gyimah-Boadi (Dakar, Senegal: CODESRIA, 1993), 176–95; E. Gyimah-Boadi, "Associational Life, Civil Society, and Democratization in Ghana," in *Civil Society and the State in Africa*, ed. J. W. Harbeson, D. Rothchild, and N. Chazan (Boulder, Colo.: Lynne Rienner, 1994), 125–48.

16. Aili Mari Tripp, *Women and Politics in Uganda* (Madison: University of Wisconsin Press, 2000).

17. Manuh, "Women, the State, and Society Under the PNDC"; Gyimah-Boadi, "Associational Life, Civil Society, and Democratization in Ghana"; Aili Mari Tripp, "Women in Movement: Transformations in African Political Landscapes," *International Feminist Journal of Politics* 5, no. 2 (2003): 233–55; Dzodzi Tsikata, "Women's Political Organizations, 1951–1987," in *The State, Development, and Politics in Ghana*, ed. E. Hansen and K. A. Ninsin (Dakar: CODESRIA, 1989), 73–93.

18. Manuh, "Women, the State, and Society Under the PNDC"; Gyimah-Boadi, "Associational Life, Civil Society, and Democratization in Ghana"; Tsikata, "Women's Political Organizations, 1951–1987."

19. Gyimah-Boadi, "Associational Life, Civil Society, and Democratization in Ghana."

20. Linda Semu, "Kamuzu's Mbumba," *Africa Today* 49, no. 2 (2002): 77–99; Lisa Gilman, "The Traditionalization of Women's Dancing, Hegemony, and Politics in Malawi," *Journal of Folklore Research* 41, no. 1 (2004): 33–60.

21. Such singing and dancing were also traditionally expected of women. In community situations, women were known to sing praises and perform dances for leaders in the community whom they felt the need to praise. Banda used this tradition to his benefit and had women praise him through their songs and dances.

22. Pat Williams, "State, Women, and Democratisation in Africa: The Nigerian Experience (1987–1993)," *Africa Development* 22, no. 1 (1997): 141–82.

23. Philomina E. Okeke-Ihejirika and Susan Franceschet, "Democratization and State Feminism," *Development and Change* 33, no. 3 (2002): 439–66.

24. Peter Landesman, "A Woman's Work," *New York Times Magazine,* September 15, 2002.

25. Peter Uvin, "Ethnicity and Power in Burundi and Rwanda," *Comparative Politics* 31, no. 3 (1999): 253–71.

26. Landesman, "A Woman's Work."

27. Literally translated as "those who attack together," these were groups of Hutu men who engaged in acts of collective violence.

28. Landesman, "A Woman's Work."

29. Uvin, "Ethnicity and Power in Burundi and Rwanda."

30. Landesman, "A Woman's Work."

31. Gerard Prunier, *The Rwanda Crisis: History of a Genocide* (New York: Columbia University Press, 1995).

32. Jean-Damascène Gasanabo, "The Rwandan Akazi (Forced Labour) System, History, and Humiliation," *Social Alternatives* 25, no. 1 (2006): 50–55; Linda Melvern, *A People Betrayed: The Role of the West in Rwanda's Genocide* (London: Zed Books, 2000).

33. The history of Tutsi and Hutu relations, along with the factors contributing to the genocide, is complex. Colonization was only one of the contributors, though an important one, to the genocide. For a more detailed explanation, see Danielle De Lame, "(Im)possible Belgian Mourning for Rwanda," *African Studies Review* 48, no. 2 (2005): 33–43.

34. Establishing the connection between colonialism and modern inequalities in Rwanda is intended to demonstrate why it is difficult to assign the term "right-wing" to Nyiramasuhuko in this context. Citing colonialism as an important source of ethnically based social and economic inequalities does not imply a justification for the genocide, nor does it in any way reduce the culpability of Nyiramasuhuko for her role in the massacres.

5

Gender, Islam, and Conservative Politics

Karla J. Cunningham

At first blush, examining the intersection of gender, Islam, and conservatism[1] appears to be a rather simple and, to some extent, futile effort. Indeed, in most analyses of societies and states where Islam dominates, the intersection of Islam and conservatism is simply assumed. Further scrutiny, however, shows that the nexus between gender, Islam, and conservatism is more nuanced—and greatly influenced by Muslim women. This chapter will provide a broad synthetic overview of women's right-wing activities in a number of Muslim areas and countries from the colonial period through the present. The term "Muslim world" as used here captures mainly Muslim women in North and sub-Saharan Africa, the Middle East, and South and Southeast Asia. Conservativism within the Muslim world is highly transnational in part because of the interconnected philosophical and intellectual traditions exhibited by the *umma,* or Islamic religious community. Shared features of Islamic feminist ideals[2] will be explored in this chapter. Nevertheless, women's experiences are influenced by the specific political characteristics of their respective countries.

The term "conservatism," when applied in the Muslim world, is often used by observers in place of the term "traditional" to avoid the value-laden and dichotomized features of the latter.[3] Religion is a central component of conservatism, especially vis-à-vis the state, and this is not unique to the Muslim world. New are contests over the proper source of religion and its role within society, suggesting that certain forms of Islamism have less to do with established tradition and more to do with power politics. As Victoria Bernal observes, "Islamic fundamentalists . . . are not so much reasserting past practices as contesting prevailing Islamic traditions and creating new ones."[4] Yet tradition itself is culturally contextual. In sub-Saharan Africa, Islam was a colonial phenomenon that introduced unequal gender constructs, replacing indigenous matrilineal kinship systems in many places, a process that was reinforced and expedited by Western, Christian, colonial powers.[5]

In the early post-colonial era, some state leaders sought to "modernize" their states through secularization. This process was intended to emulate the separation of religion from politics, economics, and society perceived to characterize Western political structures and ideology. Freeing women from ostensibly religiously based oppression became a central arena for this practice. "Women's rights were debated and legislated in the search for new ideologies to legitimize emerging forms of state power," Deniz Kandiyoti notes.[6] The effort to peripheralize religion was reinforced by the Cold War, regardless of whether the state leaned toward the former Soviet Union or the United States. Local reactions were often intense and led to various political outcomes, including revolution (Iran) and single-party states (Egypt). However, other state leaders embraced Islam to help legitimize their rule (Jordan, Morocco, and Saudi Arabia).[7] In these states, conservative Islam was essential to state survival. Finally, conservatism has been a response to a complex socio-political dynamic that has especially characterized the Arab world since independence. Multiple military defeats associated with the Arab-Israeli crisis, combined with despotic and corrupt leadership, led people to believe that they had been abandoned by God.[8] Islamism has been a powerful response to this social anomie. It was also one of the only political responses possible under state structures that controlled virtually all of the public space and disallowed political opposition. This pushed people into the mosque, as it was one of the only available venues in which to publicly gather and organize.

The concept of "right-wing" movements or structures has some interesting characteristics in the Muslim world. Secular states, intent on modernizing their populations and often aligned with the West, came into conflict with conservative forces who opposed not only the secular ideology of the state but also its methods. Thus, "right-wing" describes behavior rather than ideology. Right-wing actors are hostile to sharing public space and frequently resort to implied or overt violence to quell opposition. For opposition forces, who are often Islamist in their political orientation, authoritarian secular states are viewed as despotic right-wing actors who dominate the public sphere and deny competition (e.g., Turkey's Mustafa Kemal Atatürk, Egypt's Gamal Abdel Nasser, Iran's Reza Shah Pahlavi, and Iraq's Saddam Hussein). For external observers, right-wing states under clerical rule, such as Iran, are seen as representing the intersection of conservative religious actors and authoritarian state structures. For state leaders, extremist Islamist actors who use political violence to achieve their ends represent the right-wing extreme of political Islam and the specter of Islamic fascism. However, legitimate political opposition is often also labeled as terrorist. As Margot Badran points out, "It is highly problematic to reduce Islamism to extreme right-wing political Islam."[9] Islamism occurs across a political spectrum, from politically moderate to politically violent.

Gender has been a central component of discourse about the state throughout the Muslim world. In essence, whoever is able to demonstrate control over women signals sociopolitical control and power. This contest has not been settled in much of the Muslim world, leading to ongoing instability and unrest. In states such as Turkey (under Atatürk) and Iran (under the Shah), gender became a critical component of the modernization enterprise, especially the effort to unveil women. In contrast, women's veiling has become a potent symbol of political opposition against both colonialism (Algeria) and corrupt westernized leadership (Iran). For many secular feminists in both the West and the Muslim world, veiling is one of the most powerful emblems of the "Muslimwoman," who, veiled or not, is a symbol of monolithic Islam.[10] Veiling remains a highly charged issue for both leaders and the populace in many countries, and this issue will be returned to shortly.

The complexities associated with gender, the state, and Islam in the Muslim world bear little difference from the interplay between gender, the state, and religion in the West. At issue are allegiance to the state and the role of the family in this process. Women's second-tier citizenship is not unique to the Muslim world;[11] however, in many parts of the Muslim world the struggle between familialism[12] and nation-building remains unresolved.[13] In Sudan, as in much of the Muslim world, Islam has given Sudanese women a new sense of citizenship that other ideologies have failed to produce.[14]

In the Middle East, citizenship is constitutionally situated within the family unit, and rights frequently derive from "relational notions of selfhood. . . . The multiplicity of notions of rights, self, and family that co-reside in the Middle East complicates and cautions our attempts to search for continuities in the gendering of citizenship."[15] The role of the family and women's roles therein contrast sharply with new realities created by broadening educational attainment, the media, and altering political landscapes. The disjuncture helps explain how and why religion remains a powerful factor in helping women navigate these complex and often incongruous processes.

The divide between the family/tribe and the nationalist and increasingly globalized enterprise has been an issue since independence.[16] The state has repeatedly intervened in the family, especially in the Arab world, with two effects. First, it eroded "class patriarchy and the extended household unit" due to socioeconomic change derived from women's education. Second, it contributed to the rise of middle-class and largely Islamist movements.[17] Family law has been a pivotal area of contestation among all parties, including states, women's organizations (both religious and secular), and Islamists (both reformist and conservative).

Feminisms and Religion

I am a reformist but I am working strictly within the framework of the Shariaa [Islamic law].
—Uzma Naheed, Islamic female activist in India, quoted in Margot Badran, "The Gender of Islam"

In the Muslim world, there is a tremendous level of controversy and activity surrounding women's Islamic activism and its relationship to female empowerment. Western observers, especially feminists, frequently contend that "once a society is dominated in certain spheres by men, women will become a suppressed and passive group."[18] Yet Muslim women have formed highly influential subsocieties in the Muslim world that counter this perception of passivity and suppression. As part of this development, Islamist women have formed their own subsociety, which has become a "specific social movement" advocating an Islamic-grounded understanding of female autonomy partly derived from women's participation in the process.[19]

Muslim women are increasingly rejecting Western-based secular feminism in favor of Islamic feminist ideals. This process calls into question what it means to be a feminist and the relationship between conservatism and women's political rights. Importantly, this process includes organizations that have heretofore been considered especially hostile to women's rights, including Islamist organizations such as Hamas, Hezbollah, and Egypt's Muslim Brotherhood (Ikhwan al-Muslimun). Such organizations have increasingly targeted women with social services, educational programs that include political instruction, and, in the case of Hamas, the political mobilization of women during the 2006 election as organizers, voters, and candidates.

In the Arab world, secular "modern" feminism was a dominant discourse regarding women's rights during the 1960s and 1970s. In Turkey, the discourse emerged in the early 1980s.[20] Secular feminists pushed for a rather standard feminist agenda of equality, human rights, and economic opportunity. Often dominated by elite women, their ranks have been under attack by conservative religious leaders, especially in the Middle East, for decades. However, secular feminists also had a difficult time connecting with the majority of Muslim women, especially in the Arab world. Differences in class and culture, urban/rural dichotomies, and complex political dynamics underscored by the Arab-Israeli crisis, pan-Arabism, and related postcolonial internal and regional upheavals all combined to divide women. Secular feminism's perceived rejection of the role of religion stood in stark contrast to the centrality of religion in many women's lives. Of course, while many secular feminists were not irreligious, their impartiality to religion was enough to create a cultural gulf within their respective societies.[21]

Religion has become a powerful vehicle to challenge authoritarian and patriarchal structures in the same way that secular feminism was used decades earlier. Women are using religion to shape their identity in the same way that men do; thus, women are not simply acted upon by religion but instrumentally act upon religion to meet their needs.[22] Both women and men, boys and girls, have been in crisis in the Arab world, leading to social anomie, dislocation, and stress. While boys and men have been intensely studied, largely because crisis has contributed to political extremism, women and girls have been largely ignored. Both sexes have had to struggle with the economic and social ramifications of urbanization, broadened education, and altered employment landscapes. All of these processes have produced normative changes that often conflict with familial norms and structures.

Nowhere is this process more intense than over the roles of women. Despite better education and employment opportunities, society has widely struggled with the concept of women as intensely engaged with the public sphere.[23] This development is also linked to broader class issues. Islam has been more appealing and meaningful to middle- and lower-class women, for whom access to the public realm may become an economic and social necessity.[24] As educational opportunities have expanded for women outside of the elite classes, religion has emerged as a central component of their self-identity and relationships.

This development is not unique to women in the Arab world. In Sudan, new religious sensibilities and traditions have emerged to institutionalize new gender relationships that are the unplanned outcomes of economic change and the integration of villages with the national and world systems. While this process has been heavily driven by economic changes, the locus for understanding what it means to be a Muslim has moved from the local level to the international level.[25] For women of the Hizb ut-Tahrir (HT) in Kyrgyzstan, religiously grounded modesty and austerity are significant to poorer women, and Islam provides an essential alternative to the social stratification and social injustice perceived to emanate from capitalism.[26] In Bangladesh, women's Islamic activism is "partly a response to the perception that local and global life-worlds are increasingly wracked by violence, injustice, and oppression."[27] The failure of the liberal state to provide security and social justice has helped move women into broader nonviolent *jihadi* movements there.[28]

Islamic feminism, which ranges from orthodox to reformist, advocates a framework for gender equality for women and men derived from—and through—the Qur'an. In keeping with broader Islamist interpretations of the Qur'an, the separation of public and private realms is rejected. While both orthodox and reformist Islamic feminists use Islam as their primary frame for considering issues, the former tend to be more restrictive in their interpretations and to view issues from a more value-laden/moral perspective.[29] Islamic feminists seek not only to eliminate the strong association between patriarchy and Islam but also to restore Islam's association with gender equality.[30] Islamic feminism allows Muslim women to balance and reconcile traditionalist patriarchy and modern realities.[31] Margot Badran notes, "Islamic feminism is an inter-Islamic phenomenon produced by Muslims at various locations around the globe. There is no East/West fault line."[32]

Islamic feminism has become more acceptable in the Muslim world and has even become something of a social fashion. Egyptian actresses at the height of their careers have abandoned their celebrity and taken the veil, becoming role models for other women. The media has become an effective social mirror both reflecting and directing new forms of Islamic feminism. Televangelism is powerful in Yemen, with Egypt's 'Amr Khaled enjoying more viewers than Oprah Winfrey.[33] Also in Egypt, Heba Kotb, a conservative Muslim, has a popular sex advice show called "Big Talk," which helps reconcile sexual issues with Islam.[34]

Women's groups have proliferated, bringing women together for religious education, social and psychological reinforcement, and integration of all aspects of life—social, political, economic—with religion.[35] Women are using Islam as a means to renegotiate their position both inside and outside the family. Inside the family, religion allows young women to defy parental control[36] or to prompt better cooperation from their husbands.[37] Outside the home, women use Islam to enter new spaces that were previously denied to them. Thus, Islam is being used to challenge kinship and gender hierarchies[38] as well as political hierarchies. Women are also pushing for expanded roles within Islam itself, including more access to mosques and even to become imams.[39]

There is significant animosity among the different feminisms in the Muslim world. "The idea that women in Islamist movements may have something to contribute to women's rights is . . . rejected as preposterous by most secular Arab feminists," Omayma Abdellatif and Marina Ottaway write.[40] Many secular feminists view their religiously oriented sisters as confused or misled by male religious leaders. In contrast, religious feminists see their movements as an effort to bridge religion and gender, and they do not view the two as mutually exclusive. In Turkey, reformist and orthodox feminists are divided on how to approach various women's issues, but they still participate in the same demonstrations and belong to the same organizations.[41]

What has been powerful for religious feminists is that they have understood the importance of religion in women's lives. Even feminists "who previously struggled against female oppression in Western feminist terms have . . . now adapted to a more favourable attitude towards Islam."[42] Secularism, understood as any separation of religion from other aspects of life (i.e., politics, economics, social roles), is extremely foreign to many women, especially outside of the elite classes. Religion creates a powerful and meaningful religio-ideological framework within which women can reconcile the multiple elements that dominate their lives: family, friends, workplace, and country.

Belief and Action: How Conservatism Impacts—and Is Impacted by—Muslim Women

It is our duty as Muslim women to have a say in the politics of our country and the politics that shape our lives as women. Politics is not only the realm of men, as many men want to propagate. On the contrary, it has been made our primary concern throughout Islamic history 1500 years ago, when the women gave the Prophet their vote (Baiya) personally. We were equally addressed, and were equal partners in matters of the state. This is, however, not the notion most Muslim men carry. Somewhere, the perception of women being only bodies fit for the kitchen or the bed lingers in the back of their heads.
—Ikhwan leader, quoted in Soraya Duval, "New Veils and New Voices"

Islamist organizations have consciously and specifically targeted women to develop and expand their movements. Women have been recruited as active members and have also been indirectly targeted through the provision of key services, especially health care and education. This has enabled these organizations to build strong structures and disseminate their messages more widely within local communities.[43] In other words, Islamist organizations have done an exceptionally good job of "winning hearts and minds" by combining socially relevant services within socially acceptable structures. "Secular women's nongovernmental organizations (NGOs) led by educated women have only limited out-reach outside the urban upper class they come from," Abdellatif and Ottaway point out. "Islamist movements, in contrast, have proven themselves adept at building a broad following across social classes."[44] This process is consistent with overall Islamist mobilization efforts. For example, in Egypt, Islamists were successful at mobilizing male youth because they won hearts and minds and developed a new concept of "civic obligation."[45] Moreover, this method is not unique to Islamist movements. Women in the Ku Klux Klan "drew on familial and community ties—traditions of church suppers, kin reunions, and social celebrations—to circulate the Klan's message. . . . They spread hatred through neighborhoods, family networks, and illusive webs of private relationships."[46]

For the sake of political expediency and effectiveness, Islamic leaders have increasingly become proponents of women's rights, as long as they are consistent with Islam.[47] However, there is little consensus on what this means. Critics charge that while these movements may have provided some modest benefits to women, they remain patriarchal and oppressive, although their secular nationalist counterparts were no different.[48] As women joined Islamist movements, they began to press for additional rights and roles.

Islamist movements were unprepared for the expanding activism of women and for the fact that women would not be content to simply sit back and be second-class citizens within these organizations.[49] Thus, there is a debate within and among Islamists—led in part by women—about women's rights and roles. Islamist feminists possess a religious authenticity that imbues their advocacy with greater power and reach. It allows women to avoid accusations that they are pursuing a narrow agenda, a charge that has been effective against nationalist and secular movements. Instead, women pursuing their rights under Islam are able to frame their activities as good for the community as a whole and religiously authentic. Further, the intersection of Islam and feminism also challenges Western universality for defining women's rights.[50] While Western human rights proponents reject the notion that human rights is tantamount to a new colonialist enterprise,[51] proponents of political Islam highlight Islam's powerful anticolonial meaning, which reconciles culture, modernity, independence, and equality at multiple levels.[52]

Religious feminists, whether orthodox or reformist, have several common positions that relate them more closely and stand in contrast, at least from their perspectives, to their secular counterparts. First, religious feminists do not wish to disengage from their responsibilities to family and community, which they see their secular sisters as willing to do. Even among elite women who have observed women's liberation in the West, their self-image remains culturally infused. Soraya Duval observes that "those women want to retain the communal extended family aspects of traditional society, while eliminating its worst abuses, such as easy divorce for men and forced marriages."[53] Instead, women's rights can be achieved within and through the family, maintaining critical relational cultural factors that are often negated and/or peripheralized by many secular feminists. This approach also allows religious feminists to frame their activism as supportive of, and supported by, the community.

Second, religious feminists do not view religion as an obstacle to women's rights. Religion is not seen as the reason for women's lack of equality; rather, this is due to incorrect religious interpretation and cultural practices. In 1999 Hamas admitted for the first time that women were oppressed and had the right to struggle against discrimination. One of its 2006 candidates, Jamila Al-Shanti, stated in an interview that Hamas was willing to address the problem because it was counter to Islam and derived not from religion but from tradition.[54] Religious feminists tend to advocate for more adaptive interpretations of religious texts and focus on the role of women in early Islamic civilization. Even influential Shi'a religious leaders, such as Lebanon's Ayatollahs Muhammad Husayn Fadlallah and Muhammad Mahdi Shams al-Din, have countered more restrictive interpretations of women's rights, such as those put forth by Iran's Ayatollah Khomeini.[55] For some Islamic feminists, the Qur'an is not only an antipatriarchal text; it is liberating.[56] They believe that the Qur'an has been misinterpreted, giving sovereignty to men rather than solely to God and interpreting difference as inferiority. As a result, Muslims have become guilty of "male worship," which violates the doctrine of Tawhid, or divine unity.[57]

Third, both religious and secular feminists tend to focus on many of the same issues, including women's education, political influence, roles in the family (e.g., the right to divorce and to pick a husband), and the right to work. In more politicized and/or politically unstable settings, women often agree on broader political issues, such as Palestinian women's opposition to Israel and the "Apartheid Wall."[58] The common perception among Muslim women regarding the difference between religious feminists and secular feminists is that the former tend to focus on justice whereas the latter focus on equality. But it is difficult to separate the two ideas in reality. Fadwa Allabadi writes, "The approach of Islamist feminists is an attempt to transform past 'tradition' into a 'modern' new language to make the religious laws and doctrine accord with women's demands for liberty and equality in the present. That is to say, they call on Islam to be a more women-friendly and gender-egalitarian religion."[59]

Fourth, a nationalist framework infuses feminist discourse. Islam replaced Arab nationalism in the Middle East as the "ideology of dissent" beginning in the 1970s.[60] However, Islam and feminism were being used even earlier by Islamist women in challenging early postcolonial structures. In 1936 Zeinab El-Ghazali founded Egypt's Islamic Women's Association, which cooperated with the Muslim Brotherhood. She wished to pursue "feminism in indigenous terms" and "find feminism within Islam."[61] This was in contrast to her counterparts who sought to advance women's rights within secular, Western, and democratic frameworks. Secular feminism represented one of the more powerful examples of Western influence within the Arab world. Religious feminists view secular feminists as Western dupes, if not conspirators, who advocate a Western-style feminism that is individualistic, antifamily, anticommunity, and focused on lesbianism.[62] Islamic feminism allows women to negotiate with and accept modernity while simultaneously "nativizing" it to avoid charges of importing Western ideas.[63]

Fifth, Islam allows women the freedom to be public in a socially acceptable manner, in a way that secularism never achieved. Wearing traditional attire, especially veils or the hijab, has special saliency. Religious feminists are using the hijab as a mechanism to draw women out of the private sphere in a socially acceptable manner.[64] Traditional dress reinforces and reaffirms cultural norms and customs; it provides women—especially young, less affluent, and unmarried women—a culturally permissible route to the public sphere.[65] This has encouraged women's educational and employment opportunities, or at least permitted women to balk at restrictions to either by their families or communities. Finally, it has allowed women broader access to mosques and equipped them with a powerful tool to counter any man who opposes their presence; the man may be charged with being un-Islamic if he contests women's roles in the mosque.[66]

The complexity of the veil as a religious, social, and political symbol is captured by the ongoing debate both inside and outside the Muslim world on its use. For at least some women, a return to the veil does not represent a change in their religiosity; rather, it represents a change in the expression of that religiosity, especially as they marry and have children. For "radical fundamentalists," on the other hand, a profound shift in religious identity does occur, and their lives are clearly divided "between the days of ignorance, before they became religious, and the days of *hidaya* or the current situation."[67] In Sudan, religious attire is associated with orthodoxy and modernity, especially for younger women who have not yet established their social status through marriage and motherhood.[68] As a result, "the messages conveyed by Islamic dress (and other symbols of Islamic fundamentalism) are just as likely to be statements about change as they are assertions of tradition."[69] Even reformist clerics[70] do not see a fundamental issue with the hijab, noting that it allows a woman to enter the public sphere "'as a person not as a woman.' . . . The veil's purpose . . . is to neutralize the perception of the woman as a female in order to prioritize her status as a person."[71] In Turkey, the turban (hijab) has been highly politicized and can impact one's ability to work or go to school.[72]

Women, Political Movements, and Violence

My son became a martyr. I have a younger son who looks like my martyred son. I want the younger one to follow the same path and become a martyr. I am a poor widow; I have done hard labor to bring these sons up. Now I have heard the call of jihad. I have no money to give, but I have this treasure, these sons. Take my second son, and when he is martyred I will have the third one ready.
—A mother quoted at the annual convention of the Lashkar-i-Tayyabia,
in Farhat Haq, "Militarism and Motherhood"

Muslim women are not new participants in the nationalist and/or religious conflicts that exist within their respective countries. Women in Algeria, Iran, Chechnya, Palestine, Turkey, and Lebanon have all participated in one form or another in the violence that shook their societies. Similarly, women have always been members of conservative and even violent Islamic movements. Many conflicts within the Muslim world, at least since the 1979 Iranian Revolution, have been ascribed religious characteristics, whether warranted or not. Islam is often used for public relations, mobilization, and propaganda purposes in these conflicts to imbue them with legitimacy. Over the past decade, a new form of religious extremism has emerged within the Muslim world that is often labeled the global jihadi movement (GJM).[73] This movement has radically combined strict Islamic interpretation with violent political and social behavior. It represents the extreme outlier of the Islamic conservative movement, which is normally nonviolent, albeit not apolitical.

David Cook's 2005 argument that "to date, women fighting in *jihad* have only been a factor in these nationalist-Islamic resistance movements (Palestinian and Chechen), but not in other globalist radical Muslim warfare"[74] has less saliency today. Women have served in an array of roles in Islamist movements, from supporter to combatant.[75] Further, to reiterate, Islamist movements range from moderate to violent, and movement along this continuum is not linear.

Women's roles have also changed in some Islamist movements that have evolved over time from political violence to more mainstream political participation. Hamas has included women for many years in a variety of roles—for example, as symbols (e.g., mothers of martyrs), suicide attackers (e.g., Reem Rayishi), and candidates in the 2006 election. Like many Islamist organizations, Hamas has a substantial social services wing that directly reaches women. It has created very successful educational classes inside mosques that allow women to leave home and congregate with others in a culturally acceptable manner. Hamas also provides job training for women and educational programs to help them gain both religious and university access. It actively recruits female students at universities. In the 2006 election, Hamas emphasized that women's and men's roles in society were equal. While women should wear the hijab, they should enjoy equal rights, including the right to die in the struggle against Israel.[76]

Traditionally, Palestinian mothers have sacrificed their children, namely sons, to the war effort against Israel.[77] Beginning in late 2000 and escalating throughout 2001, Palestinian women were increasingly visible participants in a range of violent activities that presaged their role as suicide attackers, which began in 2002. Women assisted their male counterparts in planting bombs and in other types of logistical support for violent attacks against Israeli targets. Between Wafa Idris's attack in January 2002 and the end of May 2006, sixty-seven Palestinian women were involved in planning to commit a suicide attack. Of these, eight were successful, and the rest were arrested at various stages of planning. Of the eight successful suicide attackers, five were sent by Fatah, two by the Islamic Jihad in Palestine, and one by Hamas.[78]

In central Asia, women's roles are diverse. The Chechen case has produced numerous female suicide attackers. Chechnya "is linked ideologically to the global Salafi jihad but fine-tuned to fit local circumstances."[79] Salafi influence in Chechnya, and its prominent role in introducing terrorist violence, has created complex social dynamics. Salafis emerged during the second war with Russia (1999 to the present), and they have advocated a more fervent religiosity with links to the GJM. Since 2000, when the first female suicide attack occurred, women have participated in 81 percent of the total suicide attacks involving Chechen rebels;[80] men working alone carried out only 18 percent of the attacks.[81]

In contrast, Kyrgyzstan's HT is still evolving as an organization. Whether the HT will become a violent organization is unknown; the government, however, sees the Islamist group as a significant threat to its hold on power. No one is certain of the absolute participation of women in the HT, which has roughly 7,000 to 8,000 members, but some estimates put their number be-tween 800 and 2,000.[82] Islam has become an acceptable ideology for women with the collapse of communism and the lack of a cohesive replacement. Islam offers women social protection and prestige.[83] The HT contains a women's wing, which is organized at the regional level. However, the HT also organizes and delivers social services at the local level, directly impact-ing women's lives through religious education and child care.[84] Women are encouraged to be arrested along with their male counterparts,[85] but their primary roles are to provide Islamic education to their families and commu-nities and, less commonly, to participate in public demonstrations.[86]

In Southeast Asia, virtually every Islamist movement includes women, regardless of whether they are moderate or violent, reflecting a cultural fea-ture that has encouraged and permitted women's public roles.[87] The Jamaah Islamiyah (JI), an underground Islamist organization seeking to overthrow the Indonesian government, has a "local" focus that reduces links to the GJM and is more "woman friendly," focusing on kinship, marital, and familial bonds to maintain its network.[88] Nevertheless, women's roles have been largely supportive in the JI, and women have not been linked to any terrorist activity.

The less violent but still important role of women is also visible in South Asia. Pakistan's militant Islamist organization Lashkar-i-Tayyabia (LT) has a more traditional view of the role of women, advocating the centrality of motherhood to the production of future militants for operationalization in Kashmir. Farhat Haq notes that "the LT aims to reshape the private sphere of women to facilitate a new jihadi public."[89] Since the conflict is rather remote—both literally and figuratively—for most Pakistanis, the LT has to expend tremendous energy to mobilize people. Women are central not only to gaining their support for jihad but also to building on women's relational and familial ties to imbue the effort with broader legitimacy and depth.[90] The LT has an active women's wing that fields its own publications, meetings, and religious instruction for women and girls. The LT's focus on women has given it an advantage over rival Islamist organizations such as the Jaish-i-Muhammad.[91] Interestingly, while the LT originally envisioned women's mobilization within the private sphere, over time it has had to "make com-promises with regard to women's role [sic] in public life for tactical political advantage."[92]

The group that has been of greatest interest to analysts with regard to the incorporation of women—or not—has been Al-Qaeda, the epicenter of the GJM. Abu Musab al-Zarqawi, former leader of Al-Qaeda in Iraq (AQI), was the first Islamist with known links to Al-Qaeda to use women for terrorist violence. Women participated in the Sunni insurgency in Iraq almost ex-clusively as suicide attackers but were not widely or systematically opera-tionalized until 2007, with a notable increase throughout 2008. There are contradictory reports that Al-Qaeda "central" (the core of Al-Qaeda led by

Osama bin Laden and Ayman al-Zawahiri) has been training women for suicide attacks, but women are certainly involved with Al-Qaeda in more traditional roles—as mothers and wives of jihadis—and in the context of online radicalization.[93] While Iraq serves as an important new benchmark for women's roles in the GJM's jihadist war, the war in Afghanistan has not involved female militants. One of the key differences may be that the Iraq war was largely nationalist in its intent, despite the religious branding used by militants. The war in Afghanistan remains tied to the GJM and has not evoked a popular nationalist response.

The irony for even the most conservative Islamist organizations is that their operational and tactical success requires ideological retreat with regard to women's roles in the public sphere. The LT, like other Islamist organizations, needs to bring women out of the home to permit more effective mobilization of targeted men. This has inadvertently led to expanded roles—and even rights—for women.[94] The interplay between operational imperatives and ideology will remain an important feature of women's involvement, especially in the most ideologically restrictive violent organizations.

Conclusion

"We can speak of a post-Islamist stage in which Islamism is losing its political and revolutionary fervor but steadily infiltrating social and cultural life." This, indeed, is the location of the emergent Islamic feminism whose proponents are determined to influence the contours of this contested terrain.
—Nilufer Gole, Turkish sociologist and feminist, quoted in Margot Badran, "Understanding Islam, Islamism, and Islamic Feminism"

Western observers, especially in the United States, have historically had a difficult time reconciling religion and politics. These tensions are currently at issue in the Muslim world, but they are heavily influenced by broader trends, including postcolonial state structures, globalization, and sociocultural stress. The reassertion of political Islam is frequently perceived as a uniform phenomenon that is wholly negative. In reality, it is a multifaceted political occurrence that ranges from moderate to violent; it is also transnational, creating a shared experience for women from Africa to Southeast Asia. Women are central actors in this development, and the long-term implications for women's rights remain unknown.

Religion will play a central role in the political outcomes and sociocultural identity of women—and men—throughout much of the Muslim world in the decades to come. This does not mean that every state will take the path of Afghanistan's Taliban or Saudi Arabia's Wahhabi clerics. Instead, the Muslim world will experience, and exhibit, conservatism in its entire political range, and part of this diversity will be the result of the diversity that drives the process. While Muslim women are part of Islam's *umma,* they are also members of specific political regimes. The two forces will influence how women use religion to secure particular rights. Some of this will be beneficial to women, some neutral, and some quite negative. However, the tendency to assume a monolithic Islamic threat to Muslim women should be dispelled, and a more nuanced approach to how women use religion should be embraced. "Religious movements provide opportunities for women to participate in political processes," Haq writes. "Islamist movements in particular enable middle- to lower-middle-class women from traditional families to become politically active and even pursue a career since their purdah and affiliation with the Islamists make their lives in public more acceptable to their families."[95]

The struggle in much of the Muslim world is now less against religion than within religion. Undoubtedly there will be no uniform winner, but the struggle between conservative and reformist elements will continue. One potential danger for the future is that women's use of Islam could create a backlash wherein politically violent and extremist factions move toward an extremely rigid interpretation of Islam that seeks to undermine women's roles within religion and society. However, even some of the most politically violent organizations have had to relax their views toward women and become more "woman friendly." While this opens the door to women, it also has the potential to widen the impact and reach of these more violent organizations. This is a progression that bears monitoring by both internal and external observers.

NOTES

1. This term is conceptualized and operationalized for the purposes of this discussion to simply mean an inclination to maintain traditional order. This may, or may not, represent the current order within the existing political system.

2. This concept will be more fully elaborated in the following discussion. However, at the most basic level, Islamic feminist ideals constitute the perspective that women's rights can be articulated and pursued within a religious framework.

3. Laurie A. Brand, *Women, the State, and Political Liberalization: Middle Eastern and North African Experiences* (New York: Columbia University Press, 1998), 6.

4. Victoria Bernal, "Gender, Culture, and Capitalism: Women and the Remaking of Islamic 'Tradition' in a Sudanese Village," *Comparative Studies in Society and History* 36, no. 1 (1994): 40.

5. Zakia Salime, "Mobilizing Muslim Women: Multiple Voices, the Sharia, and the State," *Comparative Studies of South Asia, Africa, and the Middle East* 28, no. 1 (2008): 204.

6. Deniz Kandiyoti, "Women, Islam, and the State," *Middle East Report* (November–December 1991): 10.

7. Brand, *Women, the State, and Political Liberalization,* 252–53.

8. Soraya Duval, "New Veils and New Voices: Islamist Women's Groups in Egypt," in *Women and Islamisation: Carving a New Space in Muslim Societies,* ed. Karin Ask and Marit Tjomsland (Fantoft-Bergen, Norway: Chr. Michelsen Institute, 1997), 40.

9. Margot Badran, "Understanding Islam, Islamism, and Islamic Feminism," *Journal of Women's History* 13, no. 1 (2001): 47.

10. Miriam Cooke, "Roundtable Discussion: Religion, Gender, and the Muslim-woman," *Journal of Feminist Studies in Religion* 24, no. 1 (2008): 91–93.

11. Karla J. Cunningham, "Women, Political Violence, and Post-conflict Citizenship," in *Democratic Development and Political Terrorism: The Global Perspective*, ed. William J. Crotty (Boston: Northeastern University Press, 2005), 73–92.

12. While often perceived as advocating a Western familial (i.e., nuclear) model, famil-ialism is also a key concept in other cultures. As applied for the purposes of this discus-sion, the concept is consistent with the Confucian understanding of the importance of family cohesion and continuity, as well as the tendency to defer to the family hierarchy. See Shawn H. E. Harmon and Na-Kyoung Kim, "A Tale of Two Standards:
Drift and Inertia in Modern Korean Medical Law," *SCRIPTed* 5, no. 2 (2008): 267–93.

13. Raphael Patai, *The Arab Mind*, rev. ed. (New York: Charles Scribner's Sons, 1983), 282–83.

14. Salime, "Mobilizing Muslim Women," 210.

15. Suad Joseph, "Gendering Citizenship in the Middle East," in *Gender and Citizen-ship in the Middle East*, ed. Suad Joseph (Syracuse: Syracuse University Press, 2000), 24–25.

16. Kandiyoti, "Women, Islam, and the State," 11.

17. Valentine M. Moghadam, "Patriarchy in Transition: Women and the Changing Family in the Middle East," *Journal of Comparative Family Studies* 35 (2004): 140–41. Moghadam's use of the concept of "class patriarchy" captures the idea of a ruling class of men.

18. Duval, "New Veils and New Voices," 38.

19. Ibid., 39–54.

20. Gül Aldıkaçti Marshall, "Ideology, Progress, and Dialogue: A Comparison of Fem-inist and Islamist Women's Approaches to the Issues of Head Covering and Work in Tur-key," *Gender and Society* 19, no. 1 (2005): 104.

21. Nayereh Tohidi, "'Islamic Feminism': Perils and Promises," in *Middle Eastern Women on the Move: Openings for and the Constraints on Women's Political Participation in the Middle East* (Washington, D.C.: Woodrow Wilson International Center for Scholars, 2003), 143.

22. Wilhelmina Jansen, "Contested Identities: Women and Religion in Algeria and Jordan," in Ask and Tjomsland, *Women and Islamisation*, 66.

23. Jansen, "Contested Identities," 67.

24. Tohidi, "'Islamic Feminism,'" 135.

25. Bernal, "Gender, Culture, and Capitalism."

26. International Crisis Group, "Women and Radicalisation in Kyrgyzstan," *Asia Re-port* no. 176, September 3, 2009, http://www.crisisgroup.org/home/index.cfm?id=6296 (accessed October 1, 2009).

27. Maimuna Huq, "Talking *Jihad* and Piety: Reformist Exertions Among Islamist Women in Bangladesh," *Journal of the Royal Anthropological Institute*, n.s., 15, no. S1 (2009): S167.

28. Ibid., S168–71.

29. Marshall, "Ideology, Progress, and Dialogue," 105.

30. Margot Badran, "The Gender of Islam," *Al Ahram*, February 24–March 2, 2005, 1.

31. Tohidi, "'Islamic Feminism,'" 140.

32. Badran, "Gender of Islam," 2.

33. Sophia Pandya, "Religious Change Among Yemeni Women: The New Popularity of 'Amr Khaled," *Journal of Middle East Women's Studies* 5, no. 1 (2009): 64.

34. Associated Press, "Sex Talks on Muslim TV?" *Ynetnews.com*, December 4, 2006, http://www.ynetnews.com/articles/0,7340,L-3335705,00.html (accessed October 7, 2009).

35. Duval, "New Veils and New Voices," 47–49.

36. Jansen, "Contested Identities," 65.

37. Duval, "New Veils and New Voices," 49.

38. Jansen, "Contested Identities," 72.

39. Cooke, "Roundtable Discussion," 95.

40. Omayma Abdellatif and Marina Ottaway, "Women in Islamist Movements: Toward an Islamist Model of Women's Activism," Carnegie Middle East Center, Carnegie Papers no. 2, June 2007, http://www.CarnegieEndowment.org/pubs (accessed September 2009).

41. Marshall, "Ideology, Progress, and Dialogue," 107.

42. Anne Sofie Roald, "Feminist Reinterpretation of Islamic Sources: Muslim Feminist Theology in the Light of the Christian Tradition of Feminist Thought," in Ask and Tjomsland, Women and Islamisation, 16.

43. Abdellatif and Ottaway, "Women in Islamist Movements," 2.

44. Ibid., 3.

45. Rosefsky Wickham, quoted in Roel Meijer, "Taking the Islamist Movement Seriously: Social Movement Theory and the Islamist Movement," International Review of Social History 50 (2005): 283.

46. Kathleen M. Blee, Women of the Klan: Racism and Gender in the 1920s (Berkeley: University of California Press, 1991), 3.

47. Abdellatif and Ottaway, "Women in Islamist Movements," 2.

48. Badran, "Understanding Islam, Islamism, and Islamic Feminism," 49.

49. Abdellatif and Ottaway, "Women in Islamist Movements," 6.

50. Ibid.

51. Ann Elizabeth Mayer, "Comment on Majid's 'The Politics of Feminism in Islam,'" Signs 23, no. 2 (1998): 363–69.

52. Anouar Majid, "The Politics of Feminism in Islam," Signs 23, no. 2 (1998): 321–61.

53. Duval, "New Veils and New Voices," 38.

54. Fadwa Allabadi, "Controversy: Secular and Islamist Women in Palestinian Society," European Journal of Women's Studies 15, no. 3 (2008): 194.

55. Rola El-Husseini, "Women, Work, and Political Participation in Lebanese Shia Contemporary Thought: The Writings of Ayatollahs Fadlallah and Shams al-Din," Comparative Studies of South Asia, Africa, and the Middle East 28, no. 2 (2008): 273–82.

56. Asma Barlas, "The Qur'an, Sexual Equality, and Feminism" (lecture at the University of Toronto, January 12, 2004), http://www.asmabarlas.com/TALKS/20040112_UToronto.pdf (accessed September 20, 2009).

57. Ibid., 5.

58. Allabadi, "Controversy," 183.

59. Ibid., 191.

60. Duval, "New Veils and New Voices," 42.

61. Ibid., 53.

62. Ibid., 54.

63. Tohidi, "'Islamic Feminism,'" 139.

64. Allabadi, "Controversy," 184; Duval, "New Veils and New Voices," 68–69.

65. Salime, "Mobilizing Muslim Women," 210–11; Tohidi, "'Islamic Feminism,'" 135.

66. Duval, "New Veils and New Voices," 49–51.

67. Jansen, "Contested Identities," 60.

68. Bernal, "Gender, Culture, and Capitalism," 55.

69. Ibid., 60.

70. There are three categories of Muslim scholars who write about women: traditionalist, neo-traditionalist, and reformist. Reformists argue that Islam supports gender equality across the board and that Islam and modernity are compatible. Ziba Mir-Hosseini, cited in El-Husseini, "Women, Work, and Political Participation in Lebanese Shia Contemporary Thought," 273n2.

71. Sayyid Muhammad Husayn Fadlallah, quoted in El-Husseini, "Women, Work, and Political Participation in Lebanese Shia Contemporary Thought," 278.

72. Marshall, "Ideology, Progress, and Dialogue," 107.

73. The GJM constitutes the violent end on a continuum of a broader Salafi movement. There are three Salafi factions—purists, politicos, and jihadis—who share a common creed but differ over their understanding of the contemporary world and its problems. They thus offer different solutions to those problems. For example, jihadis take a militant position and believe that only violence can produce change. The Salafi movement includes a diverse array of people, such as Osama bin Laden and the Mufti of Saudi Arabia. Quintan Wiktorowicz, "Anatomy of a Salafi Movement," *Studies in Conflict and Terrorism* 29, no. 3 (2006): 207–39.

74. David Cook, "Women Fighting in Jihad?" *Studies in Conflict and Terrorism* 28 (2005): 383.

75. Karla J. Cunningham, "Cross-Regional Trends in Female Terrorism," *Studies in Conflict and Terrorism* 26, no. 3 (2003): 171–95; Karla J. Cunningham, "Countering Female Terrorism," *Studies in Conflict and Terrorism* 30, no. 2 (2007): 113–29.

76. Allabadi, "Controversy," 195.

77. Julie Peteet, "Icons and Militants: Mothering in the Danger Zone," *Signs* 23, no. 1 (1997): 103–29.

78. Yoram Schweitzer, ed., *Female Suicide Bombers: Dying for Equality?* (Tel Aviv: Jaffee Center for Strategic Studies, 2006), 25.

79. Anne Speckhard and Khapta Ahkmedova, "The Making of a Martyr: Chechen Suicide Terrorism," *Studies in Conflict and Terrorism* 29, no. 5 (2006): 440.

80. Anne Speckhard and Khapta Ahkmedova, "Black Widows: The Chechen Female Suicide Terrorists," in Schweitzer, *Female Suicide Bombers,* 63.

81. Speckhard and Ahkmedova, "Making of a Martyr," 468.

82. International Crisis Group, "Women and Radicalisation in Kyrgyzstan," 6.

83. Ibid., 7.

84. Ibid., 10.

85. Ibid., 6.

86. Ibid., 16–17.

87. Farish A. Noor, "Women in the Service of the Jundullah: The Case of Women Supporters of the Jama'ah Islamiyah of Indonesia" (paper for the workshop on "Female Suicide Bombers and Europe" held at the International Institute for Strategic Studies in London, March 12, 2007), http://www.iiss.org (accessed October 14, 2009).

88. Noor, "Women in the Service of the Jundullah," 12.

89. Farhat Haq, "Militarism and Motherhood: The Women of the Lashkar-i-Tayyabia in Pakistan," *Signs: Journal of Women in Culture and Society* 32, no. 4 (2007): 1033.

90. Ibid., 1027–28.

91. Ibid., 1028.

92. Ibid., 1029.

93. Tuty Raihanah Mostarom, "Al Qaeda's Female Jihadists: The Islamist Ideological View," R. Rajaratham School of International Studies (RSIS) Commentaries, February 6, 2009, http://dr.ntu.edu.sg/bitstream/handle/10220/6098/RSIS0142009.pdf?sequence=1 (accessed November 2, 2009).

94. Haq, "Militarism and Motherhood," 1030.

95. Ibid., 1033.

6

Women in Extreme Right Parties and Movements:
A Comparison of the Netherlands and the United States

Kathleen M. Blee and Annette Linden

The European far right has few women members, while the extreme right in the United States has a substantial, perhaps even growing, proportion of women. Across Europe, far-right parties have made inroads into electoral politics, taking seats in parliaments and electing candidates to local and regional offices. In the United States, the extreme right has virtually no electoral presence but exists as loosely connected and marginal groups and movements.[1]

In this chapter, we explore how women's participation on the far right is affected by the organization of national politics. Using life histories related by women members of far-right political parties in the Netherlands and women activists in white supremacist movements in the United States, we compare the ways that Dutch and U.S. women describe their entrance into and participation in extremist politics. Our findings are twofold. One is that the differences in women's participation in the Dutch and U.S. far right are due more to party/nonparty distinctions than to other contextual factors. The other finding is that the far right in both the Netherlands and the United States is highly gendered; that is, women's experiences in right-wing extremism are substantially different from those of men.

Background

The Netherlands

Fascist and Nazi ideas have always been marginal in Dutch society, and extreme right-wing organizations and parties have never been very successful, partly as a consequence of the strong and continuing societal condemnation of racism and Nazism through the 1990s. As it is illegal in the Netherlands for a political organization to be openly racist, extreme right parties must disguise their extremism. Doing so, however, creates conflict within the parties between moderates who want to maintain a respectable image to secure votes and more radical members who push for more open declarations of fascist or Nazi sentiments. Moderate party members, for example, argue that people with extremist sympathies "spoil the identity" of right-wing parties. Conflicts between radicals and moderates about the image they show "front stage" and the ideas that are nurtured "backstage" lead time and again to schism and fragmentation.

In the 1990s, many parties of the extreme right were unable to formulate clear goals or differentiate themselves from other rightist parties, shaping what J. Van Donselaar describes as "a mosaic of the extreme-right."[2] Yet, in the second half of the 1990s, the biggest extreme right party, the Centrum Democrats (CD), led by Hans Janmaat, who vowed to defeat multiculturalism in the Netherlands, obtained three seats in Parliament. At the same time, three extreme right parties won a total of eighty-four seats in city councils in large cities, including Rotterdam, The Hague, and Utrecht. These were the CD; the Centrum Party '86 (CP '86), a splinter party of the CD with a more radical ideology against foreigners; and the Netherlands Blok (NB), another splinter from the CD. Parties like the CD were state nationalistic, regarding all individuals born and raised within the territory of the state, or living within the state and willing to naturalize, as "our own population" and insisting that immigrants assimilate or leave. Parties like the CP '86 were folk nationalistic, with a more extreme ideology that insisted that all races and ethnic groups had to live in line with "their unique nature." Both state and folk nationalist parties sought a society without social mingling across races or cultures and were militantly nationalistic and anti-immigration, even supporting the forced expulsion of migrants from the Netherlands.[3]

Despite electoral victories, the opinions of leaders and representatives of the extremist parties were ignored in the overall political debates of the 1990s, and members of extreme right-wing parties were often excluded from political boards and disregarded during meetings. By the end of the 1990s, extreme right-wing parties had lost all seats in city councils and Parliament. Today there is just one extreme right-wing political party, the Dutch People's Union (NVU), and it does not attract many votes.

The United States

The strong two-party system and winner-take-all voting procedures in the United States make it difficult for extremist parties to operate, and there are currently no racially extreme parties with any significant ability to attract votes. Indeed, over the past century, the only far-right group with any substantial electoral strength was the massive racist, anti-Semitic, and anti-Catholic Ku Klux Klan (KKK) of the 1920s. Although it does not have electoral strength, the contemporary extreme right in the United States wields some power through violence and terrorism, both planned and occasionally enacted.

Today the U.S. extreme right consists of the KKK, neo-Nazis, and assorted white supremacists.[4] The KKK is a collection of small and competing groups that promote extreme racism against African Americans and hostility to nonwhite immigrants. KKK members tend to be middle-aged or older and are largely located in southern states and rural areas. Some embrace the old-style nationalism and southern-state rhetorics of early waves of the Klan, but many now adopt more internationalist ideas of a world order founded on the principles of white supremacism. The more active extreme right movements are those that embrace ideas of neo-Nazism; these are found throughout the country, although with larger concentrations on the coasts. They include white power skinhead gangs that enlist teenagers and young adults in violence on behalf of racial goals; white supremacist groups that aspire to undertake acts of terrorist violence against racial enemies and what they term the ZOG (Zionist Occupied Government); and virulently anti-Semitic followers of the doctrine of "Christian Identity" who believe that only whites are human and that Jews are the literal descendants of Satan.[5]

Life Histories

There is virtually no information on women who are active in far-right politics in the Netherlands and the United States. Not only are extreme rightists generally reluctant to provide information about themselves but, in the case of women, the layer of secrecy is thicker because the officials and spokespersons of such groups and parties in both countries are virtually all male and scholars have tended to study only male activists.

In this chapter, we report on limited but very rare data that were collected in the 1990s directly from women activists in extreme right parties and movements in both countries.[6] These data allow us to glimpse the role of women in right-wing extremism from the point of view of female activists themselves. For the Netherlands, we focus on women who play relatively minor roles in right-wing parties and make up a small percentage of the membership. For the United States, we report on women in KKK chapters, who constitute a larger proportion of Klan members but are rarely involved in shaping the strategy or direction of these groups, as well as women in neo-Nazi and white supremacist groups who are significant members, both numerically and in terms of their participation in the groups' aggressive and violent actions.

To find what drives women to become and stay involved in Dutch extreme right-wing political parties and organizations, Annette Linden conducted life-history interviews with 5 female activists. These women (along with 32 male activists also interviewed for the larger project) were selected to ensure variation in the type of party or political organization, the region of the country, and the length of time that they had been active. The women ranged in age from 27 to 67. Interviews were conducted in a variety of locations of the interviewees' choosing and ranged in length from 1 to 5 hours. Additionally, information was collected by talking to women who were present at interviews with their husbands and to women who attended protests, press conferences, and party meetings.

Information on far-right activists in the United States was gathered by Kathleen Blee through life-history interviews with 34 women in various racist and anti-Semitic movements, including white supremacist, neo-Nazi, white power skinhead, and KKK movements. Women were selected for interviews through a purposive multistage sampling technique that ensured variation in the type of movement, the region of the country, and the length of time that they had been active. The women ranged in age from 16 to 90, with a mean age of 24. Interviews were conducted in a variety of locations of the interviewees' choosing and ranged in length from 2 to 6 hours. Information was also collected through observation of extreme rightist events, such as rallies and protests, and systematic analysis of documents and propaganda produced by these movements.

Paths into the Extreme Right

To describe the paths that women took into the extreme right in the Netherlands and the United States, we use an explanatory framework developed by Bert Klandermans that identifies four stages through which activists move: investigating (finding out about the group and getting involved), socializing (meeting and hanging out with others within the group), maintaining (staying involved), and exiting (leaving the group).[7] Although each life history was unique, we identified sufficient similarities in the stages toward activism to distinguish four paths through these stages of participation in the extreme right. We refer to these trajectories as the prototypical extreme right activist careers. They are revolutionaries, wanderers, converts, and compliants.

Revolutionaries see the extreme right as an instrument to change the world and to meet with other combatants. These activists have strong ideological motives and identify with others who subscribe to the same ideology. If there were no such others, they would carry out extreme right activities themselves. Indeed, if the right-wing organization they join does not live up to their expectations, they establish new organizations or take on the activities themselves.

Wanderers are primarily looking for others who share their extreme right ideology. They are searching for political homes and constituencies of identification. If the organizations to which they adhere fail to deliver, they disengage and look for other political shelters.

Converts see themselves as having suffered wrongs. Their anger drives them more than ideology does. In the extreme right they find others who feel the same way. They are likely to quit if they find that other members are not also motivated by anger and frustration.

Compliants predominantly identify with others in the movement. They participate as long as these people continue to be involved, even if they have misgivings. There is little ideology behind their participation. Rather, they participate to maintain friendships or relationships with other members.

The ways in which women engage in the extreme right can be seen by examining their stages of involvement, from investigating and socializing to maintaining; since we interviewed current members, we do not consider the stage of exiting.

Stages of Activism in the Netherlands

None of the Dutch women can be categorized as a revolutionary activist, someone who enters the extreme right to change the world, or as a convert, someone who enters the movement to express anger; 19 of the 32 men fall into one of these categories. One woman is a wanderer, searching for a movement that shares her ideology; 8 men are in this category. Four women are categorized as compliants, participating because of their ties to someone in the movement; 5 men are in this category.

Investigating

Before they become involved in the extreme right, men generally investigate the organization or party. Most female activists, on the contrary, skip this stage and enter the extreme right to support a significant other who is already active. Eva van Veen comments on her entry into the NB: "If I were just his assistant and not married to him, I would at a certain moment say that I wanted a week's rest. But then you see him doing it himself, so what are you to do? You help again. . . . I feel, of course, responsible because it is my man's party. To be sure, I am on his payroll, but at the same time he is my man and to your man you don't say no that easy."

Since they enter right-wing politics to support someone else, these female activists recall getting involved as something that just happened to them. Looking back on this period, they state that they knew hardly anything about the parties they joined. They describe themselves before they became actively involved in political activities of the extreme right as confident, socially accepted, and active women who were engaged in voluntary work, such as teaching foreigners how to read and speak Dutch, but also as politically naive. Their lives revolved around caring for children, husbands, and relatives while developing and pursuing an independent professional career.

Many women describe their activism as having started off without their even realizing it. In their minds, it was never their intention to become active; they saw themselves as simply helping a husband, good friend, or relative who was in the movement. For example, Maria Helgers's brother, who had been a member of the CD for several years in a nearby town, nominated her as a CD candidate for the city council elections in her hometown. She was prepared to stand by her brother, explaining, "Brothers and sisters have to be there for each other. At least, that's my opinion. One day one starts to understand that as long as you help each other, you both benefit from it, you can take a next step. I mean, if I lift up the other to get hold of the biscuit tin on the top shelf, then that is the team spirit. It is something you cannot get hold of by yourself. We have always had this unique bond."

Socializing

Most male activists said that meeting others with the same ideas gave them a great sense of belonging, a sense of comradeship. For most female activists, this sense of belonging is directed toward a single individual, such as a husband, a good friend, or a close relative, not toward a party or organization. To support this individual, many female activists perform all sorts of chores in the extreme right, including handing out flyers and helping host a house meeting. In the beginning of their involvement, these women say, they were hardly engaged in politics and were not interested in ideology, only in helping their friend, husband, or relative. But the longer they stayed, the more committed to the extreme right they became, especially if the person they were helping was successful within the party or organization. For instance, Maria agreed to stand for office to support her brother. She considers her efforts to help him as a kind of social work, because with her help her brother could exert influence on decision makers in the city council. "Of course, it takes a huge lot of my time to run a campaign, stock all kinds of election posters and leaflets," she remarks. "I made the programs by myself! I'm a creative person, I have the brains, so I did it myself. I made a whole bunch of those programs, copying them, making nice layouts on the computer, etc."

Maintaining

Most female activists express initial negative feelings about their role in the extreme right. They talk of feeling uncertain about speaking in public and fearful about being attacked by antifascists. They show especially strong emotions when they recall the first time they appeared in the open as an extreme right activist. Maria, for example, remembers being overtaken by stage fright when she had to speak at her first council meeting as a representative of her party: "So there I was, standing in the council chamber, with thirty-eight members staring at me, while I tried to say something through a microphone. Very scary; it felt like being back in school when I feared to speak in public. I had a hard time those first months in city council."

Maria came to understand that her political career would become even harder over time because she would have to act on her own, as her brother—also elected as a council member—put more of his energy and time into his own business. Despite her concerns, Maria carried out her political representative responsibilities, but she continues to be afraid of speaking publicly on behalf of the extreme right: "I trained myself how to speak in public. . . . But I only speak when I'm quite sure that the subject hasn't been discussed in previous council meetings. . . . In that case, I'd rather keep silent."

During her life-history interview, Margriet Cornelissen, a member of the CD, also spoke of feeling anxious at the start of her career in the city council:

> From the moment I was a member of the council, I've had help from everywhere. It felt like I had a bodyguard on every corner. At first they even walked me to my kids' school, because strange things happened. In the beginning it was quite scary, but after a while I felt more secure. Nevertheless, people stayed to protect me, quite reassuring. . . . We were threatened in the beginning. Threatening letters we brought to the police. Letters contained messages like "We know where to find you" or "We piss on your grave." My daughter was still very young at that time, and my son was still a baby. What did you expect? I was just an innocent housewife before I became active, and the situation, then, was quite frightening.

Unlike Maria, Margriet came to feel more positive about her role in the extreme right over time as she garnered support for herself from her party colleagues, whom she looks upon as a circle of friends. She recalls, "The antifascists organized a demonstration against us, some time ago. Forty people gathered in my house at that time. Half of them I hardly knew! But they all came to support me; all those people belonged to the CD in one way or another. We had lots of fun then! The antifascists had planned to walk by my house, but the police stopped them. They anticipated the riots. . . . For me that event was very fulfilling, because I experienced the care of so many supporters." More typically, female activists become increasingly isolated and forced to act on their own over time. They long for collaboration, yet most find it difficult to trust others in the extreme right or to "find the right men with the right position," as Eva says. Eva, wife of the leader of the NB, sees her husband as the only one in the party she can trust:

> People . . . have collaborated with us in the party, but they have never stayed for a long time. It's never really possible to get commitment from someone, it seems. After some time they leave, and we stay behind. But it appears to be symptomatic for the entire movement of the [extreme] right. Like fleas, they jump up and down, from one alliance to the other, and then they quit completely because they become socially isolated, ignored by family, by colleagues, and they can't get a job, let alone job interviews, and so on and so on. It's a hard life, this party life.

Most women never develop strong positive ties with the organizations they join. For one, they dislike feeling marginalized from society and explicitly and strongly claim to oppose the use of any ideology, symbols, or behaviors associated with Nazism. Maria complains that she is labeled a Nazi and that her social and personal life is scrutinized:

> I'm absolutely not a racist. It could be that I'm looked upon as a racist, but that's certainly not the case. I hate Hitler, I detest the persecution of the Jews, really, that sort of thing makes me shiver. . . . I don't want to be associated with fascists, racists, and that kind of people. In the local press that's what happened. They compared me with those kinds of people, those rotten apples. For a long time I felt responsible, but it was hard to defend myself against that stigma. . . . In some cases the public opinion is correct. There are quite some "people haters" among us, and they admit that they are Nazis. But my sense of righteousness always made me protest against them. Those kinds of people should be rejected from the parties. Or even better, prevented from joining, by screening them before they become members of the CD.

Eva also expresses a strong distaste, even fear, of National Socialists: "They are far more extreme than we are; I don't feel at ease with those sorts of ideas. . . . I told one of them, who used to be normal before, 'Give up on that crap,' meaning he should stop with collecting all those magazines about the Second World War, all that rotten Nazi shit. They're all the same . . . shouting 'Holland should become white.'" Danielle, who combines an activist career with being a single mom and a good friend of one of the leaders of CP '86, explains her views as distinct from those of racists and Fascists:

> I'm a Nationalist. I just want the Netherlands to be for the Netherlanders. And for everybody who has a legal status in this country. Concerning those without legal status, I don't want them here. I'm no racist, no

fascist; I just have a nationalistic mind. I have no problems with colored or blacks, nor with yellow, green, blue people. I don't care what color they are painted, as long as they are willing to belong to the Dutch society. You see, I even think it is okay if foreigners live here, but they just have to adapt completely.

These extreme right activists want their parties to be seen as normal, with an established place in politics. That is why they despise activists in the movement who overtly associate with Nazism and militarism. They feel that these activists contaminate their image and further marginalize their parties. Most do not want their children to be involved in extremist politics, because they fear that they would be socially marginalized and unable to develop a successful work career if they did so. Some even compare the stigma they face with how members of the NSB, the Dutch Nazi party during World War II, were publicly shamed and blocked from a number of professions at the end of the war.

Women also find it difficult to develop strong ties to the extreme right parties and organizations to which they belong because they resent the conflicts, mutual reproaches, and fragmentation they find there. Ineke van Wijk describes herself as a brave woman who was able to conquer the negative consequences of stigmatization and find status and respect in the CD. Yet she expresses her unhappiness with the infighting over power and status in the far right:

> To correct misspellings has always been my hobby. So in the beginning I'd send the party leader corrected versions of leaflets and posters. To support the leader. And also because I think that one cannot afford to make mistakes against our language. Especially a party such as the Centrum Democrats, which is so focused to preserve the culture of the Netherlands. But the leader never thanked me for it. Quite the opposite, in fact. He (Janmaat) was insulted by me, and called me a busybody and such. So my impression of him became even more negative than before. But I carried on, because I was convinced that the day would come in which I could be meaningful for the party and for politics in general. . . . I'm sorry to say that those days haven't arrived yet, because the leader of the party is a dictator. It's true what others say, you know. I wanted to help him, in many different ways, but he has always rejected my support. I'm on my own. I'm active for the Centrum Democrats, but he keeps me hanging on. I'll never be taken seriously, I guess.

Aside from these frustrations, female activists say that they benefit from the experience of being politically active. Margriet concludes that despite the threatening situations she found herself in, activism has been worthwhile for her:

I've become more independent, in the sense that I'm not as naive as I used to be and I have opinions which I stand for. And I mean wherever I am, I feel free to express my views. Not only concerning politics, but in general; here I am, I belong somewhere and I'm free to express my thoughts and ideas. And if you don't like what I say, I now allow myself to say so. Before, I didn't have the courage, I wanted to stay friends with everyone; even if I didn't agree with others, I wanted to be accepted and liked. Now I'm not like that anymore; I've become tough.

Women claim that right-wing politics expresses their moral obligation to assist those whom they perceive as in need of help—"normal people" who bear the burden of dealing with unchecked immigration into their country. As Eva states, "It's the most rewarding aspect of being politically active. . . . The technical side of politics, so to say, is not my favorite pastime. Mainly what motivates me is to help out normal people. That has always been the case. To help those people that sit at my kitchen table, asking for help, telling me their life story, explaining to me what they have gone through. Yes, that's why I did it, for those people. Maybe that's not very idealistic, it's pragmatic. Maybe I should be more idealistically involved, but that's just not the case." The human aspect of politics gives meaning to Eva's political life, but it also absorbs her energy so that she doesn't have time for other pastimes. She explains,

Most people have a job, a wife, a girlfriend apart from their political life. But I never have somewhere else to go to, some kind of excuse not to be busy with political life. Only in very rare cases I can say "No" to my husband. Because I'm always at home, with my husband and his party. And if I have to make a choice between house chores or helping my husband with the party business, then I will do the latter. And all the other things in life, such as spending some time on my own, stay behind.

In the end, the needs and ambitions of women activists never fit into right-wing extremist parties and organizations dominated by men. Over time, women are able to gain a place in the party, primarily as helpmates, that nonetheless makes them proud to be activists and committed to the organization. But they still express frustration about being stigmatized by the wider society and unable to find a leadership role within their parties and organizations.

Stages of Activism in the United States

The Dutch women are easily categorized as mostly compliants, with one wanderer; it is more difficult to categorize the U.S. women. The far right in the

United States comprises overlapping and rapidly shifting racist groups rather than institutionalized parties as in the Netherlands. Since what defines membership in a racist group is less clear-cut than in a right-wing party, the trajectories of U.S. racist women are more ambiguous. Given this ambiguity, we tentatively classify about half of the U.S. women as revolutionaries, none as converts, a quarter as compliants, and a quarter as wanderers. This is a striking difference from the Netherlands, where none of the women interviewed are revolutionaries. Unfortunately, there are no comparable data on U.S. men.

Investigating

A number of right-wing U.S. women describe developing extreme racist ideas and looking for a movement in which they could express these beliefs. Although Dutch women generally skipped this stage, moving directly into extreme right organizations to support a significant other, about a quarter of the U.S. women report having investigated racist groups before joining them. A neo-Nazi we call Sue (all U.S. names are pseudonyms) claims, "I became very interested in my own racial heritage in high school. I am German, in fact, Aryan. I spent time working for a German neighbor and learned a lot about Germany before, during, and after World War II. I was shocked at the vast amount of disinformation the victorious side was putting out. . . . I started contacting different [racist] organizations, including the [Holocaust-denying] Institute for Historical Review for information."

Most U.S. women, about three-quarters, skipped the investigating stage and moved directly into a racist group. But unlike Dutch women, who moved into racist extremism to support a current activist with whom they had a personal tie, U.S. women almost never followed a loved one into the movement. Some were brought into extremist politics early in life by parents who belonged to racist groups. Julie, who was raised in an explicitly racist compound, had little contact with people who had other ideas. She was socialized, even homeschooled, in the racist community and thus learned racism and anti-Semitism as the guiding principles of life from an early age. After high school, she recounts, "I did consider going to college, but I figured I'd have to put up with more of what I did not [want]—indoctrination and stuff like that—than I would actually be learning something." She recalls her transition into racist activism as just part of growing up: "I was acquainted with [the racist group], of course, before. . . . I like its aggressive stance toward the need to have a movement for white people in America who are being oppressed by government action."

Other women adopted extreme racist beliefs only when they met a racist activist. That is, they learned about racism in the context of being pulled into a racist group. An example is Sarah, a middle-aged member of a neo-Nazi group. She talks about her entry into white supremacism as having occurred when a prominent neo-Nazi leader "had some papers, *Racial Loyalty*, delivered in Tampa, which caused a hullabaloo in the local *St. Petersburg Times*. They wrote him up as a villain, and I was about ripe to wake up so I wrote him. . . . This led me to reading and correspondence with my first POWs [racist 'prisoners of war'] . . . other literature, and growing convictions."

U.S. women often enter racist activism—especially neo-Nazi groups—by taking part in racial "scenes," the dynamic and loosely structured practices at the edges of far-right movements, and then slowly being pulled into membership. Some scenes are cultural in form, such as those that feature white power music.[8] White power bands, many based in Europe, tour the United States, playing in obscure venues and attracting young audience members through word-of-mouth publicity. Recorded white power music is the centerpiece of parties infused with alcohol and a sense of bravado. Other scenes are activity based. The KKK and other white supremacists host "self-help" sessions that teach techniques to bolster self-esteem and strong family ties, as well as social events that bring people together across generations and gender. Racist groups also pose as nonracial community associations and subtly embed racist ideas into campaigns for environmentalism, neighborhood safety, school quality, or even women's rights. Other activity-based scenes are based on violence. Neo-Nazi skinheads engage in displays of brutal street violence, against one another as well as against their perceived racial enemies.

Right-wing scenes have proven a powerful route for women into racist movements. Older women slip into racist movements as they are befriended by racist recruiters while working on projects they perceive as aimed at civic improvement. Young women are more likely to be lured by the aggressive, affronting spectacle of neo-Nazi violence. One young racist skinhead in the northwest said that she first became aware of white supremacism when she was fourteen years old:

> I used to go to a dance club on Friday and Saturday, and one time I heard some people mention that some skinheads were going to have a march next week. So I asked them what skinheads believed and why they were marching, and they briefly (and uneducatedly) said that skinheads were people who didn't like any other races besides whites and that they were going to march for white supremacy. I believe in that and showed up to the march. There I met a lot of skinheads and eventually learned the real reasons for the march and all the real beliefs of a true "skinhead."

Racist scenes are successful in bringing women into racist movements because they blur the boundaries between performers and audience. They differ from more traditional public appearances of racist movements, in which the roles of participant and spectator are clearly delineated. Customarily, members of racist groups reserve the right to wear racist clothing like

Klan robes and hoods, sport racist insignia like swastika tattoos, and perform racist rituals like cross burning or swastika lighting. They perform as racists for those who are watching. In these traditional racist events, spectators are sharply separated from racist performers and may be terrorized, excited, or left numb. Regardless of their reactions, those who watch cross burnings or see racists parade down streets do not regard themselves as participants or even potential participants. In these events, spectators are those to whom the message is directed. They are the recipients of racist ideas; they are not asked to formulate these ideas. They are performed for, but not asked to perform.

In contrast to traditional racist events, there is little distinction between activists and audiences in racist scenes. Casual observers are lured into participating in scenes, even when the intent or message is not clear to them. Women become active in civic groups on behalf of safe schools with hardly any awareness that these groups will eventually point to racial minority students as the cause of school problems. They join environmental groups without knowing that the groups are promoting ideas of white racial purity along with those of environmental purity. Spectators to skinhead violence also become involved, some as witnesses and others more directly as the violence spills into the crowd and stimulates anger and hostility. Scenes can engender a collective sense of identity and a buzz of emotional energy that further lure women into the racist movement. In such scenes, women can easily, almost imperceptibly, slide from scene to movement. One woman provided insight into how some racist activists understand their transition from action-scene to movement: "You don't have to 'join' one specific group (like a gang). The KKK, Christian Identity [a racist, anti-Semitic creed] skins, Odinists [a racist theology based on Nordic religions] (most of them), pro-white groups, white power skinheads, National Socialists, Church of the Creator skins, etc., are all part of the movement. It is your beliefs and your actions that make you part of the movement, not the name you go under or are associated with. As your beliefs and actions are pro-white, you are in the movement."

Socializing

Compared to the Dutch activists, racist women in the United States have more varied roles in their groups. Some, like many women in the KKK, take on supportive tasks, preparing meals and bearing and taking care of children to ensure the future of the white race. For them, this is the role of racist women. As Amy explains, "What do I see myself doing to help the [racist] movement? Well, I think one of the most important things you can do is keep our children out of the public education system. That's why I'm a teacher." Other women, particularly in some neo-Nazi and white power skinhead groups, take a more assertive posture. They are willing to fight and to stand up to the men in their groups. Suzanna says, "In order to be in the move-

ment, you have to earn your respect. . . . I tell them who I am and why I believe the way I believe. . . . If somebody hits me the wrong way or if somebody
does something stupid, I don't want nothing to do with them. And I'll plain
tell them." In either case, women express a sense of belonging to a racist
movement that transcends their attachment to a particular individual in that
movement. Bev, a KKK member, recalls that she helped her Klan leader son
by making "a couple of trips north to New York and to Chicago on various
problems . . . and helping with his robes [and allowing] meetings to be held
here in my house." But her sense of belonging to the racist movement is expressed in much broader terms as she describes her efforts "to keep the organization going [to] enlighten the public. . . . Hell, we want to win the hearts
of the people, and that can only come through disseminating your views."

Maintaining

Like the Dutch activists, right-wing women in the United States commonly
express fear about their vulnerability, especially in public protests. Susan laments that "I may not go out on the street and protest any more. . . . Do you
think I want them [her comrades] to go tell my kids that Mom's been killed
for what she believes in? . . . I just want to live for my children." Wendy describes many violent incidents in which she has been involved, concluding
that "when there's a demonstration, I'm not getting anywhere. Nobody's listening to what I have to say. I'm instantly trashed to begin with before I even
open my mouth. I mean, I got the shit beat out of me in New York, where I
thought they were gonna kill me. . . . I didn't even get up and speak yet. And
they beat the living shit out of me. And that wasn't fair."

U.S. women rarely find support among their male comrades to counteract
the attacks they fear from antiracist activists. To the contrary, they often complain about the attitudes and behavior of men in their groups. One Klan
woman says, "The men regard the women with sort of biker attitudes; they're
there to serve the man, and they keep them off the front [of the action]. Sort
of on a pedestal, but yet they can look down on them at the same time. In fact,
one woman told me that at least one group refer[s] to the women as cattle."

Like Dutch activists, right-wing women in the United States rarely develop strong ties to their groups, even if they remain committed to them for
decades. They do not worry as often as Dutch women do about the stigma of
being seen as Nazis; indeed, many of these women avidly and openly embrace Nazi symbols and ideas, which are not banned in the United States as
they are in many parts of Europe. But they find the conflict and tensions
within racist groups to be demoralizing and worry that leaders, in the words
of Eve, "have no stick-to-itiveness. If some little thing turns up that doesn't
suit them, they're quitters and you have to be very, very careful how you han-
dle them." Many express pride in their activism, but almost every woman ultimately concludes that participating in the racist movement has been costly

and largely unrewarding for them. Most revealing, perhaps, almost none are interested in convincing their daughters to follow their lead into extremist politics, although, in contrast to the Dutch women, they have little worry about their sons doing so.

Comparison and Conclusion

The national political context shapes how women participate in right-wing extremism. As shown in the contrasting cases of women's activism in the far right in the Netherlands and the United States, the structure of institutional politics influences whether women will join extremist politics as well as the role they are likely to have when they join. In multiparty electoral systems like the Netherlands, right-wing extremist parties have the potential to attract sufficient votes to gain office. These right-wing parties are highly stigmatized, as the statements of the Dutch women make clear, but they are also official and publicly recognized. In two-party electoral systems like the United States, in contrast, it is very difficult for extremist parties to achieve sufficient votes to gain office, so right-wing extremism takes the form of loosely organized groups and networks.

Structural differences between the Netherlands and the United States affect women's rightist activism in several ways, beginning with the demographics of participation. Official political parties, even those based on extremist ideologies, attract more older women than do looser extremist movements, as shown in the age difference between the Dutch and U.S. women activists. Second, institutionalized and publicly recognized political parties develop an interest in their own long-term stability and public face, more so than do more fluid movements. This is evident in the greater concern expressed by Dutch women about the stigma of Nazi symbols in their politics. Third, the nature of membership in political parties is far more clear than in movements. Women who join far-right parties in the Netherlands make an unambiguous transition from mainstream politics into extremism; their shift is evident to outsiders and authorities, who then regard them as politically extreme, even as some women activists view themselves as moderate within their parties. In contrast, membership in far-right movements in the United States is often vague, so women slide into these movements as they partake in the cultural venues and social scenes that surround racist groups. These women are often able to keep their involvement secret from outsiders, even from colleagues at work or family members.

Gender matters as well. Despite their very different national political contexts and ways of participating, right-wing extremist women in the Netherlands and the United States share similar feelings about their involvement. Almost all relate disappointment, frustration, or aggravation at how women are treated by men in their organizations. Whether they join to support a current member, to find an outlet for their ideological beliefs, or to stay within a network of friends or a cultural scene, far-right women feel that they were promised a political role that did not materialize. In both the Netherlands and the United States, such sentiments have fueled occasional expressions of gender conflict and even advocacy of women's rights by far-right women, although these are always expressed in the context of support for anti-immigrant, racist, and right-wing agendas. For example, some Dutch far-right women argue that Muslims should be expelled from Dutch society because Islamic culture violates women's rights. In the United States, white supremacist women sometimes make a similar argument, claiming that racial minority or Jewish women are prone to sexist or sexually violent behavior.

In recent years, small neo-Nazi groups and racist subcultures based on hardcore music have emerged throughout the Netherlands with women as visible and active participants, similar to those in the United States. It is likely that these are attracting younger members who are less concerned about stigma than members of extreme right political parties. If these subcultures develop into racist movements in the Netherlands and capture adherents from the extreme right parties, the differences between activists in the Netherlands and the United States may decline further. Regardless, women have established themselves in the ranks of the far right on both sides of the Atlantic.

NOTES

1. David Art, *The Politics of the Nazi Past in Germany and Austria* (New York: Cambridge University Press, 2006); Mabel Berezin, *Illiberal Politics in Neoliberal Times: Culture, Security, and Populism in the New Europe* (New York: Cambridge University Press, 2009); Mabel Berezin, "Revisiting the French National Front: The Ontology of a Political Mood," *Journal of Contemporary Ethnography* 36, no. 2 (2007): 129–46; Timothy Scott Brown, "Subcultures, Pop Music, and Politics: Skinheads and 'Nazi Rock' in England and Germany," *Journal of Social History* 38, no. 1 (2004): 157–78; Bert Klandermans and Nonna Mayer, eds., *Extreme Right Activists in Europe: Through the Magnifying Glass* (London: Routledge, 2006); Cynthia Miller-Idriss, *Blood and Culture: Youth, Right-Wing Extremism, and National Belonging in Contemporary Germany* (Durham: Duke University Press, 2009); Kathleen Blee, *Inside Organized Racism: Women in the Hate Movement* (Berkeley: University of California Press, 2002).

2. J. Van Donselaar, *Fout na de oorlog: Fascistische en racistische organisaties in Nederland 1950–1990* (Amsterdam: Bert Bakker, 1991).

3. Bert Klandermans and Nonna Mayer, "Links with the Past," in *Extreme Right Activists in Europe*, 16–27; Jacquelien van Stekelenburg and Bert Klandermans, "Radicalization," in *Identity and Participation in Culturally Diverse Societies: A Multidisciplinary Perspective*, ed. Assaad E. Azzi et al. (Malden, Mass.: John Wiley, 2011), 181–94.

4. The Tea Party and similar movements on the right are not included in this definition because they do not espouse explicitly white supremacist agendas nor advocate or practice violence or terrorism as a standard political strategy.

5. The nature of U.S. organized racism today is also detailed in Martin Durham, *White Rage: The Extreme Right and American Politics* (New York: Taylor and Francis, 2007); Pete Simi and Robert Futrell, *American Swastika: Inside the White Power Movement's Hidden*

Spaces of Hate (Lanham, Md.: Rowman and Littlefield, 2010); and Leonard Zeskind, *Blood and Politics: The History of the White Nationalist Movement from the Margins to the Mainstream* (New York: Farrar, Straus and Giroux, 2009).

6. Details of the theoretical approach and methodological strategies of the larger studies from which these data are drawn can be found in Blee, *Inside Organized Racism;* Annette Linden and Bert Klandermans, "Revolutionaries, Wanderers, Converts, and Compliants: Life Histories of Extreme Right Activists," *Journal of Contemporary Ethnography* 36, no. 2 (2007): 184–201; and Team Members, "Writing Life-Histories: Interviewing Extreme Right-Wing Activists," in Klandermans and Mayer, *Extreme Right Activists in Europe,* 51–64.

7. Bert Klandermans, "Collective Political Action," in *Oxford Handbook of Political Psychology,* ed. David O. Sears, Leonie Huddy, and Robert Jervis (New York: Oxford University Press, 2003), 670–709.

8. Robert Futrell, Pete Simi, and Simon Gottschalk, "Understanding Music in Movements: The White Power Music Scene," *Sociological Quarterly* 47, no. 2 (2006): 275–304.

PART 2

Privatizing the Public, Politicizing the Private

7

Maternalism Goes to War: Class, Nativism, and Mothers'
Fight for Conscription in America's First World War

Kate Hallgren

Addressing an audience of woman pacifists in 1924, activist Rosika Schwimmer blamed the press for the devastation of World War I. She claimed that
"no diplomat, king, etc., can make war if the Press is not supporting him and
serving him to poison the people and to inject into us all the lies through
which . . . we want to go to war and kill each other." Schwimmer's analysis
emerged from hard experience. She'd helped found a significant women's
peace movement in the United States that had drawn on the popular belief
that women's motherly and nurturing qualities made them natural pacifists.
The movement had recruited members and made headlines across the country, but its popularity had declined precipitously as the nation came closer to
declaring war.[1]

Most of the country's press, politicians, and women's leaders went from
condemning the war in 1914 to embracing it by 1917, when America declared
war against Germany. Pockets of antiwar sentiment remained, however.
Many women were apathetic about the war, and some actively opposed it. In
response, right-wing women cooperated with editors and publishers to promote the appearance of a united, pro-war American womanhood. Borrowing
pacifists' strategy, these nationalist women politicized motherhood. They exhorted American women to use their private influence to support their sons'
enlistment and then, as patriotic mothers, to become public supporters of
conscription.

This essay focuses on women's campaign for the military draft. It exposes the gendered aspects of the American draft debates that have gone
largely unexplored in a literature that is heavily weighted toward studies
of antiwar, pacifist, and leftist women. Nationalist and conservative women

were particularly active in the early weeks of the war, however. In articles and letters, a small group presented themselves as examples of loyal mothers who could speak for other American women. Many were affluent women whose sons had already voluntarily enlisted. In wartime, this gave them a special patriotic status, and they used this position to demand conscription to force suspected "slackers" and "shirkers" into the military. The women implied or stated that immigrant, working-class men were too selfish and unpatriotic to voluntarily enlist. They feared a demographic disaster if the volunteer system was maintained, imagining that the sons of their class would be killed in large numbers; they used these fears to try to manipulate other women into joining them. Their campaign for conscription was an aggressive defense of their own class and, in the Social Darwinist understanding of the term, race.

Though scholars have long debated the role of the mass media in shaping public opinion, this essay accepts the power of published stories to present a type of proof by example that can shape political debate. As scholars of both right-wing women and lesbian politics have noted, stories can influence a group's self-definition, perception of the world, and political allegiances. Stories are often particularly important to women's activism because a narrative can make public what is usually private: the links between home, family, and politics. In war, boundaries between public and private are especially liable to break down. This essay highlights right-wing women's agency in choosing to adopt the position of Spartan mother—a mother who values her nation's well-being above her child's—and the women's creative and political work aimed at persuading other women to do the same.[2]

The chapter begins with an examination of the way that American mothers figured in U.S. Congressmen's debates over war and conscription, and then looks at the pro-conscription campaign waged by nationalist women and newspapers in Chicago and New York. Though reporters named fewer than twenty women as supporters of conscription, the women's stories and claims of leading a larger movement reached hundreds of thousands of readers in their home cities. When the Associated Press chose to distribute their stories, they reached even more readers and a much wider geographic area.

In the second part of the chapter, best-selling author and mother Mary Roberts Rinehart serves as a case study. Rinehart published her account of her eldest son's enlistment in an article that used baldly classist and nativist arguments for the draft, and that positioned mothers of soldiers as patriots with a right to influence military policy. Rinehart's story was extremely influential and widely distributed. Her papers and memoir also allow us to understand the private factors that motivated her public political stance.[3] Finally, in the conclusion, we will explore some long-term effects of the war's outpouring of nationalist propaganda aimed at women and mothers.

Manning the American Expeditionary Force:
The Conscription Debates

President Woodrow Wilson asked Congress to declare war on Germany on April 2, 1917, and four days later the measure passed. The day after war was declared, Secretary of War Newton D. Baker presented the administration's conscription bill. To the Wilson administration, conscription seemed the most efficient way to raise more than five hundred thousand troops in a short time. The measure provoked determined opposition from a minority of Congressmen, however, and the debates lasted for approximately six weeks.[4]

The conscription debates were protracted in part because many constituents opposed U.S. intervention in the "European war" altogether. Historians have found evidence of opposition to the war among not only woman pacifists and working-class radicals but also many rural people, westerners, southerners, Socialists, immigrants, and urban residents.[5] Intervention tended to be most popular among a business class tied to Europe financially and an elite tied to Britain and France through educational and cultural experiences. Many of these wealthy and well-connected Americans, both men and women, were part of the "preparedness movement" before the war. Led by Theodore Roosevelt, they wanted a larger American army and navy and military training for all young American men. In addition, most newspapers supported the war, likely as a result of British efficiency in supplying news releases with stories slanted in favor of the Entente.[6]

Americans could look at two international examples of the process of passing a military draft. Great Britain's Parliament was able to pass conscription legislation after the wartime government had convinced labor unions that it would be enforced fairly. There, men and women across classes supported conscription, and prominent suffragists numbered among the war's most fervent and visible supporters. In contrast, Australia defeated conscription with a voter referendum in 1916. Many commentators said that women's votes were responsible.[7]

In view of women's political importance in other countries at war, perhaps it was natural that Congressmen debated women's attitudes toward U.S. participation. But their discussions did not focus on women as workers or even as wives. They focused on mothers—because mothers were seen as key to the recruitment of young, single men, who were considered the best potential soldiers and conscripts.

In the 1910s, before Freudian theory had been popularized, mothers and sons were expected to have a close, passionate love for each other. Ruth Slack, a Georgia mother who supported conscription, said that she "flew" to see her son in Baltimore so they could have a "love feast" before his enlistment. "Mother songs" made up an entire genre of popular music that evoked adults' longing and love for their mothers, much as popular songs today focus on lovers. Author Mary Roberts Rinehart acknowledged that mothers would dread a son's military service because mothers and sons were "always" so close. And Representative William Fields (D-KY) believed a young man's most important relationship was with his mother. Opposed to conscription for the young, he said that a nineteen- or twenty-year-old was a child who "by divine right belongs to the mother." At age twenty-one, the child became a man, and "his mother yields him, because it is his duty to go."[8]

Adding political might to their cultural influence, American mothers and other women were joined together in powerful political lobbies in the Progressive Era. The largest women's voluntary associations, with membership in the millions, based their work on maternalism, the belief that women were essentially moral and motherly, with a unique and vital role in public affairs. Politically, maternalists set the country's welfare agenda, and they successfully lobbied for mothers' pensions, in which the states distributed financial support to needy mothers to enable them to care for their young children at home. Maternalists also promoted labor laws and public health measures designed to protect women and children. Even with only partial woman suffrage, the maternalist coalition made women a political force in the 1910s.[9]

With a powerful role in family, culture, and politics, mothers would be key to wartime mobilization. Antiwar, anticonscription members of Congress initially claimed to speak for American mothers. Their irritated opponents responded with an outpouring of stories of mothers who supported the draft and their sons' military service. An exchange between two senators typified these opposing positions.

Republican senator Robert M. La Follette of Wisconsin entered the debate over the declaration of war on Germany by reading a letter from "A North Dakota Farm Woman." The author asked the Senate to consider the mother of "the poorer, thrifty classes," who had lain awake with her infant son and who had skimped on food and clothing for herself in order to feed and clothe her child. This mother did not deserve to see her son sent "to a slaughterhouse to be butchered" on the front lines of Europe. La Follette supported maternal pacifists' arguments that women and children were the greatest victims of any war, and in reading this letter he presented himself as the defender of women, children, and the working class.[10]

A strong supporter of U.S. entry to the war, Senator John Sharp Williams (D-MS), rebutted La Follette's assertions point by point. He mocked the letter from "some female farmer out in the Dakotas" and her complaints that "she had patched her boy up, and she had been taking care of him for I don't know how long," saying that her antiwar stance was "cowardly nonsense." Opposed to the woman's melding of motherly role and antiwar politics, Williams mentioned the popular song of 1915: "'I Did Not Raise My Boy to Be a Soldier' and all that nonsense. If you raised your boy right, you raised him to do whatever he had to do for his own honor or for his country's honor." Finally, he criticized the author's "false motherly love" for turning her boy into a coward, unwilling to stand up for any principles. Williams's speech attacked the basis of women's pacifism. He depicted a pacifist mother's love as corrosive to national loyalty and her son's manhood. Using a story from his own family history, Williams asserted that only men could understand the obligation to fight in time of war and that an honorable man enlisted no matter what the objections of his mother or wife.[11] Rather than question why La Follette and Williams spent their time discussing mothers, other Congressmen proceeded to share their own stories of mothers in wartime, supplied by letters from constituents, newspaper coverage of women's attitudes, or their own family history.

America's conscription debates focused not only on mothers' wartime loyalty but also on the patriotism of immigrants and the working class. Many Americans looked with suspicion on the "new" immigrant groups that had flooded into America, questioning whether they could adapt and become truly democratic citizens. Some writers and intellectuals suggested that only the Anglo-Saxon race, supposedly typified by the oldest American families, was adapted to democratic self-governance. Those who feared that blood or birth determined wartime loyalty had much to fret about. At the time of the war, the population of U.S. immigrants born in Germany and its wartime allies was significant, about 4.6 million. After the war had begun in Europe, a few acts of German sabotage occurred in the United States, and President Woodrow Wilson and former president Theodore Roosevelt made speeches criticizing disloyal immigrants, thereby casting suspicion on all immigrants. Furthermore, some immigrants were active in socialist and anarchist politics. These groups had condemned the war as an opportunity for the rich to profit while the poor fought and died. Congressmen did not openly discuss radical labor as a challenge to the draft, but they did imply that working-class and immigrant men were the most likely "slackers" who would never voluntarily enlist.[12]

Perhaps with an eye to reelection, senators only hinted as to who "slackers" really were. Senator Jacob Gallinger (R-NH) suggested that if his peers wished to see examples, they should walk "from the Peace Monument to Seventh Street on Pennsylvania Avenue [in Washington, D.C.]. . . . If he will go into the East Side of New York or the Bowery of New York or North Street in Boston he will find the slackers there." These were immigrant, working-class areas. Senator Knute Nelson (R-MN) said that slackers came from "a certain class of our population whom I do not care now to refer to by name." These senators discussed how to shape the age requirements for draft registration to catch the largest number of slackers in the government's net.[13]

As Congressmen anticipated mothers' response to the draft bill and considered the identities of "slackers," some women around the country began a campaign for the draft focused on petitions, letters, telegrams, and the press. In particular, women in Chicago and New York cooperated with newspapers and magazines to create the impression of a large-scale mothers' movement.[14]

The *Chicago Tribune* was committed to supporting both the war and conscription. The paper's owners were Republican politicians and supporters of Theodore Roosevelt and his vision of an expanded U.S. military. The *Tribune*, then, was hardly disinterested when it announced the appearance of a new "movement" among mothers, many with sons who had already enlisted, who were pushing Congressmen to support a draft. The *Tribune* presented an array of pro-conscription quotations from leading clubwomen and socialites; the women emphasized that they knew many others who agreed with them. Influential philanthropist and suffragist Louise de Koven Bowen said that she had fifty pro-conscription signatures on a petition she was circulating. Alice Bradford Wiles said that all of the clubs she belonged to supported conscription. Wiles not only was an officer in the Daughters of 1812, a small and exclusive organization, but was also active in the General Federation of Women's Clubs, an umbrella organization for all of the largest and most significant women's voluntary groups. Former head of Chicago's Civic League Mrs. B. L. Engelke claimed that every woman had a "duty" to send a telegram to her Congressmen supporting conscription, and Mrs. Heaton Owsley said that she had "induced" her female friends to join her in doing so.[15]

While Chicagoans were probably aware that the *Tribune* would support the Roosevelt Republicans as they joined the campaign for conscription, those outside the city may not have known. When the Associated Press picked up the story of a Chicago pro-conscription mothers' movement and sent it across the country, it lent greater credence to the paper's claims. When the pro-war and pro-conscription *New York Times* and *New York Tribune* each printed a story of a New York mother's support for conscription, they further contributed to the impression of a widespread movement. Though in fact only a small number of women were quoted as supporting the draft, the wording of headlines and stories indicated a much larger movement, and through these papers the women's voices reached large urban audiences. The daily circulation of the *Chicago Tribune* was 329,483; the *New York Times,* 340,904; and the *New York Tribune,* 101,611.[16]

The newspapers that printed these reports were refuting the philosophies of maternal pacifism with every example they provided of mothers who supported conscription and their sons' enlistment. Each story was peppered with short sketches of the women and mothers quoted; these stories accumulated into an impression of proof. The sketch of Mrs. Lyman A. Walton was particularly telling. She explained that she had been a member of the "peace party" and considered herself a pacifist before the declaration of war. Now her only son had volunteered to serve as a pilot. She quit the peace party and was working with a "large number" of women—she implied they were also former pacifists—to telegraph and write letters to their Congressmen in support of the draft.[17]

The newspapers emphasized the standing of the women they quoted as "social and civic leaders." The *Chicago Tribune* mentioned names its readers would know: the mayor's sister, the wife of the president of the University of Chicago, prominent suffragists and reformers. When the *New York Times* profiled a Mrs. Genet's support for conscription, readers already knew that Mrs. Genet was part of a family stretching back to the American Revolution. Newspapers made her a household name when her eldest son became the first pilot flying the American flag to be killed in France. When she was quoted as supporting the draft, she showed herself to be a true Spartan mother, part of a long line of patriotic Americans.[18]

Many of the women explained their support for conscription in terms of fairness and equality, but in fact they were attempting to use suspicion of immigrants to mobilize native-born Americans. The mothers were drawing on widespread reports that in Britain the volunteer system had killed the country's best and brightest young men first, as they had volunteered in the early days of the war, leaving the lazy and disloyal men at home. A few of the mothers openly referred to British casualties; others only hinted. Mrs. C. F. Millspaugh said, "If this is a democratic nation the sons of all should go and serve alike. It is not right that only the bravest should go first." New York mother Mrs. Henry A. Peckham remarked that she expressed "the woman's point of view" in supporting conscription as the only way to avoid sacrificing "the flower of the country" on behalf of the "slackers." Mrs. Wallace Winter, a mother of three sons with two already in military service or training, said that a volunteer army would allow "the nation's selfish and less useful citizens to remain at home in comfort and security."[19]

Editors also pushed readers to suspect immigrant and working-class men of being slackers. Next to the first *Chicago Tribune* story on pro-conscription mothers, editors placed the headline "2500 'Bos Dodge Work and War in Slacker Lane." "'Bos" was short for hobos; the article described unemployed men as lazy, angry, and unwilling to support themselves. Readers could make their own decision: the sons of "social and civic leaders" were volunteering, but should they go to war to protect America's hobos? Similarly, the April 22 issue of the *New York Times* juxtaposed Mrs. Genet's support for conscription—even after her eldest son had died in the war—with the story "Alien Slackers May Not Escape Service." The *New York Tribune* alerted readers to a supposed rush among "aliens" for "war brides" in the hope that married men would be exempt from conscription due to the need to support their wives. The same day, it published the pro-conscription letter from Mrs. Henry A. Peckham.[20]

The women named in articles on the pro-conscription movement ranged from the professional class to the extremely wealthy. Of the seventeen women from New York and Chicago, nine were listed in their city's *Social Register*, which included only high-society residents, and at least nine appeared in their newspaper's society pages. Six were active in the fight for suffrage. These were women used to wielding their money and social status for causes they supported, and who understood the value of publicity.[21]

Moreover, at least five of the women traced their ancestry back to early America; three were members of the Daughters of the American Revolution, the Daughters of 1812, or the Colonial Dames. Explicitly tying white American bloodlines to American values, these organizations placed great value on men's military service and after 1917 supported an expanded American military. Their members were self-consciously exclusive.

A further important influence on the women may have been their connection to America's educational elite. Seven of the seventeen New York and Chicago women had husbands or sons connected with the University of Chicago or the Ivy League; so did pro-conscription letter writer Ruth B. Slack of Georgia and author Mary Roberts Rinehart. Once war was declared, many American universities, including Harvard and the University of Chicago, offered military training to students. In this respect, the American elite followed in the footsteps of the British aristocracy; Cambridge and Oxford had served as active recruiting grounds. Robert R. McCormick, the co-editor and president of the *Chicago Tribune,* had attended Yale in the early 1900s; he supported the war and volunteered to serve. In America, top colleges and universities were centers of pro-war activity, and alumni networks connected powerful editors and publishers, Wilson administration officials, politicians, and their wives—many of them leaders in the fight for conscription.[22]

Members of the Woman's Peace Party provide a useful contrast to the pro-conscription women. Both groups had members descended from America's oldest families and connected to top colleges and universities, but the pacifists had a determinedly internationalist, not nationalist, orientation. The greatest difference between the two groups lay in the glittering social activities of the pro-conscription women. This supports the work of historian Barbara Steinson, who found that female supporters of a stronger American military linked the cause to their round of charity balls, luncheons, and events.[23]

In peacetime, the social whirl of the pro-conscription women was the most visible manifestation of their remarkable sense of class consciousness. In wartime, they explicitly and implicitly indicted immigrant and working-class men for their lack of patriotism. Rather than allowing men to make the choice to enlist individually, they wanted to use the coercive power of the state against the unknown "slackers." For many of the mothers, their own sons had already enlisted; other pro-conscription women had no sons to send off to war. They promoted conscription not to keep their sons from the risks of military service but to benefit their class of elite, old-stock Americans as a whole.

Contemporaries would have understood the women's words in terms of not just class but also race. In the early twentieth century, theories of Social Darwinism connected race to nation, ethnicity, and biological destiny. Before the war, a variety of social thinkers had debated ways to advance "the race" of white Americans. As immigration rose, Theodore Roosevelt created a national sensation when he criticized the falling birthrates of old-stock American families as "race suicide." War created a new eugenic threat. In Britain as well as the United States, men and women blamed Britain's volunteer military system—in place from 1914 to the start of 1916—for killing the country's best young men and endangering future generations. American and British eugenicists embraced conscription, or selective service, as a way to prevent the sacrifice of the fittest "future fathers." The pro-conscription mothers' campaign, laced with language suggestive of biology and hierarchy—"the flower of the country" and the "best" young men—must be considered against this backdrop of racial thinking and fears of race suicide.[24] In the atmosphere of haste and emergency that accompanied the American declaration of war, these women embraced conscription as a means of ensuring the survival—perhaps even the continued dominance—of their own social group.

Mary Roberts Rinehart: Reinventing the Mother's Role in Wartime

Perhaps the most influential story of a mother's support for conscription—and her son's enlistment—was also the most personal. Mary Roberts Rinehart was a gifted storyteller whose status as a best-selling author meant that editors were eager to publish her opinions and experiences in full. Her story "The Altar of Freedom" was first printed in the *Saturday Evening Post*—the most popular magazine in America, with a circulation of 1.8 million—and later reprinted in booklet form and as part of another news magazine. The right-wing National Security League selected it as one of only three publications to recommend on the subject of women's role in wartime. The article anticipated a theme that would penetrate multiple genres of wartime popular culture: the heroic nationalism of mothers of soldiers.[25]

Mary Roberts Rinehart wrote "The Altar of Freedom" as a personal narrative based on her son's decision to volunteer for the army. Its title was taken from Abraham Lincoln's letter to Mrs. Bixby, a woman who had lost five sons in the Union army during the Civil War. Lincoln assured Mrs. Bixby that her sons had been sacrificed on the "altar of freedom." During World War I, editors in America reprinted the letter as a tribute to mothers' self-sacrificing patriotism and as a prescription for feminine behavior. But while her title connected her with previous generations of women, Rinehart positioned herself—and her audience of mothers—as voters and political actors who could and should reform the American military from top to bottom. Rinehart turned her son's enlistment into a platform from which to demand military reform, and she urged other mothers to do the same. War meant that the state would disrupt the private sphere by recruiting young men for the military; Rinehart wanted mothers of soldiers to claim public authority as patriots based on what had once been their private role as mothers.[26]

According to Rinehart, soon after the United States joined the war, she received a phone call asking her to write a story to persuade "other women to give up their sons." Telegrams from the end of March 1917 show that her literary agent and the publisher of many of her books, George H. Doran, made this suggestion. Since he did not publish the article himself, he seems to have suggested it for political reasons; Doran's company also printed wartime material for the pro-war, pro-conscription National Security League. Rinehart's editor at the *Saturday Evening Post,* the powerful George H. Lorimer, applauded the idea and sent her an encouraging telegraph: "Hope you will carry out George Doran's suggestion for patriotic article for [us] at this time it would be a splendid thing to do." Lorimer, a former Yale student who had steered the *Saturday Evening Post* to embrace a stronger U.S. military before the war, pushed the magazine to promote nationalism and unquestioning support for the government during the war.[27]

Rinehart supported U.S. intervention against Germany; she blamed Germany for the war and atrocities against civilians. Yet she recalled that writing "The Altar of Freedom" was an ordeal. She locked herself in her office, cried, and wrote for twelve hours straight to meet her tight deadline. Lorimer praised the resulting story as "splendid." It had arrived at the last possible moment, and revealing the importance he placed on it, Lorimer said that "we had to double rush it" to the printers so that it would appear in the first *Post* issue responding to the declaration of war.[28]

Rinehart wrote the story as a mother addressing other mothers. She warned her readers that American mothers would be subversive to the war effort if they were too weak to give up their sons and insisted on seeing them as "little boys." Rinehart described war as a "great adventure" inherently appealing to young men, a natural step on their way to adult manhood. Mothers who opposed their sons' enlistment were selfish. Though she had reported on the war in Europe and understood the brutal conditions of trench warfare, she assured mothers that as soldiers their sons would experience the comradeship and small, intense pleasures of military life.[29]

Rinehart said that she wanted to tell her own story to help other mothers. Her son had asked both parents if he could enlist. Rinehart did not record her husband's response, but told the reader that, "womanlike," she had asked her son for more time to consider the question. He then sent his parents a telegram, asking them whether they wanted him to be "a quitter." The message surprised her. She explained, "I came to my senses then, and the necessary permission to enlist was signed and sent." It was the most difficult decision she had ever faced, but her son, by discarding her advice to wait before enlisting, had earned her respect. She said that she would "never have forgiven him" if he had not enlisted, though she knew that he had gone against her advice in doing so. Ultimately, her example instructed mothers to distrust their antiwar impulses.[30]

Though her plot had much in common with nineteenth-century sentimental novels that made a virtue of women's passive suffering and even victimization, Rinehart was a twentieth-century woman. She departed from her usual fictional and journalistic style to make her private life public through a narrative formula Susan Zeiger has called the "enlistment drama," in which the plot focuses on the mother-son relationship and a son's enlistment. Screenwriters later adapted this formula for use in many World War I films. The enlistment drama reveals the way in which war collapsed the private and public, pushing mothers to confront national duty from within the bosom of the family. Rinehart wanted mothers to take advantage of this situation. After describing her emotional struggle with her son's decision, she began to make demands. First, she asked other mothers to support conscription. She warned mothers that "for every high-spirited lad like yours and mine who goes out to fight," thousands more would remain at home. She called them men "who have no country, but only a refuge from the oppression of Europe," and promised that they outnumbered the "college boys" who would enlist voluntarily by a hundred or a thousand to one.[31]

Rinehart's appeal intended to create an "us" versus "them" mentality that was both nativist and classist. She warned mothers that it was their responsibility to prevent the wholesale destruction of the country's "best" young men; she explained that British mothers had failed to do so and were suffering the results. Rinehart dangled a nightmare vision in front of her readers, in which their sons and all of their peers were killed and the only men who remained in the country were disloyal immigrants.[32]

"The Altar of Freedom" closed by urging mothers to support a modernization of the military—an argument few women had made in such detail and in such a public forum before the war. By treating her private story as a parable of women's duty in the public sphere, Rinehart's motherhood allowed her to take an empowered position as a military critic. She had visited the European front on a reporting trip in 1915, and based on her observations, she demanded that the American army adopt major changes in its methods of recruitment, promotion, and decision making. Rinehart asked her mother-readers to support her on these points: "You who considered prayerfully the best doctor for your child when he was ill, are you going now to place his life in unskilled hands?"[33]

Rinehart proved her patriotic credentials and her capacity to write compelling propaganda with "The Altar of Freedom." After its publication, she enjoyed a special relationship with the War and Navy Departments. Officials gave her access to military training camps and bases, asking her to report on their organization and conditions. She published cheerful articles about them while also reporting on them secretly—and more completely—to officials. Rinehart was charming and famous, and she used her working relationship with top officials, such as the secretary of war, to try to gain desirable wartime posts for her eldest son and husband. Her husband worked as a military doctor in the United States. Her eldest son went to France, where he served safely on a general's staff.[34]

Nearly 120,000 Americans died in military service during World War I. In her 1930s memoir, Rinehart stated that only God could know how "terrible" it was for her to write "The Altar of Freedom" and how haunted she felt by the hundreds or even thousands of letters she'd received from mothers who sent their sons into the military and wrote her about their experiences. One mother told Rinehart that she had cancer and would die before her son could return from the war; many women wrote her after the Armistice, explaining that their sons had been killed. In the late 1930s, as war with Europe again looked likely, Rinehart urged women to support the "Peace Amendment" to the Constitution, which would require a nationwide referendum before the United States could join another foreign war.[35]

Conclusion: The Roots of Twentieth-Century Gendered Nationalism and Conservatism

The Selective Service Act became law on May 18, 1917; the House voted 397 to 24 to support it and the Senate 81 to 8. The draft apparatus worked efficiently, and 72 percent of the 3.5 million military troops were conscripted. The most significant resistance to the draft focused on registration and induction, and newspapers continued to print propaganda supporting enlistment, conscription, and Spartan motherhood throughout the war.[36]

The passage of the draft was influenced by a number of factors, and it is impossible to know how the women's campaign ultimately affected the vote. The women's words were clearly important, however, for the way they politicized many women's private lives to make heroines—and activists—out of mothers of soldiers. The women who told of their support for their sons' enlistment, and then demanded conscription, used the position of the Spartan mother to advance their own political agenda. They helped define a role for women that combined the public activism and motherly rhetoric of the Progressive maternalist with the nationalism and militarism of wartime. Historians have called this formulation "patriotic motherhood" but have usually focused on men's use of the ideology to discourage and punish antiwar women.[37]

In women's hands, patriotic motherhood proved extremely useful as a tool in wartime political campaigns. It could even be adapted for Progressive causes. Women—including both mothers and nonmothers—identified themselves as loving mothers of the nation in order to sell war bonds, win woman suffrage, campaign for equal rights for African Americans, and create antiprostitution measures around military bases. During the war, a rhetoric and symbolism of patriotic motherhood may have generated greater respect and popularity for women's causes and leaders, but it also propagated an extremely conservative vision of women's citizenship. It glorified women who put nationalism above personal ties, honored and obeyed the military, and bore sons. In other words, it relied on the most traditional Western ideals of femininity, combining a vision of women's work in the private sphere with loyalty to the patriarchal family and state.

Progressive woman leaders who adopted a rhetoric of patriotic mother-hood during the war had cause to regret this choice years later; their praise of mothers of soldiers as true mothers of the nation helped galvanize a conservative women's movement that would oppose the continuation of Progressive reform campaigns in the 1920s and 1930s. After the war, mothers and female relatives of soldiers joined groups such as the American War Mothers, American Gold Star Mothers, and American Legion Auxiliary to honor patriotic motherhood and maintain the heated nationalism of wartime. These groups paid tribute to women's traditional roles as wives and mothers and opposed what they saw as Red conspiracies designed to destroy the private sphere altogether. They fought against Progressive woman leaders who embraced disarmament, the League of Nations and World Court, and public health benefits for women and children. They blamed immigrants for left-wing radicalism and sought ever greater restrictions on immigration.

In the United States, as in many other nations, the war was a catalyst that sharpened conflicts between the political left and right. Predominant stories of a mother's nature in the pre-war years had focused on the "social house-keeping" of the maternalist and woman pacifist, who saw all of humanity as an extension of her own family. In wartime, right-wing women promoted ideals of nationalist motherhood with heroines who were fiercely protective of their own social group against suspected enemies. These conflicting definitions of a mother's nature effectively politicized motherhood and would inspire activism and conflict among women's organizations, military officials, and politicians from the 1920s through the rest of the twentieth century.[38]

NOTES

1. A. P. Davidson, *Report on Women's International League for Peace and Freedom*, Fourth International Congress, May 3, 1924, Washington, D.C., folder 10110–1935 (1 of 3), Military Intelligence Division Correspondence, 1917–41, RG 165 Records of the War Department General Staff, National Archives II, College Park, Md.

2. Ronnee Schreiber, "Playing 'Femball': Conservative Women's Organizations and Political Representation in the United States," in *Right Wing Women: From Conservatives to Extremists Around the World*, ed. Paola Bacchetta and Margaret Power (New York: Routledge, 2002), 211–23, 221–22; Shane Phelan, "(Be)Coming Out: Lesbian Identity and Politics," *Signs* 18, no. 4 (Summer 1993): 765–90, 773.

3. Mary Roberts Rinehart, *My Story* (New York: Farrar and Rinehart, 1931), 221; Rinehart, "The Altar of Freedom," *Saturday Evening Post*, April 21, 1917, 6, 37–38.

4. John Whiteclay Chambers II, *To Raise an Army: The Draft Comes to Modern America* (New York: Free Press, 1987), 130, 153–77.

5. Ibid., 143, 154–59, 206–8; Barbara Steinson, *American Women's Activism in World War I* (New York: Garland, 1982), 251–52.

6. Chambers, *To Raise an Army*, 74–79, 84, 205–8; H. C. Peterson and Gilbert C. Fite, *Opponents of War, 1917–1918* (Seattle: University of Washington Press, 1957).

7. Nicoletta F. Gullace, *"The Blood of Our Sons": Men, Women, and the Renegotiation of British Citizenship During the Great War* (New York: Palgrave Macmillan, 2002), 110–13; "Australia and Conscription," *Times of London*, December 22, 1917, 6.

8. Ruth B. Slack of LaGrange, Georgia, April 19, 1917, read by Rep. David Adamson on conscription, H.R. 3545, 65th cong., 1st sess., *Congressional Record*, vol. 55 (April 23, 1917), 984; Rinehart, "Altar," 6; House, *Congressional Record* (April 24, 1917), 1031.

9. Theda Skocpol, *Protecting Soldiers and Mothers: The Political Origins of Social Policy in the United States* (Cambridge, Mass.: Harvard University Press, 1992). Actual distribution of the mothers' pensions reflected cultural and racial bias. See Linda Gordon, *Pitied but Not Entitled: Single Mothers and the History of Welfare, 1890–1935* (New York: Free Press, 1994).

10. S.J. 1, 65th cong., 1st sess., *Congressional Record*, vol. 55 (April 4, 1917), 223.

11. Ibid., 237.

12. John Higham, *Strangers in the Land: Patterns of American Nativism, 1865–1925* (New Brunswick, N.J.: Rutgers University Press, 2002), 196–98, 213.

13. S. 1871, 65th cong., 1st sess., *Congressional Record*, vol. 55 (April 21, 1917), 915.

14. Katherine S. Johnson, "Personal Insurance," *Los Angeles Times*, April 14, 1917, sec. 2, 21; "Won't Send Sons to Save Slackers," *Washington Post*, April 17, 1917, 2. See also n. 8 above on Ruth B. Slack's letter and the sources cited below.

15. Jerome E. Edwards, *The Foreign Policy of Col. McCormick's Tribune, 1929–1941* (Reno: University of Nevada Press, 1971), 10–12; "Mothers Urge Congressmen to Order Draft," *Chicago Tribune*, April 12, 1917, 5.

16. "Volunteers' Mothers Indorse Conscription," *San Jose Mercury News*, April 15, 1917, 38; "New York Mother Urges Conscription," *New York Tribune*, April 15, 1917, 12; "Mrs. Genet for Draft," *New York Times*, April 22, 1917, 15; *N. W. Ayer and Son's American Newspaper Annual and Directory* (Philadelphia: N. W. Ayer and Son, 1917), 193, 673–74.

17. "Mothers Urge Congressmen," 5.

18. "Mrs. Genet," 15; "Genet First to Die in France Under U.S. Flag," *New York Tribune*, April 19, 1917, 1.

19. "Mothers Urge Congressmen," 5; "Chicago Mother of Three Sons Demands Draft," *Chicago Tribune*, April 18, 1917, 1; "Chicago Women in Draft Appeal to Congressmen," *Chicago Tribune*, April 20, 1917, 1; "New York Mother," 12.

20. "2500 'Bos Dodge Work and War in Slacker Lane," *Chicago Tribune*, April 12, 1917, 5; "Alien Slackers May Not Escape Service," *New York Times*, April 22, 1917, E3; "Rush for War Brides Wavers," *New York Tribune*, April 13, 1917, 16.

21. *Social Register, Chicago, 1916*, vol. 30, no. 4 (New York: Social Register Association, 1915); *Social Register, New York, 1914*, vol. 30, no. 4 (New York: Social Register Association, 1915); Albert Nelson Marquis, ed., *Who's Who in America, 1916–1917*, vol. 9 (Chicago: A. N. Marquis, 1916). Other biographical research was conducted using the ProQuest Historical Newspapers searchable database of the *Chicago Tribune, New York Times*, and other papers.

22. Edwards, *Foreign Policy*, 6; Jan Cohn, *Improbable Fiction: The Life of Mary Roberts Rinehart* (Pittsburgh: University of Pittsburgh Press, 1980), 111; "Rookie," *Chicago Tribune*, April 18, 1917, 5; Rinehart, "Altar," 6; "Hand Grenades," *Chicago Tribune*, April 18, 1917, 3.

23. Steinson, *American Women's Activism*, 212, 289.

24. Gullace, *"Blood of Our Sons,"* 112; "Conscription and Eugenics," *London Times*, July 2, 1915, 6; Gertrude Adele Reinitz, "Eugenic Conscription," *New York Tribune*, April 17, 1917, 8; Gail Bederman, *Manliness and Civilization: A Cultural History of Gender and Race in the United States, 1880–1917* (Chicago: University of Chicago Press, 1995), 25.

25. *N. W. Ayer and Son's*, 858; Rinehart, "One Woman's View of War," *Current Opinion*, December 1917, 3; Albert Bushnell Hart, *America at War: A Handbook of Patriotic Education References* (New York: George H. Doran, 1918), 64.

26. Suzanne Evans, *Mothers of Heroes, Mothers of Martyrs: World War I and the Politics of Grief* (Montreal: McGill-Queens University Press, 2007), 161–62; Rinehart, "Altar," 38.

27. Rinehart, *My Story*, 220; see n. 25 above for a sample Doran publication; Marquis, *Who's Who*, 1515; George H. Lorimer telegram to MRR, March 26, 1917, Mary Roberts

Rinehart Collection, Special Collections Department, University of Pittsburgh Library System. All Rinehart correspondence and papers cited here are held in this collection.

28. Rinehart, January 1915 Journals, entries for January 27, 28, 30; Cohn, *Improbable Fiction*, 81; Rinehart, *My Story*, 221; Lorimer to MRR telegram, March 28, 1917; Lorimer letter to MRR, March 30, 1917.

29. Rinehart, "Altar," 6.

30. Ibid., 37.

31. Ibid., 6. On enlistment as a domestic drama, see Susan Zeiger, "She Didn't Raise Her Boy to Be a Slacker: Motherhood, Conscription, and the Culture of the First World War," *Feminist Studies* 22, no. 1 (Spring 1996): 7–39.

32. Rinehart, "Altar," 6.

33. Ibid., 38.

34. Cohn, *Improbable Fiction*, 114–19; Stanley Rinehart to MRR, December 2, 1918.

35. United States Department of Veterans Affairs, "Fact Sheet: America's Wars," November 2008, http://www1.va.gov/opa/fact/amwars.asp (accessed February 14, 2010); Rinehart, *My Story*, 220–21; Rinehart, "Before the Drums Beat," *Good Housekeeping*, January 1938, 24–25, 158–59.

36. Chambers, *To Raise an Army*, 73, 170, 211–13.

37. Kathleen Kennedy, *Disloyal Mothers and Scurrilous Citizens: Women and Subversion During World War I* (Bloomington: Indiana University Press, 1999); Zeiger, "She Didn't Raise."

38. My dissertation will discuss these developments in more detail. See "The Nation's Mothers Raise the Army: Women's Activism, Popular Culture, and the Great War in America, 1914–1941" (Ph.D. diss., Graduate Center of the City University of New York, forthcoming).

8

From Suffrage to Silence: The South African Afrikaner Nationalist Women's Parties, 1915–1931

Louise Vincent

[W]e gave a good deal of money to the men. . . . We were an independent political party but we received no recognition. Most of us were in favor of women's suffrage. Hertzog decided that when the vote was granted we had to join the men. Most of us were against it. . . . General Hertzog was of the opinion that it would be dangerous for the men and women to remain separate in two strong organizations. We were always better organized than the men, for example, at elections. . . . The Women's Part[ies] built the National Party. They were the power behind the scenes.

—Mrs. M. M. Jansen, founding president of the nationalist women's party in Natal

Prior to the latter half of the nineteenth century, membership in an Afrikaner ethnic community was seldom invoked as a political claim, and South Africa itself existed as little more than a geographic expression.[1] The context for the present essay is the emergence of Afrikaner nationalism as a successful political movement that united disparate classes and interests and ultimately came to power in 1948 on an apartheid election platform. The chapter focuses on the way in which politically active Afrikaner nationalist women in South Africa in the early years of the Afrikaner ethnic mobilization both interacted with the most ubiquitous of nationalist icons—the figure of woman as *volksmoeder* (mother of the nation)—and were acted upon by it. In doing so, the chapter challenges the portrayal of nationalist mobilizing tools as the creation of the leaders of nationalist movements used to manipulate witless ordinary men and women, rather than as the outcome of complex processes of contestation. This argument is explored against the backdrop of the women-only political parties established by Afrikaner nationalist women from 1915 onward.

The history books make only passing reference to the Afrikaner women's political parties. Afrikaner nationalism is commonly assumed to have been hostile to the idea of women becoming directly involved in politics, and the volksmoeder ideology is specifically seen as having sanctioned the political disempowerment of the Afrikaner woman, relegating her to the narrow confines of home and church. While the cultural and welfare work of Afrikaner women in the early part of the twentieth century is relatively familiar, the assumption that these women were politically disengaged appears to derive largely from the fact that they were almost entirely absent from formal politics in the period after 1931. This chapter argues that the assumption that Afrikaner women's role in the building of Afrikaner nationalism was limited to the private sphere of hearth and home is a false one. Instead, women were actively engaged in the reinterpretation of what it meant to be "good mothers," arguing that their private responsibilities to their families were inextricably linked to the need for them to be politically active. Enfranchisement did not bring about the fundamental reordering of gender relationships that many male opponents had feared. National politics after women's enfranchisement remained male-dominated, and those women who did enter the political terrain "tended to devote themselves to back room party work in a supportive rather than a leadership role."[2] But in the years leading up to 1931, Afrikaner women used the vehicle of their own independent political parties to play a much more active and outspoken political role than is sometimes imagined. Rather than following a linear pattern of inexorable progression toward greater equality, however, the gains made in the 1920s were quickly and dramatically reversed—a common trend around the world in the interwar years.

The Emergence of Afrikaner Nationalism

The Transvaal and the Orange Free State (OFS) ostensibly became politically independent republics in 1852 and 1854, respectively. At this time, there were still numerous other autonomous African polities throughout the South African region.[3] Economic hegemony over all these diverse groups was in the hands of British merchant capital. The discovery of gold and diamonds served to accelerate the economic integration of the region, but it also increased the sharp differentiation of the region's people into what Leroy Vail has termed "more favored and less favored societies" and of the societies themselves into "more favored and less favored classes-in-the-making."[4] The group that would ultimately become known as "Afrikaners" was by no means a coherent ethnic community at this stage. Regional rivalries, class divisions, and religious schisms permeated the lives of Dutch-Afrikaners. The South African War (1899–1902), in which the British sought to end the independence of the Boer Republics, would change this. The war ended in British victory in 1902, but not without bequeathing a legacy that acted as a crucial stimulus to the development of a pan–South African Afrikaner nationalism.

A range of new Dutch-Afrikaner organizations emerged in the wake of the war and British attempts to impose English as the dominant language in education and other aspects of social life. These included women's groups, cultural bodies, and language associations. The establishment of the Union of South Africa in 1910 fed into emergent Afrikaner nationalism by taking the emphasis away from regional politics. Further, its constitutional provision enfranchising all white men added an additional motivation for intellectuals to devise a political program capable of redefining class interests as ethnic concerns. In 1913 the Boer general J. B. M. Hertzog formed the National Party (NP). Its platform included South African self-sufficiency, dual-medium education, and compulsory bilingualism in the public service. The new party drew together Afrikaner workers fighting to protect their relative privilege in the face of competition from unskilled black labor, small farmers threatened with proletarianization, and the middle-class intellectuals of the language movement.

For Afrikaner cultural entrepreneurs concerned with calcifying the boundaries of an ethnic community, a key area of concern at this time was the so-called poor white problem. A middle-class intelligentsia that had an overriding interest in "creating Afrikaners who would refill Afrikaner churches, attend Afrikaner schools and buy Afrikaans books"[5] was alarmed by the specter of potential members of the *volk* being lost forever as a result of the moral and cultural degeneration perceived as accompanying life in the backyard slums of the urban areas. From the outset, their attempts to theorize the problem were saturated with the ideas of Social Darwinism, eugenics, and the fear of "miscegenation." Women were seen as having a very particular role to play in the preservation of racial "purity," and in this way the private sphere of the family was infused with a wider political importance: "By instruction leading to the improvement of the individual we shall aid in preserving women for their supreme purpose, the procreation and preservation of the race, and at the same time promote that race to a better standard, mentally and physically."[6] The public/private duality of women's perceived political significance was encapsulated in the notion of the volksmoeder, which suggested not only the political significance of women's role in socializing their children but also that women were mothers to the nation and in particular to its poor. A network of women's welfare organizations emerged to minister to the moral and material needs of those regarded as the "underclass" of the Afrikaner nation. At the same time, a literature of books, plays, and magazines emerged in which the contours of an image of ideal Afrikaner womanhood were popularized and debated.

The Idea of the Volksmoeder

The volksmoeder drew on the Great Trek, the Battle of Blood River, and the South African War as favorite subjects. Women featured prominently in each of these mythic repositories of emergent Afrikaner nationalism. Tough and self-sufficient, the legendary Voortrekker women who acted as teachers, doctors, nurses, and soldiers during the Great Trek were held up as the embodiment of all the essential volksmoeder traits.[7] But it was the experiences of Afrikaner women in the South African War that most caught the popular and intellectual imagination. More than 28,000 Boers died in the war; 22,000 of these were children under the age of sixteen, and 4,000 were adult women. Most succumbed to disease in English concentration camps.[8] These events provided Afrikaner intellectuals with many of their most potent symbols as they began the process of articulating the central characteristics of the quintessential "Afrikaner woman," portrayed as religious, freedom loving, honorable, selfless, and incorruptible.

One interpretation of the role depicted for Afrikaner women in the volksmoeder ideology is that of being priestesses in the temple of the family, keeping the flame of household happiness burning and finding their greatest fulfillment in their own homes.[9] However, this early version of the volksmoeder ideology was reshaped by evolving social and political circumstances. A growing concern with poor whiteism dovetailed neatly with the idea that Afrikaner women were called to be not just mothers of their own families but also nurturers, educators, and moral instructors—in short, mothers—of the nation's poor.[10]

From the outset, poor whiteism was seen through the prism of the perceived threat to the survival of the Afrikaner volk posed by the black majority—stoking what Roger Petersen has referred to as a "resentment narrative" in his account of the role of anger, resentment, and hatred in stimulating people to participate in ethnic conflicts.[11] In the context of a troubling awareness of their minority position, Afrikaner nationalists focused on ensuring that every possible member of the volk would be gathered into the fold of the Afrikaner nation and made to feel a sense of belonging there. Afrikaner women were envisaged as having a central role to play in policing the boundaries between black and white, acting both as bulwarks against miscegenation and as a workforce to drag the "fallen" members of the volk back into the fold. By 1923 Afrikaner women's organizations began to pledge themselves to a far more thoroughgoing commitment in search of a solution to the problem of the Afrikaner "underclass." The period saw a note of paranoia enter the discourse in relation to the perceived "black peril" as newly urbanized Afrikaners found themselves in competition with black workers for jobs.[12]

The volksmoeder ideology suggested that the volk was the Afrikaner woman's wider family circle. The qualities that were required for efficient homemaking were the same qualities needed for the wider housekeeping of the state. Initially, it was expected that Afrikaner women would exercise the public dimension of their role as volksmoeders solely by way of charity work in Afrikaner welfare organizations. Key among these was the Afrikaanse Christelike Vroue Vereniging (ACVV),[13] formed in 1902.[14] While many women continued to emphasize their role in the home, even in the welfare organizations, there was growing recognition of the need for a reconceptualization of the extent and nature of women's responsibilities as depicting the state, in Marijke Du Toit's words, as "a household that needed a woman's hand to put it right," thus challenging the distinction between private and public.[15]

Cast with this emphasis, the volksmoeder ideology held huge possibilities for women to engage in a wide range of projects outside the private sphere of the home. While it is true that some women steadfastly continued to regard their participation in politics as taboo, for others it did not take long to make the connection between the issues encountered in their charity work and the key political questions of the day. While the ACVV itself officially "eschewed party politics and rather held prayer meetings for the unification of the *volk*,"[16] several of its more prominent organizers, including executive members E. C. van der Lingen and M. E. Rothmann, were among the pioneers of the Afrikaner women's nationalist political parties and their campaign for (white) female suffrage in South Africa. Using metaphors drawn from the prevailing volksmoeder ideology, these Afrikaner women argued shrewdly in their suffrage propaganda that their task was to "keep house" for the state, and that in the same way as they would not dream of neglecting their housekeeping duties in their own homes, they would not hesitate to take up the challenge of citizenship.[17]

The Afrikaner Women's Political Parties

Afrikaner nationalist women's political parties were active in the 1920s but have remained a little-known feature of South African history. Those studies that do mention them[18] find little to distinguish the women's parties from the more traditional welfare organizations that are more commonly associated with Afrikaner nationalist women. But the perception that the gender ideology of Afrikaner nationalism prohibited Afrikaner women from playing a role in politics is not entirely accurate. Leading figures in the nationalist women's parties came to redefine what it meant to be a volksmoeder, articulating a broader interpretation that allowed them to legitimize their political role while remaining within the framework of Afrikaner nationalism.

The first nationalist women's party, the Vroue Nasionale Party (Women's National Party, VNP), was founded in the Transvaal more than a decade before white South African women were enfranchised. The party's stated aim was to "create a greater political awareness among the women of our country."[19] The formation of women's nationalist parties in the other provinces of the Union followed over the next few years: the Free State women's nationalist party's first congress took place in 1923, and in the same year a women's party was formed at the Cape under the leadership of Mrs. F. W. Reitz and in Natal under Mrs. M. M. Jansen.[20] A structure to coordinate the activities of the different women's parties was realized with the inaugural meeting of the women's nationalist Federal Council on June 19, 1925, in Cape Town.

The formation of the women's parties meant that Afrikaner nationalist women could participate as an organized political force in nationalist politics for the first time. One of their most significant campaigns was their involvement in the 1924 general election. Women's party members traveled the length and breadth of South Africa, often covering vast distances alone on horseback to bring the party message to every corner of the country. It was in the course of this campaign that they won recognition for their political importance and gained self-confidence as independent political entities. The 1924 election was remembered in Afrikaner nationalism as a great victory that laid the foundation for the NP's accession to power in 1948. For Afrikaner nationalist women, the victorious 1924 election campaign was remembered as the moment of their decisive entry into political life.[21]

With the election of an NP government (in coalition with the Labor Party) in 1924, the membership of the women's parties soared. The women were quick to point out that the electoral victory marked not a conclusion but rather a starting point for the work that lay ahead. Education (particularly on the *platteland,* or country districts), dissemination of information about political issues, the burning question of suffrage, the promotion of reading among the Afrikaner population, and support for the Afrikaans language were just some of the concerns on their respective agendas.[22]

The idea that the program advanced by the women's nationalist parties was barely distinguishable from the traditional welfare concerns of Afrikaner women is called into question by the fact that legislation specifically prohibited political parties from engaging in charity work. Article 42, Law No. 11 of 1926 ruled out all philanthropic work for political organizations.[23] The new legislation initially left a sense of confusion among the women's parties, since the uplifting of the Afrikaner poor, care for the sick, and support for Afrikaner cultural activities in the fields of language, literature, and education were central to Afrikaner nationalism's *political* program, and in that sense the work carried out by Afrikaner women's welfare organizations was itself highly politically infused. Forced to reevaluate their party programs, a separation occurred. The work that could no longer be undertaken by the women's political parties became the responsibility of those already involved in the welfare field, chiefly the ACVV. For their part, rather than focusing on individual responses to localized problems, the women's parties began to acknowledge the need to look to long-term solutions and for greater influence at the level of national political decision making—"not by helping this or that case, but by using the available machinery to remove the causes of the problem."[24] Despite opposition from some quarters, membership continued to grow steadily.

Part of the women's parties' success can be attributed to the fact that they were able to reach a wide constituency. Far from being an exclusive forum for middle-aged urban housewives, their membership profile was youthful and included working women and women from the rural areas. Their emphasis on "women's issues" was popular. Determined not to be "mere fund-raisers" for the NP, they believed their goal was to encourage women to read, to improve health conditions in the towns and on the farms, to further their own knowledge and education, and to be able to offer considered opinions on the key political questions of the day. For these women, taking up their rightful place in public life did not mean simply imitating the direction followed by the NP but rather complementing it. They saw the male party as preoccupied with economic concerns, while they wanted to deal with the social and moral dimensions of the Afrikaner volk's growth and development.[25] Their agendas included a focus on addressing social questions such as liquor laws and "immorality";[26] ensuring that teachers at schools with Afrikaans medium classes were bilingual; working for the abolition of parental choice with regard to medium of instruction (it was feared that Afrikaans parents would choose English because it was perceived as the language of commerce); lobbying the government to allow girls to be admitted to agricultural colleges; and calling on religious ministers to warn parents against sending their children to Catholic schools.[27] Housing and the question of language were central to the programs of nationalist women's parties around the country.[28] Defining their priorities in this way meant that Afrikaner nationalist women could integrate their private, domestic priorities as mothers with significant public, political goals.

Language was a prime example of the coalescing of the public with the private realms of women's responsibility. Once formal recognition of Afrikaans had been achieved, the challenge was to ensure that the language continued to be actively used in daily life. For Afrikaans to remain a living language it had to be used by ordinary Afrikaners. Afrikaans speakers were urged to insist on the use of Afrikaans in commercial, political, and private life. Women, as educators of their children and as consumers, were especially important in this regard. They had to be persuaded not to educate their children in English in the hopes of increasing their chances of employment. Afrikaans had to shake off its reputation as the language of the underprivileged and present itself as the key cultural expression of a great volk. Mothers who spoke English to their children were labeled "pathetic," with only themselves to blame if English speakers treated Afrikaans with disdain.[29] The Cape women's party, the Nasionale Vroue Party (NVP), made a formal decision to support the language preservation society (handhawers), and members were urged to speak Afrikaans to the clerks and officials they encountered in places of business, in shops, at government offices, and on public transport.[30]

Health was another key area of concern that provided women with the opportunity to demonstrate that their public and private roles were intimately intertwined. It was argued that healthy young people were needed to build the nation. This went along with the perceived health threat posed by poor whites living cheek by jowl with members of "other races," including the ideologically saturated obsession with venereal disease. It was assumed that disease was somehow related to a state of fallen morality. The focus was on providing information so that people could take steps to prevent disease. Such measures included not only primary health practices but also social practices with particular emphasis on the need for segregation. Within Afrikaner nationalism's gender ideology, women were assumed to be particularly suited to addressing the health needs of the volk. The women's parties were happy to play this role, but they insisted on pointing out that real solutions had to be sought at the level of political policy, implying the need for them to be represented at that level. Among other things, they called for state institutions to monitor health and for compulsory medical inspection at schools. As the perceived importance of policing the boundaries of racial exclusivity grew throughout the 1920s, the women's parties' discussion of health came in time to focus on issues such as the racial segregation of health services and "immorality" (a reference to sexual relations across the color line), which they thought should be harshly punished.

At election time, women's party branches were directed by the national congresses to work closely with the NP to register voters. Indeed, where the NP was weak, women were urged to take the initiative in delivering lists of voters to magistrates.[31] There were also more direct calls on women's branches to produce propaganda for the nationalist cause, receive NP speakers, organize political meetings, and bring together reading circles. The women often described this work as educating them for full citizenship.[32] Increasingly, however, the electioneering, educational, self-improvement, information-gathering, and advisory role that the women's parties had outlined for themselves became a source of dissatisfaction among members. There was no disguising the women's parties' lack of real power in nationalist politics. As the president of the NVP's Naauwpoort branch, C. L. Oosthuizen, commented, "We can do nothing active. . . . We must simply give advice and help to collect money for the men but if we don't even have a say, will they think of us as competent enough to take our advice? . . . What good does all this knowledge and enthusiasm which motivates us to such undertakings do if we cannot share what we have gained? . . . In my opinion we are a mere appendage, without the right to vote or act. . . . It looks as if our party may have to undergo a radical change."[33]

Leading women's party campaigners realized that without the vote, there was little chance that their call for improved infant and maternal care, greater emphasis on education and training for women, and a range of other social legislation would be taken very seriously.[34] While they were not suffrage organizations as such, the question of the franchise lay at the heart of their political program. Contrary to the common perception of the women's enfranchisement campaign in South Africa as a campaign of English-speaking middle-class women,[35] Afrikaner women and their political parties were centrally involved in the campaign.[36] The suffrage ambitions of white South African women were finally realized when, at the conclusion of the 1929 general election, the nationalists had won a majority of seventy-seven seats. Hertzog promised white women that he would use his party's dominance to settle the "native question," which would in turn make possible the introduction of a bill enfranchising white women alone.[37] On Thursday, March 6, 1930, the parliamentary galleries were crowded with women anxious to witness the enactment of legislation that would finally allow them to register as voters and to stand for election themselves.

With enfranchisement imminent, interest in the women's parties reached a high point.[38] In the four months prior to its 1930 congress, the NVP established approximately sixty new branches, mostly on the platteland, bringing membership to more than seven thousand. In 1930 the VNP similarly added eighty new branches to its organization.[39] This early promise was not to be fulfilled, however. Precisely at the moment when Afrikaner women achieved formal political power, their independence was harnessed by the male political establishment, and the women's parties were called upon to disband in the name of a greater good. Since the time frame for amalgamation was left up to the branches, some joined with the male parties immediately, while others remained separate well into the 1950s. In 1933 Afrikaner women went to the polls for the first time, and at the early general election on May 18 of that year, Mrs. F. W. Reitz took up the NP candidacy for Parktown. Shortly afterward, on August 24, 1933, at a by-election in Wonderboom, Mrs. Kenne Malherbe won a seat in Parliament. In 1933 Mrs. M. M. Jansen was elected as deputy leader of the NP in Natal and to the Federal Council of the NP.[40] But these were women whose political leadership had been forged in the women's parties. After these parties' demise, very few Afrikaner women continued in active political life.[41]

Conclusion

The volksmoeder ideology was very powerful in the hands of Afrikaner suffragists. It claimed that Afrikaner women were an especially pure form of the nationalist ideal, particularly uncorrupted and incorruptible. Those who wanted to deny (white) women the vote argued that their purity would be out of place in the degrading world of politics. But nationalist women were able to turn this logic on its head, primarily by distinguishing between politics and nationalism. By way of this device, the good of the nation was placed above the "narrow concerns of politics." The true nationalist goal was not the sordid pursuit of political power but rather a quest for the realization of a divinely inspired project, the necessary birth of a nation. Women, who had been designated as a more trustworthy form of humanity, could then claim that they had particular responsibility for the success of this project. The women's parties' propaganda did not speak of political involvement so much as national necessity, a necessity which, it was argued, had always been close to women's hearts. What woman was not interested in the health of her children and the safety of her daughters? She now simply had to broaden her concerns to include the health and safety of that larger family, the Afrikaner volk.[42] Without her nurturing, the infant nation in the making would not be housed or educated; it would become morally degenerate and worthless.[43]

While the NP used the volksmoeder language to encourage women to become actively involved in the nationalist movement, this same language was used by women themselves to argue for greater political rights for women. Nationalist ideology contended that if women were concerned about the well-being of their families, they had to be concerned about the well-being of the state.[44] Nationalist women took this argument further, implying that suffrage was imperative for the good not only of individual women but of the entire Afrikaner nation. The Afrikaner woman, the NVP argued, had proven herself and earned her right to vote and be active in politics. Unlike her noisy foreign sisters, she was said to have gone about the business of caring for her volk with quiet dedication.[45] By presenting themselves as entirely indigenous blooms, Afrikaner nationalist suffragists could combat the contemporary view among the ranks of male Afrikaner nationalism that women's enfranchisement was a foreign idea propagated by "outsiders."[46]

The mother of the nation myth in Afrikaner nationalism echoed the imagery employed in the eugenics movement in Britain at the turn of the century, which called upon women to perform their duty to prevent the decline of the imperial nation and the "deterioration of the race."[47] A trumpet call was issued to "awaken woman to her weighty obligations, as much imperial as domestic or social."[48] Similarly, in what was essentially a euphemistic reference to "racial purity," Afrikaner women were afforded responsibility for safeguarding the "level of civilization" of the Afrikaner people.[49] The mother of the nation ideology thus operated in a dual way: On the one hand, it relegated women to a separate and subordinated social sphere. But on the other hand, it implied a politicization of the familial orbit and of women's mothering role in particular. This served to disrupt the separation between the private domain of the home, deemed to be the proper realm of women, and the public domain of work and politics reserved for men. Once nationalist politics were cast as little more than a "family affair," it became possible to argue that women had not only the right but also the duty to be active participants in the political realm.

The notion of the Afrikaner woman as volksmoeder thus emerged as a key weapon in the suffragists' propaganda armory. In congress motions, press releases, speeches, and letters, the membership of the women's parties looked forward to what could be achieved with the franchise. They saw themselves standing proudly alongside male nationalists, in control of South Africa's destiny and the welfare of the state.[50] They envisaged large numbers of women speaking with one voice and making a powerful difference in social life by means of changes to legislation.[51] However, the achievement of their goal also marked the beginning of a period of reversal and the decline of Afrikaner women's involvement in politics. Informed by the volksmoeder ideology (even at its most expansive), these women ultimately lacked the ideological coherence to fight to continue to organize separately in order to serve their interests as women. Afrikaner women now faced a fate similar to that of their counterparts in Britain, who "had to function within the confines of male constructed political parties, which were imbued with patriarchal values. . . . Women's issues tended to be swallowed up within the 'wider' policies of political parties."[52] The volksmoeder ideology, which Afrikaner women had used so effectively for their own purposes, was now wielded against them. They were called upon to display the spirit of self-sacrifice that had "always been at the heart" of the contribution they wished to make to their volk. They were reminded of their national calling and of the extent to which future generations were relying on them for the safety of white civilization.[53]

The demise of the women's parties coincided with the years of the Great Depression. When the Depression began to create greater competition in the labor market, the traditionalist strain in the volksmoeder ideology came to the fore once more, urging women back into the home: "You girls can no longer follow the path of the previous generation. It seems that a humbler task has been appointed for you. The woman of yesterday mimicked the man, tried to do the same work as him; she was inspired by the same ambitions. The woman of the young generation must create a new type of woman; must not lose sight of the differences between male and female ideals. This will bring her happiness even though her contribution will be less visible."[54] As Matthew Stibbe has commented, campaigns to remove women from the labor market in order to make jobs available to unemployed men were a typical European-wide response to the world recession of the early 1930s. In Germany, Italy, France, Belgium, Bulgaria, Greece, and the Netherlands, the interwar years saw restrictions on women's eligibility for professional positions.[55] While the First World War had seen a massive expansion in job opportunities for women, when the war ended, women were dismissed from the workforce in large numbers.

In contrast to the 1920s, which were years of ideological flux, Afrikaner nationalism entered a new phase after 1930 as it strove to find a definitive framework for itself. The Nazi-sympathizing "Shirt Movements," with their much more restrictive view of women's role in society, rose to brief prominence, and the all-male Afrikaner Broederbond began to play a much larger part in Afrikaner nationalist politics. In this context, Afrikaner women were now required to reproduce the dominant ideology of Afrikaner nationalism rather than question it, to refrain from swelling the ranks of the unemployed by competing for jobs with men, and to "do their duty" in the home.

Ironically, the device used to justify this shift was the very volksmoeder ideology that Afrikaner women had used to such good effect to legitimize their quest for greater political and social independence in the 1920s. While the volksmoeder ideology had been a convenient tool, its weaknesses were now exposed. The retention of the volksmoeder framework meant that these women were not able to fundamentally challenge prevailing gender stereotypes and their associated inequalities. In contrast to the campaign waged by the radical British suffragists, who recognized the embodied nature of citizenship and incorporated marriage laws, family life, and sexual relations into their fight for the vote,[56] Afrikaner women employed an ideological device that served to reinforce the notion that women possessed certain natural predispositions that were fundamentally different from those of men. Ultimately, this was a tool not of feminism but of ethnic nationalism. Effective as it was in empowering the Afrikaner woman for a time, the volksmoeder ideology was used to silence her when political and economic conditions changed and the nationalist movement felt that it could no longer tolerate an independent and critical voice within its ranks.

The universality and all-encompassing nature of gender differentiation make it a less cohesive and potent base for collective identification and mobilization than those of class or nation, which more readily inspire collective consciousness and action.[57] The vote having been won, white women lost the single unifying goal that had briefly allowed them to unite in a common cause as women. The hiatus in Afrikaner women's political activity that followed reflects a familiar pattern. Internationally, the period between 1920 and 1960 has been described as "years of intermission, when for the time at least, feminism seemed to have come to an end."[58] As Deidre Beddoe puts it, "The vote had united women. Now exercise of the vote was to divide them."[59] While the suffrage struggle lent women's political ambitions a certain independence from workaday party politics, Afrikaner women now once again had little to distract them from nationalism's increasingly strident summoning.

NOTES

The epigraph is drawn from an interview by F. J. van Heerden, Institute for Contemporary History, Bloemfontein, South Africa (hereafter INCH) Sound Archive, University of the Free State, cassette no. 5; my translation. Martha Jansen was the wife of advocate E. G. Jansen. Together they were active in Afrikaner nationalist cultural and political circles. As a teacher, Martha Jansen contributed in particular to the development of the Afrikaans grammar.

1. Herman Giliomee, "The Beginnings of Afrikaner Ethnic Consciousness, 1850–1915," in *The Creation of Tribalism in Southern Africa,* ed. Leroy Vail (London: James Curry, 1989), 22.

2. Cherryl Walker, "The Women's Suffrage Movement," in *Women and Gender in Southern Africa to 1945,* ed. Cherryl Walker (Claremont, South Africa: David Phillip, 1990), 340.

3. Shula Marks and Stanley Trapido, *The Politics of Race, Class, and Nationalism in Twentieth-Century South Africa* (Essex: Longman, 1987), 3.

4. Leroy Vail, "Introduction: Ethnicity in Southern African History," in *The Creation of Tribalism in Southern Africa,* ed. Leroy Vail (London: James Curry, 1989), 10.

5. Giliomee, "Afrikaner Ethnic Consciousness," 48.

6. J. E. Gemmell, Presidential Address, *Journal of Obstetrics and Gynaecology of the British Empire* 4 (December 1903): 590, cited in Anna Davin, "Imperialism and Motherhood," *History Workshop* 5 (Spring 1978): 21.

7. See, for instance, Talia [pseud.], in *Die Huisgenoot,* May 1919, 11.

8. Lou-Marie Kruger, "Gender, Community, and Identity: Women and Afrikaner Nationalism in the *Volksmoeder* Discourse of *Die Boerevrou* (1919–1931)" (master's thesis, University of Cape Town, 1991), 130–31.

9. *Die Huisgenoot,* May 1920, 6–8.

10. H. Retief (ACVV president), in *Die Huisgenoot,* October 3, 1924, 33.

11. Roger Petersen, *Understanding Ethnic Violence: Fear, Hatred, and Resentment in Twentieth-Century Eastern Europe* (Cambridge: Cambridge University Press, 2002), 2.

12. *Die Huisgenoot,* November 30, 1923, 9.

13. The organization was launched as the Zuid Afrikaansche Vrouwe Vereeniging (ZAVV) in 1904 and renamed the Zuid Afrikaansche Christelyke Vrouwe Vereniging (South African Christian Women's Organization) soon afterward, but it came to be known as the Afrikaanse Christelike Vroue Vereniging (ACVV) from 1906 onward. See Marijke Du Toit, "Women, Welfare, and the Nurturing of Afrikaner Nationalism: A Social History of the Afrikaanse Christelike Vrouevereeniging, c. 1870–1939" (Ph.D. diss., University of Cape Town, 1996), 80–88.

14. The formal launch took place later in September 1904; see Du Toit, "Women," 19.

15. Ibid., 255–56.

16. Ibid., 201.

17. In an article that appeared in the suffrage magazine *Flashlight* (published in Uitenhage by the Women's Enfranchisement Association of the Union of South Africa) in July 1930, Mrs. M. Moldenhauer described the newly won suffrage as "a cake of soap" that women would use to "clean up the dirty places of the country, and lighten darkness wherever it is possible." M. Moldenhauer, "Our Suffrage Victory and After," *Flashlight,* July 1930, 36.

18. See, for example, Kruger, "Gender, Community, and Identity"; Du Toit, "Women"; Deborah Gaitskell and Elaine Unterhalter, "Mothers of the Nation: A Comparative Analysis of Nation, Race, and Motherhood in Afrikaner Nationalism and the African National Congress," in *Women, Nation, State,* ed. F. Anthias and N. Yuval-Davis (London: Macmillan, 1989).

19. M. S. Vorster, "Opening Address to the Nasionale Vroueklub [National Women's Club]," July 1970, INCH Private Collection 614, P19, p. 1.

20. M. M. Jansen's active participation in politics began the same way as many other Afrikaner women's political careers: she supported her husband's NP candidacy in the 1915 general election. She went on to become president of the nationalist women's party in Natal and chair of its Pietermaritzburg branch. S. Greyvenstein, "Martha Mabel Jansen se bydrae op kulturele, politieke en maatskaplike gebied in Natal 1910–30" [Martha Mabel

Jansen's cultural, political, and social contribution in Natal, 1910–30] (Honors thesis, University of the Free State, 1989), 29.

21. M. M. Jansen, INCH Sound Archive, cassette no. 5.

22. C. Van der Vyver, in *Die Burgeres*, December 1927, 66. See also *Die Burgeres*, October 1927, 43.

23. "Annual Report of the Federal Council of the National Women's Parties of the Four Provinces of South Africa," *Die Burgeres*, March 1928, 8.

24. *Die Burgeres*, December 1927, 56; my translation.

25. This did not mean, however, that the NVP failed to make a financial contribution to the NP. It added £3,000 to the 1924 election campaign alone. See "Minutes of the Third NVP Congress" (Cradock, December 1925), 26, INCH Private Collection 27 (I) ½/2/2/1.

26. Constitution of the Natal Women's National Party, cited in Greyvenstein, "Jansen," 34.

27. Greyvenstein, "Jansen," 35.

28. Ibid., 36.

29. Van der Vyver, in *Die Burgeres*, December 1927, 66.

30. *Die Burgeres*, October 1927, 43.

31. J. H. Conradie, "Oor die registrasie van kiesers" [On the registration of voters], *Die Burgeres*, May 1928, front cover.

32. M. E. Rothmann, "Die werk van die Graaff-Reinet Kongres" [The work of the Graaff-Reinet Congress], *Die Burgeres*, April 1927, 6.

33. *Die Burgeres*, October 1927, 38; my translation.

34. E. C. Van der Lingen, in *Die Burgeres*, October 1930, 47.

35. See, for example, Walker, "Women's Suffrage," 318.

36. See, for example, the testimony of nationalist women such as Martha Mabel Jansen and Engela Lyon to the 1926 Select Committee on the Enfranchisement of Women. For a more detailed examination of Afrikaner women's participation in the suffrage campaign, see Louise Vincent, "Mothers of Invention: Gender, Class, and the Ideology of the *Volksmoeder* in the Making of Afrikaner Nationalism, 1918 to 1938" (Ph.D. diss., Oxford University, 1997).

37. For many years, nationalists had argued that the enfranchisement of women on the same terms that were then enjoyed by men would have the undesirable result of extending the "native" vote, as black women would then be entitled to share the limited suffrage still enjoyed by black men at the Cape.

38. "Reelingssekretaris se verslag" [Organising secretary's report], *Die Burgeres*, December 1930, 89.

39. "Jaarlikse verslag van die VNP voorbereidingskomitee" [Annual report of the VNP Working Committee, December 1929 to October 1930], *Die Burgeres*, December 1930, 87.

40. Untitled document (probably a speech by Tini Vorster), n.d., INCH Private Collection 614, P16/30, pt. 7.

41. Vroueaksie [Women's Action Committee], "Report to the National Party of the Transvaal, 1973/74," INCH Private Collection 614, P16/30, pt. 2.

42. *Die Burgeres*, February 1929, 101.

43. This idea can be traced back at least as far as the British feminist Anna Jameson, whose writings and lectures in the 1850s "claimed for women particular qualities, knowledge and aptitudes as essential to any proper reordering of society, something additional to and differing from the masculine contribution which determined public life at that time." Sandra Stanley Holton, *Suffrage Days: Stories from the Women's Suffrage Movement* (London: Routledge, 1996), 12.

44. See, for example, A. J. [pseud.] and Oplettend [pseud.], both in "Die vrou en die huis" [The woman and the home], *Die Huisgenoot*, June 15, 1928, 57.

45. *Flashlight*, April 1930, 5.

46. This was, for example, one of the arguments employed by antisuffragist and nationalist MP Harm Oost, who also contended that women's enfranchisement would undermine

the family as the foundation of national life. "Waarom ek teen die stemreg is" [Why I am against the suffrage], *Die Huisgenoot,* April 6, 1928, 29.

47. Davin, "Imperialism and Motherhood," 10.

48. A. Ravenhill, "Eugenic Ideals for Womanhood," *Eugenics Review,* 1909, 267, cited in Davin, "Imperialism and Motherhood," 22.

49. Reflecting on this traditional responsibility in a 1976 speech, Tini Vorster, for example, spoke of how the character of the Afrikaner woman had historically determined the level of civilization of the Afrikaner people ("die peil van 'n beskawing styg nie hoër as die karakter van a vrou nie"). Vorster, "Die vrou vandag en môre" [The woman today and tomorrow], INCH Private Collection 614.

50. *De Afrikaner,* November 5, 1929, cited in Greyvenstein, "Jansen," 37.

51. H. Van Der Sandt De Villiers, "Ons het die stemreg—Hoe gaan ons dit gebruik?" [We have the vote—How shall we use it?], *Die Huisgenoot,* June 13, 1930, 69.

52. Deidre Beddoe, *Back to Home and Duty: Women Between the Wars, 1918–1939* (London: Pandora, 1989), 144–45.

53. E. C. Van der Lingen, "Closing Address to NVP Congress," *Die Burgeres,* December 1930, 71–72.

54. G. Lombroso, "My raad aan die jong geslag" [My advice to the young generation], *Die Huisgenoot,* March 25, 1932; my translation.

55. Matthew Stibbe, "Women and the Nazi State," *History Today* 43 (November 1993): 37.

56. Holton, *Suffrage Days,* 29.

57. Anthony D. Smith, *National Identity* (London: Penguin, 1991), 4.

58. Olive Banks, *Faces of Feminism: A Study of Feminism as a Social Movement* (Oxford: Martin Robinson, 1981), 150.

59. Beddoe, *Back to Home,* 136.

9

Porfirista Femininity in Exile: Women's Contributions to
San Antonio's *La Prensa,* 1913–1929

Nancy Aguirre

The Ideal Woman . . . never contradicts her parents, siblings, relatives, or friends . . . has a clean
spirit . . . does not shed abundant tears at every step . . . has gazes that shed loving tenderness . . .
does not pronounce more than one hundred words per minute . . . does not spend hours fixing
her hair . . . [and] prefers her home rather than the street.
—*La Prensa,* April 24, 1913

In early twentieth-century San Antonio, Porfirista women, members of the
exiled right-wing Eurocentric elite who had supported Mexican president
Porfirio Díaz (1876–1911), asserted their conception of femininity in the
newspaper *La Prensa.* They supported patriarchy and promoted domesticity
among Mexican women. Yet their involvement with *La Prensa* and the community demonstrated that they could be political actors as well as wives and
mothers. Throughout the 1910s and 1920s, household roles, motherhood,
devotion to Catholicism, and education were central components of Porfirista
femininity. Acceptance of European culture and notions of modernity were
also fundamental. As women's roles in society changed over the course of the
decades in both the United States and Mexico, Porfiristas used the public
sphere to politicize the domestic, spreading their ideas to *La Prensa*'s female
audience in both countries. However, Porfirista women faced a conflict with
their male counterparts because they adopted trends set by modern European women, including short hair, which the men believed made them look
masculine. This gender division demonstrated that while women could publicly defend patriarchy, men would criticize them for any behavior they perceived as a threat to masculinity.

Porfirista women crossed spatial, cultural, and political boundaries. Mexico's Revolution of 1910 was a transnational conflict that affected both Mexico and the United States. As thousands of Mexicans crossed the border into the United States, the barrios of cities including San Antonio, El Paso, and Los Angeles expanded. The U.S.-Mexican border, however, was not the only "border" that these immigrants faced. In cities, Anglo discrimination against Mexicans was a reality: Mexican barrios were politically, economically, and culturally separated from the rest of the community. Moreover, immigrants had to adapt to life in the United States while contending with the effects of war and displacement. Conflict also existed within barrios, since the Revolution split Mexicans according to political affiliation, class, race, and gender. These divisions are illustrated in the pages of *La Prensa* in the different ways that male and female contributors expressed what it meant to them to be Mexican.

The Ricos of San Antonio

As revolution and war consumed Mexico between 1910 and 1920, Mexicans of all social classes and ideologies fled the violence and migrated north of the border. San Antonio, Texas, was particularly attractive because it had been a center for revolutionary activity prior to the start of the war. In San Antonio, Francisco I. Madero launched his Plan de San Luis Potosí,[1] and anarchist Ricardo Flores Magón worked on his newspaper *Regeneración*. San Antonio was not only appealing to supporters of the Mexican Revolution, however. Significant numbers of Porfiristas fled Mexico after the exile of President Porfirio Díaz in May 1911. Díaz's supporters in San Antonio were known as the *ricos,* meaning "rich," since they were the intellectual and economic elite in the Mexican barrio.

Historian Susan M. Yohn has addressed the problem of essentializing groups according to political ideology, suggesting that binaries such as conservative or liberal obscure complexities and contradictions in a person's or group's identity.[2] Moreover, conservative movements are often negatively characterized, in the words of scholar Alan Brinkley, "as the futile, and dwindling, resistance of provincial or marginal peoples to the inexorable forces of modernism,"[3] a definition that equates conservatism with a resistance to progress. This description is problematic because it suggests that conservatives are politically "backward" without critically examining this ideology.

Mexican conservatism (and liberalism) differed from the U.S. versions addressed by Yohn and Brinkley. Historian William D. Raat suggests that in the case of Mexico, "Porfirio Díaz . . . blurred the distinctions"[4] between liberalism and conservatism during his regime. Mexican liberalism, established in the mid-nineteenth century, supported individual political freedom, laissez-faire economics, and the need for a strong state to "curtail corporate privileges,"[5] particularly those of the Catholic Church. Scholar Charles A. Hale notes that conservatism, on the other hand, was fundamentally pro-clerical, skeptical of democracy, and in favor of a strong centralist government that would bring "order" to Mexico through the institutions of the Catholic Church and the military.[6] Díaz was a liberal who adopted conservative policies and supported the Catholic Church as an economic institution. During the Porfiriato, Díaz's supporters (both liberal and conservative) favored private property, believed in a strict class hierarchy, and overlooked the general welfare of the Indian population.

The most prominent group of Porfiristas, known as the *científicos,* adhered to these principles and sought to create a "modern Mexico" tailored after modern European nation-states.[7] Historian Mauricio Tenorio-Trillo notes that científicos worked for progress in finance, education, industry, and society through the use of science.[8] Moreover, they equated modernity with "whiteness." Indigenous people and their culture were ignored, repressed, or exoticized, and Europeans were favored over Mexicans in the labor sector and in government positions. Mexico's científicos held both liberal and conservative beliefs; considering Yohn and Brinkley's arguments, it is more useful to characterize Porfiristas (including científicos) as right-wing. Porfirismo was to the right of anarchism, syndicalism, antipositivism, socialism, populism, liberal indigenism, and other "ideologies of protest"[9] that had consolidated by 1910. These opposition groups were more "radical" than Porfiristas because, regardless of their specific goals, they wanted to incorporate more sectors of the population into the development of a "modern" Mexico.

Upon migrating to the United States, the ricos practiced their Porfirista ideology in Mexican barrios, where they resided with middle- and lower-class Mexicans. At the same time, they faced Anglo racism and the realities of exile. According to historian Richard A. García, "They lived between 1908 and the early 1940s in a state of exiled purgatory and with their ideological vision as *mexicanos de afuera* (Mexicans outside of Mexico), they were interested in the Mexican population in San Antonio and the Southwest, but only in broad cultural-political terms."[10] The newspaper *La Prensa,* established in 1913 by rico Ignacio E. Lozano, became the largest-selling Spanish-language newspaper in the United States, and the primary medium of expression for rica/o thought.[11] News reports, contests, entertainment columns, editorials, political cartoons, historical narratives, popular literature, and advertising constituted the content of the newspaper. Through *La Prensa,* San Antonio's elite worked to reach the Mexican immigrant population, known as *el México de afuera,* or the Mexican diaspora. Moreover, the ricos created a Habermasian public sphere, a space for debate and dialogue, within the barrio through which Mexican immigrants negotiated their identities as residents of the United States.

La Prensa was an exile newspaper written by a group of people who made it clear that the United States was not their home. It was also a transnational publication that was smuggled into Mexico, where it was censored because it was a right-wing publication critical of the Revolution and postwar revolutionary government. Nevertheless, the newspaper was read in Mexico, and leaders including Emiliano Zapata, who fought for indigenous land rights, and President Álvaro Obregón (1920–24) contributed to the publication. These men had specific plans for a postrevolutionary Mexico, and they wanted the support of Mexicans in the United States in case of any return migration. They also understood the importance of La Prensa within el México de afuera and the influence that the publication had on its readers.

In the 1910s and 1920s, Lozano and his staff, who remained nostalgic for the days of progress under Díaz, heavily criticized the Mexican Revolution and the authoritarian regime of Plutarco Elías Calles (1924–28). They supported the pro-Catholic Cristeros in their war of 1926–29 against the Mexican government. Because of the conditions in Mexico, many ricos chose to remain in exile in the United States, despite the amnesty offered to them in the early 1920s by President Álvaro Obregón. La Prensa documented the reactions of the Porfiristas to the changes within Mexico. However, it was Lozano and his male staff members who critiqued postrevolutionary Mexico through editorials, news reports, and political cartoons. La Prensa's female staff was active in the development of the newspaper, but only in a manner that coincided with Porfirista notions of femininity and women's roles in society.

Porfirista Femininity

San Antonio's ricas were highly active within the San Antonio community, helping promote education, culture, and literacy among Mexicans. For example, Alicia Lozano, wife of Ignacio, established the Sociedad de la Beneficencia Mexicana, a charity organization. She also served as director of La Prensa after her husband's death in 1953. Journalist Beatriz Blanco, who in the 1920s and 1930s directed La Prensa's "Página para el Hogar" (Page for the home),[12] worked as president of the Club Mexicano de Bellas Artes, a fine arts organization in San Antonio. These women exercised what Gabriela González deems "the politics of benevolence," the "idea that women bore moral responsibility for society."[13] The ricas raised funds and worked to help Mexicans on both sides of the border. Was La Prensa an extension of their social activism?

An examination of women's contributions to the exile publication in the years 1913–29 reveals a variety of complex dynamics within the rica community, as well as between the male and female elite. The ricas espoused the upper-class feminine ideal, which I will refer to as "Porfirista femininity." They practiced Catholicism, supported patriarchy, and were interested in promoting Eurocentric ideals of fashion, art, education, race, and culture. They also favored domesticity for women. The "Página para el Hogar," established on a permanent basis in 1918, included the latest fashion trends, advice for wives and mothers, and literature, and it reflected the ways in which ricas viewed themselves in light of the changing gender roles of this time.

During the 1920s, activists were working for suffrage and other rights for women across Mexico. North of the border, the "Jazz Age" was in full swing. "Modern" women in the United States (as well as in Europe) were wearing more revealing clothing with shorter hemlines, smoking and drinking alcohol openly, and engaging in the public sphere in an unprecedented manner. San Antonio's ricas supported women's suffrage, dressed like "flappers," and applauded women who succeeded outside the private realm, particularly in education. This seems contradictory, since the ricas advocated women's domesticity. However, within the context of gender roles during the Porfiriato, it was not so. Women were encouraged to become educated and engage in the literary sphere because it could be an outlet for their emotions. Through education, women could teach others how to be better wives and mothers. According to Lorraine Dipp de Holaschutz, by Porfirista standards, the more cultured and educated the woman, the more superior her offspring would be; ultimately, this would benefit families and the Mexican nation.[14] Thus, Porfirista femininity blurred the boundaries between the public and private and politicized the latter.

Nevertheless, *La Prensa* demonstrates tension between male and female Porfiristas because of the ongoing transformation of women's roles. Lozano and other male contributors criticized modern women. They believed that these women threatened patriarchy by engaging in "masculine" activities such as sports, wearing their hair short like men, and seeking greater participation in the public sphere. Gender, which was not initially a significant issue in the newspaper, gained increasing attention in the late 1920s.

These dynamics impacted Porfirista femininity in the early twentieth century. An analysis of rica culture as depicted in *La Prensa* will provide insight into the ways in which ricas influenced Mexican culture and the definition of *mexicanidad,* or Mexican-ness, as well as femininity north and south of the U.S.-Mexican border. More important, this study will consider the effects of being female, Mexican, exiled and discriminated against, wealthy, educated, Catholic, and supportive of patriarchy. Through *La Prensa,* Porfirista women expressed their identities and attempted to shape those of their audience during a period marked by drastic political and social change.

Women in *La Prensa:* 1913–1918

La Prensa focused mostly on the Mexican Revolution and World War I between 1913 and 1918, and women were scarcely featured in it. In 1913 *La Prensa* comprised news reports, editorials, and literature. The "Página Literaria" (Literary page) ran from 1913 to 1915. Onofre Di Stefano's study *"La Prensa* of San Antonio and Its Literary Page, 1913 to 1915"* lists more than four hundred authors featured in this column.[15] At times, authors used pseudonyms or their initials, so it was not always clear whether they were male or female.[16] Only twelve authors whose work appeared in *La Prensa* were known to be women, including seventeenth-century Mexican writer Sor Juana Inés de la Cruz and Rosario Sansores, a twentieth-century Mexican poet. Dipp de Holaschutz and Gabriela Cano suggest that Mexican women were active in writing literature and publishing magazines during the Porfiriato; women's participation in literary circles was acceptable feminine behavior, as long as they expressed "sweetness, submission and domesticity."[17] This explains why initially the only place for women in *La Prensa*—both as writers and as subjects—was the "Página Literaria." The first edition of the "Página para el Hogar" did not appear in *La Prensa* until 1918.

The literature featured in the newspaper at times focused on women, particularly their behavior and beauty. One literary piece, entitled "The Ideal Woman," states that a proper and decent woman did not speak back to any authority figure, spend hours on personal grooming, or speak more than one hundred words per minute. She was also pure of spirit and preferred the home to the street.[18] In general, when writing about women, contributors to the column emphasized their attractiveness and the importance of maintaining their Catholic values. A poem entitled "Your Eyes," for example, was written from the perspective of a man looking into a woman's eyes. The woman's gaze "erased"[19] the author's bitterness, and her eyes were all that he lived for. The beauty of the Mexican woman was also celebrated in other sections of *La Prensa*.

In a special issue in 1916 that celebrated Mexico's independence from Spain, a full-page illustration depicted Mexico's turbulent past and violent present. The future was represented by a "robust" woman with an "erect womb with which to give birth" to a new generation. This woman was "La Patria,"[20] which roughly translates to "the Fatherland," and she was a symbol of hope for a brighter future for Mexico. Although the picture emphasized the beauty of the Mexican woman, its message was more profound. Women, particularly those who took care of their personal appearance and lived according to Catholic moral standards, were given the responsibility to "re-create" Mexico by giving birth and raising children with Porfirista values. By living up to their natural role as mothers, Mexican women would repair the damage done by the Revolution. Mothers were portrayed as the potential saviors of Mexico, yet the gendered language in this issue of *La Prensa* demonstrated their position within patriarchal society. Despite being pregnant, the woman in the illustration was not named "La Matria," or "the Motherland."[21] Instead, her identity was framed within the context of fatherhood, and her purpose was to procreate for the benefit of the Fatherland.

Finally, between 1913 and 1918, women were also depicted as consumers in *La Prensa*. Products aimed toward female readers included beauty products, skin creams made to fight wrinkles, and hair dye. Women's clothing and jewelry were often advertised, and stores such as Sears & Roebuck were regularly featured in the newspaper. These varied examples of the portrayal of women reflect the general scope of their inclusion in *La Prensa* in its first six years of publication. Women were supposed to be beautiful, virtuous, and pure in order to elevate the Mexican race. More important, women's contributions to the newspaper were limited.

Before 1918, women, culture, and issues unrelated to the Mexican Revolution and World War I were not a priority for *La Prensa*'s staff. Porfiristas in the United States lived in exile due to a revolution that they opposed. They lost their position as Mexico's elite, became the object of racial discrimination in the United States, and witnessed the deterioration of Europe, which they had long considered the center of civilization. As the conflicts in Europe and Mexico began to subside in 1918 and 1919, the ricos shifted their focus more to barrio culture. Many exiles now had U.S.-born children, businesses, and other endeavors that kept them in the United States. Other Porfiristas felt that Mexico had changed too much for them to return home. *El México de afuera* was firmly in place, and the exiles forged a "home" in a transnational space in which Mexican and U.S. politics, economics, and culture were merged. *La Prensa* represented this transnationalism. The newspaper remained dedicated to publishing news from Mexico, yet children's literature, entertainment, and sports columns, as well as the "Página para el Hogar," represented European and U.S. culture.

Women in *La Prensa*: 1919–1923

Women's involvement in war industries changed the way in which gender roles were perceived at the end of World War I. According to *La Prensa*, "The woman demonstrated that she possessed the great aptitude" to carry out jobs once considered only for the "strong [male] sex." The newspaper praised women for taking the place of men in factories in times of war, because this allowed men to carry out their masculine roles as defenders of their countries. The ability of women to succeed in "masculine" jobs helps explain the increasing attention given to women in *La Prensa* beginning in 1919, and the placement of the "Página para el Hogar" under the direction of rica Beatriz Blanco in 1923. Not only could women successfully work in factories, but they could also have "intellectual jobs."[22] According to Cano, the press was a vital part of the intellectual and political development of Mexican society during the Porfiriato. Women were active in the press, even establishing their own publications. As Cano suggests, writing was considered a virtue of the educated and cultured lady.[23] However, this new respect for women in the workforce was fundamentally patriarchal. As *La Prensa* demonstrates, women were allowed to participate in the public sphere as workers, educators, writers, and community activists as long as the goal was to uphold men and improve the home, family, and nation. Hence, the ricas' involvement with the newspaper was not considered a threat to patriarchy.

The "Página para el Hogar" in 1918 and the early 1920s represented Porfirista femininity.[24] The column, which ran weekly until 1923, consistently featured the latest fashion from Europe, particularly Paris and Spain. Models were illustrated wearing expensive clothing and accessories; most of the outfits were evening gowns. The explanations of the fashion coincided with Porfirista conceptions of "classiness." Dresses featured were deemed appropriate for soirees and grand receptions, and the adjective "elegant" characterized numerous outfits. In one description, the writer stated that "every elegant socialite knows that a black soiree gown is indispensable to her wardrobe."[25] Elite fashion was also featured in advertising. An ad for El Compuesto Mitchella, a vitamin supplement for women preparing for motherhood, depicted a mother holding her infant child. The mother wore a luxurious dress and pearls, and her hair was pulled neatly into a bun.[26] The message reflected in La Prensa was clear: fashionable women and good mothers in the Mexican barrio dressed like wealthy Europeans.

Whiteness was also emphasized in the newspaper's advertising during this period. Advertisements for skin-lightening cream and skin bleach stated that "it was not necessary to suffer humiliation for having dark and ugly skin," and that "the man or woman with white skin . . . free of freckles . . . pimples, etc., would have greater success in business, love, society . . . because he/she would be more likeable."[27] This was a central quality of Porfirismo, which correlated whiteness with beauty, intelligence, and wealth. The concept of "race betterment" was of high importance to the científicos during the Porfiriato. In his work on the participation of Mexico at the World's Fairs in the late nineteenth century, Tenorio-Trillo states,

> The superiority of the white European race was so forcefully promoted by the late-nineteenth-century scientific perspective that no nation seeking to be considered modern and cosmopolitan would even attempt to propose the superiority or equality of other races. For Mexico it was a lost cause to try to prove the pure and unmixed white nature of the modern Mexican population. But all of the Mexican propaganda . . . emphasized that the Mexican upper classes were unmistakably white and, hence, that Mexico fit modernity according to one criterion established by modern societies—namely, through a well-defined class structure.[28]

Dark-skinned individuals were not depicted in the publication's advertising; rather, light-skinned people were featured to show readers the ideal skin tone that they could attain.

Although it was never explicitly stated, the contributors to *La Prensa* were reestablishing the class norms of the Porfiriato, which disappeared when Mexicans of all classes fled Mexico. In regard to class, Porfirista femininity was elitist. Porfirista women elevated European culture and high society, of which they had been a part before the Mexican Revolution. Not all Mexicans in San Antonio could participate in rico society, nor could all *mexicanas* dress like the ricas. Advertising throughout *La Prensa* featured women's clothing sold in local stores, but the section dedicated specifically to women did not feature these advertisements. Thus, the "Página para el Hogar" excluded anyone searching for information regarding local (and presumably less expensive) clothing, while simultaneously giving women a fashion standard to which to aspire.

The ricas exemplified the bourgeois feminine ideal in other respects as well. The "Página para el Hogar" included articles that specified the importance of teaching children manners; in particular, mothers were supposed to prepare their daughters for marriage.[29] Furthermore, the section "Golden Words" contained popular quotations by figures such as King Solomon and the Roman philosopher Quintilian on various topics, including marriage and gossip. Women were advised to be respectful of their husbands and not to speak poorly of others—in short, to follow Porfirista values. The "Página para el Hogar" exposed readers to biblical texts and philosophy, as well as proper moral values, demonstrating that women were supposed to be *intelligent* wives and mothers.

Women in the United States, including those of Mexican backgrounds, were becoming more active in the public sphere; their fashion was changing, and so were standards for what was socially acceptable for them. *La Prensa* illustrated these changes. In December 1923, a full-page drawing by Henry Olive, entitled "The Modern Eves," depicted a woman with her bare back exposed to the reader.[30] According to Olive, Eve, the first woman, wore little to cover her body, which symbolized that a woman's body should be celebrated and seen, contrary to popular notions of modesty. Olive's work exemplifies the changing perceptions of women, their bodies, and femininity; from then on, the image of women would undergo drastic transformation in *La Prensa*, reflecting the influence of modernity on society, gender roles, and Porfirista femininity.

Women in *La Prensa:* 1924–1929

In 1924, the "Página para el Hogar" featured recipes, popular literature by male and female authors (including the Chilean poet Gabriela Mistral), social commentary written by men and women, advertising, and fashion. Homemaking was emphasized through sewing projects and recipes, which were printed almost daily. Each edition of the "Página para el Hogar" illustrated the latest styles from Europe; in 1928, New York City clothing was also commonly highlighted. Moreover, poetry and prose, biblical stories, biographies, and editorial pieces were part of the literature presented to readers. All these elements combined to form a page from which women could learn how to improve themselves, their homes, and their families, and simultaneously learn about the world around them.

The structure of Beatriz Blanco's page remained the same throughout the rest of the decade, but the content reflected a gradual division in the ways in which men and women defined Porfirista femininity. The male ricos, who had embraced modernity, were now critical of the effects of postwar modernity on women. The ricas remained true to their Porfirista ideals, which included idealizing European culture and modernity. Ironically, this meant embracing elements of the "modern woman" that the rico men criticized. Porfirista femininity was not static; ricas encouraged women's progress and remained dedicated to advancing modernity in the United States, *el México de afuera,* and the homeland. The "modern woman" became the most significant point of conflict between Porfirista men and women. Men felt threatened by women's increasing participation in the public sphere and their ability to "look like men" by cutting their hair. Meanwhile, women asserted greater control over their bodies by choosing how much skin to expose and how they wanted to style their hair.

Ricas also practiced modernity by promoting education, which was the primary purpose of the "Página para el Hogar." Women were encouraged to learn about science, the arts, and homemaking in order to pass on this information to their children. Articles featured biographical information on artists such as Ludwig van Beethoven and Jules Massenet. Women also learned about parts of the body and their functions, and how to take care of the body. Furthermore, readers were exposed to Greek and Roman thinkers, including Plato, Aristotle, and Cicero, and contributors to *La Prensa* would use the works of these philosophers to develop their own arguments on social and religious issues. For example, "The Worker in the Time of Paganism" describes the feelings of the aforementioned philosophers toward laborers, who were supposed to "live for the master, not have personal interests, or honor, or dignity." According to the author, conditions for laborers improved "when Jesus Christ came into the world."[31] Catholicism always triumphed in philosophical debates, and it was the ideological center for women's instruction in *La Prensa.*

The Virgin Mary was the most prominently illustrated female in the "Página para el Hogar," and she was considered the ideal Porfirista woman. A wife and mother, Mary upheld the natural state of women's domesticity. Moreover, she was humble, modest, and obedient. In the "Página para el Hogar," articles instructing women to have these qualities appeared on a daily basis. One piece, entitled "Advice for my Daughter," was written by a mother who wanted her daughter to "find love, mold virtue, and love pain"[32]—all

Marian qualities. In addition, Bible stories and parables were included in this section, and every edition listed the Catholic saint for the day.

Women's education was not limited to European culture and Catholicism, however. *La Prensa* included information about foreign cultures, particularly in the supplemental edition published on Sundays. For example, one article discussed the similarities between Middle Eastern and medieval European music.[33] In 1929 a Sunday edition featured modern Turkish women. The rhetoric in the article was clearly gendered. Turkey was congratulated for becoming a republic, and its men and women were praised for becoming westernized. Turkish women were increasingly rejecting the traditional veil and wearing makeup. They also engaged in the public sphere because they now had access to divorce and were no longer "slaves" completely confined to their homes. However, the author subtly criticized the women for adopting the "masculine aspect"[34] of North American females, including short hair. The author equated freedom for Turkish women with diminishing beauty.

The "Página para el Hogar" was also a medium for social commentary. In 1924 Blanco lamented that so many young women were attracted to the Hollywood lifestyle, which she considered a "fantasy."[35] Other issues that received attention in the late 1920s included smoking by women, which was considered "ruinous for beauty,"[36] and health problems caused by obesity. Social issues were also addressed, such as the disastrous impact of book printing on trees. One article focused on the topic of justice, stating that "justice is the equilibrium between liberty and rights. Its value is superior to that of the law . . . which can sometimes be unjust."[37] Articles such as this coincided with the activism of the ricas. Alicia Lozano established the Sociedad de la Beneficencia Mexicana. Blanco was the president of the Club Mexicano de Bellas Artes, which sponsored community events and worked with *La Prensa* to help the barrio's lower classes. Other women with connections to the newspaper fought discrimination against the Mexican community and poverty in the barrio, and educated barrio residents about Mexican culture. Hence, *La Prensa* was an extension of their social housekeeping roles outside the home, which blurred the boundary for women between the public and private spheres.

At times, the ricas politicized the private by adhering to their domestic roles as a political stance. During the presidency of Plutarco Elías Calles, the Catholic Church faced violent repression resulting from anticlerical policies. Churches were closed across the nation, clergy were exiled or executed, and Mexicans were forbidden from wearing any religious symbols. In protest, between 1926 and 1929, Catholics waged the Cristero War against the Mexican government. Scholar Sister Barbara Miller, who studied the role of women in the war, notes that Cristeras helped establish a clandestine Church, cooked and cleaned for the troops, and sometimes engaged in the violence.[38] Women's organizations, including the Unión Femenina Católica Mexicana (UFCM), worked extensively for the Catholic cause. *La Prensa* closely followed the conflict, and Ignacio Lozano was highly supportive of the Cristeros. However, there was no mention of the conflict in the "Página para el Hogar," despite the ricas' piety. In fact, although there was Catholic content on the page, it seemed that the ricas were preoccupied with fashion and the upkeep of their homes. For example, on September 25, 1926, *La Prensa*'s front-page headline read, "The Laws Regarding Religious Subjects Will Be Applied with Rigor." That same day, the "Página para el Hogar" published stories on chess and Chinese checkers, the latest styles for gloves, and umbrellas. While the men were concerned with wars and ideological dissension in Mexico, the women's political task consisted largely of publicizing and celebrating the domestic sphere.

Why would the ricas, who were devout Catholics and activists in the barrio, not use *La Prensa* to express their opinions on the persecution of the Catholic Church in Mexico? According to Cano, during the Porfiriato, women were expected to be patriotic, and "feminine patriotism was not only expressed in procreation and the upbringing of children; it arose in civic participation and professional activities."[39] By promoting art, education, culture, and economic advancement, the ricas manifested their patriotism and engaged politically. This adds a different dimension to the definition of Porfirista femininity. Just as the Virgin Mary does not play a passive role in Catholicism, women were supposed to be moral and Catholic wives and mothers, as well as active members of their societies. As the men openly criticized the Mexican government, women also made a political statement by defending the home.

However, the ricas accepted cultural elements that did not conform to male Porfirista notions of femininity. The fashion depicted in the "Página para el Hogar" and the harsh critiques against women in 1928 and 1929 demonstrate the changes in Porfirismo during this time. Hemlines on dresses were slowly rising, hairstyles were becoming shorter, and dresses were showing off women's shoulders and backs. The latest fashions from Europe were increasingly revealing, as were the illustrations of women in advertising and the supplemental page in *La Prensa*. For example, in 1928 a Parisian dress was featured with a hemline ending at the model's upper thighs. That same day, a literary piece expressed the author's request for her suitor not to kiss her, so that she might maintain her purity.[40] This demonstrates that the ideas about femininity presented in the publication were *seemingly* contradictory. Short hemlines could in fact be advertised along with a story about maintaining a woman's purity because the fashion was European. The ricas were not compromising any facet of their ideas on femininity.

Another example was a 1929 advertisement for Picot Sal de Uvas, a powder that was consumed with water in order to alleviate indigestion. It showed a woman looking into a mirror while holding a glass full of the product. The woman was wearing a slip with thin straps that revealed most of her breasts, a hemline that ended at her upper thigh, and a slit that ended *above* her thigh. The woman was also wearing knee-length pantyhose and high heels. Short dresses, short hair, bare backs and legs, and heavy makeup were the standard for women's fashion, and the ricas embraced it since it was "modern." Moreover, advertising in the "Página para el Hogar" still emphasized women's beauty products, such as hair dyes, acne medication, skin cleansers, and skin bleach. From their perspective, the ricas continued to uphold the feminine ideal; they dressed like modern Europeans and reinforced the importance of whiteness, just as they had in the 1910s and before.

The ricos, on the other hand, were horrified by the "modern woman." Numerous articles criticized modernity, including one that stated that "the general opinion of [male] painters" was that the essence of the modern woman could not be captured because she did not "expose her soul," or simply had no soul. An artist could not paint the woman "because she [did] not look like one."[41] Another report suggested that modernity was stripping away the beauty of women and the entire world. These men equated attractiveness with domesticity, Christian moral values, and purity of spirit. The modern woman blurred the line between the public and private spheres because she was active in sports and entertainment, worked outside the home, participated in civic organizations, smoked, and wore revealing clothing. Stepping outside the domestic realm and exposing herself to "masculine" activities ruined her purity, diminished her femininity, and, at the extreme level, took away her soul. Consequently, *male* artists (*La Prensa* made no mention of female painters) could not do their jobs.

Moreover, according to Count Hermann Keyserling, the German founder of the School of Wisdom, feminism was destroying love in the world, and the United States was the perfect example; the more independent the woman, the less independent the man.[42] Another author expressed the basic dilemma for the modern woman. She had to choose between happiness and liberty, and if she "insisted on being too free, she would pay the price of solitude and abandonment."[43] Finally, historian John Langdon Davis predicted a grim future for men and the complete reversal of current gender roles. Davis wrote that in the future, men would become women's slaves, and they would work in offices and factories. Women, in turn, would only dedicate themselves to having fun.[44]

Porfirista Femininity in Exile

The conflict between different Porfirista notions of gender by 1929 was only one of the complex dynamics that influenced the construction and representation of rica identity between 1913 and 1929. The Mexican Revolution politicized women of various ideologies. During the conflict and afterward, women in Mexico began vocalizing their needs and opinions, and they organized in order to gain rights and improve their status. Female veterans sought bene-fits from the government, prostitutes fought for their rights as mothers, teachers in Yucatán were engaged in social reform, and Catholic women stressed the importance of domesticity.[45]

Similarly, women of varying ideologies were increasingly active in the United States. In the 1910s and 1920s, women worked to gain suffrage, to pass the Equal Rights Amendment (ERA), and to find employment outside of the home at an increasing rate. Left-wing women were not the only ones fight-ing for these issues; as scholar Kathleen Blee demonstrates, an important Klan supporter backed the ERA.[46] Yohn has cited this example to demonstrate that women cannot be neatly categorized.[47]

Like other women in Mexico and the United States, San Antonio's ricas blurred the border between the public and private spheres and set a unique standard for Mexican women in both countries. *La Prensa* was a tool through which ricas expressed their political position, namely, domesticity. The news-paper was also one medium used by these women to improve conditions in the barrio. Porfirista femininity remained unchanged by the Mexican Revo-lution yet adapted to current European and U.S. trends. The ricas continued to be elitist but reached out to women of the lower classes through commu-nity activism and the "Página para el Hogar." They also continued to stress the importance of whiteness despite the increasing acceptance of *mestizaje*, the mixing of ethnicities, in Mexico. Ricas crossed certain boundaries and maintained others, and regardless of their displacement from the homeland, they never lost sight of their position as part of Mexico's *gente decente*.

NOTES

For the purposes of this study, all of the quotes from *La Prensa*, with the exception of titles of page headings, have been translated by the author from Spanish to English.

1. The Plan de San Luis Potosí endorsed the principle of "no reelection" for the office of president of Mexico. Moreover, it nullified the 1910 election of Porfirio Díaz, named Madero provisional president, and provided instructions for a national military uprising in Mexico.

2. Susan M. Yohn, "Will the Real Conservative Please Stand Up? or, The Pitfalls In-volved in Examining Ideological Sympathies: A Comment on Alan Brinkley's 'Problem of American Conservatism,'" *American Historical Review* 99, no. 2 (April 1994): 430–37.

3. Alan Brinkley, "The Problem of American Conservatism," *American Historical Review* 99, no. 2 (April 1994): 413.

4. William D. Raat, "Ideas and Society in Don Porfirio's Mexico," *The Americas* 30, no. 1 (July 1973): 47.

5. Ibid., 46.

6. Charles A. Hale, "The War with the United States and the Crisis in Mexican Thought," *The Americas* 14, no. 2 (October 1957): 166. Also see his books, *Mexican Liberal-ism in the Age of Mora, 1821–1853* (New Haven: Yale University Press, 1968) and *The Trans-formation of Liberalism in Late Nineteenth-Century Mexico* (Princeton: Princeton University Press, 1989).

7. The científicos believed that classical liberalism had failed in Mexico, and they looked to a secular and more tangible way of promoting "progress." Positivism appealed

to this group because it emphasized demonstrable science, rather than ideology and religion, as the basis for all truth. Education was a top priority for the científicos, and they established a secular education system, which they believed developed logical individuals who would then promote social order and stability in their communities. The number of public schools in Mexico doubled during the Porfiriato, and religious instruction was replaced with a curriculum that included subjects such as physics, chemistry, history, geography, and the metric system.

8. Mauricio Tenorio-Trillo, *Mexico at the World's Fairs: Crafting a Modern Nation* (Berkeley: University of California Press, 1996).

9. Raat, "Ideas and Society," 52.

10. Richard A. García, *Rise of the Mexican American Middle Class: San Antonio, 1929–1941* (College Station: Texas A&M University Press, 1991), 222.

11. A number of prominent Porfiristas were directly associated with *La Prensa*. Nemesio García Naranjo, minister of public education under Mexican president Victoriano Huerta (1913–14), wrote extensively for the newspaper. Furthermore, Leonides González, a Porfirian exile from Durango, was the business manager for *La Prensa* from 1913 to 1957. His son, Henry B. González, served as a congressman in the U.S. House of Representatives from 1961 to 1999.

12. The page was originally entitled "Página para el Hogar," was then changed to "Página Amena para el Hogar," and by 1929 was entitled "Página para el Hogar y de Sociedad." For this study, I will refer to this section as the "Página para el Hogar."

13. Gabriela González, "Carolina Munguía and Emma Tenayuca: The Politics of Benevolence and Radical Reform," *Frontiers: A Journal of Women Studies* 24, no. 2/3 (2003): 208. Although González's work focuses on left-wing women, her usage of the term "politics of benevolence" can also be applied to the right.

14. Lorraine Dipp de Holaschutz, "Women and the Culture of Modernity in Mexico City and El Paso, Texas, 1880–1900" (M.A. thesis, University of Texas at El Paso, 2005).

15. Onofre Di Stefano, "*La Prensa* of San Antonio and Its Literary Page, 1913 to 1915" (Ph.D. diss., University of California, Los Angeles, 1983).

16. News reports and editorials were not attributed in *La Prensa* until 1914.

17. Quote in Gabriela Cano, "The Porfiriato and the Mexican Revolution: Constructions of Feminism and Nationalism," in *Nation, Empire, Colony: Historicizing Gender and Race,* ed. Ruth Roach Pierson and Nupur Chaudhuri (Bloomington: Indiana University Press, 1998), 111. See also Dipp de Holaschutz, "Women and the Culture of Modernity."

18. *La Prensa*, April 24, 1913.

19. Ibid., December 26, 1914.

20. Ibid., September 16, 1916.

21. The word *matria* was not commonly used in the early twentieth century. The phrase *la madre patria* signifies "motherland" but generally refers to Spain.

22. *La Prensa*, August 24, 1919.

23. Cano, "The Porfiriato and the Mexican Revolution," 111.

24. Before 1923, it is unclear who specifically contributed to this page, as most of the articles were not attributed.

25. *La Prensa*, July 6, 1919.

26. Ibid.

27. Ibid., October 17, 1929.

28. Tenorio-Trillo, *Mexico at the World's Fairs*, 88.

29. *La Prensa*, December 16, 1923.

30. Ibid.

31. Ibid., May 21, 1928.

32. Ibid., November 5, 1928.

33. Ibid., June 5, 1929.

34. Ibid., November 24, 1929.

35. Ibid., December 23, 1924.

36. Ibid., September 27, 1925.

37. Ibid., May 20, 1926.

38. Sister Barbara Miller, "The Role of Women in the Mexican Cristero Rebellion: A New Chapter" (Ph.D. diss., University of Notre Dame, 1980).

39. Cano, "The Porfiriato and the Mexican Revolution," 112.

40. *La Prensa,* November 13, 1928.

41. Ibid., November 3, 1929.

42. Ibid., May 21, 1928.

43. Ibid., December 2, 1928.

44. Ibid., April 28, 1929.

45. Stephanie Mitchell and Patience A. Schell, eds., *The Women's Revolution in Mexico, 1910–1953* (Lanham, Md.: Rowman and Littlefield, 2007).

46. Kathleen M. Blee, *Women of the Klan: Racism and Gender in the 1920s* (Berkeley: University of California Press, 1991), 75.

47. Yohn, "Will the Real Conservative Please Stand Up?" 434–35.

10

Domesticating Fascism: Family and Gender in
French Fascist Leagues

Daniella Sarnoff

As the essays in this book clearly show, women have been a central part of
right-wing movements throughout history. Despite works that have documented female involvement in European fascisms, the longtime understanding of fascism has been that it is an ideology and movement that puts the
masculine, and men, at the center, and the feminine, and women, at the
margins.[1] One of the reasons this has been the case is the rhetorical separation of the notions of public and private in the period and place of fascist developments. The understanding of fascism has continued to be influenced by
the masculinist interpretation that supports the premise that women in
right-wing movements or fascist organization are a paradox that must be explained. There is clear evidence that women joined fascist groups and that
fascist groups were deeply interested in gender ideology and discussed it extensively. Ignoring this aspect of interwar fascism replicates the sexist ideology of the 1920s and 1930s in Western Europe that asserted that women were
most suited—physically, temperamentally, and intellectually—for a life
bounded by private or domestic concerns, and men were best suited for the
public world of politics and business. Hence, the belief that women would be
uninterested or unwelcome in organizations that were clearly engaged in political argument, government organization, or state challenges prevailed.

If, as it appeared, fascist groups placed a premium on traditional ideas of
gender and its relationship to the public and private, then fascism, the argument continued, would not be a clear "home" for women. This view of fascism not only relegated female involvement to the margins of the discussions
and analyses of fascism, but also led those investigating the topic to believe that
one must "explain away" female involvement and account for the supposed

paradox of female activity and interest in an organization that, at times, expressed a belief that women should engage in matters of the home, not the state. And yet this view of fascism, at least as it applies to the French case of fascist leagues of the interwar years, entirely misses an essential component of fascist ideology. The moment when female partisans of fascism participated in large public rallies, marched in the streets in uniforms, and offered the fascist salute, often in the name of maternal concern and domestic preoccupations, is not the paradoxical moment of fascism but the moment it makes the most sense.

In this piece, which addresses leagues—the term used by the extra-parliamentary movements—that operated in France between 1919 and 1939, I consider women as the center of fascism, not necessarily in number but in terms of French fascist worldview.[2] It was the involvement of women and their combined interests in the operations of the French state, as well as the reproductive future of the nation, that made fascism a "logical," if compromised, choice for some French women. Women and gender were not marginal to fascist movements but fundamental to its ideology and to the fascist reordering of the nation. An investigation of women in French fascism and an analysis of the nature of public and private within fascist rhetoric and activities shed light on the operation of gender in fascism and right-wing movements more generally, and make clear the importance of women and gender in the history of fascism.

This chapter, which examines Le Faisceau and La Solidarité Française—two leagues that formed and operated between the wars—considers women to be vital to French fascist movements, as agents within the leagues and as subjects of discussion by the leagues. While women were active as leaders and members, this piece will focus primarily on the rhetoric about women, gender, and family in the leagues.[3] It is essential to bear in mind the extent to which women could be in uniform, espousing racism and violence and marching with the fascist salute, not despite the fact that they were women and mothers but because of it. Fascist leagues made important claims to female allegiance during the interwar years. To appeal to women as those most capable of regenerating France and to glorify their duties as mothers was no marginal matter to the leagues. Motherhood and family were, as the leagues often repeated, the essential cell of the nation. While male members may have been, in number of bodies, the greater force of French fascism, female members better embodied the spirit of French fascism.

To the fascist leagues of the 1920s and 1930s, the family was the focus of immense concern, and the movements spent a great deal of time writing about the "state of the family," exhorting the French to have more children and designing laws that were to help strengthen the French family. The leagues of the extreme and fascist right were not alone in engaging in discussions of the family. In many ways, they echoed much of the interwar discourse on *denatalité*, the role of government in social legislation and family law.

To the leagues, the discussions about the family were important for many reasons in addition to the link to population concerns. While certainly seen as the source of more children and soldiers for France, the family, with its seemingly timeless existence and traditionally ordered hierarchy, was also a primary unit within the organization of the fascist leagues. And, to the leagues, the family was a perfect symbol for the *patrie* itself. The entire family was to be involved in the service of the nation.

The familial or domestic interests of the leagues were often made known through the pages of the fascist press. Recipes and child-care advice were present in the papers of all the leagues and are illustrative of the interconnectedness of gender and family, hearth and home, within what were ostensibly masculine political movements. The propaganda that the leagues espoused about maternal and paternal bliss often effaced the distinction between politics and family and illustrates the ways in which fascism often collapsed the public and private spheres of French life. The leagues did also use separate spheres rhetoric and ideology. However, the leagues most often referred to the private and to family to bind together all parts of French life. Fascists were interested in organizing all areas of existence, from the most intimate to the most remote, under the rubric of the state. This meant that the leagues were intensely concerned with the operations of French family life, but also that they envisioned the family as a model for the state. This inevitably meant encouraging women to embrace the systems of fascism, as well as bringing fascism into the home. Fascism became part of the philosophy of maternal and paternal domestic harmony, and domestic bliss would be one of the aspirations claimed by league propaganda. In this way, fascist groups politicized the private and domestic spheres and considered private and domestic issues to be of great political and public importance.

The organization of the leagues themselves often gave primacy to the family unit. For example, the significant role of the family within the Faisceau, founded in 1925, is illustrated by the league's structure. Along with soldiers and producers, one of the primary organizing groups in the Faisceau was the family.[4] Georges Valois, the leader and founder of the Faisceau, supported the idea of adding the family as an important representative sector and called it "the constant force of the country, the creative force and the force that reigns for eternity." In creating a platform for the family in the league, Valois and the Faisceau noted that the assembly of family heads would be responsible for "always placing with the head of the state all the sentiments, desires, and interests which are represented in life by the cell of the nation, by the father and mother of the family."[5]

The Faisceau advocated the philosophy that the family and the nation were the same, part of an organic whole, and they did this in no uncertain terms. In their pamphlets and posters, the Faisceau often honed the theme of the nation as a family. As a 1926/27 pamphlet noted,

For fascism:
The family is the cell even of the nation
The Region is like an extension of the family home
And the Profession an extension of the family workshop
The Region and Profession must be organized with a view to the
    prosperity of the family.
The Nation, it is the assembly of families.[6]

The union and unity of the family and the nation was a general theme repeated numerous times in organization pamphlets and meetings. The Faisceau was intent on promoting the importance of the family and its role as the "primordial cell of all well-organized societies."[7]

An assembly of the Faisceau in Reims in 1926 called attention to the importance of the family, specifically the head of the family, within the structure of the Faisceau, and of all human activity:

What then is the great, the true spirit of creation? The spirit of the
    family.
Where is the great motor of human activity, of fertile activity? It is at
    the heart of the father of the family.
Where is the great faculty of saving, the great force that maintains
    the man on the land of his fathers, that makes the walls of the
    city rise? At the heart of the mother of the family.

Clearly, the family was the center of all that was right and productive in the league, in French society, and beyond. Both men and women were essential in and through their conceived roles within the family. By extension, as the Faisceau proclamation continued, it was the family that made all parts of civilization—politics, cities, and business—possible. As the assembly went on to say,

Where is the great spirit of sacrifice . . . ? In the love of the father and mother, who renounce the minutes that go by for the hour when the child could inherit the fruit of their renunciation. There is no greater force than that which moves a man for his children; there is no greater force of civilization than that which makes a mother save for her children. . . . The spirit of the family is the true founder of cities, the real force of arts and crafts. . . . It is this force that fascism wants to make represented in the national state.[8]

The primacy of the family to the Faisceau is an example of the connectedness of the private and the public. The familial philosophy espoused at the Faisceau assembly was also, of course, a proclamation of political ideology. And the family could be used for very specific political ends—to highlight the inadequacies of the current regime or to attack competing ideologies.

Other French fascist leagues also considered their proclaimed support of family as indicative of their superior political philosophy and often used the nation and family interchangeably. Or the fascist groups judged other political movements by the family ideal they espoused. The Solidarité Française, founded in 1933 by the *parfumier* François Coty and led by retired colonial infantry commander Jean Renaud, used the family ideal as a point of discussion and invidious comparison to the ideas and ideals of communism. In *Corporatisme et reforme de l'état,* the Solidarité Française author described the Marxist home: "His wife is a distress to him, his children elude him: Society seizes him. One requires, in addition, that he expel God from his home as well as his soul. He is no longer anything but a moral wreck and a puppet, stripped of all human liberty."[9]

While Marxism in this description was responsible for the worst possible family relationship, corporatism, the Solidarité Française's grand economic and social plan, claimed the inverse: "Corporatism is, to the contrary, the politics par excellence of the family as we conceive of it and as we always live it in France."[10] In the place of the greed and moral bankruptcy that fascists saw in liberal capitalism, the corporatist model was to offer communal business ties with the government; this was supposed to illustrate the benefits of group allegiance over individual selfishness. Corporatism, the fascists claimed, would offer a harmonious alternative to the class warfare and rancor of capitalism and communism. In the Solidarité Française piece, the attack on the disharmony promoted by both capitalism and communism in the public sphere extended to the domestic sphere. This rhetorical leap is not surprising given this chapter's larger argument about the intrinsic connections of the political and economic to the familial within fascist ideology. So, for the Solidarité Française, the economic strife created by both capitalism and communism had affected the family and brought it to a point of conflict. The solution would be a family and economic ideal that brought all the aspects of life, including family and business, together peacefully—corporatism. And so, for the Solidarité Française, corporatism and fascism were the ideology and politics par excellence of the family.

Beyond considering themselves advocates of the family, fascist groups were particularly interested in the role of women in the future of the French nation. Leaders of the leagues expected women to be wives and mothers, and men to be husbands and fathers, bearing the responsibility of producing more children for France. The connection of familial happiness, cooking, and fashion to the politics of fascism helped create and reinforce the idea that the domestic was political. In this way, the leagues reframed the concepts of public and private and used them for their political gain. The recasting of gender ideology and the reframing of separate spheres ideology enabled extreme right and fascist groups to support female suffrage (a seemingly progressive move) while at the same time advocating "traditional" female roles. For the Solidarité Française and Le Faisceau, domestic life was central to their reordering of the nation. Because of this, we see that the leagues directly appealed to women to be part of their individual fascist groups and the politics of the nation.

A Solidarité Française leaflet posted in Marseilles in 1934 illustrates the league's interest in domestic life, as well as the intertwining of gender and the nation:

Frenchwomen Remember!!

<u>1914</u>   The negligence of our politicians provokes the war with Germany. And the women suffer! And the mothers weep!

<u>1926</u>   The mistakes of the same politicians cause the ruin of the domestic economy. And the women work and toil!

<u>1934</u>   Always by the fault of the same politician misery settles itself in our homes! And the little ones are hungry! And the grown are without future!

TOMORROW   Civil war more horrible than the other will be in the streets! And the women will again be widows, mothers without children, girls sacrificed or defiled!!

THERE IT IS   The work of the socialist-communist Jewish-Franco-Masonic politic.

STAND UP   Brave women of France! Everyone united without distinction of social rank! None of us will be spared!

SUBSCRIBE   Without delay to the advantage of our propaganda. It is not beyond our role to want to block the route to the International, sower of Misery, of Disgrace, and of Death.

For your Children! For your Homes! For the Country!
JOIN THE WOMEN'S SECTIONS OF
SOLIDARITÉ FRANÇAISE[11]

This leaflet makes clear a number of aspects of the Solidarité Française view and its expectations of women. Women, according to the publication, are repositories of family memory. They are specifically charged with keeping the war, financial woes, and 1934 (a year of protests that saw the victory of the leftist Popular Front over the rightist and fascist antiparliamentary leagues) in mind. The mere remembrance of these events would lead women to join the Solidarité Française. Further, these political and public occurrences are cast in this poster as important because of their domestic and personal impact. The good Frenchwoman would know and remember all of this for the sake of her children, her home, and her country, which became one and the same for the Solidarité Française. As mothers and wives, women would see that the movement would help them in their familial roles, or at least understand their daily concerns of maternity and domesticity.

Within the Solidarité Française, there was frequent "comingling" of political and domestic concerns. Alongside such notices as "The freemason is the executor of the basest deeds of the Jews" and "The reform of the state means the end of Judeo-Masonic dictatorship,"[12] which lined the pages of the league's periodical, *La Solidarité Française,* one could find recipes for pork terrine, headcheese, and Irish stew. The latter appeared in the paper's elaborate women's section, "La maison et le monde," which regularly offered book reviews, articles on fashion and gastronomy, and general "words to women."

In linking the racist language of the Solidarité Française with the preoccupations of family and female life, one of the accomplishments of the women's section was the domestication of fascism. The newspaper managed to normalize a politics of exclusion, antagonism, and violence within the context of everyday concerns. The inclusion of feminine touches in the newspaper, whether in the form of sketches of the new season's plumed outfits, recipes, or advertisements, diluted the violence of the other pages; however, it also served to legitimate it. The message was that the violence of the Solidarité Française was necessary in order to respond to the dangers posed by seeds germinating in the Third Republic. According to the Solidarité Française, certain interwar forces (real or imagined)—communism, the Popular Front, the low French birthrate, the impotence of the parliamentary system— threatened to take away the comfort and stability of life, as symbolized by well-dressed wives who also made terrine of pork. The pages of the newspaper helped resolve what may strike us as a conflict between masculine political violence and assumptions of women's more pacifist and passive support.[13] *La Solidarité Française* helped weave together the political and domestic interests and concerns of fascism, and, in doing so, justified political violence when the very core of French life was being undermined. It was through the *pages des femmes* that the leagues reconfigured ideals of separate spheres. In this reconfiguration, fascist politics created a new woman and mother who was a combination of old and modern. This new woman supported the image of woman as mother, and she left her own home to attend meetings and rallies. She argued that women are and must be the moral voice of the nation, and she donned a blue shirt and beret, gave the fascist salute, and espoused violent anti-Semitism in the name of morality. She cooked and cleaned and tended to her family but also joined the Solidarité Française and attended meetings. Descriptions of this new woman often used traditional language to emphasize the need for women's public engagement in the renewal process. In this way, however, the Solidarité Française provided the terminology and the ideology that their female members could use to launch into public politics and activism.

Another equally strong appeal to women's participation appeared in August 1933 in *L'Ami de Peuple,* a paper owned by François Coty and, in addition to *La Solidarité Française,* another voice for this group. The article asserted that women had always maintained the family and domestic household, ensured children's protection, protected social mores, and guaranteed peace in the world. The author pleaded with women, "Don't disinterest yourself from the public world; we reserve for you a vast field of activity in our reforms."[14] The appeal to women clarified that their traditional world—children, domesticity, and peace—was not separate from the concerns of the public world: "Women must hurry to replace the honor in the family, and one will see in that more clearly the management of the business of the world."[15]

This sentiment was clearly expressed in a May 1934 article in *La Solidarité Française* that called upon women to join the league for a variety of reasons. It began by invoking the work that Frenchwomen had always done, according to the league: "*La Française* has always excelled in the management of her household; she has always known how to raise her children, with tenderness [and] love, and to have them understand where the real work is, to inculcate them into this marvelous public-spiritedness which earns the admiration of the world and which benefits the whole nation." In mentioning "public-spiritedness," the Solidarité Française was both invoking a general nationalism and alluding to a variant of "republican motherhood." While the Solidarité Française was not advocating republican motherhood per se (and not advocating the republican form of government!), this was a nod to women's specific skills or perceived talents to socialize their children and convey to them a sense of national belonging and responsibility.

The article continued by placing women at the center of the future of the French state:

Also, if . . . peace one day is to find its place, it will have to be at the behest of the French mother.

Mesdemoiselles, Mesdames, your work is to act on our behalf, we are a force, you are another. . . . Be with us, for you, for your children, for your husbands, for your homes, and, above all, so that France can live.[16]

This appeal to women invoked the possibility of world peace through motherhood and reinforced the idea of women as innately connected to pacifism. Indeed, the Solidarité Française believed that the French women who were most capable of securing world peace were French mothers. Further, while the beginning of the statement addresses mesdemoiselles and mesdames, the paragraph tried to convince women that they should join the Solidarité Française for the sake of their children, their husbands, and their households, which most single women would not have. Despite its original overture to married and single women, the league focused its attention on married women and mothers in particular. The political appeal to French women to join the Solidarité Française was also a political appeal to French women to have babies. In the end, the involvement of mothers is sought because of the league's conception of the nation: France lives through its mothers. This would certainly place lesbians, women who did not marry, and women who could not or chose not to reproduce outside the interest of the Solidarité Française.

The discussion of marital status of women in France, particularly the fascist view thereof, was shaped by the impact of World War I. For many years before the Great War, there had been deep concern in France about the declining population. The war exacerbated those fears at the same time that the great loss of life, especially among young adult males, made it more difficult for many young women to follow their prescribed gender role to marry and reproduce. The reality of the interwar years was that even more women would remain single, by choice or due to the demographic impact of the war. Moreover, the view of women as potential mothers was not entirely inconsistent with league attitudes toward men as fathers or potential fathers. The May 1934 appeal underscored the population concerns of the nation and acknowledged a biological necessity for mothers—that their very being meant the reproduction of the French population. The exaltation of the French mother, and the equation of the family and the nation, also reinforced the organic and reproductive nature of the *patrie,* which the Solidarité Française and other leagues promoted.

Children were also targets of league propaganda. In addition to their youth groups, the leagues appealed to children in other ways. The Solidarité Française had its Maison Bleue, where family members could enroll in jujitsu class, mothers could sew, and everyone could take gymnastics.[17] The Faisceau's attempt to attract children is clearest on the "Page de la famille" of the group's periodical, *Le Nouveau Siècle.* The paper featured cartoons, puzzles, and advertisements for toys. A 1925 article heading appeared to appeal directly to children: "A nos amis les enfants . . . et à leur parents." The article provided a primer on the Faisceau's historical and political understanding of the trials and formation of the French family:

> Here is the page which each week will endeavor to be the smile of this paper, the father's page, the mother's page, and the children's page, as the home does not exist but in view of the child and through the child. The child is the show of union between the husband and wife, the cement that binds them, the perfume that embalms them, the finery that embellishes them.
>
> But the love of our children . . . cannot stop at our own family; it extends to families of our circle, of our village, of our province, of our country. All families stand together. . . . We will examine some of the great problems that solicit our attention: *Natalité,* the education of children, the reciprocal duties of a couple, how to be a good father, a good mother, a good citizen, how to maintain and develop love.[18]

In many ways, the page was made for adults, to teach them how to build a proper household, to impart the proper gender roles to their children, and to initiate sons and daughters into the cultural propaganda of the Faisceau. However, when children read the page—lured by cartoons, the "rebus" puzzle, and advertisements for toys—they too would be inculcated with the Faisceau's cultural ideology.

Through their focus on the family, the leagues could accomplish many things. Philosophically, they could use the immortality of the family to give their own leagues a timeless and organic feeling. They could also use the family to emphasize an ideology that shirked individual expression, which most fascist groups maligned as emblematic of decadent liberalism. They could use the traditional hierarchy of the family to legitimate the hierarchy within fascist movements while still opening up the movement to women, as women were central to the function of family. And they could use the rhetoric of family, the replication of bourgeois language on family, to give the leagues respectability and perhaps to validate a politics of exclusion and antagonism in the name of the family.

The centrality of women to the continuity of the nation was clear, and indeed fascists were well aware that this also made women central to the conception and operations of the state, including representation in the structures of government. By engaging in child rearing and politics, the domestic and the political, the private and the public, women strengthened the nation. The fascist belief in the interconnectedness of those areas of life was the reason why the leagues could and did support female suffrage, a right not yet held by French women. In fact, at a time when many moderate and leftist parties did not wholeheartedly support female enfranchisement, many fascists did. Many right-wing and fascist groups could also support female suffrage with the hope and belief that women would vote more conservatively than men. The belief in women's supposed conservatism was likewise held by leftist groups and was an often unspoken argument for their lackluster support of women's suffrage. And some fascist leaders were opportunists to a certain extent. It seemed inevitable that French women would share this right with their English, German, and Scandinavian sisters, so in anticipation of this eventuality, these leaders believed that perhaps it would be best to court them on the topic. The question of female suffrage was certainly part of public discourse in France in the 1920s and 1930s.[19] However, an even more complete answer to the question of why fascist groups would support female suffrage, and why they would find female partisans who not only shared a fascist ideology but also took seriously the possibility of women's political engagement, is that women's maternal and domestic identities and concerns were entirely compatible with fascist notions of politics and the state. In fact, many fascist leaders and organizations considered female enfranchisement to be the essential component of French political and moral regeneration.

And so, in speaking to women as important political actors, fascist groups were not merely being opportunists or exposing a paradox of their ideology, but rather bringing a view of women's political activity into alignment with fascism's ideology. As argued throughout this piece, fascist rhetoric and ideology often broke down the distinction between the political and the private.[20] This left women with a great deal more access to politics than traditional conservative, liberal, or communist views offered. Fascists supported female enfranchisement because they believed that it was a way to clean up politics—just as women cleaned up households—but also because they could insert familial concerns into politics. Both of these reasons were consistent with fascist views of the *patrie* as a *grande famille*.

Conclusion

Seeing the family and the domestic as the organizing and stable principle in French fascism meant that there could be movement and opportunity for women in these leagues. It also meant that the operation of gender and the role of women in leagues were complicated. The primacy of the family and women in fascist doctrine is one of the reasons why and one of the ways in which the leagues eradicated the distinctions between public and private spheres. All of the leagues examined in this chapter had female members. Women could be part of the group's internal police force, or they might be involved exclusively in its social work—raising money for children's summer camps and collecting clothing for the poor and unemployed. And they could be involved in both. Women's participation was essential to carrying out the plans and programs of the leagues. Part of league organization work was to create and enforce the power of the family, both symbolically and in the state; to turn the movement into a large family; and to turn the state into a grand family. To that end, all members in the league were essential components of the league family, playing their distinct roles in molding the workings of the group. However, women were particularly important, as their presence already lent itself to the sense of the league as a family.

Family and domestic ideology and imagery permeated all areas of the leagues. French fascists considered the family, which women represented, to be the center of their universe. To the leagues, all aspects of French life—politics, history, economics—could be understood through the family: The Great War's horror was partially measured by its destruction of the French family. The Parliament of the Third Republic was reprehensible because it did not support the family. Parliamentarians, Jews, and Masons were intent on destroying real French homes. The weak franc was ruining homes. The structure of labor did not encourage large families. And women were the family.

This is not to say that men were not an essential part of the French family, nor that patriarchy was absent from fascist ideals. The centrality of women and the family to the fascist leagues' vision of the future France did not necessarily mean that women would achieve emancipation and equality through

French fascism. Yet it was through family, women, and gender relations that fascists made sense of their world, and, as such, women and domesticity were not marginal to the fascist project but were its core. Through their structure—having women work for the movement, attend public rallies, give speeches, and write for the press—it is clear that the leagues depended on women's public action.

Further, the feminine traits that the leagues emphasized—nurturing, sympathy, quiet sedentary interests—were matched by supposedly nonmaternal ones, as expressed by female members who marched in the streets in uniform and gave fascist salutes at league parades. The combinations of these female activities and traits—nurturing and giving fascist salutes—may strike us as tense juxtapositions and unsustainable contradictions; however, considering these qualities and actions through the lens of fascist domestic ideology helps us resolve those conflicts. There *were* great tensions within league discussions of women and their role in the movement, as well as their role in the nation. The adulation of family and of domestic activities helped ease those tensions and made sense of the woman who had short hair, helped support her family with wage labor, or agitated for female suffrage. Fascists could accept flexible female roles and identities. These female identities could be understood and justified when the protection and strengthening of the family was invoked. And this could be an easy charge for fascism, as the philosophy of the groups revolved around the family: recognizing it, reinforcing it, promising its exaltation.

Women's roles or potential roles as mothers were what made them—in the logic of French fascists—natural partisans of fascism. That they were innately suited to the movement was evident in their desire to care for children and husbands, run the household, and serve proper food. Women's reproductive and domestic concerns and abilities could explain and justify their engagement in all areas of service to the nation. Women as well as men would be called upon to rid the nation of the forces that appeared to be standing in the way of their natural calling—to form families—whether these be Jews, Socialists, Parliament, or the unstable franc.

By speaking about women, family, domestic life, and politics in the way that they did, fascists also presented women as essential to the future of the France they envisioned. As symbols of the family, women would be at the center of French fascist life and the center of the nation. It was in this manner, which included collapsing the ideas of discrete public and private realms, that French fascists were successful in both privatizing the public and politicizing the private.

NOTES

Unless otherwise noted, all English translations from French are the author's own.

1. Roger Griffin, *The Nature of Fascism* (London: Routledge, 1993); Michael Mann, *Fascists* (Cambridge: Cambridge University Press, 2004); George Mosse, *The Fascist Revo-*

lution: Toward a General Theory of Fascism (New York: Howard Fertig, 2000); Stanley G. Payne, *A History of Fascism, 1914–1945* (Madison: University of Wisconsin Press, 1995); Robert Paxton, *The Anatomy of Fascism* (New York: Knopf, 2004); Robert Soucy, *French Fascism: The First Wave, 1924–1933* (New Haven: Yale University Press, 1986) and *French Fascism: The Second Wave, 1933–1939* (New Haven: Yale University Press, 1995); Zeev Sternhell, *The Birth of Fascist Ideology* (Princeton: Princeton University Press, 1994) and *Neither Right Nor Left: Fascist Ideology in France* (Berkeley: University of California Press, 1986); Michel Winock, *Histoire de l'extrême droite en France* (Paris: Editions du Seuil, 1993) and *Nationalism, Anti-Semitism, and Fascism in France* (Stanford: Stanford University Press, 1998). All of these texts consider fascism, in France and beyond, as nearly exclusively male. In addition to Victoria de Grazia, *How Fascism Ruled Women: Italy, 1922–1945* (Berkeley: University of California Press, 1992), and Claudia Koonz, *Mothers in the Fatherland: Women, the Family, and Nazi Politics* (New York: St. Martin's Press, 1987), some works on France, and beyond, give attention to women and gender. See Martin Durham, *Women and Fascism* (London: Routledge, 1998); Melanie Hawthorne and Richard Golsan, eds., *Gender and Fascism in Modern France* (Hanover: University Press of New England, 1997), which focuses on culture; Samuel Kalman, *The Extreme Right in Interwar France: The Faisceau and the Croix de Feu* (Aldershot: Ashgate, 2008); Cheryl Koos, "Fascism, Fatherhood, and the Family in Interwar France: The Case of Antoine Rédier and the Légion," *Journal of Family History* 24, no. 3 (July 1999): 317–29; Kevin Passmore, ed., *Women, Gender, and Fascism in Europe, 1919–45* (Manchester: Manchester University Press, 2003); and Daniella Sarnoff, "In the Cervix of the Nation: Women in French Fascism, 1919–1939" (Ph.D. diss., Boston College, 2001). There have also been a number of books looking at women in racist and extreme right politics in the United States during the same period: Kathleen M. Blee, *Women of the Klan: Racism and Gender in the 1920s* (Berkeley: University of California Press, 1991), and Glen Jeansonne, *Women of the Far Right: The Mothers' Movement and World War II* (Chicago: University of Chicago Press, 1996).

2. "League" was the designated term for these organizations, which, by their own choice, were not political parties, as a criticism of political parties was inherent in their existence. A law of 1936 would force many of them to reform into official political parties.

3. See Sarnoff, "In the Cervix," for a discussion of all aspects of women in French fascism.

4. Archives Nationales de France (hereafter AN) F7/13208, pamphlet attached to police report of November 13, 1926.

5. *Le Nouveau Siècle*, special issue, February 1926, AN F7/13209.

6. Pamphlet from Bordeaux Faisceau, 1926, AN F7/13210. See also Le Prefet de la Marne à Ministre de l'Interieur, report, Chalons, April 25, 1927, AN F7/13212.

7. *Bulletin du Faisceau des Combattants et des Producteurs du XVII Arrondissement,* premiere année, no. 1, March 1, 1927, AN F7/13212.

8. *Le Nouveau Siècle*, June 19, 1926.

9. Louis Mouilleseaux, *Corporatisme et reforme de l'état—Méthode—Programme—Action—La Doctrine économique et social de la S.F.* (Paris: Editions documentaires de la Solidarité Française, 1935), 126–27.

10. Ibid.

11. "Françaises Souvenez-vous!!" Solidarité Française poster, stamped December 18, 1934, Direction Générale de la Sûreté Nationale, AN F7/13239.

12. *La Solidarité Française*, June 23, 1934, and May 18, 1934.

13. On the masculinity of nationalism, see George L. Mosse, *Nationalism and Sexuality: Middle-Class Morality and Sexual Norms in Modern Europe* (Madison: University of Wisconsin Press, 1985). For appeals to women based on pacifism, see Christine Bard, *Les filles de Marianne: Histoire des féminismes, 1914–1940* (Paris: Fayard, 1995).

14. *L'Ami de Peuple*, August 2, 1933, AN F7/13238.

15. Ibid.

16. *La Solidarité Française*, May 12, 1934.

17. Physical training classes did have practical purposes for a paramilitary group, of course, but they are discussed more as an innocent childhood interest and indulgence, rather than in the name of fitness for political ends.

18. *Le Nouveau Siècle,* December 13, 1925.

19. In the interwar period, the suffrage campaign took on a new force and tone as French suffragists saw women in many other countries gain the right to vote. In 1919 the Chamber of Deputies voted in favor of extending the right to vote to women. After years of debate, the Senate rejected the bill in 1922 and did so again in 1925, 1932, and 1935. For more general discussion, see Steven C. Hause with Anne R. Kenney, *Women's Suffrage and Social Politics in the French Third Republic* (Princeton: Princeton University Press, 1984), and Bard, *Les filles.*

20. Paul Smith offers an examination of the left, right, and center political parties that gives some sense of the similarities among them with regard to feminism and the general reluctance to thoroughly support female suffrage. See Paul Smith, *Feminism and the Third Republic: Women's Political and Civil Rights in France, 1918–1945* (Oxford: Oxford University Press, 1996), 63–103.

11

The Volksgemeinschaft and Its Female Denouncers in the Third Reich

Vandana Joshi

As an undergraduate in German studies in the 1980s, when I started looking for material on Nazi Germany it was commonplace to find pictures of ecstatic, exuberant groups of German women swooning at the sight of the führer, some of them extending their hands to reach out and touch him. I often wondered what was so appealing about Hitler that he was able to play the pied piper, seducing the womenfolk as rats to their destruction. Or was it just clever propaganda of the Third Reich? When I read accounts of feminist historians, the reality of the Third Reich seemed just the opposite. Women were projected in this narrative as victims of an extreme right-wing regime that deprived them of the rights hitherto won through a concerted feminist movement. This account of a backward march usually started with the description of the women's emancipation movement before 1933, outlined its gains, and then presented an endless list of antifeminist measures: a ban on double earners; the introduction of marriage loans for those willing to give up jobs, marry, and procreate; a compulsory labor service; a restriction on female students to 10 percent in the universities; recognition of women primarily as childbearing machines, and so on. Psychological and Freudian explanations existed on both sides of the spectrum. The conservatives projected Hitler as an object of desire for the female masses, while the feminists steered clear of anti-Semitism by declaring it a men's disease that resulted from their unresolved Oedipal crisis. Represented by Margarete Mitscherlich, this latter view looked for unconscious psychological motives for the development of anti-Semitism, such as the projection of hate for fathers, the shifting of incestuous desires onto a different group of people (i.e., Jews), aggression, and rivalry, all of which were of relevance primarily to the male psyche.

Most such early feminist efforts to save women from the evildoings, seen as primarily male, were tied to a feminist identity-building project, whose hallmarks were escapism at worst or victimhood at best. The question of female agency in Nazi crimes could not be ignored for long, however. It surfaced in a *Historikerinnenstreit* (women's historians' dispute) of sorts with the publication of American historian Claudia Koonz's book *Mothers in the Fatherland* in 1987 and German historian Gisela Bock's scathing criticism of it. I shall return to this debate later. Even there the question of the roles and responsibilities of women in the Third Reich was cast in a paradoxical manner, swinging between proverbial Madonna and whore. Women were either portrayed as innocent victims or villains.

This chapter breaks this mold and trudges through the grey zone in which women are seen sometimes defending themselves against abuse and other times getting others into trouble in the name of serving the regime. In any event, they acted as cogs in the wheel to make the persecution of social outsiders possible. The Third Reich is generally considered an example of an extreme right-wing totalitarian dictatorship, which commanded total subservience from its people. This chapter, however, will draw attention to ordinary people's—specifically women's—consent and collaboration rather than coercion as a key aspect of the functioning of the totalitarian regime. It shows how women themselves opened up most intimate and private spaces for policing and investigations. In other words, the chapter demonstrates how the right-wing politics of racial and political intolerance spread far beyond the committed cadre and state functionaries to encompass ordinary, seemingly apolitical citizens, who voluntarily collaborated with the regime in very intimate and personal spheres of life.

I have divided the chapter into two sections related to two different kinds of spaces in which women acted as willing agents of the Nazi state by hounding out the "suspects" and opponents to create a *Volksgemeinschaft* (people's community) free of internal enemies. I start with the most intimate sphere, the family, and then go on to explore spaces in semipublic or public domains of assembly, work, and socialization. This is done by placing women in the context of their mundane existence and studying a particular mode of behavior, namely denunciation, that turned private women into political citizens. The chapter goes beyond exemplary and spectacular cases, such as the much-talked-about profiles of Helene Schwärzel and the blonde Jewish underground denouncer Stella in Berlin, or the few selected cases of female denouncers discussed by psychologist Helga Schubert in *Judasfrauen*.[1] In this work, she contested the assumption that women are merely sensitive, tender, motherly, sympathetic, creative, and authentic. They were also evil and dangerous in their own way. Schubert chose her cases from the dossiers of the Volksgerichtshof (Nazi Supreme Court), which handed out mostly death penalties to the defendants. All her denouncers were invariably females, and all the victims were males. This helped her create a stereotypical and essentialist image of women as scheming and vicious to the extreme of taking their victims' lives.

My work is founded on the assumption that the Nazi system operated at many judicial, extrajudicial, and arbitrary levels, and the phenomenon of denunciation cast its shadow far beyond the Volksgerichtshof. My research base is therefore much wider, encompassing ordinary women caught in the web of interpersonal relationships in their private world of domesticity. As a result, I have arrived at an understanding that is far more nuanced and complex. However, before proceeding further, let me first elucidate the meaning of denunciation.

The term "denunciation" entered the German penal code for the first time in the postwar era as a legal concept. It was declared a crime against humanity. The Kontrollratsgesetz Nr. 10 of December 20, 1945, mentioned denunciation in Article II, Section 1c as "persecution on political, racial, or religious grounds without considering if it damages the national right of the country, in which the act has taken place." Citizens often presented their denunciations as support and loyalty for the regime. In official correspondence, this is called *Anzeigeerstattung* (reporting in a neutral sense) rather than *Denunziation,* exalting it as citizens' duty to the state, even though the Nazi officialdom was aware of its real nature. After the collapse of the Nazi regime, it was clearly seen as an act of political collaboration. However, this "political act," more often than not, had a hidden agenda.

Drawing on 366 samples from the surviving 6,808 Gestapo files on the city of Düsseldorf, my study contends that the Gestapo was omnipotent and omnipresent, and it opens a window onto discreet spaces, which were being policed by ordinary citizens who invited Gestapo officers as dispensers of justice.[2] Even though not every denunciation resulted in high-level drama and executions—as in the spectacular cases of denouncers such as Helene Schwärzel, Stella, and those featured in *Judasfrauen*—every denunciation resulted in some kind of drama played out at the level of the family, neighborhoods, and community on a regular basis. I reconstruct some of these small dramas of everyday life here.

I have selected a few representative cases for detailed treatment in this chapter. For an essay of this length, I prefer this approach to a statistical survey, as flesh-and-blood stories communicate the workings of the system better than faceless data. The practice of denunciation revealed some explosive situations within the family, where raging battles ensued between its members over power and influence in the household. A disconcerting yet fascinating finding in the Gestapo files was the denunciation of husbands by their wives. It was a red thread that ran through almost all selected categories, including the Jews, racially foreign workers and minorities, Communists, and the Law Against Malicious Gossip. A close examination of such cases suggested that there were gender troubles at the core of most of them.

The female accusers reported the infractions in two phases. They started with the erring behavior of their husbands, which led to regular quarrels at home and often ended in bouts of physical violence against the other family members. Subsequently, the husbands were portrayed as enemies of the state, regularly cursing the regime and its leaders. The basic agenda was, therefore, presented in a camouflaged manner by labeling husbands as opponents of the state. I now turn to a few examples.

Denunciation in the Private Sphere

Frau Hof filed the following report at the office of the police chief in Düsseldorf, and it found its way into the Gestapo records on June 10, 1939.[3] The text contained grammatical errors and the language was not very refined, which could be expected of a woman from a working-class milieu. Frau Hof's complaints were as follows:

> This report concerns my husband. I am forced to take this step, for there is no other way out. I married him in 1926. I have been fond of him though he used to drink a lot, which he continues to do even today. Soon after our marriage, he told me one day, "I have not married you to feed you, you lazy pig! Go and work!" For the sake of peace I went to work as a cleaning woman. Before I got to know him, he had lived with a whore. He looks at all women as whores, including me. I have recently got to know that he lived with such a woman. He also suffers from venereal disease. He himself never told me all this when we got married. He often beat me up. He has always been left oriented, now even more so than earlier. I have reported him to the health authorities to find out if he still has the disease, but to date I do not know the status. On May 12 he beat me again, and on June 6 he beat me half dead. He sprang upon me like a wild beast and kept hitting me till I turned blue, and on September 17, 1933, he hit me with a bucket and broke my leg. I got three stitches, and a small side bone was fractured. No one can love such a man. I have filed a divorce case against him where I also enclosed the statement of the doctor.
>
> And now to the main point: he is left oriented; I cannot take it any longer. He always curses the government. He says that he would never become a National Socialist. He has a loaded pistol and often threatens to shoot. On June 6, when he beat me, he took out the burning coal from the fireplace and wanted to set the house on fire. He wanted to kill me. He said that Hitler and Göring were criminals, the government would soon go down, and the reds would come; all those who were ruling would be hanged.[4]

The Gestapo inquired in all seriousness into the matter and came to the conclusion that Frau Hof had denounced her husband for private reasons, and that all charges of maltreatment leveled against him were correct. However, since he issued seditious statements before his wife in private, there was no fear of spreading discontentment in public. He was fined for keeping an unauthorized weapon and allowed to go home after a warning. One could clearly decipher from the rather bulky file that Frau Hof's personal troubles outweighed the political ones. The choice to denounce her husband came as a last resort after the long, drawn-out process of negotiations. Herr Hof himself admitted that she had filed a divorce suit and sought physical protection from him. But when he prepared to leave, she stopped him. This story was a classic one of an oppressed wife whose self-respect and dignity were hurt time and again, yet she put up with it. All bonds of love broke the day she realized that her husband had cheated on her and contracted venereal disease from a prostitute. Beyond this point, she could no longer make peace, and she reported him to the health authorities. The husband's subsequent beating and bullying traumatized her completely and led her to resort to police protection.

Here the female body became a site of power relations—of domination and subordination in the conjugal life—and, interestingly, a site for resistance and subversion. Frau Hof's denial of access to her body was an act of resistance, which led to intensified physical violence. It was at this point that Frau Hof sought the intervention of Nazi authorities to "discipline and punish" her husband on two levels. At one level she invited the medical authorities to examine her sexually diseased husband, and at another level she sought the intervention of the political police, who might put her home "in order" by disciplining her morally erring, drunk, and violent husband. In appealing to the health authorities, she was responding to the eugenic propaganda and policies of the regime that had the concept of a "healthy racial body" at their core. Reporting a sexually diseased husband as unfit for intercourse and reproduction might have helped the regime implement its eugenic policies just as much as it would have helped the wife out of the "sexual disorder" at home. However, the dossier does not contain further information on the follow-up action taken by the health authorities.

Such cases of battered and mishandled wives surfaced even in instances where they had long divorced their husbands but used this newfound opportunity to teach them a lesson. In the following case, the matter became complicated, as it involved an ethnic Pole named Herr Schmidt. In 1940 his ex-wife accused him of issuing seditious statements, listening to foreign broadcasts, and being sympathetic to Poland.[5] The witnesses included her son (Schmidt's stepson) and his girlfriend, as well as the wife's neighbors. They all had something to report against the accused. The stepson's girlfriend, who was Polish in origin but later Germanized, testified against Herr Schmidt, lending credibility to accusations against him.

In his defense, the accused projected himself as a responsible divorcee who "laid his weekly salary before his wife on the table" but objected to the immoral relations between his stepson and his girlfriend. He thought that they were seeking revenge upon him. However, his self-defense, a good report from his office, and his responsible attitude toward his family did not suffice because of his Polish origins. He was sentenced to six months of imprisonment on charges of malicious gossip and listening to foreign broadcasts. This was a classic case of a wife gaining added strength as a mother and successfully using her son as a witness to get the "interfering" divorced husband out of her way.

It cannot be reconstructed from the sources how aware the wives were of the consequences of their denunciations, or whether they had really wished for the verdict. It was as if the wives removed all blinds and curtains from the glass windows of their houses for the inquisitive and searching eyes of the Gestapo functionaries. This exposed their lives and troubles to observers and investigators, who then forced entry into their homes. Equipped as these onlookers were with arbitrary powers, it was difficult for the wives to determine what the Gestapo functionaries could lay their hands on and what they would spare. Subsequent searches, interrogations, and houses turned upside down snatched the agency from the initiator of the process. The accusing wives could not wind back the process. But at the same time, it is worth noting that they neither withdrew their cases (except for one against a mother-in-law) nor appealed for mercy.

Wives sometimes used denunciation as a communication strategy, sometimes as a defense mechanism, and yet other times as a weapon to discipline and punish their husbands in "incorrigible cases." This is indicative of their subjective perceptions of conjugal relations, which they politicized, thereby breaking the taboo attached to talking about household violence or abusive behavior. The sources do not permit us to reconstruct how they lived "unhappily ever after" or coped with the loss of their incarcerated husbands' income, as in the case of Frau Schmidt.

These and many other everyday dramas enacted within the four walls of the home give us vital insights into the private-public dichotomy in the National Socialist regime from three vantage points—that of the Gestapo, the accuser, and the accused. For the Gestapo, it was the seriousness of the political crime that mattered. If the husband was just drunk and abusive, it did not matter much. However, it was problematic when a "serious enemy" of the state, such as a Communist, a Pole, or a Jew, went unreported. Even if it led to the breakup of the family, the state did not hesitate to intrude into the private realm, exhibiting total disregard for the marriage partners' right to privacy and for breach of trust by the spouse.

The same privacy of the household, however, became dangerous, isolating, and alienating for a wife who was being beaten, deserted, or betrayed by her partner. Consequently, she herself chose to invite political intrusion into the private realm. Though these power struggles originated in the family, the whole discourse entered the realm of the state and politics as soon as state agencies, witnesses, and onlookers entered the scene. The power that a woman thus acquired and practiced was a sociopolitical one, in that political and social concerns were drawn into the private realm. The "big world" of politics operated in miniature form in the "small world" of the family.

In the husbands' behavior, one indeed sees the big world of politics quietly moving into the small world of the family when the public realm became dangerous. These husbands, who led a public life at work, were living a dual existence of obedience in public and defiance in private. The dictatorship silenced them in political matters, which compelled them to withdraw into the inner realm of privacy at home. Comments typical of the Gestapo, such as "politically the accused has not come into notice before," bore testimony to this silence in public. The husbands came home frustrated and drunk and criticized their leaders, the state, and whatever else they thought was wrong with the system. Husbands saw the household as a space for unmasking, for releasing tensions and anxieties that accumulated during the day's work. It is another matter that even this private realm became so colored with the hatred and aggression of the outside world that it no longer remained safe for the act of unmasking. The political did not remain isolated from the private, domestic, and personal. The big world of politics did not stand above the small world of family. The two became inextricably intertwined.

Women used denunciation not only against their husbands but also against his relations. Parents-in-law and sisters-in-law often fell prey to the avenging daughters-in-law. There was an added dimension of racial victimization here. On May 13, 1941, a Jewish woman named Frau Frankenberg approached the serving vice president to tell her tale of woe.[6] She was chased out of every rented house soon after she moved in. A Gestapo officer, she claimed, informed her landlord that she was wanted by the police. This officer was acting at the behest of her sister-in-law, an Aryan, who did not want her to live in peace. Frau Frankenberg said that this forced her to change houses more than fifty times. On May 10, 1941, she was arrested by the Gestapo for concealing her identity and later shifted to Ravensbrück, where she eventually died on September 14, 1942. The Gestapo reports portrayed her as a mentally unstable person unfit for any questioning. The Gestapo also reported that she tried to jump out of the deportation transport.

Another Aryan sister-in-law urged her brother to denounce his Jewish wife, which resulted in her death.[7] Mr. P. married the Jew Frau P. on March 18, 1908. They were colleagues before marriage and were initially happy. But twenty years later, in 1928, Frau P. apparently began to create trouble, which may have been due to menopause. She became nervous and jealous and picked fights with her husband. In 1934 Mr. P. filed a divorce case, which he withdrew upon his wife's apologies. In 1944, however, Mr. P.'s sister Frau K. moved into their house after hers was bombed, and the fights began all over again, this time more frequently between the sisters-in-law. On February 18, 1944, Frau P. asked Frau K. to leave the house after a fight. The Nationalsozialistische Deutsche Arbeiterpartei (NSDAP) block leader "volunteered" to help the family. Frau K. hesitated at first but later accompanied her brother to see the block leader, and they both spoke, among other things, of Frau P.'s antistate attitude. The block leader advised Mr. P. to divorce his Jewish wife.

In March 1944, as the situation at home became "unbearable," Frau K. denounced her Jewish sister-in-law for sedition. Mr. P. supported his sister in front of Gestapo officers and, on March 20, 1944, filed for divorce. The case was decided on April 5, 1944, declaring Frau P. to be the guilty party. She was arrested by the Gestapo on March 22, 1944, and sent to Auschwitz in July, where she ended her life in October.[8] In this case, Frau P. became a stranger in her own home when her Aryan sister-in-law moved in. She was an "undesirable" element in the house, which her Aryan guest "rightfully" snatched from her.

Denunciation in Semipublic and Public Spaces

From the realm of the family we now turn to the neighborhood and other semipublic or public spaces where ordinary Aryan women acted as racial watchdogs of the Volksgemeinschaft in hounding out Jews. In the following case, various neighboring women first fought their own battles with a Jewish woman living in mixed marriage and then eventually joined hands in 1943 to persecute her collectively. The file on the fifty-three-year-old Jew Frau Gurke, married to an Aryan, opened with charges of regularly cursing the neighbors and the state and disturbing the peace of the neighborhood.[9] The denunciation letter urged the Gestapo to take appropriate action against the "Jew."

The complainants characterized the Gurke couple as asocial and seditious. The Gestapo's inquiry revealed that the Gurkes had served an eviction notice on their tenants, the Rosenthals, who turned hostile toward them. Constant harassment led Frau Gurke to file a defamation suit against Frau Rosenthal. The inquiry concluded by saying that it was a case of trivial domestic gossip. According to neutral parties, the fighting couples had lived in perfect harmony for years. The Gestapo nonetheless instructed Frau Gurke to exercise restraint as a Jew, and the case was suspended.

The case file opened again in September 1943 with a letter from the Security Service Head Office to the Gestapo urging them to take action against Frau Gurke. The most interesting part of the file was a denunciation letter signed by the Gurkes' neighbors Frau Rosenthal, Frau Eberwald, and Frau Jochum and enclosed with the Security Service letter. These women were determined to get rid of the Jew and her Aryan husband at a time when the deportation of Jews was in full swing. The letter was written in Frau Eberwald's handwriting on her husband's letter pad, denoting the denouncer's professional middle-class standing. It was not addressed to any particular office or person, so it could be assumed that it was posted to various authorities who might take action; ultimately, an army welfare officer took the initiative of forwarding the letter to the Security Service. The letter read,

> As a soldier's wife (a prolific mother with six children), I hereby make a request to sternly warn my neighbor, a full Jew, for once. It has been observed that the Jew has adopted a particularly provocative stance in the last few months of war. Ever since my husband has become a soldier, the situation has become unbearable. The Jew pours two barrels of liquid manure on the hedge on hot days so that one cannot sit outside. I work a lot outside and even eat there. She continuously belches loudly with open mouth, making me feel sick. This goes on the whole day. But she does not do this while talking to others nor while sitting for hours in the bunker. It is only toward us that she turns provocative in every way.
>
> In these times one is happy if one got an hour of relaxation, but one does not get it and boils in rage. I have been patient for many years, but it has become too much now and I cannot bear it any longer. On top of this comes the preferential treatment that the Jew enjoys when the firewood is being distributed in the nearby bunker. Another neighboring woman whose forty-five-year-old husband has been a soldier for the past four years asked the polisher for some firewood. She did not get it, and the Jew got two carts full. . . . Let it be known that Herr Gurke is a cheat. One should revoke his war invalid's card, which he has obtained through unfair means. If something is not done fast, we, soldiers' wives of the neighborhood, would resort to self-help and take action against the Gurkes. There is no other way out.
>
> Hail Hitler,
> Frau Eberwald
> Frau Rosenthal
> Frau Jochum
>
> Note: Frau Rosenthal is a war widow from 1914. Her son-in-law died in Russia, leaving three children behind. Her own son is at the front. The party has warned Gurke three times. The fourth time she was not there, and we have no idea about what followed. . . . Frau Jochum is the soldier's wife I mentioned in connection with firewood.

It was a crafty, well-thought-out letter by a highly aware and literate Aryan housewife who knew what kind of ingredients a denunciation letter required to make it a palatable recipe for authorities. She consciously conjured up black-and-white images of the denounced and the denouncers, assigning all evil to the Jew and her husband and all virtues to the denouncers, projecting the latter as prolific mothers and self-sacrificing soldiers' wives. The Jew, on the other hand, was portrayed as a mischief maker and a quarrelsome woman constantly inventing tricks to annoy the neighbors. While the denouncers were deprived of essential items like firewood, Frau Gurke was apparently living in abundance and luxury.

Equally interesting in the letter was the silencing of some of the facts, which may have distorted the neat projections. Repeated mention was made of the war years and the resultant hardships for ordinary Aryan women like the denouncers, but the letter was silent about the fate of the Jews during this period. The letter demanded that the Jew be "warned sternly," even though the denouncers were aware that the couple had already been warned thrice and that the Gestapo were still searching for them. While Frau Eberwald wrote with much pride that all the complainants were soldiers' wives, she completely overlooked the fact that Frau Gurke was a soldier's wife too. It is the Gestapo remarks that inform us that Herr Gurke was a war veteran who sustained major injuries in World War I, incapacitating him for the rest of his life. The denouncers not only disregarded his sacrifices for the fatherland but even projected him as a cheat. They were totally unaffected by the couple's serious illnesses. Frau Gurke was a diabetic and was under medical observation when the Gestapo visited her. Similarly, the invalid Herr Gurke suffered from heart problems and epileptic fits. One wonders how such politically vulnerable and physically ailing people could afford to be provocative toward their neighbors all the time. The denouncers hardly bothered to fabricate seditious charges against them, something that was done in similar cases. Anti-Semitism coated the social envy of some and the differences of others. As a Jew, Frau Gurke was taught to behave herself and not indulge in fights of these kinds with her neighbors if she wanted to avoid harsher state police measures. Throughout the case, the Gestapo seemed to be more considerate toward the denounced couple than the denouncers. They had to be so, tied as they were to their obligation toward an invalid war veteran. If Frau Gurke survived the Third Reich, it was because her invalid Aryan husband supported her to the bitter end.

Another denunciation letter was written on September 15, 1941, and was addressed to the Schwarzes Korps, the SS mouthpiece. It read as follows:[10]

Dear Schwarzes Korps,

After much thought, I have decided to write to you, to inform you of a matter relating to the Jewish question and in strict confidence. Before this, I must point it out that it is not now that my Aryan consciousness has awakened. In 1903, when I was a young woman, a gentleman came to visit us and asked me if I had listened to the beach concert. I said, "I did not go there."

He said, "How sad! There was German music there."

"What was that?" I said.

"Pieces of Meyerbeer!"

I replied, "Since when has Meyerbeer become a German? He is a 'Jud' [a derogatory reference to a Jew]." And then I gave a piece of my mind to them on the question of race. . . . Now back to the point, I want to know who is obliged to wear a star? Is a Jewish woman [though converted since her childhood], and married to an Aryan freed from wearing the star? [The Gestapo remark in the margin said yes!] I find that disgraceful. I feel that she should wear the star and her husband should do the same. For me, an Aryan who marries a Jew is a thousand times more condemnable than the Jewish spouse. In our neighborhood there are two rich Jewish sisters living with their Aryan partners. One of them has often been seen without a star; the other one is not seen in public at all. The Aryan husbands had to give up their jobs as conductors after the Jewish laws were passed. One of these couples travels a lot, and the Jewish woman lives in Aryan hotels. Is it allowed?

The family in our neighborhood possesses a house with thirty-two rooms. They have two Aryan maids, other helpers, and two central heating systems. My daughter and I are both widows. We have a small house, not even enough coal to heat our house properly, and we have to manage with that.

Hail Hitler

Frau Wonder

The author presented herself as a convinced fighter for her racial community who apparently required no racial indoctrination. Her letter was written at a time when it was mandatory that Jews wear the Star of David on their breasts, making vulnerable all those who could have otherwise hidden their identity through their highly assimilated existence in large parts of Germany. Many such cases came to light due to active policing by neighbors and relations.

Professional rivalry among women working in the same firm could also lead to sly denunciations, as the next case demonstrates. A thirty-five-year-old sales girl named Miss Wollenberg was repeatedly denounced in her workplace. The first denunciation letter was sent anonymously, but in the second one, two names appeared. This second letter, written on March 2, 1943, was a rather crude piece of writing containing innumerable grammatical errors that have been corrected in the following translation:[11]

We have been writing repeatedly to the district party leader, but till today without any follow up. I would now like to very politely request you to urgently take up the matter of Miss Wollenberg, employed in the firm Brenningmeyer. Miss Wollenberg has relations with men from the Gestapo that involve intimate matters. Her father is a full Jew; so are her mother and brothers. She travels to Litzmannstadt, from where she gets news and smuggled objects. One can make out from her conversations that she is oriented against the present government. She presents a danger through exchange of letters from Litzmannstadt. She hides all that she gets from different Jews, like money, clothes, silver, and other stuff. Frau Wollenberg does not deserve a place as sales girl in the firm. There are definitely more upright women who can take her place. . . .

With German greetings,
Two sales girls from the same firm

We would like to also request you not to name us before Wollenberg.

Signed by
Frau Hess
Miss Persil

Professional rivalry, jealousy, cultural inferiority, fear of reprimand from the boss, who seemed to be cultured and favorably disposed toward the accused, and fear of the apparently high and mighty who were allegedly also on good terms with Miss Wollenberg compelled the denouncers to remain faceless at first. Yet their desire to harm Miss Wollenberg was so intense that when anonymous denunciation did not work, they filed a signed report. However, they turned faceless again when confronted with an inquiry, which was initiated immediately. Within ten days, the Gestapo came up with the following findings about the accused woman.

Miss Wollenberg was racially Aryan and was orphaned at the age of two, after which her aunt, married to a Jew, assumed her guardianship. This mixed couple had two sons, one of whom left for France in 1938. The other was evacuated to Minsk after he married a Jew. Both sons were considered first-degree *Mischlinge* (offspring of a mixed couple), as they belonged to the Jewish community. Miss Wollenberg referred to her foster parents as her own parents and their sons as her brothers. Although she had her own house at the time of the action taken against the Jews in 1938 (*Reichskristallnacht*), she kept returning to her foster parents' house. She frequently went to the authorities to learn of her brothers' whereabouts. According to her employer, who seemed quite satisfied with her work, she had lately been deployed in the air force as a news assistant and sent to Hamburg.

The Gestapo report ended by saying that since Miss Wollenberg had become Jewish in her ways, she was no longer fit to serve in the air force and should be dismissed. Thus, her former female colleagues were eventually successful in robbing her of her new job.

Conclusion

Let me now delve a little deeper into women's tendency to target people within their "separate sphere," primarily their neighbors, relations, and colleagues. I wish to place this problematic "separate sphere" within the broader context of gossip and its function in a racial society, and within the traditional sphere of motherhood and housewifery. These issues were in the eye of the storm during the *Historikerinnenstreit* that ensued between Claudia Koonz and Gisela Bock in the late 1980s.[12]

Bock launched a scathing attack on Claudia Koonz for locating women's guilt in Nazi crimes in their "separate sphere," that is, in their functions as dutiful wives and nurturing mothers. For her part, Bock exonerated all housewives and mothers, arguing that most female perpetrators were active in "nontraditional functions outside the home" as unmarried, paid workers employed in the destructive state machinery. Therefore, what was at stake for Bock was not their quantitative participation, which was comparatively low, but rather the qualitative attitudinal change in women, which she ascribed to the brutalization of the female sex as part of their socialization in the Nazi public domain. In what follows, I argue that this brutalization of the female sex extended to their private sphere as well, and that it was in this sphere that they were more visible in comparison to their professional counterparts.

When Bock talked about housewifery as a profession, she only took into consideration the work that it entailed, leaving out the leisure activities that were part and parcel of women's everyday lives. Gossip was an integral part of this. It bound women together and excluded all others who did not fit into the Volksgemeinschaft. Gossip peppered with anti-Semitic prejudice became a palatable recipe for the Gestapo and the media alike. These agencies considered it worthwhile to religiously write down all denunciations, at least for the purpose of further inquiry. So, a practice that was earlier confined to oral tradition acquired the status of the written word and was institutionalized by the state and its agencies. Oral exchange of information, which was at once recorded by the Gestapo, worked to the advantage of working-class and lower-middle-class women, who were more likely than men to be locked up in a largely oral world. The Gestapo's willingness to record their denunciations telephonically and orally encouraged even less articulate women to present themselves and feel important.

This informal power of housewives and mothers, which was elevated to the level of the state and politics, ought to be taken seriously. This variant of the politicization of the private and the privatization of politics[13] needs to be accounted for when dealing with the question of women's roles and responsibilities, especially in the context of right-wing dictatorships, which in the traditional feminist understanding deprive women of all agency or reduce them to just obliging housewives and mothers. The private realm did not just involve housekeeping, cooking, and looking after children; it also involved keeping a watch on the neighbor, cooking up malicious stories, eavesdropping, and guarding the neighbor's morality and sexuality—things that housewives and mothers seemed to be doing with much relish in the Third Reich. This activity required no formal gathering at a fixed place. Shop floors, house floors, doorsteps, staircases, and bunkers provided space enough for gossip to do its rounds. This showed in Frau Wonder's concern about the disturbing prosperity of the Jews living next door, and in Frau Hess's and Miss Persil's sly reporting of Miss Wollenberg in an attempt to make her jobless. Such denunciations entailed conniving with other anti-Semitic, anti-Polish, anticommunist, and antisocialist neighbors and converging all material and personal interests to harass them. This became evident in Frau Eberwald's, Frau Rosenthal's, and Frau Jochum's repeated acts of denunciation against their Jewish neighbor Frau Gurke on frivolous grounds. Conversations across the coffee table and over the fence took on anti-Semitic coloring, just as living rooms turned into venues for drafting letters of denunciation signed by groups of disgruntled Aryan women.

While at the top institutionalized power flowed from the Gestapo headquarters, where men were the majority, denunciatory practices show how power was exercised by ordinary people at the informal levels of household and community—and that the regime provided ample scope for ordinary women to do so. It is the duality of denunciations that make them fascinating for social historians. One component is political (real or fabricated), but the other is social and may reflect personal, moral, domestic, sexual, civil, or gender discords. This double edge explains why the practice of denunciation was so widespread. Had it not offered the possibility of hiding the social behind the political, its use might have been far more restricted. This aspect of denunciation broadened the consensual social spaces of the dictatorship and offered ordinary people a chance to play the game of power once in a while. This power eventually merged with the formal, institutionalized state police power. Thus, the process of politicization did not work from above alone; it was equally activated by people, frequently women, from below. This unleashed a process of criminalizing interpersonal relations in everyday life in the Third Reich. In all these informal situations, gender power was not just visible; it was almost fatal.

NOTES

This chapter is largely inspired by my earlier work and is published here with the kind permission of Palgrave Macmillan. See Vandana Joshi, *Gender and Power in the Third Reich: Female Denouncers and the Gestapo, 1933–45* (Basingstoke: Palgrave Macmillan, 2003).

All English translations from German are my own, and all the names of individuals discussed in the chapter are pseudonyms.

1. Cf. Inge Marßolek, *Die Denunziantin: Die Geschichte der Helene Schwaerzel* (Bremen: Temen, 1993). In this work, Marßolek presents a detailed case study of an ordinary

woman who gained prominence and media attention because she denounced Carl Gordeler, who carried a huge prize on his head as one of the main conspirators of the July 1944 bomb plot to assassinate Hitler. Schwärzel won the money but could not enjoy it, and she faced a prison sentence once the war was over. In *Stella* (New York: Simon and Schuster, 1992), Peter Wyden tells the story of a high-profile Jewish woman who denounced many underground Jews and acquired the name "U-Boot," or "the submarine of Berlin." See also Helga Schubert, *Judasfrauen: Zehn Fallgeschichten von weiblicher Denunziationen im Dritten Reich* (Berlin: Aufbau, 1990).

2. The Gestapo files on which this chapter is largely based are housed in the Düsseldorf State Archives (hereafter HStAD) and vary in size and treatment. The Gestapo relied more on oral communication and informers where dangerous enemies (e.g., Communists) were concerned. On the other hand, detailed inquiries through personal testimonies were made for minor infractions. The reports presented a sanitized version of the events, having no trace of torture and third-degree measures widely used to extract information. Nevertheless, reading between the lines could render clues as to the sense of brutalization and intimidation the victims may have suffered.

3. HStAD RW/58–13944.

4. I have corrected grammatical and other errors in the translated quote for smoother reading.

5. HStAD RW/58–24739. For the same individual, I found a file in Schloß Kalkum (situated on the outskirts of Düsseldorf) containing the judgment of the Special Court. Schloß Kalkum reference: Ger. Rep.114/Nr.1737.

6. HStAD, RW/58–64395.

7. Rita Wolters, *Verrat für die Volksgemeinschaft: Denunziantinnen im Dritten Reich*, Forum Frauengeschichte Band 19 (Pfaffenweiler: Centaurus, 1996), 61–63.

8. It is important to note that spouses living in mixed marriages had the protection of law if the Aryan spouse continued to support the Jewish one.

9. HStAD RW/58–22416.

10. HStAD RW/58–2908.

11. HStAD RW/58–45964.

12. This debate can be followed in the journal *Geschichte und Gesellschaft*. See Giesela Bock, "Die Frauen und der Nationalsozialismus: Bemerkungen zu einem Buch von Claudia Koonz," *Geschichte und Gesellschaft* 15, no. 4 (1989): 563–79; Claudia Koonz, "Erwiderung auf Gisela Bocks Rezension von 'Mothers in the Fatherland,'" *Geschichte und Gesellschaft* 18, no. 3 (1992): 394–99.

13. Cf. Alf Lüdtke, "Formierung der Massen, oder Mitmachen und Hinnehmen? Alltagsgeschichte und Faschismusanalyse," in *Normalität und Normalisierung*, ed. Heide Gerstenberger and Dorothea Schmidt (Münster: Westfälisches Dampfboot, 1987), 26.

12

Mothering the Nation: Maternalist Frames in the
Hindu Nationalist Movement in India

Meera Sehgal

Since its emergence in the early twentieth century, the Hindu nationalist movement has worked to make a monolithic, exclusionary vision of Hinduism the basis of Indian citizenship. Based on a religious right-wing view of the nation, this movement espouses Hindu supremacist and xenophobic ideas, to be achieved through an authoritarian and militaristic political culture. Its preferred state would relegate all non-Hindus to second-class citizenship. Since the mid-1980s, women's organizations in the Hindu nationalist movement have been faced with the task of recruiting and retaining women in a hypermasculinist movement whose dominant collective action frames typically did not address the life experiences of women. Given these constraints, Hindu nationalist women's organizations have mobilized women by constructing maternalist frames that valorize and politicize women's reproductive capacity and have thereby carved out more active roles for their constituents in civil society and within the larger movement.

The ascendance of Hindu nationalism, achieved only in the closing decades of the twentieth century, accompanied the rise of feminist and women's rights discourses in India, and the latter provided the immediate context in which the former fashioned its newly viable political project. This situation presented the challenge of how to transform a deeply patriarchal movement into one that could engender an active, public loyalty among Hindu nationalist women, while keeping them in a subordinated position vis-à-vis Hindu men. This challenge has been met through organizational strategies deployed by Hindu nationalist women's organizations that appropriate notions of women's empowerment, but in forms largely denuded of meaningful consequence. Central to the success of the Rashtriya Sevika Samiti (National

Female Volunteers Association; hereafter the Samiti), a Hindu nationalist women's organization and the focus of my research, has been its ability to make the popular discourse of "Mother India" resonate with the everyday life of its members. It does so by blurring the distinction between public and private spheres so that women's reproductive activities are framed as a core aspect of Hindu nationalism.

The Mother India master frame,[1] in which the Indian nation is imagined as a mother, has been hegemonic in India since the 1940s and has been used by a variety of social movements ranging from religious reform to anticolonial. The male-centered Hindu nationalist movement uses this master frame to represent India as a Hindu mother (of the nation's heroic sons), victimized by foreign (read Muslim) invaders and in need of protection (in turn provided by her sons). This framing of Mother India aims to attract men's devotion and ultimately confers social power and political agency on men.[2] It reinforces the public/private divide, situating Hindu nationalist men within the public sphere as powerful actors and relegating women to the private sphere as passive victims. In contrast, the Samiti constructs maternalist frames[3] that reorient the Mother India master frame to extend women's roles as nurturers and caretakers from the home front to the public sphere as society's mothers.

My analysis is based on ethnographic research in north India that extended over twenty-one months in 1995–97 and included participant observation at rallies, neighborhood meetings, festivals, and a paramilitary camp; twenty-eight in-depth interviews and approximately thirty informal extended conversations with Samiti activists; and an analysis of primary documents, including lectures, physical training manuals, inspirational life stories of legendary women, and periodicals.[4] The Samiti is a hierarchical, militarized, cadre-based women's organization with more than a million members, and it plays a powerful, agenda-setting role for women within the larger Hindu nationalist movement.

The Samiti's maternalist frames bridge the public/private divide by highlighting women's contribution to sociocultural reproduction at macro, meso, and micro levels. At the macro level, by reconstructing Mother India as the "mother of the universe," the Samiti discursively transfers power and agency from men to women. At the meso level, the Samiti represents itself as a mother—the ideological creator and sociocultural reproducer of Hindu nationalist female subjects, the future mothers of the Hindu nation. Finally, at the micro level, ideal Hindu nationalist women are framed as mothers of individual Hindu children. Motherhood becomes a social movement activity that spans the public/private divide, making it impossible for participants and observers to ignore women's key role in the movement.

This chapter is divided into three sections. In the first, I provide an overview of the gender politics of the Hindu nationalist movement and situate the Samiti within this context. In the second, I examine the significance of the Mother India master frame and how the Samiti transforms it to suit its goals.

In the third, I focus on a Samiti leader who amplified aspects of the maternalist frame to justify her activism, highlighting her attempts to resolve the inconsistency of advocating motherhood for Hindu nationalist women while choosing to remain childless herself.

The Samiti and the Gender Politics of the Hindu Nationalist Movement

In spite of its millions-strong membership and extensive political power, the Hindu nationalist movement paints its constituent base as a preyed-upon majority desperately needing defense against non-Hindu "Others," particularly Muslims (less than 14 percent of the population), who are represented as dangerous to the Indian nation. It manufactures a siege mentality among its followers, a collective emotional and embodied habitus of fear and persecution in relation to various "Others" who are framed as the cause of virtually all of the Hindu community's problems.[5] The homeland, strictly understood to belong to Hindus, is presented as vulnerable to defilement by "outsiders" and therefore in need of defense by fearless, virile Hindu nationalist men. This narrative has enabled a long history of violence by Hindu nationalists against Muslims in India, including riots and pogroms.[6] The movement reinterprets and homogenizes the diversity of Hindu practices and texts to construct a militantly aggressive masculinity. The "failures" of Hinduism have been connected by Rashtriya Svayamsak Sangh ideologues to "indisciplined . . . effeminate, weak" Hindu men and their inability to protect the Hindu motherland.[7] These men were to be fashioned anew by the training of mind, body, and intellect into disciplined, unified, and militant men dedicated to the Hindu nation.[8]

The most important organization within the movement is the RSS, an all-male body boasting a membership of several million men. Since its establishment in 1925, the RSS has created a diversified network of affiliate organizations, reflecting the movement's expansion into civil society, political party processes, and local and state governance. The most significant organizations created by the RSS are the World Hindu Council (VHP) and the Indian People's Party (BJP). Each organization has women's wings that deal with "women's issues," but these are lower in the hierarchy of the movement. Women were largely invisible in the movement until the mid-1980s, following a strategic shift that sought to target women, "untouchables," and the poor for recruitment.[9] The post-1980s period was characterized by the intensified, militant, highly visible activism of various women's wings.

The tactical recruitment of female participants required a reframing of women's traditional roles as central to the movement's agenda. This was accomplished in gender-segregated women's wings like the Samiti, where Hindu nationalist concepts have been reinterpreted to suit the needs of female recruits who primarily come from upper-caste, middle-class, petit bourgeois urban Hindu families that see their caste and class interests as jeopardized by neoliberalism and caste-based affirmative action. This reinterpretation involves a considerable degree of stigmatization and appropriation of elements from widespread discourses in Indian society, which are then recombined with elements of the Hindu nationalist ideology, thereby modifying and reinventing them.[10] In gender-segregated spaces, women reinterpret religious epics and Hindu nationalist concepts in ways that valorize the feminine, resonate with their lives, and locate their concerns as primary and significant to the movement and the nation.

Female activists in the movement travel to often distant cities unaccompanied by family members, bond with other women, assume leadership positions, move their bodies in nontraditional ways (through physical exercises), and receive validation for expressing their anger against Muslim men. By widening the scope of women's customary practices, valorizing women's reproductive labor, and reinterpreting women's power as extending beyond the home, these female wings enable women to feel valued for performing familial roles about which they oftentimes have little choice. The brahminical Hindu ideology of *pativratya* (literally "husband worship"), which "historically has informed the institutional structures and social practices of Indian society," is subordinated to reproductive labor, now valorized as essential to the movement's success.[11] The Samiti's reinterpretation of traditional myths and legends in ways that are relevant to modern life plays a significant role in making the movement attractive to women. Participation in the movement gives traditional women a legitimate opportunity to engage in politics.

The Hindu nationalist movement increases its legitimacy by having female participants. They help normalize its hate-filled agenda by subtly weaving it into the everyday fabric of Indian society, by ensuring that its ideology gets discussed in the bedrooms, living rooms, and kitchens of ordinary people and percolates into children's socialization.[12] For this, the movement capitalizes on women's roles as reproducers of biological and cultural systems. Women run their households according to Hindu nationalist dictates, teaching their children and neighbors songs, stories, and games that propagate Hindu nationalist conceptions of morality; boycotting Muslim-owned shops; using informal networks to spread rumors about Muslim violence during riots; and providing food and managing children at Hindu nationalist rallies, campaigns, and meetings.[13]

The Samiti is the most powerful of the women's organizations in the movement. It was founded in 1936 to function as parallel but subordinate to the all-male organization, the RSS. It maintains intimate ties with the RSS through informal networks, and its membership is composed predominantly of the female relatives of RSS men. Most women in leadership positions in the movement have received the Samiti's training before circulating to other organizations. It is hierarchically and geographically organized into branches at the neighborhood, city, district, state, and national levels.

The Samiti's main activities include neighborhood meetings, annual camps (teacher training and paramilitary), conferences, festivals, marches, demonstrations, and hunger strikes supporting a variety of Hindu nationalist campaigns. It owns a publishing company that produces hagiographies, activist training manuals, magazines, pamphlets, and books on female role models, Hindu nationalist history, geography, songs, prayers, and games. Through its organized activities and publications, the Samiti promotes an activist ideal of "Indian womanhood." Role models replete with symbols from the life stories of historical and legendary women exemplify the ideal politically active Hindu nationalist woman.

At the national level, the Samiti has twenty-eight full-time organizers (*pracharikas*)—celibate single women who work in different zones of the country. This position is vested with considerable power and moral authority. All organizers are expected to dedicate their lives to providing direction to the movement. Using single celibate women helps the Samiti address the dilemma of running a separate women's organization with female leadership positions that require a full-time commitment when its ideology states that a woman's primary obligation is to her family.[14]

Celibacy desexualizes these organizers and decreases anxieties about their sexuality. In upper-caste Hindu society, the sexuality of single women is widely viewed as potentially "dangerous," requiring containment within heterosexual patriarchal boundaries. The Samiti's pracharika position draws on a long-standing Hindu tradition of renunciation and asceticism, which frees women and men from familial obligations[15] and symbolizes spiritual purity and selflessness. Still, most Samiti activists do not choose nor are asked to renounce their families or to take vows of celibacy. The RSS has approximately four thousand celibate male organizers, compared with the Samiti's twenty-eight.

An examination of the Samiti's literature over time reveals a shift in emphasis from wifehood as the model for virtuous Hindu womanhood to the elevation of motherhood above all other feminine roles. In 1996 the Samiti published a book titled *Motherhood, Leadership, Action* devoted exclusively to the stories of women classified as exemplary mothers and leaders. These stories were based on an older 1990 Samiti publication (*Women to Remember Every Morning*), from which the category of ideal wives was removed and the remaining tales were reorganized to emphasize maternity and leadership.[16] This change aligns with the Samiti's increasing deployment of motherhood as a tool in the Hindu nationalist movement's arsenal.

The Samiti's Maternalist Frames

Constructing maternalist frames that politicize motherhood is not unique to the Samiti. In modern history, women have frequently been portrayed by nationalists as biological and cultural reproducers of the nation. As is the case with these movements, the Samiti has used maternalist frames to transcend the Hindu nationalist movement's prescriptive gender ideology, which limits women's primary role to that of caretaker of children.[17] Historian Carolyn Strange points out that maternalist ideology can mobilize women for movements with radically different goals, ranging from Nazism to maternal pacifism. The tactical advantages of using the idiom of maternalism are considerable. The imagery of mothers taking to the streets makes their message more acceptable to a broad spectrum of observers and has been one of the most potent devices to mobilize previously apolitical women.[18]

The Samiti's discourse of motherhood builds on a preexisting nationalist master frame that portrays the Hindu nation as an embodied, gendered, anthropomorphic entity—a young woman. In the Hindu nationalist movement, the Mother India frame is represented through the visual iconography of a map of India in which a Hindu feminine body symbolically represents the Indian nation. Two dominant versions of this iconography are used in movement literature. The first displays a woman, with the bearing of the goddess Durga, sitting on a tiger and holding aloft the Hindu nationalist flag; she is superimposed on the map of "Greater India" (encompassing neighboring nation-states). In contrast to this idealized, "pure" Hindu past is the image of Mother India in chains and torn into parts, superimposed on a fragmented, partitioned map of contemporary India. These images are prominently displayed on booklets, posters, calendars, leaflets, stickers, and New Year cards that circulate in the movement.

Mother India represents the personification of the nation as female, "where the motherland is a woman's body and as such is ever in danger of violation—by 'foreign' males/sperms,"[19] requiring the protection of male citizen warriors. By using this imagery, the Samiti evokes a gendered portrait of the nation metaphorically located in space and time. Thus, the image of India as a young mother and a nation "expresses a spatial, embodied femaleness: the land's fecundity, upon which the people depend, must be protected by defending the body/nation's boundaries against invasion and violation."[20] The Mother India image also expresses a temporal metaphor in that "the rape of the body/nation not only violates frontiers but also disrupts—by planting alien seed or destroying reproductive viability—the maintenance of the community through time."[21] Rape of women therefore becomes a metaphor of national or state humiliation.[22] Among Hindu nationalists, the 1947 Partition of India is symbolically portrayed as the rape and dismemberment of Mother India by "alien" and "sexually predatory" Muslim men. This is an emotionally powerful hegemonic trope that encapsulates the sense of victimization and humiliation of the entire Hindu community.[23] As Bacchetta puts it, "The Sangh presents her as a chaste mother, victimised (by Muslims) and declares that she needs the protection of her 'virile' sons, the 'men with the capital M.'"[24]

Although the Samiti symbolically constructs both "the Hindu woman" and India as mother of the universe, its macro-vision of motherhood is not laden with the typical masculinist Hindu nationalist overtones of female victimization (the raped and brutalized Mother India) that requires protection or revenge by male citizen warriors. Instead, the Samiti's maternalist frames project a powerful vision of mothers who calmly assert their right to operate in the public sphere as part of their supposedly "ancient" Hindu tradition.

This powerful image of motherhood at the macro level consequently merges the nation, the family, and the home so as to extend and justify a more direct and active role for women in the public sphere. As Usha Tai Chatti, the head of the Samiti in 1996, explained, "India's land is mother-like. . . . Each and every woman from here is looked upon from a maternal point of view. Mother, mistress of the household, inspiration of the home—she is the incarnate form of India's land. This universe is my home, the entire society is my family—this view has been given to us by Hindu culture. This only is mother-India's feeling of motherhood."[25] In this view, the duty of Samiti activists is to harness the power of mothers and to envision themselves as universal mothers. In another publication, a Samiti leader exhorts rank-and-file women with these words: "All you activists of the Samiti have to fill your hearts with tenderness and accordingly transmit this feeling of service and care, not only to each corner of India but also to foreign countries. Only a mother can, through her loving touch, stop the destruction born from the womb of materialism and can change the direction of social life."[26]

In this vision of global Hindu supremacy, India, by virtue of being a "mother," should spiritually lead other nations. Here the Samiti draws upon an orientalist vision of India as an essentialized land of spirituality, with women representing the source of spiritual virtues.[27] Explaining to its members that "mother-India was the progenitor of the universe in the past and can still be in the future," the Samiti skillfully amplifies and extends the Mother India frame to address the impact of corporate globalization on middle-class urban Indian women in the 1990s: "When we observe the increasing impact of multinational companies on the nation's life, consumerism, materialism, the fall of immortal Hindu life values, the various kinds and forms of women's exploitation, cultural pollution, the absence of a national character, and the threat of hostility from foreign nations, then we remember the words of the Samiti's founder and leader, revered Lakshmibai Kelkarji—'that from an emotional, intellectual, spiritual, and cultural perspective, India has been the mother of the entire universe.'"[28]

In its 1996 magazine *Vishambhara* (Mother of the universe) commemorating the Samiti's sixtieth anniversary, an editorial points out the centrality of this macro-vision of motherhood for the Samiti's roles for women: "The name of the convention's commemorative volume, indicative of the preceding sixty years of the Samiti's doctrinal and general work, has been kept *Vishambhara*. *Vishambhara*—the one who nurtures the universe, the one who gives a womanly life perspective—mother. The Rashtriya Sevika Samiti has regarded mother-Durga, the mother-India-like progenitor of the universe, as its revered god. That all Indian women may ultimately don *Vishambhara*'s mantle of intelligent motherhood in the form of the universal mother has been the Samiti's continuous effort." The Samiti reconstructs the Mother India master frame as a motivational frame by splicing together goddess worship traditions and nationalism to make it resonate with its members' experiences: "I am present in many forms in all the workings of the entire universe. I only am Lakshmi, Saraswati—I am the ensconced ruler among all the gods. The entire universe takes birth through me and ultimately coalesces back into me. Actually this only is the self-knowledge of the Indian woman. It is this self-knowledge that presents to her universal role."[29]

At the meso level, the Samiti is equated with a mother whose responsibility is the cultural reproduction of ideal Hindu nationalist women, the future mothers of the Hindu nation. The Samiti uses motivational frames to portray itself as contributing to women's development by fulfilling the duties of a mother toward her children. A national leader framed the Samiti's contribution to women's development as having accomplished "the work of awakening. . . . We have done the work of creating a human being."[30]

This interpretation of the Samiti's organizational role mirrors women's reproductive roles in a heteropatriarchal society and implicitly invokes the analogy of mothers (the Samiti) and fathers (the RSS) providing each other with support in an ideal family (the Sangh Parivar)—the micro-model for the future Hindu nation. The Samiti depicts its mothers not as passive embodiments of the nation but as actively engaged in the task of reproduction, providing leadership and guidance to all, including men in the Hindu nationalist family.

At the micro level, the Samiti engages in what Jill Vickers labels the "battle of the nursery," which involves ensuring that children are bred in culturally appropriate ways in order to ideologically reproduce the group.[31] As sociocultural reproducers, mothers are required to transmit group and family histories, cultural practices, and values that socialize children into the imagined identities of the group.[32] Thus, the Samiti stipulates that women in general and mothers in particular need to make sure that their behavior, homes, and the socialization of their children are in accordance with "Hindu traditions" and not "influenced by westernization."[33] The Samiti specifies the rules covering a wide range of domestic practices, such as food, clothing, language, children's names, birthday celebrations, hospitality codes, and symbols of Hindu tradition necessary for all Hindu homes.

Virtuous and cultured mothers are those who inculcate Hindu nationalist values in their progeny "because children are the nation's future citizens."[34] Mothers are portrayed as immensely powerful, small-scale gurus with their own special captive audience of disciples. A Samiti activist argued, "Can we have a better school, university, or teacher than one's home presided over by an enlightened mother? What a blessing it is to be such a mother, who is also a guru to her own children. Such a mother passes on to the society her benediction in the form of spiritually enriched and enlightened children who would grow into responsible citizens."[35] Here the Samiti valorizes women's sociocultural reproductive roles by connecting them to the role of the guru, a culturally renowned and powerful position in Hindu society. However, unlike the typical gurus in the multitudinous sects of Hinduism—who are supposed to be learned in a variety of scriptures, disciplined through years of asceticism, renunciation, and celibacy, and live in ashrams with a retinue of disciples[36]—the Samiti's recasting of this guru role makes ideological space for married heterosexual mothers to achieve the same kind of power, social esteem, and reverence without renouncing their families or leaving the comforts of home.

The universal mother of the nation supersedes the individual mother, and this conceptualization of motherhood allows women to help create a violent masculinity within the home. This is evident in the Samiti's expectation that mothers teach their children, particularly sons, their heroic duty to the nation—to be manly warriors defending the nation's honor and their "mother's honor" unto death. In a character sketch published by the Samiti, warrior-queen Vidula sternly rebukes her son for running away from battle to save his own life. She explicitly explains that her love for him is conditional on his defense of the "warrior-mother's honor." The preservation of her honor, and by extension that of the nation, is more important to her than her son's life:

> I am your mother. Loving one's son is a mother's duty. . . . But if I remain silent even after seeing you so wretched and dispirited, my motherhood will get dishonored. I take pride in being a brave warrior-mother. The warrior who turns his back on a battle is not worthy of being called a warrior. Shame on such a mother who calms and satisfies her cowardly and lazy son with love. . . . For once prove yourself a worthy son of a warrior-mother. Crush your opponents with your might and valor. . . . Then . . . see how much love there is in your mother's heart toward you.[37]

This is an extreme form of maternalist nationalism that draws on the generic masculine nationalist framing of the motherland as female and the state and its citizens as male; the latter are required to prove their "political manhood" through defense of the motherland.[38] In this story, Vidula models what women need to do in order to culturally reproduce male citizen-warriors, and she frames male reluctance to take on the role of warrior-aggressor and protector as cowardice. Thus, it is the mother's love for the nation that provides her with the capacity to withstand the pain of her son's possible demise on the battlefield. This capacity to bear extreme emotional pain makes her a "brave warrior-mother."

The moral of the story is that a mother's love for her children should be conditional on their serving the nation and that such motherly sacrifices were the cause of India's past glory. The character sketch concludes that "it was only due to mothers who were willing to gamble with their sons' lives by sending them to the battlefield in order to protect their ideals that India was able to become world renowned."[39] This is the Samiti's version of what Hindu nationalist leaders advocate at large public rallies when they call upon Hindu men to defend the besieged motherland.[40] The Samiti maintains that its politicized mothers should incite their sons to commit acts of violence as their duty. Thus, mothers need not commit actual acts of violence themselves, having fulfilled their own patriotic duty by setting up the preconditions for a violent masculinity within the safety and sanctity of their homes.

Motherhood Exemplified: A Celibate, Unwed Mother's Account

Dr. Sunita (a pseudonym), one of the Samiti's twenty-eight full-time organizers, was a prominent female leader in Uttar Pradesh, the most populous state in India, where she regularly organized two concurrent paramilitary camps every summer, beginning in 1990. She also headed the movement's educational wing for girls. In her early forties, she took pride in her Ph.D. in Sanskrit and signed her published articles with "Dr." preceding her name (as opposed to the typical "Mrs." or "Miss" that other Hindu nationalist women use).

Tall, broad-shouldered, and barrel-bodied, with a gruff, booming voice that could be heard across a field, she looked like an army sergeant major, notwithstanding her crisply starched cotton sari, the *bindi* on her forehead, and a ponytail. She had a no-nonsense steely gaze, commanding persona, and self-assured body language, in that she occupied large amounts of space with her feet wide apart and shoulders held straight back and walked with a loose-limbed, well-coordinated, confident, tough, almost macho swagger. She wore no jewelry.[41] She was the unmistakable queen, or rather general, in whose presence women trembled, shook, and fell silent, and whom women hated and loved with equal passion. An impressive figure, renowned in Hindu nationalist circles all over India, she inspired respect and awe.

Dr. Sunita came from a dyed-in-saffron Hindu nationalist family; her father, four sisters, and three brothers were high-level, old-time members of the RSS, Samiti, and other branches of the movement.[42] Nevertheless, when she decided to become a full-time celibate organizer in the Samiti, her family strenuously objected. Her parents were particularly unhappy that she did not want to get married. Ultimately, she rebelled, leaving her home in 1989 to become an organizer. When I met her, she lived on her own in a small three-room house, out of which she ran the regional Uttar Pradesh headquarters of the Samiti (this is atypical in the Indian context, as most women live with their families—either their parents or husbands). As an organizer, she was constantly traveling across India to monitor local Samiti branches and organize workshops for Hindu nationalist schoolteachers.

Dr. Sunita extended the Samiti's maternalist frame to justify a very active role for herself in the public sphere. For her, biological motherhood was an insufficient prerequisite for being a complete mother—rather, a woman was not truly a mother until she fulfilled her maternal duties to the nation. She made the following argument in response to my question about how Hindu nationalist women could have the time to be "good mothers" if they spent a lot of their time outside the home working for the Samiti:[43]

> The aim of becoming a mother does not mean becoming the mother of one or two children. Actually, we want to become and make such mothers—we want to give them such a consciousness that they can become the mothers of not only their individual families but also . . . the mothers of the nation. So, when can they become the mothers of the nation and society? When they start thinking of removing societal problems right along with their families' problems; when they offer their support to the nation during periods of national adversity; or when [a woman] plays a role in helping rid the nation of misfortunes— only then can she become a mother.

This recasting of motherhood helped Dr. Sunita resolve the inconsistency of telling women that their main duty was to be virtuous mothers of good Hindu nationalist children and yet drawing them out of their homes for campaigns, leaving them with less time to socialize their children. Moreover, Dr. Sunita's conception of motherhood was not limited to women alone or to biological motherhood. A woman need not give birth or have sexual relations, as she explained to me, thereby justifying her unmarried, celibate, yet maternal status: "Does a girl become a mother merely by giving birth to a child? That is not so. Every girl has a mother hidden inside her."

Ultimately, for her, a mother doesn't necessarily have to be female:

> [A mother can be] a man, too, when he dons the emotional disposition of motherliness; then his anger, his spite, and feeling that I am so great—all these emotions start getting finished. And when the special qualities of femininity, the special qualities of a woman's soul, come within him—tenderness, compassion, moderation, restraint, and self-control—when these special qualities start coming within him, then he becomes a saint. This only is the nature of a saint. How can a saint talk about the welfare of a society? Because a mother sits in his mind. How did the great men or great women of our country make their voices resound about the problems of our society or our country—how did they work to resolve these? Because there was a mother sitting inside them.

Here Dr. Sunita made three main assertions: that the emotions associated with motherhood are quintessentially feminine; that the feminine principle is superior to the masculine; and that the superiority of the feminine is caused by women's maternal capacity. She clearly recognized and subtly denounced male domination, in terms of their feeling and enactment of superiority over women. Thus, from her perspective, a man could become a saint only when imbued with the emotional qualities of a maternal femininity. Not only did she gender emotions, but she classified the emotions she valued highly as feminine.

Furthermore, she linked artistic and spiritual creativity to this conception of motherhood: "This mother, she does not become a mother only by giving birth to children. Motherhood is intelligence. It is an emotional disposition. . . . The one who creates, that is, composes—this is the emotional quality of a mother. When you sculpt a statue, which feeling will you sculpt it with? Or does a sculptor have a different emotional consciousness? A sculptor, too, does not have a different consciousness—that, too, is a mother's consciousness." This interpretation creates unity among Samiti members—linking schoolgirls (the potential future mothers) with biological mothers and celibate leaders (the metaphorical mothers)—through the platform of motherhood.

Thus, mothers are expected to serve and lead both their families and the nation: "We want our country's young girls to become such mothers who, along with being devoted to their families, can also be devoted to the nation. By getting women out of the house to work for the nation, I am not saying that women should neglect the family and the children. Only by creating cultured children in a cultured family can the nation be cultured and be taken care of. During times of national adversities women should take time to work for the nation with complete resolve." Dr. Sunita skillfully wove together emotional orientation and intelligence, tying work/resolve, feeling/doing, and devotion/service into packages. And lest one think that motherhood is a one-dimensional straitjacket, she points out that in her and the Samiti's understanding, motherhood needs to be multidimensional: "Women have so many capabilities. Today she has been reduced to a one-dimensional role only—looking after her children and husband. When she will become multidimensional, her personality will automatically become conscientious."

Conclusion

In casting motherhood as a higher stage of evolution, the Samiti diverges from classical Hindu texts and folk traditions, in which motherhood is considered less important for ordinary women than being ideal wives. In these texts and traditions, females are dually represented in "the roles of wife (good, benevolent, dutiful, controlled) and mother (fertile, but dangerous, uncontrolled)."[44] Susan Wadley notes, "The wifely role is preeminent in Hinduism, the maternal only secondary. Thus, whereas mythology and law books provide endless models of the good wife, there are no prime examples of the good mother."[45] Although mother-goddesses exist in the Hindu pantheon and are worshipped for their benevolent capacities and feared for their malevolent powers, they are clearly domesticated and seen as consorts of powerful gods.[46] Prabhati Mukherjee argues, "Proceeding down the ages we find that the ideal held up before women is to be a submissive, dutiful and loyal wife."[47] Mothers, even when transformed into mother-goddesses, do "not represent proper or ideal behavior" for women.[48]

The Samiti's divergence from traditional Hinduism can be understood in the context of a gendered Hindu nationalism. Similar to other forms of nationalism, the Samiti recognizes the necessity of women as the biological and sociocultural reproducers of the nation. Thus, it valorizes motherhood over and above "wife-hood." Though motherhood is abstractly venerated in Hindu society, "it is because it results in the production of future fathers and not mothers."[49] Motherhood is celebrated and wives are given respect only when they give birth to sons. Wives who give birth to daughters are blamed for bringing ruin upon the family.[50] While the Samiti does not directly propagate the idea that the ideal mother is a mother of sons, eight of its thirteen ideal mother stories are about mothers of sons, and the other seven are stories of mothers who, though not biological mothers, adopted sons or demonstrated their motherly qualities in relation to male characters. The Samiti is curiously silent about what might be the duties of mothers toward daughters in a larger context that explicitly devalues female children. Its silence and implicit propagation of sons make sense when viewed within the context of women as reproducers of the nation operating within the confines of a heterosexist Hindu patriarchy that stipulates which "breeders" and which "breeds" are to be valued.[51] Thus, heterosexual, married, upper-caste, middle-class Hindu women who bear sons and socialize them to be citizen-warriors are upheld as role models.

As participants in the hypermasculinist gender politics of the male-dominated Hindu nationalist movement, Hindu nationalist women and their organizations perform predominantly reproductive and supportive roles in the movement. These activists accept these essentially subservient roles because their organizations use maternalist frames that valorize women's reproductive capacity in order to carve out active political roles for them, thus blurring the boundaries between the private and public. In right-wing movements, the rhetoric of motherhood often garbs conservatism and antifeminism. Nira Yuval-Davis convincingly argues that nationalism and maternalism are almost always linked, because nationalists need biological and cultural reproduction to supply members to "the nation."[52] The Samiti reproduces a feminine collective identity, in which women are embodied as the carriers of culture, the conduits through which hierarchical social relations and systems are transmitted to each new generation.

NOTES

Unless otherwise noted, all translations from Hindi are my own.

1. Master frames are generic, broad in interpretative scope, characterized by inclusivity, flexibility, and cultural resonance, and hegemonic in particular societies at specific historical time periods. For excellent analysis of Mother India, see Radha Kumar, *The History of Doing: An Illustrated Account of Movements for Women's Rights and Feminism in India, 1800–1900* (New Delhi: Kali for Women, 1993); Paola Bacchetta, *Gender in the Hindu Nation: RSS Women as Ideologues* (New Delhi: Women Unlimited, 2004); Christiane Brosius, *Empowering Visions: The Politics of Representation in Hindu Nationalism* (London: Anthem South Asian Studies, 2005).

2. Brosius, *Empowering Visions*, 173; Bacchetta, *Gender in the Hindu Nation*, 27.

3. Frames refer to "interpretative schema" that link Samiti members, their belief systems, and their personal experiences to the goals and objectives of the larger Hindu nationalist movement. For more, see David Snow, "Framing Processes, Ideology, and Discursive Fields," in *The Blackwell Companion to Social Movements*, ed. David Snow et al. (Malden, Mass.: Blackwell, 2007).

4. Meera Sehgal, "Reproducing the Feminine Citizen-Warrior: The Case of the Rashtria Sevika Samiti, a Right-Wing Women's Organization in India" (Ph.D. diss., University of Wisconsin–Madison, 2004); M. Sehgal, "Manufacturing the Feminized Siege Mentality: Hindu Nationalist Paramilitary Camps for Women in India," *Journal of Contemporary Ethnography* (special issue on Racist Right-Wing Movements) 36, no. 2 (2007): 165–83; M. Sehgal, "The Veiled Feminist Ethnographer: Fieldwork Among Women of India's Hindu Right," in *Women Fielding Danger: Negotiating Ethnographic Identities in Field Research*, ed. Martha Huggins and Marie-Louise Glebes (Lanham, Md.: Rowman and Littlefield, 2009).

5. Sehgal, "Manufacturing the Feminized Siege Mentality," 167.

6. For information on the Hindu nationalist pogroms against Muslims in Gujarat in 2002, see K. Chenoy et al., *Gujarat Carnage 2002: A Report to the Nation* (New Delhi, 2002); V. Nagar et al., *Ethnic Cleansing in Ahmadabad: A Preliminary Report* (SAHMAT Fact Finding Team to Ahmadabad, 2002). On the involvement of Hindu nationalist women in these pogroms, see S. Hameed et al., *How Has the Gujarat Massacre Affected Minority Women? The Survivors Speak* (Ahmadabad: Citizen's Initiative, 2002); P. Advanni et al., *Report of the Committee Constituted by the National Commission for Women to Assess the Status and Situation of Women and Girl Children in Gujarat in the Wake of the Communal Disturbance* (Delhi: National Commission for Women, 2002); People's Union for Civil Liberties and Shanti Abhiyan, "Women's Perspectives on the Violence in Gujarat," in *Gujarat: Laboratory of the Hindu Rashtra* (New Delhi: Indian Social Action Forum, 2002).

7. Chetan Bhatt, *Hindu Nationalism: Origins, Ideologies, and Modern Myths* (New York: Berg, 2001), 143–44.

8. Ibid.

9. Bacchetta, *Gender in the Hindu Nation*.

10. Christophe Jaffrelot, *The Hindu Nationalist Movement in India* (New York: Columbia University Press, 1998).

11. Vanaja Dhruvarajan, "Hinduism and the Empowerment of Women," in *Gender and Society in India*, vol. 1, ed. R. Indira and Deepak Kumar Behera (New Delhi: Manak, 1999); Vanaja Dhruvarajan, *Hindu Women and the Power of Ideology* (Granby, Mass.: Bergin and Garvey, 1989).

12. Kathleen Blee, *Inside Organized Racism: Women in the Hate Movement* (Berkeley: University of California Press, 2002).

13. This information is drawn from personal interviews with Samiti activists and participant observation at rallies, campaigns, and meetings, 1996–97.

14. These are crucial positions because male leaders would not be able to recruit women, particularly young women, given Indian norms around gender.

15. For more information on this tradition, see Meena Khandelwal, *Women in Ochre Robes: Gendering Hindu Renunciation* (Albany: SUNY, 2004).

16. Rashtriya Sevika Samiti, *Prateh smarniya mahilayen* [Women to remember every morning] (Nagpur: Sevika Prakashan, 1990); Rashtriya Sevika Samiti, *Maatritva, netritva, kartritva* [Motherhood, leadership, action] (Nagpur: Sevika Prakashan, 1996).

17. M. Bahati Kuumba, *Gender and Social Movements* (Walnut Creek, Calif.: Altamira Press, 2001), 57.

18. Carolyn Strange, "Mothers on the March: Maternalism in Women's Protests for Peace in North America and Western Europe, 1900–1985," in *Women and Social Protest,* ed. Guida West and Rhoda Blumberg (New York: Oxford University Press, 1990).

19. V. Spike Peterson, "Sexing Political Identities/Nationalism as Heterosexism," in *Women, States, and Nationalism: At Home in the Nation?* ed. Sita Ranchod-Nilsson and Mary Ann Tétreault (New York: Routledge, 2000), 68.

20. Peterson, "Sexing Political Identities," 68.

21. Ibid.

22. Jan Jindy Pettman, *Worlding Women: A Feminist International Politics* (New York: Routledge, 1996), 49.

23. Amrita Basu, "Feminism Inverted: The Gendered Imagery and Real Women of Hindu Nationalism," in *Women and the Hindu Right: A Collection of Essays,* ed. Tanika Sarkar and Urvashi Butalia (New Delhi: Kali for Women, 1995); Bacchetta, *Gender in the Hindu Nation,* 2004.

24. Bacchetta, *Gender in the Hindu Nation,* 27.

25. Usha Chatti, "Letter to the Activists of the Samiti," in *Vishambhara (Mother of the Universe): A 60th Anniversary Commemoration,* ed. Sharad Renu (Nagpur: Sevika Prakashan, 1996), 2.

26. Sharad Renu, "Samiti Editorial," in *Vishambhara,* 3.

27. Partha Chatterjee, *The Nation and Its Fragments: Colonial and Postcolonial History* (Princeton: Princeton University Press, 1993); Uma Narayan, *Dislocating Culture: Identities, Traditions, and Third-World Feminism* (New York: Routledge, 1997).

28. Renu, "Samiti Editorial," 3.

29. Ibid., 4.

30. Author's interview with Dr. Sunita [pseud.], Mathura, India, January 31, 1997.

31. Jill Vickers, "At His Mother's Knee: Sex/Gender and the Construction of National Identities," in *Women and Men: Interdisciplinary Readings in Gender,* ed. Greta Hoffman Nemiroff (Toronto: Fitzhenry and Whiteside, 1990).

32. Nira Yuval-Davis, *Gender and Nation* (London: Sage, 1997).

33. Rashtriya Sevika Samiti, *Bodh sarita* [River of knowledge] (Nagpur: Sevika Prakashan, 1988), 23.

34. Author's interview with Dr. Sunita.

35. M. Kakshmikumari, "Empowerment of Women—the Vivekanand Way," in *Vishambhara,* 52.

36. For more on gurus, see Khandelwal, *Women in Ochre Robes.*

37. Rashtriya Sevika Samiti, *Prateh smarniya mahilayen,* 17–18.

38. Peterson, "Sexing Political Identities," 69.

39. Rashtriya Sevika Samiti, *Prateh smarniya mahilayen,* 17–18.

40. Tapan Basu et al., *Khaki Shorts and Saffron Flags: A Critique of the Hindu Right* (New Delhi: Orient Longman, 1993).

41. Jewelry is an integral aspect of feminine identity in India across religion, caste, class, and region.

42. Hindu nationalists have adopted saffron as a symbol of their collective identity.

43. All the quotes in this section are from my interview with Dr. Sunita.

44. Susan Wadley, "Women and the Hindu Tradition," *Signs* (special issue on Women and National Development: The Complexities of Change) 3, no. 1 (Autumn 1977): 117.

45. Ibid., 119.

46. G. N. Ramu, "Femininity and Maternity: The Case of Urban Indian Women," in *Gender and Society in India,* vol. 1, ed. R. Indira and Deepak Kumar Behera (New Delhi: Manak, 1999); Bacchetta, *Gender in the Hindu Nation.*

47. Prabhati Mukherjee, *Hindu Women: Normative Models* (New Delhi: Orient Longman, 1994), 16.

48. Wadley, "Women and the Hindu Tradition," 119.

49. Ramu, "Femininity and Maternity," 185.

50. This devaluation of female children is reflected in India's skewed sex ratio (936 females per 1000 males)—a result of the neglect of female children, sex-selective abortions, and female infanticide.

51. Peterson, "Sexing Political Identities," 65.

52. Yuval-Davis, *Gender and Nation.*

PART 3

Countering the Left

13

"It Takes Women to Fight Women": Woman Suffrage and the
Genesis of Female Conservatism in the United States

Kirsten Delegard

At the beginning of 1927, a group of women in Huron, South Dakota, convened a special meeting of the local chapter of the Daughters of the American Revolution (DAR), the most prestigious of the hereditary associations
founded at the end of the nineteenth century. This extra session was devoted
to neither historic markers nor genealogical research, the activities most
commonly associated with the women's organization, whose members were
required to trace their lineage back to supporters of the American Revolution. Rather, these women came together in South Dakota to support an in-
tensifying crusade against communism. They gave little time that winter
morning to the work of avowed revolutionaries, focusing instead on developments they viewed as more insidious. They passed resolutions opposing two
legislative measures: the Sheppard-Towner Maternity and Infancy Protection
Act and the proposed constitutional amendment to ban child labor. In the
first decades of the twentieth century, the DAR had lent its support to female
reformers' efforts to persuade the federal government to assume greater responsibility for maternal and child welfare. By the winter of 1927, however,
the members of the hereditary association in Huron had come to see federal
bans on child labor and programs to disseminate health information to pregnant women and mothers as "state socialism." Passage of this legislation
would embolden "Red" organizations and push the country closer to Bolshevism, according to Francis Cone, who spearheaded the group's campaign to
root out "subversive movements . . . in various South Dakota cities" and illuminate "the 'Red' menace to our institutions."[1]

The DAR's exchange of what has been called "maternalist" politics in the
United States for an activist anticommunist agenda was prompted, at least in

part, by the passage of the Nineteenth Amendment, which gave American women the right to vote. Suffragists had predicted that female enfranchisement would usher in a new era of political engagement; none of them anticipated that it would encourage what one activist characterized as a "movement organized for the purpose of destroying the power of women."[2] The triumph of Bolshevism in Russia converged with the new responsibilities of the franchise to mobilize conservative women like Cone, who surprised the nation in the decade after the suffrage amendment by attacking the organizations and initiatives most identified with female political influence. After making common cause with other conservative Americans who were determined to elucidate the global Bolshevik threat, DAR leaders turned against female reformers.[3] Antisuffragists helped transform the activism of the DAR and other established hereditary and veterans' organizations, which enlisted their large memberships to block child welfare measures that had enjoyed almost universal popularity among civic-minded women before the specter of revolutionary radicalism loomed so large.

In the first decade of female suffrage in the United States, new conservative activists reshaped popular assumptions about what it meant to be a politically active woman. Before the Nineteenth Amendment, middle-class women's activism was perceived to be uniformly progressive. Female reformers had been the animating forces behind what is known as the Progressive Era, when many women came of age politically in campaigns to improve child welfare and clean up cities. During those years, women's clubs and settlement houses taught women the skills they needed for public participation, giving them a framework to identify social problems and pioneer solutions. Female activists perfected the art of pressure group politics, learning how to shape policy from outside the electoral system. The welfare state that emerged in the early twentieth century was largely a product of these activists, who made powerful appeals to local, state, and national officials to remedy persistent social problems. Their efforts reconfigured the relationship between the individual and the state, pushing the federal government to shoulder new responsibility for the health and welfare of its citizens.

The 1920 passage of the Nineteenth Amendment was itself in many ways an outgrowth of these interlocking campaigns for reform. For veteran activists, the vote was a tool for social justice; it would make it easier for women to demand legislation that would transform politics and government. Yet, in the decade that followed, women's access to the ballot box seemed to give no additional momentum to the movement to expand the American welfare state. "So far as federal legislation is concerned," reformer and academic Sophonisba Breckinridge observed in the early 1930s, "the cause of Child Welfare . . . has advanced little, if any, since 1921."[4] Indeed, women's political influence, as measured in legislative reforms, seemed to diminish. The paradox of contracting influence in the context of expanding political rights has puzzled historians, who have wondered, as Anne Firor Scott articulated,

"What happened to the verve and enthusiasm with which the suffrage veterans set about to reorganize society?"[5]

The fervor for social justice remained undiminished among female reformers in the 1920s.[6] But these committed activists came up against a new nemesis: other middle-class women who believed that they were best situated to halt what they saw as the expanding influence of the left in American life. They used the mantle of moral authority they enjoyed as middle-class clubwomen to challenge female reformers, who had built their political influence on their claim to represent all women. Driven by anxiety about revolutionary radicalism, these women had become wary of all manifestations of progressive change. They recast "social housekeeping" as patriotically suspect, denouncing the legislative reform that had won nearly universal support from women's organizations before the Nineteenth Amendment. Their efforts not only blocked key legislation that would have funded maternal health programs and banned child labor but also eviscerated the women's coalition that had provided popular support for progressive reforms.

It was not only in the United States that new women voters embraced conservatism. Historian Claudia Koonz sees a relationship between female suffrage and the ascendance of conservatism, arguing that significant progressive victories tend to be followed in modern representative democracies by mobilizations from the right to defend traditional hierarchies.[7] She cites the 1918 enfranchisement of German women, which was also hailed as the dawn of a new era for social justice. As in the United States, suffrage did little to improve the legal and economic status of German women, who lost interest in electoral politics as economic and political turmoil overwhelmed their nation. Those who did vote cast their ballots for parties on the right, which emphasized women's importance to the traditional family.[8] New women voters in Latin America were also drawn in large numbers to fascist and conservative parties, which had advocated female enfranchisement as the best way to defeat Bolshevism and ensure "national salvation."[9] Determined to protect home and nation, conservative women embraced this new tool. "Whether or not you approved the franchise, it came to you and with it the solemn obligation to use it," argued Anne Rogers Minor, one of the leaders of the DAR.[10]

In these different contexts, enfranchisement catalyzed conservative women to organize politically, lending legitimacy and urgency to their activism. In Germany, women voters came to see themselves as a bulwark against the left. "The Revolution called us into political life," German leader Gertrud Bäumer asserted. "But now we are also called on to oppose the Revolution."[11] In the United States, the Nineteenth Amendment forced antisuffragists to jettison their ambivalence about sustained female political engagement. Mary Kilbreth, the last president of the National Association Opposed to Woman Suffrage (NAOWS), vowed to fight the feminist remaking of politics imagined by reformers. "The best way to have defeated Feminism would have been to have prevented woman suffrage," Kilbreth conceded in 1921.

"But . . . Anti-Feminists [cannot] submit to the Sex Revolution simply because suffrage forces have succeeded in crossing a boundary line."[12] Suffragists, asserted Kilbreth, had turned to lobbying in order to "establish vast Feminist Bureaucracies," which could "be used as in the Russian Propaganda System, as channels of Revolution."[13] Kilbreth decided to meet this new threat by reconstituting her antisuffrage organization as the Woman Patriot Publishing Company (WPPC), which dedicated itself to lobbying and the publication of a small newspaper, *The Woman Patriot*.[14]

While the women in South Dakota were not formally affiliated with the WPPC, the DAR and similar hereditary associations fell under the sway of this small band of former antisuffragists in the 1920s. This group went on to have an influence in American politics out of proportion to its tiny membership. The WPPC's warnings about "revolution by legislation" struck terror in the hearts of women already unsettled by the Bolshevik Revolution, including one member of the National Congress of Parents and Teachers Association (PTA) who asserted that Sheppard-Towner and the Child Labor Amendment had been conceived by radicals who had sworn they would force clubwomen to "'dig their own graves.'"[15] The WPPC found a receptive audience among women who had concluded that Bolshevism was the most pressing problem of the day.

While dispatches from the Bolshevik Revolution had left many Americans shaken, the fate of women in the new state came under special scrutiny in 1919, when Congress convened hearings to investigate conditions in the revolutionary regime. Witnesses before what came to be known as the Overman Committee testified that Bolsheviks had sanctioned soldiers' rape of women and legalized abortion to facilitate female promiscuity. It had enacted divorce laws that encouraged men to discard their wives. It had supposedly "nationalized" women and children, placing children in state institutions to be raised and forbidding women to "belong" exclusively to one man. The witnesses swore that Bolsheviks also forced women to register at the government "Bureau of Free Love," where they were made available to any and all men, regardless of their feelings.[16] This assertion grew out of a decree issued by the workers' soviet in the city of Vladimir during the brief period of social experimentation that followed the 1917 revolution. But any limited manifestations of "free love" quickly gave way to terror and repression. And revolutionary edicts did not rip children from the arms of loving parents. Civil war left millions dead and brought an epidemic of sexual violence. War left children without parents, women without male providers, and most people without adequate food, shelter, or medical care, miseries that were blamed on Bolsheviks' supposed determination to pervert the traditional family.[17]

The riots, strikes, and bombings of 1919 signaled to some Americans that a Soviet-style revolution threatened the United States. Leaders of hereditary and veterans' groups responded to this possibility by rallying their members with variations on the "nationalization of women" myth, admonishing women at chapter meetings and national conventions that unless they fought back, what happened in Soviet Russia would happen to them.[18] The DAR was one of the women's groups that began denouncing radicalism with ferocity, condemning both the Soviet Union and "all forms of sovietism, socialism, communism and bolshevism."[19] The hereditary association's robust organizational structure and deep pockets made it the shining star in a constellation of women's organizations that embraced the campaign against communism as essential for the protection of women and children. "When women thoroughly understand how Bolshevism menaces their sex they will take up arms against it and fight it incessantly to destruction," declared Ida Vera Simonton, president of the Women's Military Reserve of the United States. "Governments so far have been powerless against it, and it remains for the women to help the Government against this new terror."[20]

The Woman Patriot became an ideological wellspring for women like Simonton, who were determined to protect women and children from the ravages of radicalism. Activists all over the United States coalesced around the newspaper's priorities as they built the first explicitly conservative movement of women in the United States. Female antiradicalism—as this movement came to be called—aimed to publicize the plight of women under communism and purge all forms of radicalism from American life. At times it seemed like the movement was hiding in plain sight, as these new conservative activists established few new groups. They advanced their political agenda by building on the existing institutional framework of women's organizations, creating committees within groups such as the Daughters of 1812 and the American Legion Auxiliary.[21] Neither achieved the power and influence of the DAR's National Defense Committee, which sprang to life under the watch of DAR president-general Lora Haines Cook. The 1925 Continental Congress voted to fund this new committee, which was charged with defending the nation from enemies "from without and enemies from within the Republic," especially "Moscow International Communist organizations."[22] While it played a critical role in crafting and promoting a culture of anticommunism among its members, the work of the National Defense Committee would also reverberate well beyond the ranks of the DAR.

The influence of the DAR's National Defense Committee was perhaps most obvious in the Women's Patriotic Conference on National Defense (WPCND), a coalition initially sponsored by the American Legion Auxiliary. While this group's inaugural convention brought together women from sixteen groups claiming to represent one million women, it expanded over the course of the decade to encompass thirty organizations. It would spur the growth of female antiradicalism as a social movement, shaping the grassroots activism of women in all of its associated groups and remaining vigorous into the Cold War.[23] Hereditary associations like the DAR, the United Daughters of the Confederacy, and the National Society of Colonial Dames rallied with veterans' organizations like the Ladies of the GAR, the American

War Mothers, and the Service Star Legion to show that "it takes women to fight women." According to Claire Oliphant, the founding mother of the WPCND conference and 1925 national president of the American Legion Auxiliary, the conference was inspired by the conviction that "the women pacifists and women radicals of America" could only be stopped by their antiradical sisters.[24]

The WPCND was set up to be a counterweight to the Women's Joint Congressional Committee (WJCC), a lobbying organization established in November 1920 to help middle-class women's organizations advocate for legislative reforms. This consortium of women's groups, which came to be known as "the most powerful lobby in Washington," immediately focused on passing the Sheppard-Towner Maternity and Infancy Protection Act.[25] To reduce the nation's infant mortality rate, which ranked near the top of twenty developed nations, this measure required the federal government to match funds provided by states for health clinics, visiting nurses, classes on nutrition and hygiene, and lectures for pregnant women and new mothers. These relatively modest programs were seen as tremendously significant for veteran social reformers like Florence Kelley. "Of all the activities in which I have shared during more than forty years of striving," Kelley declared, "none is, I am convinced, of such fundamental importance as the Sheppard-Towner Act."[26] Her enthusiasm seemed to be shared by a majority of American women. "I think every woman in my state has written to the Senator," said one senator's secretary.[27] Wary of antagonizing new female voters, politicians from across the spectrum claimed the measure as their own. It easily won approval in 1921.[28]

The seeming popularity of Sheppard-Towner did not discourage the antisuffragists associated with *The Woman Patriot,* who were determined to develop an ideological framework that would illuminate the links between this type of reform and Bolshevik revolution. In 1922 the group issued what became a widely distributed manifesto, "Organizing Revolution Through Women and Children," which was published in *The Woman Patriot.*[29] The article focused on the connections drawn by Friedrich Engels between the private family and private property, building on his assertion that revolution would not be complete without the emancipation of women. *The Woman Patriot* reversed Engels's logic, claiming that the weakening of the patriarchal family structure laid the foundation for revolution. Radicals in the United States, the publication asserted, had decided that "communism can be accomplished as *surely* by poisonous propaganda against the family as by armed uprisings against private property."[30]

According to the scheme explained by *The Woman Patriot,* radicals hoped to undermine the family by eliminating its usefulness as an economic unit; to that end, they promoted the "social 'care for all children, legal or illegal'" and "'endowment of motherhood' so that the 'proletarian' wife becomes 'economically independent' of her 'bourgeois' husband." Though federal programs providing aid to mothers and national laws restricting the right of children to work were designed by reformers to strengthen the traditional family, *The Woman Patriot* countered that such programs disrupted this institution, loosening paternal control as women looked to the state, rather than individual men, for guidance and support. State provisions for women and children, the publication argued, would turn husbands from breadwinners into dangerous agitators.[31]

The women behind *The Woman Patriot* were ill equipped to mobilize significant numbers of grassroots women around these concerns. Their ideas developed a popular following only after they forged an alliance with the DAR, which stood at the epicenter of the burgeoning movement for female antiradicalism. The DAR accepted the connections between reform and revolution illuminated by the WPPC and came to endorse its view that Sheppard-Towner and a constitutional ban on child labor would make the nation vulnerable to Bolshevik takeover. "Collectivity and bureaucracy would snatch the child from the nursery and make of it an un-American citizen," according to Mrs. William Sherman Walker, the chairman of the group's National Defense Committee.[32] The DAR adopted an official stance that condemned the "unwarranted extension of Federal activities" that had created "autocratic bureaucracy, in direct contravention of the American system of government devised by the founders of the Republic."[33]

The DAR leaders of the 1920s never acknowledged that their determination to defeat social welfare legislation represented a repudiation of their organization's previous support for the agenda championed by female reformers associated with the U.S. Children's Bureau.[34] The DAR had endorsed the initial Sheppard-Towner bill, urging its members to contact their congressional representatives to speed its passage.[35] Its members had also lobbied vigorously to ban child labor, which one of its officers described in 1908 as an "evil" that menaced "the institutions the fathers founded."[36] Yet, by 1925, the rising specter of revolution came to overshadow what had been a nearly universal commitment among middle-class female activists to child welfare reform. Narratives of Russian terror had galvanized the conservative clubwomen of the DAR to transform the political priorities of their organization. In this era of global revolution, these women came to oppose social welfare measures, which the WPPC convinced them were part of the radical campaign to expand government control over family life. In the world of women's politics, fears of a Bolshevik-inspired revolution crescendoed into the second half of the 1920s, belying historians' claim that antiradical anxieties declined after the federal government retreated from Red hunting.[37]

As Congress took up the question of whether to approve the Sheppard-Towner Act again in 1926, the WPPC issued a new manifesto. The *Woman Patriot*'s "petition" asserted that Sheppard-Towner was part of a careful "program of revolution by legislation," as menacing as a plot "to overthrow a government by force and violence." The petition declared that this idea had been "put into practice by the Bolsheviks in Russia." It explained that since the revolutionary government had made "women and children the wards of the state," it had removed "the 'economic foundations' of marriage and of morality." The document attacked not just Sheppard-Towner but the whole women's movement for social welfare reform, claiming that socialist reformer Florence Kelley had hoodwinked the General Federation of Women's Clubs, the League of Women Voters, and the PTA into a campaign to sabotage the republic and further radical communism.[38]

Delaware senator Thomas F. Bayard introduced the petition into the *Congressional Record*.[39] This made it a "public" document, shielded from libel suits and eligible for subsidized government reprinting.[40] Once it was "printed and circulated as a Government document," the petition had a reach and a legitimacy that made it devastating, according to the executive secretary of the League of Women Voters.[41] It reached all corners of the country, thanks to conservative women's groups like the DAR, which sent out the petition with a letter calling on members to defeat the "unconstitutional and vicious law."[42] This missive prompted "scared groups" to debate "its awful import with many an 'Oh,' 'Ah,' and 'How Terrible!,'" according to the well-known suffragist and reformer Carrie Chapman Catt.[43] Advocates of the federal maternity program who worked at the state level reported their struggles to contain the agitation that followed as the petition circulated hand to hand through the nation's women's clubs.[44]

Descriptions of Bolshevik terror had shifted the political equilibrium within women's organizations like the DAR, making members receptive to the message of Mary Kilbreth and her compatriots. "It is encouraging to see how alive men now are generally to the underground Communist aspect to these measures which they would have ridiculed a year ago," the leader of the WPPC boasted.[45] Her group's campaign against social welfare legislation provided an immediate target for the women agitated by radicalism. The DAR was joined in its effort to defeat Sheppard-Towner by the American War Mothers, which sent Congress a protest against the renewal of Sheppard-Towner that declared, "The next logical step after communizing the child is to communize the mother."[46] The Daughters of 1812 also condemned the bill after one of its leaders called on members to be on guard against "the viper creeping slowly and surely into the very vitals of our form of government in the insidious form of Maternity Bills, Child Labor Bills, Education, Equal Rights—all communistic."[47]

Congressmen opposed to social welfare legislation drew courage from evidence of waning support for Sheppard-Towner among the nation's women. In early January 1927, almost exactly a year after Congress began deliberating Sheppard-Towner's renewal, Senate antagonists of the Children's Bureau launched a nine-day filibuster aimed at defeating the maternity act and discrediting the federal bureau that had written the legislation. Senators drew on testimonials assembled by *The Woman Patriot* to show that the nation's women opposed maternity legislation and its "Bolshevik ideas." Utah senator William H. King asserted that the "maternity act" was not designed for the "benefit of the babes and of the mothers of the country." Instead, it was intended "for the conscious purpose of setting up State control of maternity and childhood," as in Russia.[48] When King and his allies demanded the "liquidation" of the federal agency, the Children's Bureau agreed to a compromise that saved its life; the resulting legislation extended Sheppard-Towner for two years and then mandated an end to the maternity program on June 30, 1929.[49]

Female conservatives ensured that the 1921 passage of the Sheppard-Towner Act was the only legislative victory enjoyed by reformers during the 1920s.[50] Yet federal social welfare measures were only the first casualties of female conservatives. As copies of the WPPC's petition flooded the nation's women's clubs, rank-and-file members began questioning the political agendas of their organizations. Doubts about reform came to preoccupy all the groups associated with the WJCC. League of Women Voters president Belle Sherwin revealed in February 1927 that "attacks of one form or another keep us busy most of the time."[51] Conservative propaganda dragged national leaders and grassroots women alike into the acrimonious controversy over the true nature of legislative reform and the political sympathies of the groups that endorsed these measures. Members of the League of Women Voters and the PTA quickly tired under these assaults. "I am through fighting now," Mrs. Fred Hoffman, a supporter of both the League and the PTA announced in November. "Personally, I never have been in favor of some of these measures, but worked for them through a sense of loyalty to the organization."[52] One Detroit woman revealed that she was "stirred . . . most deeply" by the charge that the League of Women Voters endorsed the legislative program of Soviet Russia. Though she wanted to support child welfare and peace, she was adamant that she could not ally herself "with any organization or disseminate any propaganda which can in any measure be construed as 'Red.'"[53]

Groups varied in their reaction to this kind of grassroots pressure. The national League of Women Voters remained defiant, assembling a "Defense Kit" to help its local branches cope with ongoing assaults.[54] It was one of the only groups, however, to remain true to the legislative agenda laid out by the WJCC at the beginning of the decade.[55] The PTA, by contrast, remained associated with the WJCC but abandoned its commitment to legislative reform.[56] The group had laid aside its concern with social change by the time its president asserted in 1930 that most of the problems of children could be solved by the education of mothers rather than political or social transformation.[57] Other groups sought relief from attacks and chose to abandon the WJCC. One of the oldest and largest American women's organizations—the Women's Christian Temperance Union—was the first to make its exit in 1927. The most serious blow to the WJCC came in 1928, when the huge General Federation of Women's Clubs decided to cut its ties.[58] These groups, which had sought social, cultural, and political change for more than thirty years, now drifted away from the priorities developed by Progressive Era female reformers. These defections signaled that female antiradical assaults had sapped support for national legislative reform from the oldest and largest women's clubs. The WJCC continued as only a shadow of its former self, limping along until it finally disbanded in 1970.[59]

Historians have traditionally interpreted the twin defeat of the Sheppard-Towner Act and the Child Labor Amendment as merely a temporary setback for female reformers, who went on to carry the agenda of the Progressive Era forward into the New Deal.[60] Indeed, the desire for progressive social change did remain strong among reformers associated with the Children's Bureau, who helped write the 1935 Social Security Act, now seen as the cornerstone of the modern American welfare state. This measure helped restore funding to Sheppard-Towner–style maternal and infant health programs, in addition to adding new services for disabled and neglected children and federal funding for mothers' pensions, which became known as Aid to Dependent Children.[61] But the ultimate success of the New Deal overshadows the fact that the campaign against female reform during the 1920s removed grassroots support for social welfare measures at a critical point in the development of the federal bureaucracy.

In the aftermath of the Bolshevik Revolution, new women voters contributed to the marginalization of reforms once embraced by the political mainstream. Their anticommunist campaign forced broad-based women's organizations to abandon their support for social welfare legislation, vitiating these organizations' political zeal. Their efforts forced a fundamental change in the political culture of women's organizations; by neutralizing them as a force for progressive change, conservative women weakened popular support in the United States for the expansion of the welfare state. While the Social Security Act was in some ways the culmination of female reform efforts, the success of the 1930s came in spite of the waning power of grassroots women's organizations. These reforms were only possible because of the cataclysm of the Great Depression, which shook the assumptions of many Americans and allowed New Deal administrators to craft a new relationship between individuals and government. In less tumultuous times, federal bureaucrats could never have mustered enough political influence to win passage of these long-sought measures. And even at this moment of supreme satisfaction, scars were obvious from antiradical attacks, which left Children's Bureau administrators "perpetually anxious," according to one historian. Discarding Sheppard-Towner's efforts to reach all women, regardless of income, the Social Security Act institutionalized means testing in federal welfare programs to avoid the kind of controversy that had dogged them in the past. Means testing ultimately made it impossible for Aid to Dependent Children to build the kind of broad constituency enjoyed by Social Security.

As a result, it was easily assailed, undermining the ability of the American welfare state to ensure social justice for women.[62]

The New Deal ushered in reforms long championed by women, but it did not revive the women's political institutions from which such initiatives had flowed. A few women's groups—the National Consumers' League, the Women's Trade Union League, and the League of Women Voters—continued agitating for progressive legislation during the New Deal. But these smaller organizations could not mobilize the millions of women affiliated with more centrist groups. Individual reformers also remained politically active through the New Deal. Yet enthusiasm for social change would never be revived in more mainstream women's organizations, even by the desperate conditions of the Great Depression. Women's groups, so vital in driving the reforms of the Progressive Era, were largely absent from the New Deal. Progressive politics lost a vital set of advocates, a fact that went largely unnoticed at a moment when the possibilities for dramatic social change seemed rosier than ever.

The passage of the Nineteenth Amendment opened a very different era for social welfare reform than the one envisioned by suffragists in 1920. Instead of allowing female reformers to expand federal support for social welfare programs, female enfranchisement made it more difficult for the American left to achieve the goals formulated during the Progressive Era. It served as a catalyst for a new conservative movement, which emerged from the same world of female voluntary associations that had supported female reformers. Moved to action by the sense of civic duty conferred by the vote and impassioned by descriptions of a Bolshevik dystopia, this coalition of veteran clubwomen was well positioned to exert pressure within the world of middle-class women's politics. These new conservative activists seriously eroded the commitment to social welfare reforms that had animated women's clubs since the beginning of the twentieth century. In a lesson that would be repeated many times over the course of the twentieth century, progressive women discovered how difficult it was to exercise political influence in the face of female foes who rallied to defeat subversion under the banner "It takes women to fight women."

NOTES

1. Cone to Tuttle, frame 831; Chaffee to Wells, January 21, 1927, frames 828–29; Cone to Hoffman, frames 888–89; Feige to Wells, June 29, 1927, frames 871–72, all in National Office Subject Files, 1920–32, Papers of the League of Women Voters, microfilm edition, University Publications of America (UPA) (hereafter LWV Papers), series A, part 3, reel 9. Cone to McNider, Washington, D.C., February 7, 1927, Central Decimal Files, 1926–39, RG 407, Office of the Adjutant General, National Archives and Records Administration, Washington, D.C. (hereafter NARA), box 2316, National Defense file 381.

2. Hoffman to Cone, LWV Papers, series A, part 3, reel 9, frames 888–89.

3. Cone to McNider, February 7, 1927; Chaffee to Wells, January 21, 1927; Feige to Wells, June 29, 1927; Memorandum from Miss Wells Re Propaganda against the League in South Dakota reported October 1926, LWV Papers, series A, part 3, reel 4, frames 744–45.

4. Sophonisba P. Breckinridge, *Women in the Twentieth Century: A Study of Their Political, Social, and Economic Activities* (New York: McGraw-Hill, 1933), 264.

5. Anne Firor Scott, "After Suffrage: Southern Women in the Twenties," *Journal of Southern History* 30, no. 3 (August 1964): 298–318.

6. Robyn Muncy, *Creating a Female Dominion in American Reform, 1890–1930* (New York: Oxford University Press, 1991); J. Stanley Lemons, *The Woman Citizen: Social Feminism in the 1920s*, 2nd ed. (Charlottesville: University of Virginia Press, 1990); Nancy Cott, *The Grounding of Modern Feminism* (New Haven: Yale University Press, 1987).

7. Claudia Koonz, "Motherhood and Politics on the Far Right," in *The Politics of Motherhood: Activist Voices from Left to Right*, ed. Alexis Jetter, Annelise Orleck, and Diana Taylor (Hanover: University Press of New England, 1997), 231.

8. Renate Bridenthal and Claudia Koonz, "Beyond Kinder, Küche, Kirche: Weimar Women in Politics and Work," in *When Biology Became Destiny: Women in Weimar and Nazi Germany*, ed. Renate Bridenthal, Atina Grossman, and Marion Kaplan (New York: Monthly Review Press, 1984), 33–65; Julia Sneeringer, *Winning Women's Votes: Propaganda and Politics in Weimar Germany* (Chapel Hill: University of North Carolina Press, 2002); Raffael Scheck, "Women in the Non-Nazi Right During the Weimar Republic: The German Nationalist People's Party (DNVP)," in *Right-Wing Women: From Conservatives to Extremists Around the World*, ed. Paola Bacchetta and Margaret Power (New York: Routledge, 2002), 141–54.

9. Margaret Power, *Right-Wing Women in Chile: Feminine Power and the Struggle Against Allende, 1964–1973* (University Park: Pennsylvania State University Press, 2002); Sandra McGee Deutsch, "Spartan Mothers: Fascist Women in Brazil in the 1930s," in *Right-Wing Women: From Conservatives to Extremists Around the World*, ed. Paola Bacchetta and Margaret Power (New York: Routledge, 2002), 141–54.

10. Anne Rogers Minor, "Why I Am a Daughter of the American Revolution," June 12, 1930, quoted in Christine Erickson, "Conservative Women and Patriotic Maternalism: The Beginnings of a Gendered Conservative Tradition in the 1920s and 1930s" (Ph.D. diss., University of California, Santa Barbara, 1999), 30.

11. Quoted in Bridenthal and Koonz, "Beyond Kinder, Küche, Kirche," 41.

12. Mary G. Kilbreth, "The New Anti-feminist Campaign," *The Woman Patriot*, June 15, 1921, 2.

13. Ibid.

14. "National Association Moves to Washington," *The Woman Patriot*, October 9, 1920, 2; Kilbreth, "New Anti-feminist Campaign," 2–3; "Antis Will Renew Fight," *New York Times*, May 2, 1920, sec. 8, p. 2; "Fight on Suffrage Goes on," *New York Times*, July 3, 1919; Eleanor Flexner and Ellen Fitzpatrick, *Century of Struggle: The Woman's Rights Movement in the United States* (Cambridge, Mass.: Belknap Press of Harvard University, 1996), 300–317; Molly Ladd-Taylor, *Mother-Work: Women, Child Welfare, and the State, 1890–1930* (Urbana: University of Illinois Press, 1994), 169; Muncy, *Creating a Female Dominion in American Reform*, 124–57; Lemons, *Woman Citizen*, 153–67; Joseph B. Chepaitis, "Federal Social Welfare Progressivism in the 1920s," *Social Service Review* 46, no. 2 (1972): 213–29; Breckinridge, *Women in the Twentieth Century*, 257–74.

15. Mrs. A. N. Hoy to National PTA, Washington, D.C., December 12, 1926, Congress of Mothers, Correspondence, 1926, Elizabeth (Hewes) Tilton Papers, Schlesinger Library, Radcliffe College, Cambridge, Massachusetts, box 9, folder 248.

16. "Bolshevism Bared by R. E. Simmons," *New York Times*, February 18, 1919, 4.

17. Wendy Z. Goldman, *Women, the State, and Revolution: Soviet Family Policy and Social Life, 1917–1936* (New York: Cambridge University Press, 1993); Mikhail Stern with August Stern, *Sex in the USSR* (New York: Times Books, 1980), 20–36.

18. Oregon speech (September 26, 1924) by Mrs. Anthony Wayne Cook, "State Conferences," *Daughters of the American Revolution Magazine*, January 1925, 37–43; Address of Mrs. William Sherman Walker, Ohio State Conference of the Daughters of the American Revolution, Columbus, March 16, 1927, Helen Tufts Bailie Collection, Sophia Smith

Collection, Smith College, Northampton, Massachusetts, box 1, folder: Publications—DAR; Mrs. William Sherman Walker, "Keep Yourself Informed About Radicalism," *National Republic*, no. 4 (July 1925): 25.

19. *Proceedings of the Thirty-Third Continental Congress of the National Society of the Daughters of the American Revolution*, April 14–19, 1924, 541.

20. "Plans to Halt Bolshevism," *New York Times*, April 13, 1919, 22.

21. "The Report of the President National at the Thirty-Fifth Associate Council" (April 24, 1927), *National Society United States Daughters of 1812, News-Letter* 5, no. 1 (June 1927): 12, 18; no. 3 (March 1928): 27; no. 11 (March 1930): 18; no. 14 (December 1930): 8; all in United States Daughters of 1812 Library, Washington, D.C. See also Frank Ernest Hill, *The American Legion Auxiliary: A History: 1924–34* (Indianapolis: American Legion Auxiliary, 1935), 122–23, 243–53; Mrs. Jos. H. Thompson, *National American Legion Auxiliary*, vol. 1, *1921–24* (National American Legion Auxiliary, Jackson-Remlinger, 1926), 63.

22. *Proceedings of the Thirty-Fourth Continental Congress of the National Society of the Daughters of the American Revolution*, April 20–25, 1925, 471–72.

23. *Souvenir Edition, First Women's Patriotic Conference on National Defense* (Washington, D.C.: American Legion Auxiliary, 1925); "Program of Women's Patriotic Conference on National Defense" and "Organizations Participating in Conference with Number of Delegates," Numerical File 1921–42, War Department General Staff, G-1 (Personnel), RG 165, Records of the War Department General and Special Staffs, NARA, box 53, file 9650; Elisabeth Ellicott Poe, "The Woman's Patriotic Conference on National Defense," *Daughters of the American Revolution Magazine*, April 1927, 270–73.

24. Mrs. O. D. Oliphant, "Rallying for National Defense," *American Legion Weekly*, August 21, 1925; *Souvenir Edition, First Women's Patriotic Conference on National Defense*.

25. Quoted in Jan Doolittle Wilson, *The Women's Joint Congressional Committee and the Politics of Maternalism, 1920–30* (Urbana: University of Illinois Press, 2007), 1; Dorothy E. Johnson, "Organized Women as Lobbyists in the 1920s," *Capitol Studies* 1 (Spring 1972): 41–58; Charles Selden, "The Most Powerful Lobby in Washington," *Ladies Home Journal*, April 1922; Lemons, *Woman Citizen*, 154; Ladd-Taylor, *Mother-Work*, 170.

26. Quoted in Josephine Goldmark, *Impatient Crusader* (Urbana: University of Illinois Press, 1953), 93.

27. Dorothy Kirchwey Brown, "The Sheppard-Towner Bill Lobby," *The Woman Citizen*, January 22, 1921, 907–8; Lemons, *Woman Citizen*, 158; Ladd-Taylor, *Mother-Work*, 170.

28. Ladd-Taylor, *Mother-Work*, 173; Lemons, *Woman Citizen*, 165; "The Maternity Bill," *Capitol Eye*, October 1921, 3–12.

29. "Organizing Revolution Through Women and Children," *The Woman Patriot*, September 1 and 15, 1922, 3–8. For distribution, see "Propaganda Against Our Women's Organizations, Who is Madame Kollontai?" Mary Anderson Papers, microfilm edition of the Papers of the Women's Trade Union League and Its Principal Leaders, Schlesinger Library, Radcliffe College, reel 4, frames 310–11; and Summary of Report of Special Committee, Signed by Mrs. John D. Sherman et al., Maud May (Wood) Park, Woman's Rights Collection, microfilm edition, Women's Studies Manuscript Collection from the Schlesinger Library, Radcliffe College, series 1: Woman's Suffrage, part D: New England, UPA, 1993, reel 44, frames 1032–53.

30. "Organizing Revolution Through Women and Children," 3–8. For Engels's argument, see Friedrich Engels, *The Origin of the Family, Private Property, and the State* (New York: International Publishers, 1972).

31. "Organizing Revolution Through Women and Children," 3–8.

32. Address of Mrs. William Sherman Walker, "Americanism Versus Internationalism," in *Proceedings of the Thirty-Seventh Continental Congress of the National Society of the Daughters of the American Revolution*, April 16–21, 1928, 446.

33. *Proceedings of the Thirty-Sixth Continental Congress of the National Society of the Daughters of the American Revolution*, April 18–23, 1927, 420–21.

34. See Central File, 1925–28, box 321, folder 11–0-11, in the Records of the Children's Bureau, RG 102, NARA; Grace Brosseau to Madam State Regent, December 16, 1926, published in 69th cong., 2nd sess., *Congressional Record* (January 8, 1927), 1280–81.

35. Alice Bradford Wiles, Report of the Chairman of Committee on Legislation in U.S. Congress, *Daughters of the American Revolution Magazine*, April 1921, 236.

36. *Proceedings of the Seventeenth Continental Congress of the National Society of the Daughters of the American Revolution*, April 20–25, 1908, 542–50.

37. See, for example, Robert K. Murray, *Red Scare: A Study in National Hysteria, 1919–1920* (Minneapolis: University of Minnesota Press, 1955).

38. "A Petition for the Rejection of the Phipps-Parker Bill Proposing an Extension of the Maternity Act," Board of Directors of the Woman Patriot Publishing Company, 69th cong., 2nd sess., *Congressional Record* (July 3, 1926), 12918–52.

39. Ibid.

40. "Patriot Petition Now Public Document," *The Woman Patriot*, September 1, 1926.

41. Harris to Atwater, June 8, 1927, LWV Papers, series A, part 3, reel 15, frames 276–78.

42. Grace Brosseau to Madam State Regent, December 16, 1926; see Records of the Children's Bureau, Central File, 1925–28, box 321, folder 11–0-11.

43. Carrie Chapman Catt, "Lies-at-Large," *The Woman Citizen*, June 1927, 10–11, 41. For the reach of the petition, see Records of the Children's Bureau, Central File, 1925–28, box 321, folder 11–0-11.

44. See, for example, Anne E. Rude, Los Angeles, California, January 26, 1927; Dr. Josephine Piece, President, Ohio Federation of Women's Clubs, to Grace Abbott, March 6, 1927; Dr. Mary Riggs Noble, Commonwealth of Pennsylvania, to Miss Grace Abbott, September 30, 1927; all in Records of the Children's Bureau, Central File, 1925–28, box 321, folder 11–0-11.

45. Mary Kilbreth to Alexander Lincoln, April 23, 1926, Alexander Lincoln Papers, Schlesinger Library, Radcliffe College, box 2, folder 9.

46. "American War Mothers Denounce Maternity Act," *The Woman Patriot*, May 1, 1927, 71.

47. Mrs. Reuben Ross Holloway, "Correct Use of the Flag," *National Society United States Daughters of 1812, News-Letter* 4, no. 10 (June 1926): 15; "Resolutions," *National Society United States Daughters of 1812, News-letter* 4, no. 12 (March 1927): 13; both in United States Daughters of 1812 Library, Washington, D.C.

48. See 69th cong., 2nd sess., *Congressional Record* (January 8–12, 1927); Speech of Hon. William H. King of Utah, "Abolition of the Children's Bureau," 69th cong., 2nd sess., *Congressional Record* (January 11, 1927), oversized encapsulated box, Mrs. Reuben Ross Holloway Collection, Fort McHenry, Baltimore, Maryland.

49. Chepaitis, "Federal Social Welfare Progressivism in the 1920s," 222.

50. Breckinridge, *Women in the Twentieth Century*, 263.

51. Sherwin to Wells, February 11, 1927, LWV Papers, series A, part 3, reel 9, frames 840–41.

52. Chaffee to Wells, January 21, 1927; Cone to Hoffman; Hoffman to Feige, November 1927, LWV Papers, series A, part 3, reel 9, frame 887.

53. Ladd to Park, March 12, 1924, LWV Papers, series A, part 3, reel 4, frames 768–69.

54. Suggested Defense Kit, reel 9, frames 866–69; Adkins to Harrison, National LWV, March 5, 1927, reel 4, frames 739–40; both in LWV Papers, series A, part 3.

55. Cott, *Grounding of Modern Feminism*, 259.

56. Circular Letter to State Presidents from Elizabeth Tilton, March 15, 1927, Tilton Papers, box 9, folder 249; Watkins to Zillmer, March 1928, Records of the Children's Bureau, R6102, Central File, 1921–28, box 265, folder 1-7-2; Ladd-Taylor, *Mother-Work*, 64.

57. Ladd-Taylor, *Mother-Work*, 65. For more on this transformation, see Elizabeth Tilton to Mrs. Moulton, Tilton Papers, box 9, folder 250.

58. Edwards to Breckinridge, March 9, 1933, frame 488; Maule to Atwater, October 22, 1927, frame 27; Maule to Atwater, March 21, 1928, frame 162; Boole to WJCC, November 26, 1927, frame 80; all in Records of the WJCC, microfilm version, Library of Congress Manuscripts Division, Washington, D.C., reel 2; "Women's Clubs Ask Congress Inquiry," *New York Times*, May 30, 1928, 21.

59. Wilson, *Women's Joint Congressional Committee*, 1.

60. Muncy, *Creating a Female Dominion in American Reform;* William Chafe, "Women's History and Political History: Some Thoughts on Progressivism and the New Deal," in *Visible Women: New Essays on American Activism*, ed. Nancy A. Hewitt and Suzanne Lebsock (Urbana: University of Illinois Press, 1993), 101–18.

61. Linda Gordon, *Pitied but Not Entitled: Single Mothers and the History of Welfare, 1890–1935* (New York: Free Press, 1994), 257.

62. Ibid.

14

Women's Work in Argentina's Nationalist Lexicon, 1930–1943

Mariela Rubinzal

Fearing the growth of Communist organizing, right-wing Nationalists in Argentina in the conservative period from 1930 to 1943 reached out to female workers, although in limited ways. This chapter examines the cultural strategies that Nationalists used to appeal to women, including their cultural representations of women workers in fiction and journalism.

On September 6, 1930, the first coup d'état in Argentine history took place against the Radical president Hipólito Yrigoyen. The coup forces, led by General José Félix Uriburu, brought together various rightist sectors that had collaborated in the conspiratorial meetings along with the military. For their part, the political parties shared a negative diagnosis of the Yrigoyenist experience, and they had hopeful expectations for movements within the army. They thought that the president's personalist style of governance and interference in the political system had polluted democracy and, therefore, it was necessary to clean up the constitutional order. Debilitated by internal intrigues and the world economic crisis, which had seriously affected the agro-exporting economy, the Radical government fell almost without offering resistance. Nationalist groups proclaimed the end of modern democracy—which had started with the law of secret, mandatory, and universal suffrage in 1912—and the beginning of a new political order in which the army and the Catholic Church would play fundamental roles. Repressing leftists and moderates, the Uriburu government lasted barely two years due to the pressure exerted by democratic political forces for the return to constitutional rule. It gave way to a succession of conservative governments that resorted to various fraudulent mechanisms to control the electoral processes. In 1943 a new military regime again persecuted the left, proscribing communism, intervening in the General Confederation of Workers (CGT) and universities, dissolving antifascist parties and associations, and installing religious education in public schools.

This period witnessed the expansion of Argentine Nationalism as its associations and organs of doctrinal dissemination proliferated and its social base grew.[1] The Nationalists' main preoccupation was to halt the advance of leftist ideologies that they believed were very close to achieving social revolution. The various groups within Nationalism disagreed with one another, engaged in polemical internal debates, and caused internal fractures that derailed attempts to unify. Nevertheless, they shared some fundamental traits: they were antiliberal, antileftist, and corporatist. In general, they openly expressed anti-Semitism and wanted a hierarchically ordered society. Nationalists occupied posts in government and public administration and influenced military, educational, and cultural circles. They also fought leftists and union members in the streets.

The "crusade" that the Nationalists began in defense of the nation included the objective of returning women to their homes and reproductive functions.[2] They claimed that "dissolvent" ideologies threatened to destroy the family by "promoting divorce laws, free love, and proclaiming equal rights for women."[3] They declared it urgently necessary "to save Argentine women from being burned at the stake,"[4] particularly the workers, who were especially exposed to the advance of communism. Antonio Varela, a Nationalist and Catholic writer, warned about the life of women in the Soviet Union. By granting females the same labor rights and duties that men possessed, Communists had converted the woman into a "sad and ridiculous carnivalesque figure."[5] Varela thought that anarchists, Socialists, and Communists fought for equality between the sexes "to speculate with the advantages that the doctrine of free love signifies for men."[6] Seeking to emancipate women from the domestic realm, Socialists contributed to "prostituting" women, who were left defenseless in the face of their bosses' sexual harassment. Similarly, Communists, who also fought for women's liberation, in reality were "pushing" them to have abortions. Determined to weaken workers' ties to the left, Nationalists would use images of the degradation and immorality of women who had abandoned the security of their Christian homes.

Nationalism also took up an idea widely shared by the society of the interwar period: namely, that capitalism was destroying the biological conditions necessary to reproduce by exposing women to corporal excesses typical of the male labor force. Although leftists also denounced the impact of capitalist exploitation on female bodies, unlike Nationalists they did not defend the traditional social order. Nationalists expressed their concern over the disruption implied by the expansion of the feminine presence in the labor market, and they related it to the decrease in the birthrate and marriage. For them, this was "an extremely serious, far-reaching social problem that must be remedied with effective government measures."[7] Another topic they emphasized was the displacement of men from their jobs, since women accepted lower salaries, thereby generating a "radical upheaval in the Christian system of Argentine society."[8] As these problems occupied a central place in the Nationalist agenda, one must ask, how did Argentine Nationalism react to the increasing numbers of women in the labor market and the spread of communism among them?

In this chapter, I will analyze some of the strategies that Nationalism used to incorporate female workers into the movement and to channel their participation within certain defined limits. Toward this end, I will examine the variety of representations of women laborers in Nationalist literature and journalism, mainly formulated by men. How Nationalist women themselves, as writers, workers, militants, and readers, helped construct images of the world of female labor will also be discussed.

Nationalist literature directed to the general public, especially novels aimed at women, provided images and representations designed to avoid the spread of Communist influence. It was hoped that women would identify with the protagonists of this literature and grasp the teachings that Nationalists tried to disseminate in the private realm of Argentine homes. Newspapers also offer a privileged means of analyzing Nationalist images of the world of work and of labor conflicts. Through their press, Nationalists paid special attention to the problems of women and propelled the creation of Nationalist female entities. Women's place in Nationalist newspapers and novels is related to a larger phenomenon—the shaping of a mass culture that implied, among other things, the incorporation of the popular sectors as consumers. As shall be seen, Nationalists used various mass media to disseminate their ideas and influence female workers. Nonetheless, Nationalist discourse was often contradictory. In fact, its journalistic support for strikes and the promotion of anticommunist female unions frequently conflicted with the representations it spread through the media.

Rightist groups backed some female unions that demanded better salaries and denounced poor labor conditions, and, at the same time, they promoted a series of representations that opposed the participation of women in the world of work. The contradictions of a discourse that aspired to mobilize women yet simultaneously proclaimed the "return of women to the home" prompted the failure of this crusade. In addition, the progressive ideas that were deeply rooted in the workers' movement limited the rightist organizations' ability to compete with leftist predominance in the working class before the advent of Peronism.

Workers and Nationalism: Strategies Against Communist Advances

Nationalists employed several strategies in order to contain Communist unionization in the factories. On the one hand, they criticized the government for relying too heavily on simple coercion—for example, by repressing worker protests, expelling foreign militants, and jailing strikers and labor leaders.

On the other hand, they tried to attract workers by creating Nationalist unions that would defend their rights, as Nationalists defined them. Through their newspapers, Nationalists defended certain strikes and denounced the social injustice that working-class sectors experienced. Nationalist journalists and writers visited factories so that they could describe in newspapers and other publications the poor working and health conditions in which laborers performed their tasks.

The most important Nationalist groups of the period organized festivals in popular neighborhoods and massive public demonstrations for May 1, or Labor Day. These mobilizations are particularly revealing of the Nationalist goal of mobilizing ample sectors of society and competing with the left to represent workers. Nationalists tried to give this date on the workers' calendar a new meaning, one opposed to internationalism and to the notion of leftist revolution. In the Labor Day rallies, women played a vital role. Viewing them through the lens of Marianism and maternalism, male Nationalists thought that these women added a tone of Christian sacrifice and piety to the male parade, much like nurses selflessly attending their patients. As a Nationalist reporter observed, "They entered the [marching] column with simplicity, as tomorrow they will begin to serve. That service of aid, of Christian love, of watching over and caring for the wounded, that makes you forget every difficulty, every pain, every betrayal. The Fatherland is reflected in them, just as it is, resolute, combative, active, courageous, and compassionate. Christian like we want her."[9]

These women represented the opposite of the politicized female workers and Communist militants, characterized by one journalist as hotheaded and lascivious, with "hooked noses, bestially sensual lips, and pig-like eyes."[10] Nationalist women were considered the natural defenders of the family, work, patriotism, and religion.[11] The function performed by Nationalist female groups generally tended toward palliating the misery of the impoverished through charitable actions, such as soup kitchens, food, and clothing giveaways, as well as visits to the poor. The objective, as a Mrs. Padilla explained, was to avoid the propagation of communist ideas among the needy: "As women, our mission should be one of unity and harmony, smoothing things over, combating malicious acts [and] dissolvent ideas, defending the prestige and peace of the home, watching over the moral health of the children threatened by exotic ideas, alleviating social ills, and contributing to harmony among all who inhabit our generous soil."[12]

Nationalists tried to attract female workers through the notion that all women, as potential mothers, acted as transmitters of moral and social values in the home unit, which represented the nation in small scale. As shown in various studies, mothers were seen as the most appropriate vectors to "transmit" Nationalist principles to their spouses, parents, siblings, and offspring.[13] For this reason, including female workers was fundamental for a movement that was trying to compete with communism to attract women.

The dissemination and fixation of certain images through the Nationalist media and literature was especially important, since representations, as a process of building social meanings, are involved in identity formation. Representations operate in daily life, since they "also contribute to the construction of myths in the measure in which the images multiply until they achieve the status of truth."[14] The construction of identities was critical for Nationalists, who were preoccupied with the multiculturalism of Argentina, with its large foreign-born population. The immigrants who made up the labor force contributed their customs, expressions, interpretations, languages, and images, among other cultural manifestations, to their spaces of sociability. Nationalists viewed this situation as a dangerous "contamination" of the national character that required immediate attention. They proposed various tools to solve this problem, from expelling members of "undesirable" communities, such as Jews, to controlling the production and consumption of cultural goods.

The production and dissemination of mass culture expanded rapidly during the interwar period. For example, around 1930 there were approximately one thousand movie theaters located in various cities.[15] Women were among the new consumers, especially in the most dynamic urban areas. Magazines aimed at the female audience, films, and radio dramas featured protagonists who offered images and representations of working women.

Nationalists regarded the cultural industries as strategic devices, since they directly influenced working-class homes by "intoxicating" family morals, in their view. Nationalist Antonio Varela believed that cinema facilitated "the hidden but known intention of extremists, Jewish or non-Jewish, of corrupting the family and Christian society," while the theater had ceased to be art and now became "a simple store counter."[16] Varela believed that only the state was capable of regulating cultural production and circulation, thereby ensuring, for example, that 40 percent of movies would be national and that all schoolbooks would be checked and modified according to Nationalist doctrine.

Radio had a more extensive reach: according to official estimates, by 1938 there were 1,100,000 receivers, which meant one radio for every ten people.[17] Nationalists used this medium to reach Argentine homes in a massive way. Nationalist priest Virgilio Filippo's radio programs are especially well known, since they were compiled and published in several volumes. Filippo was determined to "offer scientific proof of the myth of the Jewish world conspiracy."[18] Nationalist women also had their space on the radio, titled "Nationalist Culture." The Sunday broadcasts by "a distinguished lady and prestigious Argentine intellectual," whose pseudonym was Carola, exhorted women to interest themselves in their husbands' concerns. Carola believed that women directly influenced their spouses' political opinions, and this conferred upon them the responsibility of guiding the men in a rightist direction. Women should convince men with the following arguments: "You are responsible for our distress and our misfortune, you are the only one responsible, because you with your vote, believing that friendship obliged you to obey the plea of a workmate or a superior, you have chosen innocently and ingenuously the one that only sought to soar to power, and he has used you, caring neither about his duty nor his country."[19]

Carola did not demand equal social and political rights for women, as leftist women and feminists did. Her discourse was aimed at feeding women's interest in political issues, but only so that they were able to persuade their husbands effectively. For their part, feminists denounced the fact that women workers suffered a "double subordination" (as women and workers) thanks to the "clever propaganda deployed by women from the aristocracy."[20]

As for written production, the publishing industry experienced growth and consolidation in this period. Indeed, new firms specializing in various thematic areas emerged in Buenos Aires and other cities. They published works by Argentine authors and translations of works by foreign writers, which joined the periodicals aimed at the general public. The National Registry of Intellectual Property of 1936 recorded the publication of 823 registered works; almost half of these were of a literary nature.[21]

Nationalists were concerned about the proliferation of works aimed at the masses: "Today much is written, too much, especially novels. It could be said that this genre has been abused and continues to be abused because it is a composition easy to popularize." Nevertheless, they considered that some literary books served to "counteract the pernicious effects" of vulgar novels that poisoned the soul.[22] One of the consequences of "erotic literature," as they called it, was that it fed an excessive preoccupation with material goods, "which had been deified." The expansion of female participation in the labor market, not only in industry but also in government administrative posts and in business, implied—among other things—the consumption of superfluous goods. According to Nationalists, "Jews hid" in beauty parlors and the fields of fashion and cosmetics, where they enriched themselves by eroticizing women.

The "edifying" literature that Nationalists promoted to counter the profusion of "bad" literature is varied and comes from various disciplines, such as politics, philosophy, theology, and fiction. The novels aimed at the lower classes, which center on the "social question," are particularly important for their representations of women, since they systemically treated labor, affective, and other daily issues concerning women during the 1930s.

Women and Work in Anticommunist Literature

The corpus of literature that I analyze consists of two novels and several short stories by Juan Carlos Moreno, one of the most important Catholic Nationalist writers of the interwar period.[23] It also includes a narrative by Sara Montes de

Oca, a Catholic writer who shared Moreno's dramatic style of relating women workers' stories. Penned by two well-known authors, these writings illumi-nate the most common topics of a literary current aimed toward the popular sectors, one that expanded during the 1930s. These works shared the goal of re-Christianizing the poor and protecting them from leftist influence. The historical context for the appearance of these literary texts was one in which import-substitution industrialization was deepening and communism was growing in the workers' movement.

Tiempos amargos (Bitter times, 1935) was one of the most widely publicized novels in Nationalist newspapers, which praised Moreno's sensibility in de-scribing the hellishness of working-class life as well as his antileftist pro-gram: "He makes his characters speak at the very scene in which the action takes place, and puts in their mouths the solution to the problems he contem-plates. They argue, talk about a fair salary, and propose improvements. They defend social justice, not with socialist or extreme left chimeras, but instead by taking up again the teaching of the immortal [Pope] Leo XIII's [encyclical] Rerum Novarum."[24] Set in the early years of the 1930s, the novel recreates life in the factories and in the city of Buenos Aires with a clearly decadent tone. Nevertheless, at the end of the text, pessimism gives way to an extensive pro-grammatic proposal to change the political and social order. The pedagogic style with which Moreno constructed the narration—which lacks any sophis-tication of language—manifests his notion of an audience that possessed few tools to decode a novel. The language is simple and direct, seeking iden-tification between the ideal readers and the characters in the novel, who were both from the popular sectors.

The main character, Pedro Frías, was an accounting clerk at an electrical appliance factory owned by an Italian, who, with his family, managed the firm. Frías had additional jobs to supplement his meager salary, which was the only source of income for his family, comprising his mother and his sister, neither of whom worked outside the home. His employers led a dissipated life—taking vacations in Mar del Plata, journeying to foreign countries, and wearing expensive clothes—that contrasted with the work-ers' impoverished existence in tenements, lower-class neighborhoods, and shantytowns.

Moreno voiced the old and widely disseminated idea that male unemploy-ment resulted from mechanization and female work, "because women will settle for a lower salary, and a position occupied by a woman is a position lost by a man. That's why unemployment is not a female problem, but a male problem."[25] Drama permeated the lives of women who were forced to enter the world of labor. For instance, when her father lost his job, a middle-class teen-age girl had to abandon her schooling and begin work in a stocking factory. Her duties consisted of checking that the machine did not break down or be-come entangled, which demanded an excessive degree of concentration that harmed the eyes. Besides this, she had to endure her boss's constant sexual overtures. Employers' sexual abuse appears in Moreno's tales as a daily occurrence in various workplaces.

Working-class women also suffered low salaries and the mechanization of work processes; they became automatons and slaves of the machine. In the meatpacking and cigarette industries, women workers were "yellowish, hunched over, with sunken chests, sad, wilted."[26] In spite of it all, Moreno did not construct a passive image of women; on the contrary, they participated in strikes just as men did. For example, Moreno described the police repression in an *alpargata* (footwear worn by the poor) factory located in the Villa Crespo neighborhood, where female strikers protested that "instead of protecting us, the police take side with the bosses, who have gotten in good with the police commissioner. We, the poor, have no one to defend us!"[27]

Conflict in the streets and in the factories is a constant in the novel. But strikes—organized by some leftist workers—did not offer a solution, since they could cause loss of jobs and further worsen the workers' situation. The organized labor movement is absent in the novel, despite the fact that the General Confederation of Workers (CGT), a representative entity of the Argentine working class, arose during this period.[28] Moreno described a fragmented world of work, without mediations between merciless abuse by employers and individual penuries of workers. The solution was to establish a corporatist state, which would protect workers in particular, since capitalists already had resources to defend themselves. In this way, the intrinsic injustice of the capitalist system would be corrected, although social differences would not be eliminated. At any rate, Moreno and other Nationalist authors claimed that class struggle was based on an "illusory equality."

In the short story "Una obrera" (A female worker, 1943), Moreno narrated the life of Lucía, starting with the firing of her husband, Eugenio Ramírez, who worked at a meatpacking plant in the city of Avellaneda. At first, Eugenio did not want his wife to work at a factory because it would disrupt family life. In response Lucía said, "I have thought it over well. God will help us. I will get up earlier than usual. In one hour I will clean the house, bathe the children, and prepare breakfast. I will ask the neighbor to watch them while I'm at work. Later I will come back to prepare lunch, and by 1 P.M. I'll be back at the plant. When I come back, I'll have more than enough time to tend to you and the children and make dinner. Many married women do it that way."[29]

As clearly seen, women workers suffered the double day of family and factory work. They could not hand over domestic chores to anyone else. In a short time, the job of cleaning and classifying the dirty bristles of the animals weakened Lucía's health, as the dust emitted when the skeins were cleaned entered her lungs and progressively deteriorated them. "A woman's body cannot resist such a heavy load as is demanded by attention to the home, offspring, and factory work, without shattering," said a doctor who examined Lucía. "The workshop or factory kills or denaturalizes her."[30] This story imparts one of the basic principles that rightists upheld: married women should not work. "Regarding this point," recommended author Antonio Varela, "Nationalist doctrine should remain intransigent, like a closed fist."[31]

The image of female professionals—such as doctors, lawyers, intellectuals, and writers—was one of "masculinized" women, "inverted men," monstrous creatures that defied the natural order of things. In Varela's view, these professional women acted "with the malice of circus monkeys and the vacuous seriousness of parrots."[32] Women should only discuss matters related to maternity and create a "corporation of mothers" to talk about "pregnancy, lactation, child rearing, things which we men will never experience."[33] This corporation would be one of the entities making up the "constitutional dictatorship" proposed by Varela, whose model was Italian fascist corporatism.

The short story "Oveja descarriada" (Lost sheep, 1939) described women who started on a path of economic independence and personal realization. Here Moreno related the story of Carolina, a young woman from the province who moved to Buenos Aires to fulfill her dream of bettering herself economically and enjoying urban cultural attractions. "Carolina was not a bad person," the narrator constantly repeated, but she was ambitious and pretty, two qualities that made her fall for the temptations of worldly life and forget about "her town, her mother, her sister, even herself. Her soul was asleep; she didn't have time for reflection. The diversions of the big city distanced her from her soul to make her surrender to the world."[34] While living in a pension without finding honorable work, she became a dancer in a cabaret and later in a variety show, where she was forced to engage in acts contrary to her morals, such as dancing semi-naked onstage, singing coarse songs, and imitating a daring foreign dancer. "It would have been better for her if she had been a vulgar girl, neither ugly nor pretty, one who did not draw attention, one who worked in a shop or at her mother's side," the narrator stated. "She would be poor, it's true, but she would have peace and humble dreams."[35] Finally, a priest advised Carolina to return to her town, devalue her physical attractiveness, and nourish spiritual beauty, so that she might lead a humble life "in conformity with poverty."[36] The solution was to forget her desires and resign herself to a modest existence.

The dangers of modern life in a cosmopolitan city reappear in the short story "El piso 16" (Sixteenth floor, 1939).[37] The life of a middle-class couple and child changed when they moved from outlying Villa Crespo to a modern apartment downtown.[38] In her new home, Ramona began to enjoy socializing with her friends, who now visited her more often, as well as her outings to downtown stores, where she bought all kinds of objects. These new habits endangered her idyllic family life. Ramona, like other women in Moreno's tales, appeared as a weak spirit, easily broken, who succumbed to vices and the superficiality of modern existence.

The exception was Enriqueta, the main character of the novel *Frente al mundo* (Facing the world, 1933). She was a young professor of drawing and painting who had to enter the labor force because of a family misfortune, her parents' premature death. Her studies were only a pastime until she was ready to marry. Moreno wrote, "Enriqueta observed with distress that the majority of the women workers were taciturn, pale, timid, in spite of the rouge that disguised them a bit; they seemed tired, they had inexpressive eyes, many of them stripped of that vivacity and delicateness that constitutes the charm of all women. Would she become like them, in time?"[39] However, in spite of encountering this and other tragic situations—such as being stalked by her aunt and enduring poverty, illness, loneliness, and unsuitable labor situations—Enriqueta never abandoned her principles and Christian morals.

This tour through Juan Carlos Moreno's literature provides us with a series of representations of women workers that circulated through wide sectors of society. Argentine painters, musicians, and writers with differing ideological convictions and life paths agreed on the destructive aspect of women's exploitation in the factories and the misery in which they lived, threatened by fatigue, hunger, and poor health. As Mirta Lobato has pointed out, "Women condemned to work, with tension between honor and virtue, the bosses' despotic and bloodthirsty power, are the most widely disseminated images of female laborers."[40] Nonetheless, in Nationalist literature, women workers appeared not only as exploited but as disturbers of a rigid social order. They were morally weak beings who had to be confined to the realm of the home.

The literary texts of female Catholic writers, such as Sara Montes de Oca, were not out of tune with the stories I have just analyzed. In *La sirvientita* (The little maid, 1936), Montes de Oca narrated the misfortunes of a teenager from the country's interior, who started working as a maid for a provocative and sensual foreign woman—often Nationalist code words for Jews. The "savior" of the young Angelina was a woman belonging to the Catholic Action organization, who took her to work in her own home. As Omar Acha notes, the girl's social status did not change; her salvation consisted of working in the household of a morally irreproachable Catholic employer. This type of literature emphasizes a "Nationalist ethnic discourse"[41] that frequently identified Jews as being usurers, doctors who performed abortions, or union activists and labor agitators.

Women and Work in Anticommunist Newspapers

Nationalist women had access to all types of written publications; they also organized their own libraries and meetings to read together. At these meetings, they exchanged opinions and discussed different themes of interest. The task of reconstructing their ideas and readings is arduous since these women's direct testimonies are not plentiful.[42] Nevertheless, their letters to the Nationalist press give us a partial idea of how they received the representations of women.

In general terms, these letters affirmed the notions of female work that rightists promoted. Nationalist women sent expressions of gratitude and information about their activities to the newspapers. However, dissenting expressions also appeared. This was the case for a female administrative employee who argued with a columnist of the Nationalist newspaper *Crisol*. The reader underlined the journalist's fallacy in considering women as inferior to men and hardly qualified for labor tasks. This woman also refuted the thesis of male unemployment as a product of women entering the labor market. Her argument was the universal right to life and to reproduce daily life: "Since work is not a privilege created exclusively for men, but simply the means of ensuring life, then it would be the last straw to claim that men have more of a right to life than women do."[43]

In any case, this letter, which disagreed with male opinion, was an exception. Usually, female workers asked journalists to investigate and inform the community about the abuses and substandard conditions that women endured in textile factories and meatpacking plants. The relationship among newspapers, columnists, and Nationalist women workers was one of empathy and cooperation. These women used the press to express their problems and concerns, communicate their activities, and declare their adherence to the movement. For example, in August 1941, a delegation of Catholic Nationalist Women Workers visited the *Crisol* offices to thank the staff for its campaign in favor of a law regulating work performed at home.[44] That same year, a woman reader who worked at the Armour meatpacking plant decried the conditions for women who labored in this industry and submitted her story to the Nationalist press for dissemination. The inscription under the photo of the front of the Armour building that accompanied the article said, "Façade of the establishment where the greatest crimes are committed in the name of the wrongly called Argentine Democracy, against the mothers of our future soldiers. And to think that they say that the female sex is treated with certain considerations!"[45]

Rightist journalists and writers visited factories and meticulously described the situation of women workers. Their literary and journalistic descriptions coincided on more than one occasion. This is explained by the fact that some of the most important writers, such as Juan Carlos Moreno, assiduously collaborated with Nationalist reporters. It is also evident that other columnists used literature as material for their newspaper articles. It is not surprising to find criticism of liberalism in their denunciations of working conditions for women: "Democracy lacks, then, a social conscience; it lacks real activity in defense of workers, and it lacks the indispensable State control."[46] To this was added the idea that communism took advantage of the situation to attract laborers and the unemployed. As Nationalist women explained, it was necessary to "take a word of encouragement and hope to those unfortunate wretches" since misery "is fertile ground for the germination of that bad seed that is sowed everywhere by the enemies of order."[47]

Working conditions and conflicts in the textile industry aroused the attention of Nationalist journalists. This was because the industry grouped together a significant number of immigrant workers, the large majority of whom possessed few skills and over two-thirds of whom were women and girls.[48] Besides, many company owners in this sector were of Jewish origin. Nationalists argued that the mistreatment of workers was a Jewish principle, as it was what "the Protocols of the Elders of Zion demanded."[49]

Nationalists were also concerned by the Communist influence in the unions that represented the sector's workers. The most important of these was the Textile Worker Union (UOT), headed by Socialist and Communist militants who shared the leadership from 1936 to 1941.[50] To counter this threat, rightists created or strengthened antileftist unions, such as the Catholic Union of the Needle; the Union of Seamstresses; the Advisory Board of Ducilo, one of the biggest textile factories in the country, located in the locality of Berazategui (south of the federal capital); and the Group of Textile Workers, which adhered to the Junta of Coordination Against Communism.[51] Among the Catholic organizations, we should recognize the role played by the Association of Women of Catholic Action (AMAC), which worked to obtain regulation of work performed in the home, higher salaries for women, and the right to seek vocational training, among other petitions to the authorities. Victoria Arana Díaz, delegate of the AMAC, clarified that its objective was not to oppose employers but to contribute to the formation of "serious organizations" that respected others' rights[52]—thus differentiating them from leftist unions, in her view.

In general, the newspapers presented themselves as supporters of workers' demands and denounced police repression. An example of this is the conflict that took place in the summer of 1940 in the Argentine Cotton Manufacturer company. The Nationalist newspaper *El Pampero* insulted the mounted police for brutally suppressing the male and female strikers and hindering the reporters whom the newspaper sent to the factory.[53] The Nationalist newspapers' backing in workers' struggles was one of the multiple strategies used to reach out to nonunionized laborers. Yet this pro-worker discourse was often presented in an ambiguous manner. Rightist journalists made an extremely confusing differentiation between fair demands and "revolutionary gymnastics," supporting the former while opposing the latter.[54]

Final Considerations

Like other social sectors and the state, Nationalism was preoccupied with the worrisome situation of women workers during the interwar period. This constituted one of the most important issues for the movement, which had developed a special interest in the "social question." Through their books, lectures, and newspapers, its members denounced the degradation of female bodies and morality in factories and offices. Nationalists associated female labor with prostitution and the eroticization of women and claimed to see Jews lurking behind this degeneracy. In their view, Jews were lascivious employers inclined to corrupt their servants, doctors who provided abortions for lower-class women, and leftists who exploited female workers' poverty and the lack of welfare programs to achieve Moscow's hidden aims. Nationalists regarded female writers and professionals as an abominable characteristic of modern times, since they believed that women intellectuals adopted male traits. Nationalists thought that the liberal state was incapable of resolving the problems of women and that government agencies dedicated to labor affairs were ineffective. For them, the most important menace was communism, which during these years had spread among the working class and encouraged women's unionization.

To halt the dispersion of communism among female workers, Nationalists elaborated diverse strategies to apply to the world of labor. They developed a radicalized rhetoric to support workers' demands in literature and in the press and tried to create and consolidate a few anticommunist unions to defend their rights. They included women in numerous political and cultural activities, such as the organization of festivals that took place in the working-class neighborhoods of Buenos Aires, and they summoned them to participate in Labor Day rallies. Furthermore, they allotted spaces in their newspapers in which to address women's problems and provide women with opportunities to express themselves. Nevertheless, the representations that they disseminated through Nationalist literature and newspapers imposed the notion of women returning to the home.

It is interesting to note that Nationalists could have devoted more attention to organizing women workers. Instead, they concentrated their efforts on creating male unions in the industrial and service sectors and among teachers, actors, small merchants, and other occupations. This accorded with the ideology of a predominantly male movement that assigned determinant roles to masculinity and physical violence.

The results of Nationalist strategies to co-opt women workers were very much below the expectations of Nationalist militants. Part of the explanation for this failure lies in the evident contradictions of a discourse that recognized women as protagonists in the labor force yet considered work, politics, and union activity to be exclusively male spaces. One must also note that the limitations of Nationalist social programs, in addition to the street violence in which Nationalist militants engaged, helped impede the propagation of worker-oriented Nationalism in the 1930s.

NOTES

I thank Sandra McGee Deutsch for her constant support and her invitation to contribute to this volume, and Juan Suriano and dissertation writers of the Instituto de Altos Estudios Sociales for their comments and suggestions.

Translations of quotes from the Spanish were supplied by Rafael Núñez and Sandra McGee Deutsch.

1. On the popularization of the Nationalist movement, which had once been elitist, see Sandra McGee Deutsch, *Las derechas: La extrema derecha en la Argentina, el Brasil y Chile, 1890–1939* (Buenos Aires: Universidad Nacional de Quilmes Editorial, 2005), and Mariela Rubinzal, "Del elitismo al nacionalismo obrerista: La derecha argentina y la cuestión obrera en los años treinta," *Entrepasados*, no. 30 (2006): 67–85.

2. In this aspect they were not original; other social discourses of the period, including some from the left, also adhered to principles of the ideology of domesticity, affirming that domestic chores defined feminine identity. See Mirta Lobato, *Historia de las trabajadoras en la Argentina (1869–1960)* (Buenos Aires: Edhasa, 2007).

3. *Crisol*, June 19, 1936, 1.

4. Anónimo, *Bandera Argentina*, August 17, 1932, 3.

5. Antonio Varela, *Las hordas comunistas* (Buenos Aires, 1932), 210.

6. Antonio Varela, *El nacionalismo argentino y los obreros socialistas* (Buenos Aires: Imprenta López, 1935), 179.

7. *Crisol*, July 2, 1938, 1, 3.

8. *Crisol*, November 6, 1938, 1.

9. *Crisol*, May 7, 1939, 1.

10. *Crisol*, May 3, 1936, 1.

11. Sandra McGee Deutsch has shown that many Nationalist women had previously participated in Social Catholicism; thus, many of them entered the extreme right as an extension of their activities within the Catholic Church. See Deutsch, "Spreading Right-Wing Patriotism, Femininity, and Morality: Women in Argentina, Brazil, and Chile, 1900–1940," in *Radical Women in Latin America: Left and Right*, ed. Victoria González and Karen Kampwirth (University Park: Pennsylvania State University Press, 2001), 223–48.

12. *Bandera Argentina*, November 23, 1932, 3.

13. Deutsch, "Spreading Right-Wing Patriotism," 245; Marcela Nari, "El feminismo frente a la cuestión de la mujer en las primeras décadas del siglo XX," in *La cuestión social en Argentina (1870–1943)*, ed. Juan Suriano (Buenos Aires: La Colmena, 2000), 279.

14. Lobato, *Historia*, 298.

15. For this statistic and other information in this paragraph, see Leandro González Leandri, "La nueva identidad de los sectores populares," in *Nueva Historia Argentina*, vol. 7, *Crisis económica, avance del estado e incertidumbre política (1930–1943)*, ed. Alejandro Cattaruzza (Buenos Aires: Sudamericana, 2001), 234.

16. Varela, *El nacionalismo*, 167.

17. González Leandri, "La nueva identidad," 234.

18. Daniel Lvovich, *Nacionalismo y antisemitismo en la Argentina* (Buenos Aires: Ediciones B, 2003), 417.

19. Radio station L.S. 1, "Para la mujer argentina. Conferencia radiotelefónica," Nationalist cultural program sponsored by the Gobierno Provisional de la Nación, Buenos Aires, 1941.

20. Mirta Lobato, "Entre la protección y la exclusión: Discurso maternal y protección de la mujer obrera, Argentina 1890–1934," in *La cuestión social en Argentina (1870–1943)*, ed. Juan Suriano (Buenos Aires: La Colmena, 2000), 254.

21. A total of 372 literary works were published throughout the country. That number can be divided into (a) 149 works of prose fiction; (b) 77 works of philosophy, criticism, and essays; (c) 77 works of poetry; (d) 69 works of drama and comedy. See Eustacio A. García, *Historia de la empresa editorial en Argentina: Siglo XX* (Buenos Aires, 1999). I thank the Cámara Argentina del Libro for showing me this study.

22. *Crisol*, February 6, 1936, 3.

23. Juan Carlos Moreno wrote columns in the periodicals *Crisol* and *Criterio*. He was the author of numerous books on the Malvinas Islands and other themes. In 1962 his

book on Catholic Nationalist Gustavo Martínez Zuviría was published by the Ministry of Education and Justice in its Ediciones Culturales Argentinas collection, promoted by the General Board of Culture.

24. *Crisol*, February 6, 1936, 3.

25. Juan Carlos Moreno, *Tiempos amargos* (Buenos Aires: Cabaut, 1935), 76.

26. Ibid., 216.

27. Ibid., 18.

28. By 1929 there were four union federations: the Regional Argentine Labor Federation (anarchist), Argentine Labor Confederation (Socialist, created in 1926), Argentine Syndical Union (USA, syndicalist, founded in 1922), and Committee of Classist Syndical Unity (CUSC, Communist, created in 1929). The Socialists and syndicalists decided to build unity within the labor movement by creating the CGT in 1930. See Hugo Del Campo, *Sindicalismo y peronismo: Los comienzos de un vínculo perdurable* (Buenos Aires: CLACSO, 1983).

29. Juan Carlos Moreno, "Una obrera," in *El potentado y el niño* (Buenos Aires, 1943), 58.

30. Ibid., 63.

31. Varela, *El nacionalismo*, 170.

32. Ibid., 173.

33. Ibid., 171.

34. Juan Carlos Moreno, "Oveja descarriada," in *Cuentos del campo y la ciudad* (Buenos Aires: Editorial Patagonia, 1939), 20.

35. Ibid., 22.

36. Ibid., 30.

37. Juan Carlos Moreno, "El piso 16," in *Cuentos del campo y la ciudad* (Buenos Aires: Editorial Patagonia, 1939), 73–82.

38. In the 1930s, the city of Buenos Aires was transformed architecturally. Tall apartment buildings with modernist profiles of white skyscrapers proliferated, altering the urban physiognomy, especially in the central zone. The technological modernization of dwellings profoundly transformed domestic habits. See Anahí Ballent and Adrián Gorelik, "País urbano o país rural: La modernización territorial y su crisis," in *Nueva Historia Argentina*, vol. 7, *Crisis económica, avance del estado e incertidumbre política (1930–1943)*, ed. Alejandro Cattaruzza (Buenos Aires: Sudamericana, 2001), 143–200.

39. Juan Carlos Moreno, *Frente al mundo* (Buenos Aires: Cabaut, 1933), 147.

40. Lobato, *Historia*, 294. According to this study, the image of the "poor little female worker" would predominate until the appearance of Peronism, which ruptured the common representations of female labor.

41. Omar Acha, "Catolicismo social y feminidad en la década de 1930: De 'damas' a 'mujeres,'" in *Cuerpos, géneros e identidades: Estudios de historia de género en Argentina*, ed. Paula Halperín y Omar Acha (Buenos Aires: Ediciones del Signo, 2000), 223–24. Both Montes de Oca and Moreno expressed ethnic hostility in their writings, and Moreno used anti-Semitic stereotypes. See Sara Montes de Oca, "La sirvientita," *Anhelos*, no. 10 (August 1936), cited in ibid.

42. For a reflection on the reasons for the insufficiency of female sources in different periods, see Michelle Perrot, *Mi historia de las mujeres* (Buenos Aires: Fondo de Cultura Económica, 2008).

43. *Crisol*, March 2, 1941, 4.

44. *Crisol*, August 1, 1941, 4.

45. *Crisol*, July 31, 1941, 4.

46. *Crisol*, October 18, 1938, 4; November 30, 1939, 1.

47. *Bandera Argentina*, November 23, 1932, 3.

48. Torcuato Di Tella, *Perón y los sindicatos: El inicio de una relación conflictiva* (Buenos Aires: Grupo Editorial Planeta, 2003), 278. Industrial statistics for 1935 showed that in the textile and apparel industry, women represented 57.8 percent of the labor force throughout the country. See Lobato, *Historia*, 47.

49. *Crisol,* May 27, 1936, 3.

50. In 1939 Communists drove Socialists out of the union's general secretariat. In 1941 the Socialists finally separated from the union and formed a UOT parallel to the Communist one.

51. Of these *gremial* associations, those registered in the National Department of Labor were the Catholic Union of the Needle, with 1,890 members, and the Union of Seamstresses, with 1,200. As was true for other Catholic unions, their statutes declared that they worked for God, fatherland, family, and property in accord with Christian sociological principles. See Departamento Nacional de Trabajo, *Asociaciones obreras y patronales* (Buenos Aires: Ministerio del Interior, 1941), 35.

52. Acha, "Catolicismo social," 218–21.

53. *El Pampero,* January 17, 1940, 1.

54. Mariela Rubinzal, "Los conflictos obreros en la prensa nacionalista: Itinerarios de un ambiguo acercamiento al mundo del trabajo (1935–1943)," *Papeles de Trabajo* 2, no. 3 (June 2008), electronic journal of the Instituto de Altos Estudios Sociales of the Universidad Nacional de General San Martín.

15

"To Tell All My People": Race, Representation, and
John Birch Society Activist Julia Brown

Veronica A. Wilson

In June 1962, Julia Clarice Brown, a middle-aged African American woman
and former Communist, went public with her story of serving nine years as
a Federal Bureau of Investigation (FBI) informant within the Communist
Party of the United States (CPUSA). For three days, she testified before the
House Committee on Un-American Activities (HUAC), describing her experiences as a Communist and "undercover agent" in the Cleveland area.
Brown identified more than one hundred persons whom she knew or believed to be CPUSA members or sympathizers. During these hearings,
HUAC subpoenaed eighteen accused individuals to answer Brown's charges
before the committee. All pled the Fifth Amendment against self-incrimina-
tion, refusing to discuss alleged party memberships, radical political activities or convictions, or any personal knowledge of Brown. Despite this, HUAC
members praised Brown for her patriotic service, emphasizing her important contribution to the struggle against communism.[1]

Brown's testimony was but the beginning of her life as an anticommunist
activist and public speaker. Indeed, her FBI and HUAC contacts, with the
support of other committed anticommunists, enabled her to create a lucrative career as a professional, conservative anticommunist. By 1963 Brown
was a full-time speaker for the right-wing John Birch Society, which in 1966
published her memoir of her years in the CPUSA and FBI.[2] By 1964 she was
an outspoken opponent of the entire civil rights movement and, in particular, the Reverend Dr. Martin Luther King Jr. A decade after King's assassination, Brown again testified before Congress, opposing the creation of a
national holiday commemorating him. Brown's passionate anticommunism
outweighed her concern that African Americans suffered second-class citi-

zenship in the United States. Her identity as a crusader against the CPUSA and its allies seemingly "trumped" her racial identity at a time when identity politics became increasingly central to U.S. politics and society.

This essay traces Brown's anticommunist career from its inception to her final appearance before Congress in 1979, analyzing how her right-wing opposition to the civil rights movement grew even as mainstream public opinion moved in the opposite direction. I examine Brown's transformation from a liberal anticommunist to an avid supporter of George Wallace and Richard Nixon, dedicated to countering both liberal and left-wing movements. I also analyze the considerable influence Brown had within right-wing circles, despite the fact that she is virtually unknown in U.S. history today. Finally, I conclude with questions for further analysis of Brown and her impact on American politics and the civil rights movement.

When Brown appeared before HUAC in 1962, she was virtually unknown to the American public and the national Communist Party. Within Cleveland CPUSA and civil rights circles, however, she had played an active role for more than nine years. Brown began her left-wing activism in 1947, soon after moving to a middle-class area of Cleveland with her husband, J. Curlee Brown. White neighbors William and Elizabeth Cooper befriended the Browns, discussing racial problems in the city and nation with them. Julia claimed that she had rarely experienced discrimination but was appalled at the Coopers' stories of police brutality, housing discrimination, segregation laws, lynchings, and other racial injustices.

The Coopers introduced her to like-minded friends, and Brown was attracted to their egalitarianism. Later she explained, "So here, I thought, is a group of white people on my side. . . . Absolutely no difference. No segregation. It was just as if they didn't know the difference between Negro and white. It's only when you are deeply embedded in the party that you find out what's behind all this." In late 1947, Brown joined the Civil Rights Congress (CRC), an organization of liberals and Communists who provided attorneys to fight civil rights violations against African Americans and leftist radicals. Around Christmastime, she also joined the CPUSA.[3]

Initially, Brown felt restricted by her limited education and political naivete. Needing to work for a living, she had left high school after the tenth grade and moved from Atlanta to Chicago. Throughout adulthood, much of her time was spent helping Curlee build his truck-hauling business and purchase and manage rental properties. Through long hours and hard effort, the Browns had achieved middle-class status by 1947—something Julia believed made her an attractive communist recruit. At any rate, she claimed to know little about communism when she joined the CRC and CPUSA. Her commitment was not to a working-class revolution but to improving conditions for African Americans—or, as she called them, "her people."[4] Brown believed that the CRC's focus would be the prevention of lynchings and police brutality. Yet often it concentrated on providing legal defense for CPUSA leaders arrested for alleged conspiracy to advocate the overthrow of the U.S. government.[5] In addition, Brown came to believe that the CRC's propaganda was misleading and anti-American. Claiming to have neither witnessed police brutality nor experienced such violence against friends or family throughout her years in Atlanta, Chicago, and Cleveland, Brown decided that the CRC exaggerated the problem to stir up black resentment toward police and state authority. She surmised that this was part of the conspiracy to manipulate African Americans, foment civil strife, and effect the overthrow of the U.S. government.[6] In a metaphor she repeatedly employed, Brown said, "The Communists use civil rights as the sugar to catch the flies for the poison. Civil rights is the sugar to entice the people. And after they get an audience, then they feed them the poison."[7]

Brown claimed that the CPUSA was more interested in using African Americans for communist ends than in fighting to improve actual living conditions for black people. Not only did the party and CRC spend more time working on behalf of white communist leaders than against segregation or inferior housing, but they also discriminated against Brown and others she knew, despite their pretense of egalitarianism. Although she lived in the southeast area of Cleveland, she was required to join a party section group in the northeast area of the city, because, she said, that group was integrated while the southeastern group remained lily-white. Furthermore, her duties consisted of menial secretarial and chauffeur work for Frieda Katz, the Cleveland area's CRC organizer, in addition to the chores that rank-and-file members routinely performed, such as distributing pamphlets and selling subscriptions to the *Daily Worker*.[8]

By late 1948, Brown had had enough. She believed that the CPUSA did not genuinely support reforms to assist the civil rights cause and that the party was "teaching us to hate our employer" and "trying to destroy everything that I stood for."[9] She removed the sign on her house supporting the presidential candidacy of Henry Wallace and instead posted a placard for Harry Truman. She refused to donate one hundred dollars toward CPUSA defense expenses and felt intimidated by party leaders who pressured her for the money. Brown quit the party despite Katz's alleged threats, and she decided to tell all she knew to the FBI. The special agent to whom she spoke seemed unsurprised by her tales of Cleveland communist activities. Brown later vividly explained her sense of letdown after the meeting, as well as her desire to prove her patriotic bona fides:

> The Communists had made a fool of me by playing on my desire to be a good citizen. Finally, discerning the evil intent that lurked behind such phony facades . . . , I had naively assumed that I was alerting the nation to a secret peril. I felt the FBI man had also made a fool of me, letting me ramble on so, when he could have told me straight away that the Bureau knew all about the Red conspiracy. . . . Except for a very

understanding husband, I had no one to console me, no one with whom I could talk. . . . Friends and acquaintances in my neighborhood had long ago ostracized me because of my association with people they knew or suspected were Communists.[10]

Eventually, Brown made new friends, attended church again, and enjoyed the free time that life outside party duties provided. As a Communist, "so subtle had been my enslavement" of "mind and soul," she claimed, "that I had not realized how completely I had been mastered."[11] She reveled in ball games, theater, and caring for their rental properties.[12] Then, in July 1951, the FBI called her. An agent interviewed Brown and, after several hours, asked her to rejoin the CPUSA as an undercover informant for the FBI. The agent stated that she would be performing a great service to her country and thereby convinced Brown to do it. Feeling like "Joan of Arc and Paul Revere all done up in one patriotic package," she phoned former CRC comrades to begin getting back into their good graces.[13]

Within weeks, Brown was reimmersed in party life, joining the CRC-affiliated Sojourners for Truth and Justice, a black women's organization intended to raise awareness of racial discrimination. The Sojourners urged officials to offer redress for lynchings, segregation, police brutality, and poverty—as well as for especial CPUSA concerns, such as the government's revocation of radical black singer Paul Robeson's passport and its war against communism in Korea. Brown claimed that the Sojourners were actually too successful at mobilizing black women at the grass roots, resulting in the organization's 1956 dissolution because noncommunist members wanted to work for civil rights reforms in alliance with "moderate" groups such as the National Association for the Advancement of Colored People (NAACP). Furthermore, noncommunist Sojourners protested expenditures of time and money on issues tangential to civil rights, such as raising money for Communists indicted under the Smith Act. The Communists did not help their case by pressuring Sojourners to elect communist officers. Brown believed that noncommunist Sojourners "were really trying to fight for civil rights," while Communists refused to support a reformist organization, regardless of whether it genuinely helped African Americans. Once they began losing control over the organization, they dissolved it.[14]

Finally, Brown was appalled at CPUSA efforts to "infiltrate" the NAACP, whose leadership had purged most suspected party members or sympathizers from its ranks and expelled its few Communist-dominated local chapters in the 1950s. Even the staunchly racist FBI director J. Edgar Hoover routinely assured lawmakers and the public that the NAACP was not "communist infiltrated or controlled," despite Red attempts to join the association. Hoover's staff constantly investigated the NAACP and assured that "persons identified with the Communist Party and the NAACP have, in the past, acted jointly and frequently engaged in parallel activities. However, it must be kept in mind that the ultimate aims of these two groups are totally distinct." The CPUSA sought "to foster discord and discontent among the Negro race by agitation and propaganda." By contrast, the NAACP worked for "full racial integration and equality within the present form of government." The bureau praised the NAACP for its "non-cooperation with communist-controlled groups" and refusals to accept communist members.[15]

Like her FBI superiors, Julia Brown interpreted even limited and ineffective CPUSA attempts to infiltrate the NAACP as a threat to the association's independence. No doubt her Cleveland handlers, required to conform to Hoover's dictates, encouraged such hypervigilance. At any rate, Brown's fears of NAACP infiltration grew throughout her time in the CPUSA. She told HUAC that "the Communist Party wanted to take over . . . in place of the NAACP," to "discredit the NAACP and barge in on the NAACP's activities."[16] By the time she joined the John Birch Society, her fears had become conspiratorial paranoia, and she rarely differentiated between NAACP and CPUSA tactics and goals.

After nearly nine years of reporting to the FBI, Brown moved to Los Angeles in 1960, ceasing her undercover work for the bureau. She claimed that the stresses of her double life had exhausted her. The CPUSA had tightened internal security as a result of the ongoing Smith Act trials and, as Brown's presence confirmed, justifiably feared potential FBI spies in its midst. Brown had fallen under suspicion once or twice when comrades caught her taking notes during Ohio party conventions.[17] When she moved to Los Angeles, she began writing her memoir and preparing for her appearance before HUAC.

Once Brown's HUAC testimony was complete, she became a public figure and soon a fixture on the anticommunist lecture circuit. By 1963 the John Birch Society (JBS) added her to its stable of right-wing spokespersons travelling the country to lecture educational, civic, and patriotic organizations about the alleged communist threat. Unlike "mainstream" anticommunists, the JBS insisted that the *internal* Red conspiracy posed a graver danger to U.S. interests than Soviet expansion abroad, maintaining that most American leaders and institutions were already co-opted by communism. This paranoid view was the JBS "party line" at its 1958 founding by businessman Joseph Welch, and it remains the JBS's official stance to this day. Despite growing opposition to JBS conspiracy theories and secretive practices, the society flourished, largely due to Cold War anxieties.[18] By 1965 the JBS had approximately eighty thousand members, several hundred local chapters, four hundred bookstores, its own publishing house (Western Islands), and dozens of speakers in its American Opinion Speakers Bureau—including Julia Brown.

Before becoming a JBS speaker, Brown spoke to black journalists who admired her commitment to anticommunism and civil rights. In a 1961 interview with *Ebony* magazine, Brown maintained that the CPUSA was "not interested in the Negro's struggle for civil rights" but rather in "prostituting the legitimate grievances of Negroes to further its own end." She emphasized that African Americans must understand that the CPUSA was dedicated to violent revolution, not civil rights reform. Yet her tone was optimistic. "The Communist Party is weaker today among Negroes than it was 10 years ago," she maintained. "The party is preaching but not practicing. There is as much prejudice in the Communist Party as there is in Mississippi. They pick a few Negroes to represent all the rest. . . . Communists pretend that they don't believe in white chauvinism, but there is plenty of segregation in the party." In Cleveland, New York, and Chicago, between 1948 and 1951, she stated, "there were a goodly number of Negro members. So many of them are not active today, are not paying their dues and are not attending meetings. Over the entire United States, I feel sure there are no more than a few real dyed-in-the-wool Negro Communists. There are loads of sympathizers, of course, and a lot of fellow-travelers, but there aren't many dyed-in-the-wool Negro Communists."[19]

Brown warned that the CPUSA constantly tried to change this situation, but she reiterated her faith in patriotic black Americans, especially leaders of the NAACP. She believed that Communists had "little or no" influence on the NAACP as a whole. At one time, she claimed, Communists had infiltrated the Chicago NAACP chapter. However, Executive Secretary Roy Wilkins had subsequently "moved in and cleaned up" that organization. The Communists, she nevertheless warned, "attempted to infiltrate every Negro organization. . . . The last meeting I went to, they were talking about infiltrating the churches more. They want members to join the church and be active in the clubs and societies." To achieve their ends, the CPUSA relied on "sex bait," especially white women, to lure in members: "They use dances, house parties, anything, to get people in the party. . . . They use women as bait."[20]

Brown's optimism also lay in her belief that "the extent of Communist penetration among Negroes is sometimes exaggerated by well-meaning but uninformed persons." She disagreed with former president Harry Truman, who was quoted as saying that the sit-in movement was Communist inspired: "Truman was wrong. The Communists would have never inspired a movement based on passive resistance. They don't believe in that. They don't do anything that's decent. But after it started, they tried to jump on the bandwagon."[21] She concluded, "I'm 100 percent with the NAACP and I think they are doing a wonderful job." In fact, after she joined the NAACP during her time as an informant, one of its officials recognized her as a Communist and spread the word. "They didn't say anything to me," she explained, "but you could feel the air getting cold. They didn't allow me to move in any direction. Oh, they are smart guys down in Cleveland, those NAACP guys."[22]

In 1962, Brown spoke with cautious optimism to *Sepia* magazine: "The Communist Party is definitely exploiting the Negro—the ones they can get into the party. Anywhere they can find a dupe, they will find him. I was one." She added, "I feel that American Negroes are awakened to the menace of

Communism." After the CPUSA leadership went underground as a result of the Smith Act trials, Brown opined, "I feel that most of those who have gotten out of the party are people of my race. Most of my people (Negroes) are religious people—very religious. Religion and Communism are just like gasoline and fire. They don't mix."[23]

Already, however, a new bitterness and pessimism crept into her words. "Mrs. Brown," the *Sepia* interviewer stated, "has suffered considerable persecution from Negroes because of her role as a communist spy for the FBI, which was disclosed in national news stories not long ago. 'So many of my people seem to be angry with me because I have exposed my people along with others,' Mrs. Brown says. 'Some seem to think that just because I'm colored, I shouldn't have exposed our people, too.'" My research has uncovered no early commentary critical of Brown's role in the FBI, but she may have already received the sort of phone threats and hate mail she later claimed to receive as a JBS speaker. Perhaps friends or family disapproved of her secret double life with the bureau or supported communist civil rights efforts. At any rate, a new self-righteous tone appeared in Brown's rhetoric and performances.[24]

More ominously, Brown criticized African Americans whom she believed shared communist purposes. In her *Sepia* interview, she made this "startling disclosure": "The aims of the Communist Party and those of the Black Muslim movement are apparently similar in many respects. The Communists have ordered party members to encourage and aid Negroes to establish separate states within the United States. I was surprised to learn that the Black Muslims, purportedly a religious organization, would be following the line of an atheistic ideology."[25] Here Brown failed to differentiate between the aims of black nationalism (which encouraged African American self-sufficiency) and the CPUSA goal (abandoned in the 1960s for its impracticality) of establishing a separate, black socialist nation in the South. Virtually equating these philosophies, Brown overlooked the fact that Communists routinely emulated the rhetoric, strategies, and goals of more popular organizations. Just as Communists had proposed the 1920s separatist "black belt nation" theory to attract members from Marcus Garvey's "back to Africa" movement, they also echoed black nationalist rhetoric in the 1950s and 1960s, including ideas and language promoted by Malcolm X.[26] As for Brown, this was a foreshadowing of tactics to come.

In 1963, Brown was hired by the JBS's American Opinion Speakers Bureau. Making at least one hundred dollars per speech, she delivered dozens of speeches every year from 1963 to 1971 (with an estimated fifteen speeches per month in 1968 and 1969) and sporadically between 1972 and 1979. Brown forged a lucrative career, making far more money than she could have in almost any other job she might have obtained as an African American woman with a tenth-grade education.[27] Indeed, Brown's FBI handlers groused that she was "financially ambitious"—a quality, these white men implied, unbecoming in a black woman.[28] Finally, her book, *I Testify*, sold several thousand copies upon release in 1967 and at least several thousand more at Brown's JBS appearances. Audience members who found her a "spellbinding" speaker—something even her critics proclaimed—often queued up to purchase her memoir.[29]

Yet *I Testify* was hardly an accurate text or a consistent representation of Brown's earlier attitudes toward civil rights. Reflecting the preferences of her publisher, JBS's Western Islands, Brown's largely ghostwritten memoir echoed the JBS "line" on civil rights as a communist plot to divide and destroy the United States. A text that marks Brown's (d)evolution from a pro–civil rights, pro-integrationist activist to her later incarnation as a right-wing JBS fixture and supporter of George Wallace, *I Testify* praises the NAACP's anticommunism and attempts to work within the legal system. It also, however, exaggerates communist "infiltration" of the civil rights movement, painting a far grimmer picture than Brown had done a few years previously in her HUAC testimony and magazine interviews.[30]

Moreover, *I Testify* promotes African American self-help (rather than direct-action protest or political pressure on lawmakers) as the best remedy for segregation and discrimination. In the tradition of Booker T. Washington, Brown advises that bigotry "can best be fought with . . . a dignified determination to defeat discrimination by better example." Civil disobedience, or "bad behavior," she added, "can always be cited as a justification for continued discrimination. I want my people to be accepted, not just tolerated."[31] The memoir implies that nonviolent protests are as "undignified" and unattractive as the behavior of white racists attacking civil rights activists. In keeping with JBS priorities, *I Testify* sees communism as the ultimate threat, and bigotry as a more minor concern that can be fought gradually, over time, by blacks eventually earning whites' respect.

Brown reminds readers that she had never witnessed police brutality. "On the other hand," she had seen "incidents where every effort was made by misguided Negroes to provoke law enforcement officers into some action which might be propagandized as police brutality. You may be certain that [they] were doing this under instructions from some directing force. . . . In general, the people of my race have a profound respect for authority. They will not deliberately challenge that authority unless incited to it by diabolically clever brainwashing."[32]

Brown's implications are chilling: police brutality is a myth; rabble-rousers lure well-meaning police into reprisals that radicals capitalize on to condemn government authority; and, in so-called normal conditions, African Americans would not be disorderly, no matter how desperate their situations. Published two years after the Watts riot that rocked Los Angeles and at the height of the urban riots of 1965–69, *I Testify* argues that black uprisings had nothing to do with unemployment, substandard housing, poverty, and true police brutality, nor with viable grievances against public officials. Instead, "diabolical" radicals used naive African Americans to foment racial strife and destroy social harmony.

Throughout her career, Brown repeatedly played upon the anxieties of white Americans traumatized by the Cold War, urban riots, and the civil rights movement. Her speeches were popular in large measure because she was telling white folks what they wanted to hear: outside agitators were responsible for the upheavals; the majority of African Americans were not angry or capable of violence; and if the Red menace were defeated, black demonstrations and violent white backlash would stop. Here Brown's rhetoric fit into a longtime southern tradition of blaming "outside agitators"—northerners, civil rights activists, Communists—for black dissatisfaction. Speaking mostly to whites horrified by the *Brown v. Board of Education* decision and the 1964 Civil Rights Act, Brown supported their suspicions that such changes were un-American. By the mid-1960s, a majority of Americans polled believed that Communists had infiltrated civil rights groups and caused the riots; Brown and others exploited, reinforced, and encouraged such conspiratorial thinking.[33]

By 1964 the Reverend Dr. Martin Luther King Jr. and his disciples became Brown's primary target. Like many other JBS speakers (and FBI officials), Brown insisted that King was part of the communist conspiracy to destroy the United States through racial tensions leading to a violent, socialist revolution. In hundreds of speeches (with titles such as "To Tell All My People," "I Too Have a Dream," and "America Blackmailed by Threats of Violence"), Brown expanded on this theme throughout the 1960s even as King's influence grew within the movement and society as a whole. Warning audiences of the dangers he allegedly posed as a Red dupe whose appearances triggered racial clashes that negated his supposed nonviolent philosophy, Brown called King the "most violent non-violent man in America" and "the biggest enemy of my people." She also accused President Lyndon Johnson, who signed the Civil Rights Act and Voting Rights Act into law and created programs to assist poverty-stricken Americans, of doing "more for Communism than any other president."[34]

Brown repeatedly reinforced the message delivered by now-conservative black journalist George Schuyler of the *Pittsburgh Courier,* who claimed, "Negroes had been doing well before the current civil rights movement upset smooth racial relations." Civil rights leaders, he stated, made blacks "look ridiculous" by "harping on minor annoyances and the rare brutalities in which a few Negroes were involved." He urged, "Let us bring an end to racist, Marxist agitation and disorders and resolve in the aftermath that we've got a good thing going in America."[35] Brown argued, "I have been in the camp of the enemy, and the enemy knows he must destroy the United States before they can destroy the world." Given the magnitude of the crisis, the United States could not afford a divisive civil rights movement masterminded by the Reds; American civilization and global freedom were at stake.[36]

Brown reiterated that she hated discrimination and wished it to end, but the present civil rights movement was too politically and morally compromised to bring about positive change. A "genuinely anti-Communist civil rights movement" would gain her full support. But the current movement was "a fight against patriotic Negroes. Most good Negroes have not taken part in it." Throughout her career, Brown echoed *I Testify*'s theme of African American self-improvement and self-empowerment: "Moscow places all Negro troubles at white doors. This removes all responsibility from the Negro by making him feel sorry for himself and ignore opportunities." The best solution was for blacks to build their own businesses and promote free enterprise instead of "inferiority complexes." Communists had convinced African Americans that "a Negro section of a city is necessarily a ghetto." This view "helps stop Negro self-improvement by making Negroes see their dwelling places as inferior and thus paralyzing Negro initiative." In regard to the 1965 Watts riot, Brown insisted, "There are no real slums in Los Angeles, little or no discrimination, little or no segregation. Those who refused to work were getting welfare" (this was a slap at Great Society antipoverty programs), so "there was little or no poverty. What did these people want that any law-abiding citizen could not have?"[37]

JBS chapters arranged Brown's speaking engagements to precede or coincide with King's visits to southern cities, and they claimed that King sometimes canceled his appearances rather than deal with the suspicions Brown aroused in the black community. I have found several claims of this nature and suspect that King's cancellations were often coincidental, but Brown prided herself on swaying African Americans away from demonstrations. Whenever King failed to show, or to muster a large grassroots response, Brown and the JBS interpreted it as an anticommunist victory.[38] There is virtually no mention of Brown in the civil rights histories I have examined; whether this indicates her irrelevance to the movement or the embarrassment she caused King's crusade, I do not know.

Regardless of Brown's direct impact on King's plans, however, she undoubtedly reinforced racism and the violent white backlash, just as JBS opposition to the civil rights movement and to the 1964 Civil Rights Act and 1965 Voting Rights Act did.[39] Yet Brown did not recognize this possibility. Instead, she insulted, shouted at, and ignored audience members who tried to bring such issues to her attention. Relying on information gleaned from FBI and JBS sources (some of whom were allied with the Klan), Brown constantly repeated charges that King attended a "communist training school" in 1957, surrounded himself with communist advisors, and received funding from the Southern Conference Educational Fund, whose leaders included leftists Carl and Anne Braden.[40] It is difficult to gauge how much Brown's career hurt the civil rights cause. It is fair to say, however, that her remarks not only echoed but also helped shape the white backlash of the late 1960s and 1970s—one that resulted in the rise of the new right and its opposition to affirmative action, the public repudiation of busing (another of Brown's favorite targets) to desegregate northern schools, and lawmakers' rejection of substantive antipoverty programs and additional civil rights legislation.

Toward the end of her life, Brown attempted to prevent the creation of a national holiday commemorating King's birthday and life's work. Even after King's assassination, Brown portrayed him as Communist led and Communist inspired, arguing that the Communists must have killed him when he did not "do things their way" (which begged the question of how "duped" King could have been in the first place). She claimed that alleged assassin James Earl Ray had been part of a Red conspiracy to eliminate the civil rights leader Communists had once manipulated for their diabolical ends. Baseless suppositions, such as "King was getting soft" and "the Communists had used him all they wanted to," peppered her later speeches.[41]

Brown's musings inspired many right-wingers' conclusions about King's activism, his death, and the urban riots following his assassination. "King was probably murdered by a Communist," wrote a woman to the *Billings Gazette* in Montana. "Of course his death will add more to the atmosphere of hatred and violence, than he could have done alive." Everywhere King went, he was "accompanied by sex orgies in the streets, riots, arson, looting, killing and contempt for civil authorities." Why was it "up to patriotic organizations such as the John Birch Society" and people like Brown to "bring the facts to light"?[42] By 1969 Brown began claiming that Communists had assassinated Robert Kennedy too, and for similar reasons.[43]

Lest we write off Brown as a nonsensical crank with little impact, I should point out that she regularly spoke to packed houses. My research has uncovered dozens of letters to newspaper editors citing Brown as an authority on the alleged CPUSA-King conspiracy and the civil rights movement in general, as well as more than two hundred newspaper stories reporting her message in neutral or favorable terms. Contemporaries were impressed that this "light-brown skinned" woman, who looked like "the cultured wife of a successful businessman, an active laywoman in her church or a prominent clubwoman," was actually a former FBI informant. Some who disbelieved portions of her message began to question their own opinions, for they enjoyed her spirited speeches and snappy rejoinders.[44] Some believed that she lived in danger of Red retaliation. "Brown is risking her life every day just by speaking wherever she is invited," opined a Michigan woman.[45]

In 1978 and 1979, Brown made some of her last public appearances, testifying before Congress in opposition to the proposed Martin Luther King Jr. commemorative holiday. Sponsored by South Carolina senator Strom Thurmond and Georgia congressman (and JBS member) Larry McDonald, Brown urged Congress not to honor King, whom Hoover had once called "the most notorious liar in the country." She concluded, "If this measure is passed . . . , we may as well take down the stars and stripes . . . and replace it with a red flag."[46]

Protesting Congress's deliberations, JBS members and other right-wingers flooded newspapers with letters proposing black Americans who might be honored instead. Especially popular were Booker T. Washington, an accommodationist advocate of black self-improvement; George Washington Carver, who "did so much with the lowly peanut"; and Julia Brown, heroine of the far right.[47] Modestly, Brown did not offer herself as a candidate, but she was no doubt pleased by others' suggestions.

Brown's career perhaps leaves us with more questions than answers. Other than reading about letters to the editor, packed houses for her speeches, and praise from right-wing Americans, how are we to measure her influence? It is impossible to know how many people "converted" to her message, or how many were already predisposed to believe her through their affinity for the JBS, White Citizens' Council, George Wallace, and so on. Yet, as right-wing author Alan Stang points out, the mainstream "liberal" press has virtually ignored Brown's story. She is not the sort of reformer or feminist whom women's historians admire, nor the kind of activist most African Americans would wish to acknowledge. She is rarely mentioned, much less taken seriously, in the civil rights histories I have consulted, yet she may have had a tangible impact on the movement nonetheless. Certainly, she negatively impacted the individuals she named before HUAC as a result of her time in the FBI, but even sympathetic histories of American communism say little about her; they are loath to acknowledge her existence or the damage that this "stool pigeon" caused the party.

In all her performances, Brown's pride in her own accomplishments and in those of "her people" was quite clear, so it seems fallacious to write her off as a self-hating black woman or a victim of false consciousness. Historians must grapple with how to explain right-wing African Americans and strong-willed, independent women who reject liberal or leftist political positions normally associated with feminism. My research on Brown and her allies continues, for such projects, no matter how frustrating, are critically important to more fully understanding the fraught, interconnected workings of race, gender, and right-wing politics in American history.

NOTES

1. *Hearings Before the Committee on Un-American Activities: Communist Activities in the Cleveland, Ohio, Area,* 87th cong., 2nd sess., June 4–6, 1962 (Washington, D.C.: U.S. Government Printing Office, 1962). Henceforth referred to as HUAC.

2. Julia Brown, *I Testify: My Years as an F.B.I. Undercover Agent* (Boston: Western Islands, 1966).

3. HUAC, 993–1003; "I Was a Spy for the FBI," *Ebony,* March 1961, 96.

4. HUAC, 1003.

5. The Justice Department hoped to destroy the party through intimidation and bankruptcy. CPUSA allies protested the arrests and trials from 1949 until the 1950s, when the Supreme Court effectively overturned the Smith Act. See Gerald Horne, *Communist Front? The Civil Rights Congress, 1946–1956* (Rutherford, N.J.: Fairleigh Dickinson University Press, 1988).

6. HUAC, 1004–5. Brown's middle-class status may have sheltered her from police violence, particularly in urban ghettos. Or she may have overemphasized her argument to gain the favor of HUAC's conservative members.

7. Ibid., 1032.

8. Ibid., 1001–3.

9. Ibid., 1009–10.

10. Brown, *I Testify*, 34–35.

11. Ibid., 35–36.

12. Brown said, "The residence we had purchased on 123rd Street was actually a triplex, and we rented apartments on the second and third floors. The income thus derived, added to the profits from the operation of Curlee's trucks, enabled us to live comfortably and to bank an appreciable sum each month." Ibid., 36.

13. Ibid., 32, 39–41. Brown used tearful appeals to overcome Katz's suspicions. Soon she became the treasurer of several Cleveland party-affiliated organizations, sharing documents, party strategies, and other information with the FBI. See ibid., 42, 44, 50–51, 58, 88; and HUAC, 1017, 1032–33, 1038–43.

14. HUAC, 1030–39.

15. "The Communist Party and the Negro" (1956), FBI report, cited on FBI scholar Ernie Lazar's blog *John Birch Society's Endless Enemies,* http://birchers.blogspot.com; see his "Report on the John Birch Society," http://ernie1241.googlepages.com/jbs-1. See also Richard Gid Powers, *Secrecy and Power: The Life of J. Edgar Hoover* (New York: Free Press, 1987); Kevin A. Leonard, "'I Am Sure You Can Read Between the Lines': Cold War Anticommunism and the NAACP in Los Angeles," *Journal of the West* 44, no. 2 (Spring 2005): 16–23; and Brown, *I Testify*, 87–9, 100–103, 124–27.

16. HUAC, 1041.

17. Ibid., 1094–95, 1103. The FBI had so infiltrated the CPUSA that by the late 1950s, perhaps one-third of the party was secretly in the bureau's employ. In identifying alleged Communists, Brown accused another black informant. With FBI permission, Melvin Hardin admitted that he had been an informant for eight years, and his wife for four. See "A Communist for F.B.I. 'Exposes' Another One," *New York Times,* June 7, 1962.

18. By 1965, "responsible" conservatives condemned JBS connections to anti-Semitic and white supremacist groups. The JBS publicly denied such bigotry. Some individual members, however, joined racist groups such as the Ku Klux Klan and the Christian Identity movement. See Sara Diamond, *Roads to Dominion: Right-Wing Movements and Political Power in the United States* (New York: Guilford Press, 1995); Benjamin R. Epstein and Arnold Forster, *The Radical Right: Report on the John Birch Society and Its Allies* (New York: Random House, 1967); and Richard Gid Powers, *Not Without Honor: The Story of American Anticommunism* (New York: Free Press, 1995).

19. "I Was a Spy for the FBI," 94–95.

20. Ibid. FBI officials doubted Brown's "sex bait" claim. See M. A. Jones to Cartha DeLoach, January 16, 1961, FBI file HQ 100-382107-70.

21. "I Was a Spy for the FBI," 95.

22. Ibid., 102.

23. "Communist for the FBI," *Sepia,* September 1962, 12.

24. Ibid., 11.

25. Ibid., 12.

26. Bureau officials thought that Brown should only discuss activities about which she had firsthand knowledge, opining that she "is not qualified to assert herself as a

spokesman for what is happening in the CP across the country." See M. A. Jones to Cartha DeLoach, January 16, 1961.

27. For fees, see "Negro Speakers at Birch Group 'Seminar' Assail Rights Drive as Red Plot," *New York Times*, March 21, 1966.

28. Agents worried that she might "capitalize on her experience in the Communist Party to her financial advantage, and for the prestige she may believe such publicity will afford her." See SAC (special agent in charge) Cleveland to SAC Los Angeles, Julia Brown FBI Los Angeles File, serial #A-12.

29. JBS supporters often purchased multiple copies for school and public libraries, to counter "communist" views on civil rights.

30. Brown, *I Testify*, 48–59, 106–56. Brown lamented that ghostwriter Carleton Young expressed views of the "lunatic right," yet her speeches included paragraphs excerpted from *I Testify*. Brown never repudiated the book and thanked Young in her acknowledgments. Brown, *I Testify*, v; SAC Los Angeles to J. Edgar Hoover, August 8, 1963, FBI Los Angeles File, serial #A-129; SAC Los Angeles to J. Edgar Hoover, March 28, 1963, FBI Los Angeles File, serial #A-119.

31. Brown, *I Testify*, 59.

32. Ibid., 160–61.

33. Jeff Woods, *Black Struggle, Red Scare: Segregation and Anti-communism in the South, 1948–1968* (Baton Rouge: Louisiana State University Press, 2004).

34. "Communist Movement Told," *Lima (Ohio) News*, April 26, 1964; "Former Counterspy Says Nation Infiltrated with Reds," *Nashua (N.H.) Telegraph*, May 28, 1964; "King a Pawn, Says Negro," *Kingsport (Tenn.) News*, September 14, 1965.

35. "Negro Speakers at Birch Group 'Seminar' Assail Rights Drive as Red Plot," *New York Times*, March 21, 1966.

36. "Speaker Says Communist Party Seeks to Destroy United States," *Manchester (N.H.) Guardian*, January 20, 1966.

37. "Infiltration Tactics Told by Ex-Communist," *Lebanon (Ohio) Daily News*, March 10, 1967; "Negro in Birch Talk Hits Rights 'Dupes,'" *Long Beach (Ca.) Press-Telegram*, September 25, 1964; Brown, *I Testify*, 280–81.

38. Brown spoke in Petersburg, Virginia, in preparation for King's appearance. A JBS spokesman said, "We do frankly hope that [Brown's] appearance will lead to King's trip here being cancelled." *Petersburg Progress-Index*, March 21, 1968. Former JBS activist Alan Stang sometimes accompanied Brown to help "explain the scheme before [King's] terrorists arrived to foment animosity." In Sandersville, Georgia, Brown and Stang "told them . . . which organizations and people [King] worked with and fronted for . . . , what his purpose was. We explained that he was trying to divide the races and foment violence." See Stang, "'Martin Luther' King, Jr.: Communist Fraud," Ether Zone, January 16, 2004, http://www.etherzone.com/2004/stang011604.shtml.

39. "Calls for Large Attendance, Boycott Asked for Julia Brown's Free Speech," *Danville Register*, March 24, 1968. Brown's appearances sparked opposition. Officers of the Blanks Club in Danville, Virginia, urged "citizens of good will to refrain from attending" her speech. The Blanks Club was "composed of some of the city's most influential and successful Negro business and professional leaders"—evidence of Brown's limited appeal to middle-class, "respectable" blacks.

40. The "communist training school" was the Highlander Folk School in Monteagle, Tennessee, which trained activists for pacifist and civil rights work. King visited the school on Labor Day in 1957 and was photographed near a known CPUSA member. The photographer, Klansman Edwin Friend, followed King on behalf of the Georgia Commission on Education, which wanted "evidence" of a Red conspiracy to discredit the civil rights movement. See Catherine Fosl, *Subversive Southerner: Anne Braden and the Struggle for Racial Justice in the Cold War South* (New York: Palgrave Macmillan, 2002). The Georgia commission's report can be accessed online at http://mdah.state.ms.us/arlib/contents/er/sovcom/result.php?image =/data/sov_commission/images/png/cd06/041961.png&otherstuff.

41. "TACT Speaker Claims Civil Riots Red-Led," *Tucson Daily Citizen,* August 3, 1968.

42. "'Facts' On King," *Billings Gazette,* April 12, 1968.

43. "Charleston Loaded with Reds, Former FBI Informant Feels," *Charleston Gazette-Mail,* February 16, 1969.

44. *Waterloo (Iowa) Daily Courier,* February 7, 1971, 4.

45. "Great Black Americans Listed," *Benton Harbor (Mich.) News-Palladium,* January 21, 1972.

46. "Famous Black Birchers: Red, White, and Blue American" and "An Anti-communist Negro Makes This Appeal: Please Don't Help Glorify Martin Luther King," The John Birch Society, http://www.jbs.org.

47. "King's Legend," *Pasadena Star-News,* February 3, 1976; "Raising Doubts About Dr. King," *Doylestown (Pa.) Intelligencer,* January 21, 2004.

16

Leading the Nation: Extreme Right Women Leaders
Among the Serbs

Carol S. Lilly and Jill A. Irvine

In mid-1992, shortly after images of emaciated Bosnian Muslims in Serb
concentration camps shocked the world, Biljana Plavšić made a series of out-
rageous statements to the Serbian press. As vice president of the breakaway
Serbian Republic in Bosnia-Herzegovina, she urged that all Muslims be expelled from Eastern Bosnia and given a small piece of land where they could
be kept separate. But it was how she described the Bosnian Muslims that
established her credentials as a leader of the extreme right. According to
Plavšić, a biologist and former dean of natural sciences and mathematics at
the University of Sarajevo, those Slavs who had long ago embraced Islam
were now made up of "genetically deformed material." Their "defective
genes"—probably brought over from North Africa—made them inherently
incapable of reason, and therefore they must be opposed on all fronts by all
means and removed from Serbian lands.[1]

This chapter examines the role of women leaders in extreme right movements in Serbia and Bosnia-Herzegovina during and after the conflicts of the
1990s. It focuses on Mirjana Marković, president of the Yugoslav United Left
Party; Maja Gojković, vice president of the Serbian Radical Party; and Biljana
Plavšić, leader of the Serbian Democratic Party and vice president of the Republic of Serbia in Bosnia-Herzegovina. Although these three women had
important differences in their backgrounds and views, all of them endorsed
exclusivist, ethnonationalist political platforms and accepted the use of violence to achieve their political goals. They also all embraced "hypermasculinity," the need for Serbian men to recapture their essential masculinity in
order to save the Serbian nation. Yet women's roles and especially the extreme right themes of motherhood, family, and religion in defending the

nation were of far less interest to them. We argue that while these three leaders and their supporters countered the left in their political projects, they also overlapped with the left in crucial ways.

The Fall of Communism and Emergence of the Extreme Right in Serbia and Bosnia-Herzegovina

The fall of the Berlin Wall in 1989 and subsequent loss of power by communist parties throughout Eastern Europe and the Soviet Union were greeted with enthusiasm in the West as an indication of the victory of democracy. Within a relatively short time, however, it became clear that the space opened up by the collapse of state socialism had been occupied not only by liberal democratic parties but also by those on the extreme right with ethnonationalist agendas. Further, the end of censorship resulted in the revival of national tensions and grievances reaching back to the Second World War and beyond. Nowhere were these tensions and conflicts more evident than in Yugoslavia, which disintegrated into a brutal civil war from 1991 to 1995. At its outset, the former League of Communists of Serbia, now renamed the Socialist Party of Serbia (SPS), transformed itself into the main bearer of nationalism. Its dominance and the legacy of socialism within Yugoslavia inevitably influenced the policies of other right-wing parties operating in the same region. Accordingly, it becomes difficult to use the traditional terms "left" and "right" in reference to the conflict in the Balkans. Rather, the relevant political poles in the region during this period were nationalist versus antinationalist. For as we shall see, while some of the SPS's policies clearly conformed to our notions of the extreme right, others remained consistent with its more leftist roots.

Extreme right movements and parties emerged in the former Yugoslavia in the context of the first multiparty elections held in 1990 and the outbreak of war in the summer of 1991. Three main political parties represented extreme right and ultranationalist views among Serbs in Yugoslavia. The first, as noted above, was the SPS, which endorsed a nationalist political program after Slobodan Milošević's rise to power in 1987. This communist-turned-nationalist party spearheaded the campaign to carve out a Greater Serbia from the remains of the Yugoslav state as it began to disintegrate in 1990, although party leaders continued to blend their ultranationalism with leftist rhetoric. The SPS ruled throughout the 1990s with the support of the Yugoslav United Left (JUL), headed by Milošević's wife, Mirjana Marković. Through her leadership of this officially leftist party, Marković promoted a de facto program of Serbian nationalism and authoritarianism. This connection between the extreme right and the previous left-wing (communist) party with its new satellite party, JUL, had important implications for the SPS's views on gender equality.

The SPS, in condominium with JUL, maintained its control throughout the decade, but it was always in danger of being outflanked on the right by the Serbian Radical Party (SRS). Established shortly after the first multiparty elections in 1990, the SRS, under the leadership of the charismatic Vojislav Šešelj, garnered 20 percent of the vote in 1992. The SRS ran on a platform of supporting Serbs outside Serbia proper. Šešelj called on Serbs to establish a Greater Serbian state, free of such "cowardly" and "spoiled" people as the Croats and Muslims. The SRS's paramilitary force, the Chetniks, was instrumental in achieving this goal through the policy of ethnic cleansing. During the next several years, the SRS's portion of electoral support rose steadily, despite periods of repression by the SPS and JUL. Maja Gojković, a close associate of SRS president Šešelj, played an important role in this steady climb to power.

A third Serbian party was founded in 1990 to represent the interests of Serbs outside Serbia proper. The Serbian Democratic Party (SDS) represented Serbs in Croatia and Bosnia-Herzegovina and received 33.8 percent of the vote in Bosnia-Herzegovina—almost the entire Serbian community there. Although most Muslims and Croats had advocated independence for Bosnia-Herzegovina after the outbreak of fighting in Croatia in July 1991, Radovan Karadžić, the SDS leader in Bosnia-Herzegovina, vociferously opposed it, arguing that the Serbs there wished to remain connected to the Serbs in rump Yugoslavia. In the fall of 1991, Karadžić, along with such important SDS leaders as Biljana Plavšić, announced the formation of the independent Serbian Republic of Bosnia-Herzegovina. Well before that, Serb paramilitaries in both Bosnia-Herzegovina and Serbia had begun stockpiling arms for the impending outbreak of hostilities there. Once the fighting broke out in April 1992, Karadžić, Plavšić, and the SDS became deeply complicit in the brutal campaign of ethnic cleansing that ensued during the next three years of war.

The elections of 1990 and all subsequent elections established the dominance of extreme right political parties and views on the Serbian political scene.[2] These parties and their supporters espoused what are usually associated with radical or extreme right ideologies, including ethnonationalist and authoritarian views. Ethnonationalist, or what Cas Mudde aptly calls "nativist," views hold that the "state should be inhabited exclusively by members of the native group ('the nation') and that nonnative elements (persons and ideas) are fundamentally threatening to the homogenous nation-state."[3] Serbs on the extreme right endorsed the creation of a Greater Serbian state encompassing Montenegro, Macedonia, and large portions of Bosnia-Herzegovina and Croatia, which would be only for Serbs.

Gender ideologies constituted an important element in the extreme right and the ultranationalist projects of these three political parties. All three used images of women's defilement by enemy ethnic groups to mobilize support. Such gendered images played a vital role in the process of ethnic mobilization in Serbia before multiparty elections in 1990. During the late 1980s, Serbian newspapers featured almost daily discussions about alleged rapes of Serbian women (and men) by Albanians in Kosovo and the violation of all Serbs that these rapes represented.[4] The SPS, SRS, and SDS launched campaigns for demographic renewal, calling upon Serbian women to produce more sons and daughters for the nation. Legislation was passed in Serbia to promote a higher birthrate among Serbs while restricting it among enemy ethnic groups such as Albanians.[5]

Nevertheless, the SPS, SRS, JUL, and SDS generally avoided explicit calls for women's social and political subordination. In contrast to many extreme right movements, Serbian parties of this tendency did not emphasize women's traditional roles for at least three reasons. The first was the fact that the state socialist League of Communists of Serbia had sponsored ethnic mobilization. Because the SPS (and its partner JUL) were ostensibly leftist, gender equality remained at least part of the official program of this and other emerging right-wing parties. And while the SRS and SDS did not bear the same leftist traditions as the SPS and JUL, their party leaders seemed to recognize that the Yugoslav population had been raised and educated for over fifty years within a framework that promoted gender equality and women's rights; this framework could not be easily or instantly eliminated. This is not to say that the ruling party actually promoted such equality. On the contrary, one of the most pronounced features of Serbian political life under Milošević was the deterioration of women's social, economic, and political position.[6] The second reason had to do with the Serbs' opposition to Muslims in Bosnia-Herzegovina and Kosovo. As Nikki Keddie has pointed out, religious nationalist movements, in contrast to religious fundamentalist movements, "may not take conservative positions on women and, insofar as their enemies are Muslim, may even stress their gender-egalitarianism as compared to Muslims."[7] Serbian extreme right forces attempted to use the image of their more "modern" women to distinguish themselves from "'primitive, oppressive' Muslims."[8] Finally, while women's roles were a part of extreme right messages, the real thrust of their gender component in Serbia had to do with men. Serbian radical rightist parties employed a gender strategy that was aimed at reversing the "demasculinization" of the previous period and, according to one scholar, "reconstructing a new nationalist and war-oriented notion of masculinity."[9]

Women's Support for Extreme Right Parties

A great deal has been written about the ways in which the collapse of state socialism and the outbreak of war worsened the position of women in the Balkans. Women were hurt by the deteriorating economic situation and the rise of ultranationalist and extreme right ideologies, and, in areas where conflict took place, they suffered in particular ways as targets of sexual violence and forced migration.[10] Nevertheless, women also participated in ultranationalist and radical rightist movements and political parties. Although the wars in the Balkans have sometimes been described as men's wars, launched on behalf of a male elite, women often supported the attitudes and policies that contributed to them.[11] In Serbia, women held extreme right views at equal or greater rates than men. For example, according to 1994 survey data, 16.9 percent of women and 14.8 percent of men strongly agreed with the idea that "Serbia should be for the Serbs."[12] Similarly, Serbian women expressed strongest support for the idea that "one should be willing to fight for one's country without questioning whether it is right or wrong" (55.4 percent of women, 49.1 percent of men). Roughly equal numbers of women (23.5 percent) and men (24.4 percent) in Serbia placed a high priority on ensuring the protection of Serbs outside Serbia (in Bosnia-Herzegovina and Croatia).

Women in Serbia translated these opinions into electoral support for nationalist and extreme right parties. In the 1990 elections, women voted overwhelmingly for nationalist parties. Indeed, throughout the 1990s, women supported the SPS at higher rates than men, although they also consistently displayed less interest and involvement in politics than men.[13] Women also supported far-right leaders at high rates. When asked about their opinion of Slobodan Milošević in 1994, 54.3 percent of women in Serbia rated him extremely favorably, compared to 47.7 percent of men. Roughly equal numbers of women (9.2 percent) and men (9.8 percent) gave the leader of the radical rightist SRS, Vojislav Šešelj, an extremely favorable rating.[14] According to Belgrade scholar Žarana Papić, "The majority of women in Serbia have, in fact, been 'seduced' by One Man [Milošević] as their despotic patriarch and willingly surrendered themselves to the 'destiny' prescribed by the nationalist program."[15] Thus, Serbian women from all socioeconomic backgrounds, in both rural and urban areas, supported extreme right positions, parties, and leaders at roughly the same rates as men, constituting an essential source of their success.[16]

Extreme Right Women Leaders

Women's leadership in politics has been the focus of considerable research in recent years, but the study of women leaders in extreme right political parties has attracted less attention.[17] Recent scholarship on women world leaders, however, suggests certain commonalities concerning their backgrounds and paths to power. First, such women at the highest level generally come from privileged socioeconomic backgrounds and possess a high level of education.[18] Second, they assume political leadership as a result of their connections to male relatives at a higher rate than men, whether through the "widow's walk" or other surrogacy paths.[19] Indeed, such connections aid in overcoming the gender handicap in many traditional cultures. This appears to be true of powerful extreme right women in Europe today, who are often related to important male leaders.[20] Finally, as Amrita Basu illustrates in her study of preeminent women in the Hindutva movement, ultranationalist women leaders embody iconic cultural images, drawing on them to incite men to violence.[21]

Extreme right women's relationships to the gender ideologies of the movements to which they belong are often fraught with complexities, in part because of the double standard but also because they often understand themselves as working against the gender inequality within their own parties.[22] Moreover, as previously mentioned, extreme right movements that focus primarily on ethnonationalist or racist concerns may not emphasize women's subordination, even when they espouse essentialist views, but concentrate instead on the discriminatory and oppressive behavior of their "primitive" enemies.[23] While historically some radical rightist women have also seen themselves as feminists, such an explicit coupling of views has been less likely in the political context of postcommunism, where the concept of feminism was associated with the former state socialist regimes. The gender-emancipatory context of socialist Yugoslavia and the leftist roots of several extreme right parties in Serbia, however, mitigated the antifeminist positions of the radical right there.[24] How the three extreme right women leaders profiled here have situated themselves in relation to gender equality is a question we will tackle below.

Mirjana Marković

One might assume that Mirjana Marković, like so many women in political leadership, gained her positions through association with her powerful husband, Slobodan Milošević. It is just as likely, however, that he gained his positions partially through association with her, though he most visibly rode his mentor Ivan Stambolić's coattails to power. Marković was born into a powerful and prominent communist family. Her parents were devoted procommunist Partisans during the Second World War, and her father, Moma Marković, was declared a "people's hero" after the war.[25] Her uncle, Draža Marković, also rose high through party ranks, and her aunt, Davorjanka Paunović, had been Tito's personal secretary and mistress during the war.[26]

According to biographer Adam LeBor, some observers have speculated that Marković's political ties were the initial source of Milošević's attraction to her.[27] They met as high school students and soon became inseparable, described by their schoolmates as "Romeo and Juliet."[28] It seems that from that point on, Marković used Milošević as the focus of her ambitions, as much as he used her connections to further his own. It was indeed a symbiotic relationship. It has been suggested that Marković saw in Milošević "raw material that she could shape into a future leader."[29] A story is frequently told, though Marković denies it, that in 1968 when in Zadar with a cousin, as they gazed at a photo of Tito in a shopwindow, Marković said, "That's where my Slobo's picture will be one day."[30] Thus, Marković reflects the situation of many women leaders in that she came from a politically powerful and privileged family and used those connections to further her husband's political career and then used his to build her own.

Although Marković was always a powerful force behind the scenes through her husband, and probably achieved her greatest influence in this way, she launched her own political career during the first multiparty elections in 1990 with the formation of the "general's party," the League of Communists—Movement for Yugoslavia (SK-PJ), which she headed. This party joined with several others in 1995 to form the JUL, with Marković once again at its head. JUL derived its power not through electoral success (it had no parliamentary seats) but through closeness to the ruling party. In a relatively short time, JUL filled up with gangsters, corrupt officials, "entrepreneurs," and movie stars. As one observer put it, "Marković became known as the patron saint of profiteers, sycophants, and wretched cowards."[31] JUL grew into a party of thugs, enriching the Miloševićes and their supporters through bribery, extortion, and other means. In the analysis of one scholar, "The strategy pursued by Marković and JUL was not to abolish the Serbian private sector but to assert their control over it."[32] Thus, Marković, as the leader of JUL, became closely identified with strong-arm tactics and power politics. While she may have spoken frequently of her children and attempted to cultivate a softer image in public (she always wore a flower in her hair), Marković was generally seen as an utterly corrupt politician who contributed greatly to the worsening of Serbian political culture during the 1990s.

JUL may have been a party of thuggery, with very little emphasis on ideology of any kind beyond supporting the militaristic and nationalistic policies of Milošević, but the question of Marković's political views is a perplexing one. Marković is known for saying of herself, "Communism is in my genes."[33] If so, how can we speak about her in a chapter on women on the right? If we go only by what Marković has said and written, she appears to be a fairly consistent leftist and antinationalist. From December 1992 to July 1994, Marković's "diary" was published in the popular Belgrade weekly news magazine *Duga*. On many occasions, she openly derided the media's recent obsession with ancient Serbian history and Serbs' national victimization as vulgar, counterproductive, and misguided. She particularly attacked those Serbian politicians, like Radovan Karadžić, Vojislav Šešelj, and Biljana Plavšić, who clearly represented the extreme right and whose nationalist propaganda she described as nothing less than criminal. She regarded Biljana Plavšić's 1993 call for the ethnic division of Bosnia as "Nazism pure and simple," adding, "I am afraid that the Serbian people are too complacently convinced of their own high mindedness to recognize the viper in their bosom represented by the hatred of other nations and the potentiality of fascism."[34] In her

writings, she consistently and explicitly opposed the nationalist policies promoted by her husband's regime without, however, ever mentioning her husband or the regime. In one early entry, she referred to "the Yugoslav politicians
behind the war" and then listed Franjo Tudjman from Croatia; Alija Izetbe-
gović, the Muslim leader from Bosnia-Herzegovina; and Radovan Karadžić
from the Serb Republic of Bosnia-Herzegovina. Stunningly absent from this
list is, of course, Slobodan Milošević, the man who was later extradited to the
The Hague and tried for genocide and crimes against humanity.[35]

And yet, how can we reconcile such open direct attacks on Serbian nationalism with the fact that Marković's husband, over whom she apparently had
such enormous influence, was entirely complicit in the war and in the production and encouragement of those very nationalist sentiments? It is perhaps no surprise that she continued to support communism. Not only was it
part of her "genetic structure," but in contrast to much of the rest of Eastern
Europe, in Serbia, the Communist Party, though renamed, remained in
power and under the control of her husband long after its demise or transformation elsewhere. However, though the SPS retained some vestiges of its
leftist orientation, by the late 1980s it had thrown itself squarely behind a
program of ethnic mobilization and ultranationalism. It was part of the sur-
reality of Serbian politics during the 1990s, helped in no small part by
Marković's murky ideological pronouncements, that the ruling party and its
yet more orthodox partner JUL often officially endorsed brotherhood and
unity, as well as social solidarity, even as they were acting in blatant disregard
for both.

Marković's strong support for women's equality also stemmed from her
leftist background and appeared genuine. She wrote frequently in her diary
on a wide spectrum of women's issues and saw herself as promoting a solidly
feminist perspective. She insisted always on the intellectual equality of
women and men, in the workplace and in politics. Marković derided, for example, the degeneration of International Women's Day into a holiday that
offered "syrupy sentimental homage to women as mother figures, with soft
hands and blue eyes, self sacrificing and working their fingers to the bone."[36]
She also deplored the impact of war on women and children.

And yet, when it came to men, her views remained stubbornly essentialist
and nationalist. She frequently attacked SRS leader Vojislav Šešelj in a way
entirely at odds both with her declared opposition to the war and with her
belief in the equality of both nations and sexes. She sneered at him for spending his time in Belgrade attacking her, a poor, defenseless woman, when he
should have been fighting at the front himself. He didn't want to take on a
man with a gun, she said, "but he can take on me, five foot two, who does not
even know how to use a can opener." "Instead of waging war in Belgrade
against one woman," she continued, "he would be better advised to go to war
in Bosnia and fight against men."[37] His cowardice and refusal to do so, she
added some time later, only proved that he was nothing more than a "reincar-

nated Turk in Belgrade." Šešelj, it turned out, "is not a Serb. He is a Turk, in the most primitive historical edition. Or perhaps he just is not a man. Although, to be honest, I think that he is neither one nor the other. Neither a Serb nor a man."[38]

Maja Gojković

Like the other extreme right women considered here, Maja Gojković came to her political perspective through family connections. She is descended from a well-known family of lawyers with a strong pedigree within the nationalist Serbian Chetnik movement.[39] She eventually followed in the family tradition and went to law school, completing her degree at the University of Novi Sad in 1987 and joining her father's law office shortly thereafter. By 1991 she had joined a new party formed by Vojislav Šešelj, the SRS.

Gojković rose quickly in the leadership of the party. Participating in the SRS paramilitary force, the Chetniks, was essential to acquiring leadership credentials, and almost immediately after she joined, Gojković spent six months at the front in Slavonija.[40] In 1992 Gojković was elected to the Serbian Parliament and soon became recognized as one of the most effective members of the SRS within that body. It was not long before she was elected vice president of the Executive Council of SRS. That same year, she was also elected to the Federal Parliament and served for over a year as vice president of its Council of Citizens. In her capacity as a lawyer, Gojković not only defended SRS President Šešelj when he was imprisoned by the Serbian government in the fall of 1994 but also played a major role in running the party during his absence. After Šešelj voluntarily turned himself over to the Hague Tribunal in 2002, Gojković acted as his personal lawyer. In 2004 she was elected mayor of Novi Sad, serving in this position until 2008.

Gojković clearly belonged to the "hard line" and most radical contingent of the SRS.[41] She was without doubt an ardent Serb nationalist who strongly supported the SRS program based on the unification of all Serbian lands, however long that might take; indeed, she considered such a unitary state to be the only means for Serbian national survival. Gojković also expressed her support for ethnic cleansing, stating openly that it was in Serbia's national interests for fewer Albanians to be living in Kosovo and that the SRS planned to colonize the region.[42] Gojković never wavered in her support of the wars in Croatia, Bosnia-Herzegovina, and later Kosovo or her convictions about the need to use force to attain national goals. In one interview, she expressed approval of the Yugoslav Army's bombing of the Croatian capital of Zagreb: "Of course I approve the bombing." "But," the interviewer cut in, "there are mothers and children there too!" "Yes," she responded, "but they support the policies of their President Tudjman and must pay for it."[43] Gojković also vehemently denounced SPS's and JUL's later support for various diplomatic plans to halt the fighting in Bosnia-Herzegovina. "Peace," she insisted, "was not the greatest Serb national interest."[44]

Perhaps because of the militancy of her views, Gojković earned a reputation as a no-nonsense politician with a "manly," decisive voice. Among the many titles given her were the "Iron Lady" (in a deliberate comparison to Margaret Thatcher), the "First Lady of the Opposition," and the "Lady Who Can Stop the Danube."[45] SRS leaders and publications took great pains to emphasize her professionalism and individual merit, reporting at length in the party newspaper on her contributions and accomplishments in the National Assembly. This is not to suggest that the SRS neglected the themes of motherhood on behalf of the nation in its publications, but it also treated Maja Gojković as a woman capable of leading according to her own merit.

Gojković herself reflected this perspective concerning her suitability to lead as a result of her own capabilities and firm extreme right convictions. She is perhaps the best example of a radical rightist leader profiled here, as her views on nationalism and militarism were clearly in line with those of extreme right ideology, and yet her ideas on women in politics resonated with the support for women's equality officially endorsed by the previous communist regime. In many ways, her ideas about women's equality are most consistent with a liberal feminist perspective. That is, she endorses the notion that equal opportunities should be open to women, who can compete for them on the same terms as men. Thus, a woman should be elected to political office only if she is the most qualified candidate, not simply because there is a quota system in place, a system supported by the communist regime. When interviewers asked about her family life or how she dressed, Gojković always deflected the question and insisted on responding in purely professional ways. Similarly, she insisted on referring only to the professional qualifications of her female rivals. Although admitting that Serbia was a patriarchal society where many still did not want to admit to women's political skills, Gojković refused to focus on "women's issues," preferring to concentrate on matters of what she considered "national importance."[46]

Gojković did not focus on a return to women's traditional roles, but she did call for a return to traditional masculine values and behavior. Although she was the least likely of all the women leaders considered here to hold essentialist views about women, she did so about men. The SRS frequently decried the loss of Serbian manhood, a loss it associated directly with the threats to Serbia from neighboring enemy nations.[47] Gojković echoed these calls for Serbian men to return to the Serbian warrior ideal of bravery and dedication to the nation. For example, when asked what should be done to encourage higher birthrates among Serbian women, Gojković, unlike most Serb nationalists, did not insist that women must learn to do all for the nation and fulfill their natural function. Rather, while agreeing that the state should institute a more proactive maternal policy, she insisted that for women to bring new life into the world, they must be inspired by men. "It is impossible to ask women to bear children to men who have capitulated before every threat or misfortune in advance," she stated. "If we wish to increase natality, we must develop a spirit of heroism, we must help Serbian men to be that which nature and tradition has determined."[48]

While Gojković was generally uninterested in talking about the characteristics of the ideal woman, she had a great deal to say about those of the ideal man. A true man, she said, was "a Serb. A man like Saint Sava, inspired, handsome, and noble like Stefan Lazarević, prepared to sacrifice for Serbdom like Miloš Obilić, brave like Captain Gavrilović. . . . He remains at the defense of his nation, even should he perish alone and against the entire world. I am happy," she continued, "that I now know that this is not just an ideal but reality. . . . The external indicator of such men is the uniform of a volunteer, the two-headed eagle."[49]

Biljana Plavšić

Like many others drawn to the right, the attraction in the case of Biljana Plavšić seemed in part due to family connections. Her family of wealthy merchants lost thirty-four members during the Second World War, along with substantial funds and property when the Communists came to power. Nevertheless, despite her apparent distrust of communism (Plavšić never became a party member), she benefitted from the regime's promotion of women's education and employment. In her career path, she followed in her father's footsteps. He had been a scientist who then became director of the Sarajevo Botanical Gardens. Plavšić completed her Ph.D. in botany, with an emphasis on plant viruses, at the University of Zagreb in Croatia in 1967. She had begun teaching at the University of Sarajevo in 1956 and became an internationally known scholar of plant pathology during her more than three decades of teaching.

Plavšić's first direct involvement in politics came in 1990 when she joined the SDS. Within a very short time, the SDS elected her to serve as its representative to the Socialist Republic of Bosnia and Herzegovina's presidency. From 1990 to 1992, she was the highest-ranking SDS official within the government of Bosnia-Herzegovina. During the wartime years from 1992 to 1995, she served as vice president of the Republic of Serbia in Bosnia-Herzegovina. After the war, she broke with her former colleagues in the SDS, including SDS leader Radovan Karadžić, whose place she took as the president of the Republic of Serbia in Bosnia-Herzegovina, and undertook the task of implementing the Dayton Peace Accord. After learning of her indictment by the International Criminal Tribunal of the Former Yugoslavia (ICTY) on charges of crimes against humanity and genocide, she surrendered to the tribunal in 2001. Initially denying the charges, she later admitted to one count of crimes against humanity and expressed her remorse for promoting hatred against non-Serbs during the war. Her trial garnered a great deal of attention because she was the first woman to be indicted by the court and the first high-ranking official to admit guilt. She was released from prison in Sweden in October 2009 after serving six years of her eleven-year sentence and moved to Belgrade to take up residence there.[50]

From the outset of her political career, Plavšić became implicated in Bosnian Serb preparations for violent conflict, including the use of ethnic cleansing. Indeed, Plavšić, like other SDS leaders, expressed her clear support for the SDS's political goals of establishing a Serbian territorial unit within Bosnia-Herzegovina through the use of force. She also endorsed what would be the major tool in achieving this goal, ethnic cleansing. According to the "Factual Basis for Plea of Guilt" issued by ICTY prosecutors, Plavšić "embraced and supported the objective" (of ethnic cleansing) and "contributed to achieving it," although she had less to do with its execution than other leaders of the SDS.[51] Plavšić expressed her support for such a policy on more than one occasion, stating, "I would prefer completely to cleanse eastern Bosnia of Muslims. When I say cleanse, I don't want anyone to take me literally and think I mean ethnic cleansing. But they've attached this label 'ethnic cleansing' to a perfectly natural phenomenon and characterized it as some kind of war crime."[52] Exhorting Serbs to fight to achieve their national goals, she is reputed to have said, "There are twelve million Serbs and even if six million perish on the field of battle, there will still be six million to reap the fruits of the struggle."[53]

Plavšić justified the policies of ethnic cleansing with theories of racial and ethnic superiority. As a biologist, she was particularly inclined to speak in Social Darwinist terms. As Plavšić put it, "It was genetically deformed material that embraced Islam. And now, of course, with each successive generation, this gene simply becomes concentrated. It gets worse and worse. It simply expresses itself and dictates their style of thinking and behaving which is rooted in their genes."[54] In contrast, she considered the Bosnian Serbs ethnically and racially superior not only to Muslims but also to Serbs from Serbia, because they had developed special defensive mechanisms in the course of evolution. She stated, "I know as a biologist that species that are surrounded and threatened by other species develop a higher level of adaptation and survival."[55] Perhaps because of her ethnic intolerance and her repeated and explicit endorsement of violence, Plavšić became known as the "Iron Lady" of Bosnia, and she was doubtless pleased by the recognition she received from soldiers in Bosnia, who referred to her as the "Iron Lady" or "Empress/Tsarina Biljana" and often painted her name on their tanks or machine guns.[56]

Like her counterparts in Serbia, Plavšić did not direct her attention to women and their role in carrying out the Serbian national project. This was at least partially due, as we have argued, to the fact that right-wing nationalist politics emerged out of the left in Serbia, which officially endorsed gender equality and provided the context within which extreme right Serbian parties operated. Instead, Plavšić focused on the behavior of Serbian men and the need to recapture the lost spirit of the Serbian warrior-hero. The regeneration of the Serbian nation, which was largely up to men, was of the utmost importance, according to Plavšić. "The Serbs have become so de-Serbianized over these past fifty years," she wrote. "They have insisted so much and in such an ugly way that they are not Serbs. They have blasphemed so much and denigrated the Church and clergy so much. . . . The Serbs have defiled themselves terribly."[57] Reversing this degeneration would require men to become warrior-heroes once again. Plavšić publicly lauded paramilitary leaders who carried out ethnic cleansing in Bosnia-Herzegovina. One well-known photo of Plavšić in 1992 shows her stepping over the body of a dead Muslim soldier to kiss Željko Ražnjatović Arkan, the notorious Serbian war criminal whose paramilitary soldiers were known to be responsible for some of the worst atrocities committed throughout Bosnia-Herzegovina.[58] As she planted the kiss on his cheek, Plavšić declared Arkan to be "a real Serbian hero. He is a real Serb. We need men like him."[59] He returned the favor and named his Belgrade coffee shop after her. Plavšić also praised indicted war criminal Ratko Mladić as "a great man" in her 2005 memoir.[60]

Conclusion

This overview of extreme right women leaders in Serbia after 1990 suggests that the reemergence of the extreme right in the context of the collapse of state socialism and ethnic mobilization shaped its gender ideology. While the fall of communism in Eastern Europe and the Soviet Union undoubtedly led to the resurgence of far-right and nationalist ideologies, in Serbia "left" and "right" labels cannot be consistently applied to the gender policies enacted by extreme right parties and movements. Thus, extreme right women countered the left, but they also overlapped with it. Because the SPS had sponsored ethnic mobilization during the previous several years, it became the most important radical rightist party on the political scene after multiparty elections in 1990; not only did it retain much of its leftist gender-egalitarian rhetoric (though the same cannot be said of its practices), but it shaped the rhetoric of the explicitly anticommunist rightist parties. The SPS's sponsorship of ultranationalist ideologies meant that left and right overlapped in the Serbian context and that Serbs tended to be less anticommunist than the populaces of many other East European countries. While the political position of women undoubtedly worsened during this period, the extreme right was primarily interested in contrasting its more modern gender practices with the perceived oppressive and backward practices of its ethnic enemies. This blurring of left and right views, combined with anti-Muslim gender discourse, shaped the way in which the right imagined women, both constraining its gender positions and making it possible for extreme right women to become leaders.

The extreme right in Serbia had a number of high-profile women leaders. These right-wing women resemble powerful women of other political persuasions in that they came to their political positions through "normative heterofamilial lines" and brought with them considerable familial (in the case of Marković), educational, and professional resources. While Marković came from a communist background and claimed to represent this position even as she enacted ultranationalist views, Gojković and Plavšić came from anticommunist, nationalist families. All three women endorsed a political program based on ultranationalism, hypermasculinity, and the use of violence to achieve political ends. While these women essentially led as honorary males, they reserved their most emotionally charged discourse for men, inciting them to true warrior masculinity and violence against their ethnic enemies.

NOTES

Translations from Serbian, Croatian, and Bosnian are the authors' own.

1. Michael Sell, "Kosovo Mythology and the Bosnian Genocide," in *In God's Name: Genocide and Religion in the Twentieth Century*, ed. Omer Bartov and Phyllis Mack (New York: Berghahn Books, 2001), 189; Mira Marković, *Night and Day* (Canada: Quarry Press, 1995), 111; Janine Di Giovanni, *Madness Visible: A Memoir of War* (New York: Alfred A. Knopf, 2003), 243.

2. The Serbian Renewal Movement (SPO), led by Vuk and Danica Drašković, also ran on a nationalist platform in the 1990 elections. Dejan Anastasijević and Anthony Borden, eds., *Out of Time: Drašković, Džindžić, and the Serbian Opposition Against Milošević* (London: Institute for War and Peace Reporting and Beta News Agency, 2000).

3. Cas Mudde, *Populist Radical Right Parties in Europe* (Cambridge: Cambridge University Press, 2007), 19.

4. Wendy Bracewell, "Women, Motherhood, and Contemporary Serbian Nationalism," *Women's Studies International Forum* 19, no. 1/2 (1996): 25–33; Wendy Bracewell, "Rape in Kosovo: Masculinity and Serbian Nationalism," *Nations and Nationalism* 6, no. 4 (October 2000): 563–90.

5. Žarana Papić, "Women in Serbia: Post-communism, War, and Nationalist Mutations," in *Gender Politics in the Western Balkans: Women and Society in Yugoslavia and the Yugoslav Successor States*, ed. Sabrina P. Ramet (University Park: Pennsylvania State University Press, 1999), 153–70; Jill A. Irvine and Carol S. Lilly, "Negotiating Interests: Women and Nationalism in Serbia and Croatia, 1990–1997," *East European Politics and Societies* 16, no. 1 (Winter 2002): 109–44.

6. Nanette Funk and Magda Mueller, *Gender, Politics, and Post-communism* (New York: Routledge, 1993); Marilyn Rueschemeyer, ed., *Women in the Politics of Postcommunist Eastern Europe* (New York: M. E. Sharpe, 1998).

7. Nikki R. Keddie, "The New Religious Politics and Women Worldwide: A Comparative Study," *Journal of Women's History* 10, no. 4 (Winter 1999): 11.

8. Jill A. Irvine and Carol S. Lilly, "Boys Must Be Boys: Gender and the Serbian Radical Party, 1990–2000," *Nationalities Papers* 35, no. 1 (March 2007): 93–120; see also Bracewell, "Women, Motherhood, and Contemporary Serbian Nationalism."

9. Papić, "Women in Serbia," 160.

10. Rada Iveković and Julie Mostov, *From Gender to Nation* (New Delhi: Zubaan, 2004); Beverly Allen, *Rape Warfare: The Hidden Genocide in Bosnia-Herzegovina and Croatia* (Minneapolis: University of Minnesota Press, 1996).

11. Mirjana Morokvasic, "The Logics of Exclusion: Nationalism, Sexism, and the Yugoslav War," in *Gender, Ethnicity, and Political Ideologies*, ed. Nickie Charles and Helen Hintjens (New York: Routledge, 1998), 65–90.

12. United States Information Agency (USIA) Survey 1994, Croatia/Serbia, authors' copy.

13. Center for Political Studies and Public Opinion Research, Institute of Social Sciences, Belgrade, unpublished survey data provided to the authors by Ljiljana Bačević Iveković, May 2002.

14. USIA Survey.

15. Papić, "Women in Serbia," 167.

16. Irvine and Lilly, "Boys Must Be Boys."

17. For example, see Laura A. Liswood, *Women World Leaders* (Washington, D.C.: Aspen Institute, 2007); Faroda Jalalzai, "Women Political Leaders: Past and Present," *Women and Politics* 26, no. 3/4 (2004): 85–108.

18. Liswood, *Women World Leaders.*

19. Jalalzai, "Women Political Leaders."

20. Mudde, *Populist Radical Right Parties in Europe,* 90–118.

21. Amrita Basu, "Feminism Inverted: The Real Women and Gendered Imagery of Hindu Nationalism," *Bulletin of Concerned Asian Scholars* 25 (1993): 25–36.

22. Paola Bacchetta and Margaret Power, introduction to *Right-Wing Women: From Conservatives to Extremists Around the World,* ed. P. Bacchetta and M. Power (New York: Routledge, 2002), 1–18.

23. Kathleen M. Blee, "The Gendered Organization of Hate: Women in the U.S. Ku Klux Klan," in *Right-Wing Women: From Conservatives to Extremists Around the World,* ed. Paola Bacchetta and Margaret Power (New York: Routledge, 2002), 101–14.

24. For a discussion of gender-emancipatory revolutions in communist countries, see Valentine M. Moghadam, "Gender and Revolutionary Transformation: Iran 1979 and East Central Europe 1980," *Gender and Society* 9, no. 3 (June 1995): 328–58.

25. For a discussion of Marković's controversial mother, see Adam LeBor, *Milošević: A Biography* (New Haven: Yale University Press, 2002), 20; Duško Doder and Louise Branson, *Milošević: Portrait of a Tyrant* (New York: Free Press, 1999), 18; Slavoljub Djukić, *Milošević and Marković: A Lust for Power* (Montreal: McGill Queen's University Press, 2001), 4–5; Lenard Cohen, *Serpent in the Bosom: The Rise and Fall of Slobodan Milošević* (Boulder, Colo.: Westview Press, 2001), 46.

26. Djukić, *Milošević and Marković,* 5; Cohen, *Serpent in the Bosom,* 46.

27. LeBor, *Milošević,* 21.

28. Doder and Branson, *Milošević,* 19.

29. LeBor, *Milošević,* 21.

30. Djukić, *Milošević and Marković,* 11.

31. Ibid., 65.

32. Robert Thomas, *Serbia Under Milošević: Politics in the 1990s* (London: Hurst, 1999), 230.

33. Doder and Branson, *Milošević,* 20.

34. Marković, *Night and Day,* 113.

35. Ibid., 20–22.

36. Ibid., 36.

37. Ibid., 134.

38. Ibid., 242.

39. Teodora Pavlović, "Radikalsa 'Gvozdena Ledi,'" *Velika Srbija* 5, no. 16 (May 1994): 9.

40. Aleksandra Jovanović, "Bez dlake na jeziku," *Velika Srbija* (special edition) 7, no. 161 (October 1996): 21.

41. Pavlović, "Radikalsa 'Gvozdena Ledi,'" 11.

42. "Maja Gojković u emisije 'Intervju Gledalaca,'" *Velika Srbija* (special edition) 7, no. 161 (October 1996): 4–5.

43. Ibid., 13–14.

44. Maja Gojković's speech at the Fourth Congress, held May 18, 1996, "Četvrti Otadžbinski Kongres," *Velika Srbija* 7, no. 109 (June 1996): 11–12.

45. Jovanović, "Bez dlake na jeziku," 20.

46. Slobdan Nagradić, *Neka istorija sudi: Razgovori sa liderima Srpske Radikalne Stranke* (Banja Luka: Vikom, 1995), 341; Maja Gojković, "Olovka piše srcem—Staljin i Mugabe," *Velika Srbija* 7, no. 83 (April 1996): 17.

47. Irvine and Lilly, "Boys Must Be Boys."

48. Pavlović, "Radikalsa 'Gvozdena Ledi,'" 14.

49. Jovanović, "Bez dlake na jeziku," 20.

50. Marlise Simons, "Albright Testifies in War Crimes Case," *New York Times*, December 18, 2002, http://www.nytimes.com/2002/12/18/world/crossing-paths-albright-testifies-in-war-crimes-case.html; Daniel Simpson, "UN Tribunal, with Surprise Guilty Plea, Rivets Bosnians," *New York Times*, October 4, 2002, http://www.nytimes.com/2002/10/04/world/un-tribunal-with-surprise-guilty-plea-rivets-bosnians.html; Ian Traynor, "Leading Bosnian Serb War Criminal Released from Swedish Prison," *Guardian*, October 27, 2009, http://www.guardian.co.uk.world/2009/oct/27/bosnian-serb-war-criminal-freed.

51. The International Criminal Tribunal for the former Yugoslavia in the Trial Chamber, case no. IT-00–39&40-PT, "Factual Basis for Plea of Guilt," http://www.icty.org/x/cases/plavsic/custom4/en/plea.pdf.

52. *Svet* (Novi Sad), September 6, 1993, cited in Slobodan Inić, "Biljana Plavšić: Geneticist in the Service of a Great Crime," available online from *Srebrenica Genocide Blog*, September 15, 2009, http://srebrenica-genocide.blogspot.com/2009/09/crime-pays-biljana-plavsic-to-get-early.html.

53. "Biljana Plavšić: Serbian Iron Lady," *BBC News*, February 27, 2003, http://news.bbc.co.uk/2/hi/1108604.stm.

54. Sell, "Kosovo Mythology and the Bosnian Genocide," 189.

55. Mitja Velikonija, *Religious Separation and Political Intolerance in Bosnia-Herzegovina* (College Station: Texas A&M University Press, 2003), 248.

56. Ibid., 247.

57. *Republika* (Belgrade), October 16–31, 1993, as cited by Inić, "Biljana Plavšić."

58. "Biljana Plavšić: Serbian Iron Lady."

59. Di Giovanni, *Madness Visible*, 243.

60. "Jailed Plavšić Writes Bosnia Book," *BBC News*, January 19, 2005, http://news.bbc.co.uk/2/hi/europe/4189695.stm. See also Biljana Plavšić, *Svedočim* (Banja Luka: Trioprint, 2005).

Dilemmas of Representation: Conservative and Feminist
Women's Organizations React to Sarah Palin

Ronnee Schreiber

A curious thing happened on the way to the polls in November. Conservatives claimed a victory of sorts in having a woman on the ticket and feminists chided everyone to remember that "Ms. Palin does not represent us."
—Women Against Sarah Palin, http://www.womenagainstsarahpalin.blogspot.org

When Republican John McCain nominated Sarah Palin to be his running mate in his bid for president of the United States in 2008, reporters speculated that he had done so to woo disaffected supporters of Democratic candidate Hillary Clinton. For many feminists, this idea seemed like pure folly. Palin, a staunch conservative, was unlikely to attract votes from the women who stood behind Clinton, a liberal feminist, in the Democratic primaries. Indeed, feminists were right. With Clinton out of the race, few Democratic women voted for McCain/Palin; most backed the Democratic ticket of Obama/ Biden in the general election. Although the assessment of the female electorate in this case was inaccurate, it was derived in part from journalists who recognized that the relationship between gender identity and representation can be salient in elections. That is, women elected officials do behave differently from their male counterparts, and citizens take this into account when they go to the polls. It is typically assumed, and supported by data, that women elected officials feel a special obligation to represent women's interests. As such, feminists have traditionally called for the election of more women to office. With Palin, however, there was a twist. Those in favor of her nomination were conservative women, eager to have Palin representing them.

In this chapter, I examine how conservative women's organizations reacted to Palin's nomination, highlighting how they used her run for office to make claims about their organizational goals and their own abilities to represent women. For them, Palin is a fitting symbol. She champions a range of conservative causes and invoked her gender and maternal status on the campaign trail. Her political views reflect both economic and social conservatism, meaning that she can speak to, and for, a range of conservative activists. She supports free-market policies that limit regulations on businesses and reduce taxes. Palin also opposes legal abortion, same-sex marriage, and restrictions on gun ownership. Although she is a former city council member, mayor, and governor of Alaska, she boasts of entering politics through her involvement with the local Parent Teacher Association (PTA), implying that her political ambition derives from dedication to her children. Palin is married and the mother of five children, including one with Down syndrome. She featured these aspects of her life in her bid for vice president, drawing praise from many conservative women for her public commitment to motherhood. Palin claims to be a populist and chastises "elites" for allegedly trying to cast her as provincial and unintelligent. She aims to connect with her audience by invoking short, catchy phrases and winking at the crowds. In the year since Barack Obama was elected, Palin has spent her time traveling the country to promote her autobiography and rally supporters of the Tea Party, a newly formed network of conservative grassroots organizations in the United States.

The conservative women's organizations under study here found that having someone like Palin on the ticket provided them with an opportunity to counter the left and challenge feminist groups for not supporting a woman's bid for the nation's second-highest office. Conversely, feminist organizations were put on the defensive, having to explain to opponents and the public why this particular woman did not fit within their agenda to elect more women to office.

I consider conservative women's groups to be those that promote social conservative issues, such as opposition to abortion rights and same-sex marriage, and/or economic conservative issues, such as tax cuts and limited regulation of businesses. These women's organizations also contest the existence of intentional or institutional discrimination and specifically challenge the goals and successes of the feminist movement. They might be termed "right-wing," but because they explicitly and directly engage with institutions of government (e.g., Congress), other interest groups, and the media, I do not consider them to be extremists. Feminist organizations are those that either self-identify as feminist, support women's equal rights under the law, and/or believe that women's oppression relative to men is the result of discrimination. In addition, feminists believe that women's status is predominantly shaped by processes of institutional and structural inequality, not individual actions or circumstances. Like their conservative counterparts under study here, these groups are "mainstream" in that they work directly with government institutions and political actors.

To begin my analysis, I put Palin's nomination in the context of debates about identity and representation, arguing that this case affords a chance to evaluate the process of political representation in a more dynamic fashion.

The Politics of Identity and Representation

A substantial amount of research has been published in the United States on the relationship between the gender of an elected official and her/his actions in office.[1] The impetus for this body of work derives from the expectation that elected women will act differently from their male colleagues, and it assumes that the gender of elected officials will correlate to policy priorities and goals. Most studies of women elected officials support these hypotheses and conclude that women can better represent other women. Data on women state legislators, for example, show that women uniquely contribute to the political process and tend to be more supportive of women's issues, broadly defined.[2] Research also demonstrates that within their respective parties, women place a higher priority and spend more time on equity issues as well as policies related to women's traditional roles as nurturers and caregivers. Women vote differently than their male colleagues, feel a special responsibility to represent women, and work together to advance a collective agenda.[3] Although the gender of elected officials appears to be able to predict some behavior, there are important caveats, especially given the diversity among women. For example, Michele Swers finds that "ideology is the strongest predictor of voting for women's issues," although she also notes that "congresswomen are more likely to vote for women's issue bills than their male colleagues even when one controls for ideological, partisan, and district factors."[4] Given these findings, this broad collection of research can guide how we evaluate and understand a conservative woman's run for political office.

What motivates scholars to explore women's behavior in office is the assumption that descriptive representation is a valid and beneficial process for the promotion of women's interests. As defined by Hanna Pitkin, descriptive representation depends on a "representative's characteristics, on what he is or is like, on being something rather than doing something."[5] In this way, the representative is "acting for" others by virtue of her/his identity. Substantive representation is the notion that representatives need not share an identity with those they represent; instead, representation is based on the content or guiding principle of a person's actions regardless of who she/he is.[6] In this case, the representative is "standing for" her/his constituents. While Pitkin distinguishes between these two processes, there can be a direct relationship between them. That is, "acting for" can follow from "standing for." Like the research detailed earlier, this relationship is based on the assumption that a person who shares a social location with another is more likely to understand and support that person's interests and act accordingly. Claims that there is a relationship between descriptive and substantive representation are thus also epistemological ones; they suggest that people with like identities can better know the needs of others like themselves because they have had similar experiences.

The idea that the identity of a representative should be salient has its critics. Pitkin, for example, argues that descriptive representation is too focused on the composition of legislative bodies and not enough on what they are actually doing.[7] Others have argued that assuming a direct correlation between identity and interests elides differences among those within the identity-based group. Such essentialism, as it has often been called, suggests a homogeneity of interests and experiences that may only reflect a portion of the group for whom representatives claim to be speaking. Identity politics, they contend, runs the risk of assuming that all women have a "true essence—that which is most irreducible, unchanging, and therefore constitutive of a given person or thing"[8]—that is, that such politics are "essentialist."

Critiques of descriptive representation notwithstanding, several scholars have argued that there are merits to both descriptive and descriptive-substantive representation.[9] Answering a "contingent 'yes'" to the question of whether blacks should represent blacks and women represent women, Jane Mansbridge contends that descriptive representation can give a group "de facto legitimacy by making citizens, and particularly members of historically underrepresented groups, feel as if they themselves were present in the deliberations."[10] Thus, descriptive representation can have social meaning and attain the laudable goal of greater political participation. In this conceptualization, representation is considered from the viewpoint of the represented, providing a more dynamic assessment of the process whereby interests are articulated and debated in the public sphere. Following this line of reasoning, some scholars have called upon us to critically evaluate how we talk about representation and urge us to think about the concept in less static ways. That is, they argue for moving beyond a linear analysis that merely considers whether elected officials are representing a set of interests to a broader set of questions. These scholars encourage us to contextualize the process in which representation is taking place and to analyze "the multiple possible actors, sites, goals and means that inform processes of substantive representation."[11] Michael Saward argues for "seeing representation in terms of *claims to be representative* by a variety of political actors, rather than (as is normally the case) seeing it as an achieved, or potentially achievable, state of affairs as a result of election."[12] To these ends, careful attention should be paid to the effects, purposes, and processes of identity politics and its corresponding claims of representation.[13] For activists, this could mean "getting specific" in defining who they are and for which goals they are striving, to negotiate between the need for identity politics and the problems it can create.[14] As I show, feminist organizations employed this strategy in responding to Palin's nomination.

My evaluation of how national conservative and feminist women's organizations reacted to the candidacy of Sarah Palin provides insights into how, and to what ends, representative claims are deployed. I analyze not only specific claims of representation by these political actors but also the implications of these claims. That is, in what ways do representative claims about Palin advance (or not) the agendas of these groups? What are the political effects when conservative women's organizations counter feminist organizations' claims of representation in this case?

Conservative women leaders touted Palin as a symbol of their own successes and political relevance. For them, Palin beautifully exemplifies the significance of descriptive representation. For feminist groups, however, Palin's candidacy presented a predicament. These organizations argue for the need for more women in political office (i.e., they promote descriptive representation) but are at odds with most of Palin's policy goals. Thus, it was no surprise that groups like the feminist National Organization for Women (NOW) did not leap to her side. What remains unclear is exactly how conservative and feminist women's organizations framed Palin's candidacy in light of several factors. First, as noted, conservative women's groups have been conflicted over whether to devote resources to electing more women to office.[15] Although they believe that it is important to have conservative women making political claims to counter those of feminists, they are at times wary of anything that smacks of affirmative action, a policy that favors increasing the economic and political status of underrepresented groups by taking factors like a person's race or gender into account. Conservative women's organizations have also criticized feminist groups for engaging in identity politics.[16] Thus, embracing descriptive representation requires them to navigate these tensions and clarify how Palin's nomination benefits women. Conversely, feminists have long argued for the inclusion of more women in politics. But supporting Palin presents obvious problems because of her issue positions. Opposing her, however, requires that feminist organizations publicly articulate the costs of descriptive representation, an action that makes these identity-based groups vulnerable to criticism. As I show, feminist groups negotiated these tensions by being specific—by arguing that what matters is that elected officials support feminist policy goals, not that elected officials be female.

I situate my analysis within the realm of national women's organizations because they shape public discourse about feminism, conservatism, and women's interests. As they frame issues and construct their identities, they give meaning to women's interests and thus animate scholarly debates about representation and identity politics. Data come from public statements made by national conservative and feminist women's organizations in major newspapers, press releases, blogs, fund-raising letters, e-mails, and websites between August 29, 2008 (the day McCain announced Palin's nomination) and December 31, 2008 (to take into account postmortems on the election). I considered any national organization that claims to represent women, conservative women, or feminists for this paper (see the appendix for information about the groups). I consider an organization to be a women's group if it explicitly claims to represent women and/or if many of its issue priorities specifically reference women's interests (e.g., Title IX, Equal Rights Amendment, reproductive health issues). Any document that mentioned Sarah Palin was analyzed. In addition, I examined press releases from the feminist organizations that endorsed Barack Obama as they alluded to Palin's candidacy but did not mention her by name (see the appendix).

Conservative Women React to Palin

When McCain chose Palin to be his running mate, conservative women's groups were eager to react. In many ways, Palin's nomination provided national conservative women's organizations—such as Concerned Women for America (CWA), Independent Women's Forum (IWF), and Network of enlightened Women (NeW)—with a canvas on which they could project ideas about who they are and how they represent women. Indeed, one mission of these organizations is to counter feminist claims of representing women—that is, they argue that feminists do not speak for most women. Another goal is to demonstrate the importance of women in conservative politics and to show that conservatives and the Republican Party care about women's interests.[17] Claiming that Palin represents them helps these political actors further these goals. Specifically, conservative women's groups framed her candidacy in pro-women, antifeminist terms and also used this significant political moment to promote other conservative causes.

Pro-Palin, Pro-Women, Antifeminist

Conservative women's organizations cheered Palin's nomination as a victory for conservative women in general. After the election, in December 2008, the Clare Boothe Luce Policy Institute (CBLPI) sent out a Christmas card featuring a large group of young women lovingly deemed the "next generation of Sarah Palins." The National Federation of Republican Women (NFRW) declared Monday, November 24, 2008, to be "Sarah Palin Appreciation Day" and asked its members to write Governor Palin to "thank her for her principled leadership, both as the Republican Party's first female vice presidential candidate and as governor of Alaska."[18] But Palin was not just touted as a political symbol who represents conservative women. She was also presented as a formidable challenge to feminists. IWF's president, Michelle Bernard, branded Palin the "everywoman" who "might not win the votes of left-wing feminists, but [who] appeals to average women and men across the country."[19] Similarly, CWA applauded Palin's nomination while using it to take a jab at feminists: "It is particularly significant that a conservative woman was nominated for the nation's second highest office. For years the feminist movement has acknowledged for leadership only those women who embrace a radical agenda. How refreshing that now we have a woman who reflects the values of mainstream American women. . . . Take that feminists."[20]

As noted, a central aim of conservative women's organizations is to cast feminists and feminism as out of touch, too radical, and ultimately hostile to the real needs of women. McCain's picking Palin afforded conservative women's groups an opportunity to promote this message while expressing delight that a woman would represent them. The organizations suggested that criticism of Palin was sexist and hypocritical, and in effect attempted to illuminate cracks in feminists' arguments about women's rights, political opportunity, and equality. For example, an IWF blogger claimed that "much of the leftist opposition to Sarah Palin amounts to just plain sexism."[21] IWF's Carrie Lukas contended that "it is not surprising to see feminist organizations like the National Organization for Women dispute the term 'feminist' as it applies to Gov. Palin. . . . After all, groups like NOW have worked for years to redefine 'feminism' to fit their liberal agenda. Anyone who exposes conservative views is not welcome in their feminist club."[22] Adding to the mix, Bernard criticized feminist reaction to Palin by charging that "there were bountiful substantive issues dividing the candidates, all of which warranted a thorough and even tough debate. But some of the attacks on Governor Palin were blatantly sexist cheap shots—questions about how she could be both mother and vice president, for instance. . . . Many of these attacks came from many so-called feminists."[23]

In similar terms, CWA's Janet Shaw Crouse contended that "even feminists—who supposedly promote women's equality and the so-called 'women's rights' agenda—are questioning a female candidate's ability to get the job done. It's past time for the bullying to stop."[24] Karin Agness, founder of the conservative NeW, took NOW to task in an editorial on the conservative website townhall.com: "Vigorous debate is valuable in American society. Yet, it is improper, unnecessary and discrediting for NOW to completely disown Palin. She is, after all, a living example of what second wave feminists claimed to be about: empowering women to make choices and giving them the opportunity to do so. NOW, women and all Americans should celebrate Palin for the woman she is and the possibilities she symbolizes for women. She is truly a liberated woman."[25]

For these organizations, framing criticism of Palin as antithetical to feminist values and goals serves two purposes. First, it casts liberals and Democrats as hypocrites, thus putting forth the notion that Obama's party and his supporters should not be trusted. This strategy makes sense during a high-stakes presidential election. Second, it helps these conservative women's groups distinguish themselves from feminist organizations but still project to the public that they care about women. In addition, their representative claims challenge the public to scrutinize and debate the meaning of feminism, calling into question feminist movement goals, priorities, and values and raising the question of what constitutes women's interests and who can speak for them. In so doing, conservative women activists can take some credit for promoting the feminist goal of equal opportunity for women in politics and other professions, while distancing themselves from other issues that feminist organizations support but conservatives oppose. IWF summed up this idea by claiming,

> Yesterday, NOW released a plea for support as they struggle to control what a small minority of women believe feminism is. With working-class women flocking to the Palin camp, it appears they are fighting a battle they have already lost. NOW's president, Kim Gandy finds it ironic that the word "feminist" has been spoken in public so many times since the Palin explosion. However, what's ironic, is that a true feminist suddenly arrived on their playground, and because she is a conservative, anti-abortion, pro-gun, mother of five, they don't want to play.[26]

Central to conservative women's groups' ability to make representative claims about women is the degree to which they successfully characterize feminists as being out of touch with the majority of women. In this case, siding with Palin and arguing that feminists are hypocrites can raise doubts about whether feminists really care about all women, or just those who follow their agendas. As IWF argued in a fund-raising letter, Palin "proves that you don't have to hold the political viewpoints and cultural prejudices of the Left to succeed as a woman. And she does it all with grace and charm."[27] In addition, these groups can more easily claim that Palin, a woman, represents them and their interests, because in this case there is ideological consistency. Here the correlation between descriptive and substantive representation is a clear one. However, by impugning feminists, conservative women's organizations are also inadvertently pointing to the challenges of equating identity with interests. By contesting the meaning of feminism and women's interests, they demonstrate the contingent value of descriptive representation and the need to better understand the ways in which the concept is deployed.

Affirming Conservative Credentials

Conservative women's organizations also used commentary about Palin and whom she represents to shore up support for their core political values. That is, the groups highlighted that a woman nominated to be vice president could be conservative, thus contesting the idea that there is a positive relationship between being female and holding liberal policy preferences. For IWF, this meant using the discussion about Palin to reaffirm its free-market ideology as well as to contend that its political goals are not necessarily antithetical to feminism. This was in part a paradoxical political move, since IWF never claimed to be a feminist organization but heralded Palin as a "free market feminist"[28] nonetheless. An IWF fund-raising letter sent after the election touted Palin as "a dream come true for us here at Independent Women's Forum. She perfectly exemplifies the type of strong, independent woman who loves her country and its limited government ideas . . . *the type of women who we represent at IWF*."[29]

Here IWF uses claims of representation to highlight differences among women and promote the idea that women can be conservative. It adds the additional twist of redefining feminism to be consistent with its economic conservative ideology. While there are certainly economic conservatives who consider themselves to be feminists, IWF confounds the meaning of feminism itself and suggests that the economic conservative belief in "free choice," individual-level decision making, and responsibility should be central to feminism. This line of reasoning has been disputed by the feminist organizations under study because it ignores how sexism shapes and may constrain women's personal and professional options.[30]

Socially conservative women's groups were also quick to use the Palin nomination to further their beliefs and suggest that social conservatism is welcoming to women. When talking about the nomination, organizations like CWA and CBLPI employed language that celebrated the differences between women and men. To be clear, for these social conservatives, accepting that there are distinctions between the sexes does not mean that they believe women should refrain from running for office or having career goals. It does mean, however, that they think women bring something unique to politics. On a broad level, that women offer something new is not necessarily different from feminist claims about the need for more women in elective office. In this way, conservative women's groups are promoting descriptive representation; however, they do so for conservative ends. For example, CWA framed Palin's success in terms of family support and femininity: "[Palin's] success means that a woman with intelligence and inherent leadership abilities, who is hard working and has a family willing to work together, can reach the highest levels of professional attainment and exude (as well as exert) natural authority with a feminine touch."[31] Following this theme of "femininity," Michelle Easton, president of CBLPI, praised Palin for holding her baby onstage during her campaign appearances, because this shows that Palin "publicly embrace[s] being a woman in all its facets."[32]

Conservative women's organizations have been criticized by feminist groups for allegedly encouraging women to be stay-at-home mothers while simultaneously rallying around Palin. These conservative activists suggest, however, that any tensions caused by women working outside the home are mitigated when their families are on board. This argument is actually consistent with the views of many social conservatives. Studies of evangelical Protestant women and men (CWA is mostly composed of evangelical Protestants) show that despite some contradictions with their theological beliefs, evangelical Protestant couples are generally supportive of women's engagement with "public" life.[33] In line with these findings, CWA has argued that although women are natural primary caregivers, their political participation is critical for their interests to be heard.[34] As such, families should negotiate roles and duties to balance these needs, as Palin has allegedly done. Thus, for social conservatives, Palin's determination to embrace her maternal status and run for office is framed in ways that represent conservative views about motherhood and public service.

As they publicly applauded Palin, conservative women's groups had company from conservative women pundits. For example, conservative commentator and blogger Michelle Malkin asked her readers to send a message of support to Sarah Palin after McCain's staff leaked negative comments about her behavior during the campaign. They did so because they were dismayed by her weak performances during televised debates and interviews and thus felt that she was a liability to McCain. Malkin noted that "tons of readers are asking me how to get a personal message to Sarah Palin and offer her support in the face of all the ugly, anonymous attacks from back-stabbing blabbermouths on the McCain campaign. Here's a quick petition site I created where you can sign and leave your comments."[35] Some notable conservative women did openly oppose her nomination and called upon her to step down,[36] but the general publicized sentiment about Palin among organized groups of conservative women was positive and supportive. Palin's nomination presented conservative women's groups with a special opportunity to articulate who they are and how they differ from feminists, as well as to showcase the centrality of women to conservative politics. Feminist organizations, on the other hand, were put on the defensive.

Feminists React to Palin

Jane Mansbridge argues that the push for descriptive representation comes with costs.[37] Feminists have generally been willing to pay these costs to engage in identity politics and make collective claims about women's impact and interests. In addition to forming women's organizations, they have established groups that encourage, train, and raise money for women to get elected to office. In general, these tactics have paid off. Feminist groups can point to decades of success in getting more women elected to office, changing government policies, and setting the tone for what constitutes "women's interests." Palin, however, presented a significant challenge to these feminist organizations. As noted, conservative women's organizations called on feminist groups to at least recognize that having a woman on the Republican ticket had social meaning. Palin forced feminist organizations to do what critics of descriptive representation and identity politics have argued—to specify what they mean by women's interests and to delineate for whom they speak. It thus became incumbent on national feminist groups like NOW and the Feminist Majority Foundation (FMF) to articulate why they would not support Palin. Simply opposing her would not have worked because of their longtime commitment to working for the inclusion of more women in politics. Indeed, NOW's original mission statement refers to the need for more women in public life and calls for more women to participate "fully in the selection of candidates and political decision-making, and running for office themselves."[38]

When it formed a political action committee to raise money for candidates, NOW did clarify that its goal was to support *feminists*. However, the mission statement goes on to equate feminism with support for "women's rights": "As NOW advocates for women's rights, electing feminists is a crucial part of our strategy. In 1997, NOW's political action committees (PACs) launched the Victory 2000—The Feminization of Politics campaign with the aim of electing 2,000 feminist candidates at all levels of political office by the year 2000. This campaign builds on our decades of electoral work which has increased the presence and clout of candidates who support *women's rights*."[39]

In clarifying why NOW did not support Palin, NOW president Kim Gandy reiterated the connection between feminism and women's rights: "I am frequently asked whether NOW supports women candidates just because they are women. This gives me an opportunity to once again answer that question with an emphatic 'No.' We recognize the importance of having women's rights supporters at every level but, like Sarah Palin, not every woman supports women's rights."[40] Although the phrase "women's rights" has often been associated with feminism, it can be used by conservative women's groups to mean something quite different about women's interests.[41] Thus, while NOW did move toward clarifying that descriptive representation is "contingent" (and in this case not worth the costs), it did not completely erase the conflation between feminist and women's interests, further exemplifying the tensions inherent in promoting descriptive representation as a strategy. Indeed, there was evident grappling with the concept of representation when NOW bemoaned that a mother of five could not speak for women: "Governor Palin may be the second woman vice-presidential candidate on a major party ticket, but she is not the right woman. . . . The fact that Palin is a mother of five who has a 4-month-old baby, a woman who is juggling work and family responsibilities, will speak to many women. But will Palin speak FOR women? Based on her record and her stated positions, the answer is clearly No."[42]

There were moments, however, in which feminist groups did aim to get more specific, detailing the substantive interests they favor. On September 16, 2009, several liberal/feminist national women's organizations endorsed Obama at a press conference and used the occasion to articulate what they mean by women's interests. Leaders from the FMF PAC, NOW PAC, Business and Professional Women (BPW) PAC, National Association of Social Workers

(NASW) PAC, National Congress of Black Women (NCBW), and Women's Information Network (WIN) stood together to offer their support for the Obama/Biden ticket. It was noted during the press conference that these groups rarely endorse presidential candidates.[43] Although none of the speakers specifically cited the presence of Palin on the ticket as their reason for making this overt gesture, they did allude to her candidacy and their subsequent need to support candidates who are "running on the strongest platform for women's rights of any major party in USA history."[44] Eleanor Smeal, president of FMF, also proclaimed that "we don't think it's much to break a glass ceiling for one woman and leave millions of women behind,"[45] clearly referring to Palin's bid for office. BPW analyzed the positions of both presidential candidates on issues like the expansion of sick leave and the Family and Medical Leave Act, enforcement of equal pay for women, reproductive rights, and violence against women and concluded that Obama strongly supported "working women and their families."[46]

In addition to the press conference, the National Women's Political Caucus (NWPC), a bipartisan group that encourages the election of more women to political office, issued this statement in reference to Palin: "While [McCain's] selection of Governor Palin as his running mate on the Republican presidential ticket is a recognition of the importance of women's support and votes in this election and an acknowledgment of the leadership capabilities of women, it is unfortunate that their position on issues of fundamental importance to our members preclude us from supporting her."[47] Palin's candidacy also generated the formation of a netroots group that called itself Women Against Sarah Palin. Their original call to action on September 6, 2008, asked women to respond to Palin's candidacy and put her nomination in the context of representation: "First and foremost, Ms. Palin does not represent us. She does not demonstrate or uphold our interests as American women. It is presumed that the inclusion of a woman on the Republican ticket could win over women voters. We want to disagree, publicly."[48] The two women co-founders of the group also felt it necessary to clarify why they were opposing a woman on a major party presidential ticket:

> We usually feel we should support our female compatriots with as much encouragement as we can. However, Sarah Palin's record is anti-woman. Feminism is not simply about achieving the power and status typically held by men. It's about protecting and supporting the rights of women of all classes, races, cultures, and beliefs. Palin's record and beliefs do not align with this. She was chosen by John McCain specifically because he believes that American women will vote for any female candidate regardless of their qualifications. He is wrong.[49]

Ultimately, the case of Sarah Palin forced these feminists to argue that what matters in electoral politics is not gender identity per se, but where candidates stand on issues. In other words, Palin's nomination pushed feminist groups to acknowledge the risks of descriptive representation and identity politics. In so doing, it required them to specify what women's interests mean to feminists and what feminism means in general. This is not necessarily a negative outcome, but it did put feminist organizations in a reactionary position.

To be clear, feminist organizations did also talk about the 2008 election in ways that illuminated the sexist and gendered nature of politics. NWPC noted that Palin's nomination had social meaning and should be considered important in terms of the need for more gender equity in electoral representation: "There are many highly qualified women in the political pipeline today whom we enthusiastically support and work with to get elected or appointed to office. We will continue our work to achieve gender equity in politics and look forward to the day we have our first woman president who supports the principles we believe to be fundamental to the equality of women."[50] NOW also expressed concern that reporters might not be fair to Palin because of her gender and noted that it would "monitor the media and call them out for their sexism directed at Palin. A woman slurred, regardless of her party or stances, is a woman slurred."[51] Here NOW's deference to Palin demonstrates the group's concern with the treatment of women in politics, which reinforces its overall premise that institutions perpetuate sexism, regardless of the ideological perspective of its targets.

Conclusions

That conservative women's organizations countered the left by battling feminist groups over whether Palin represented them forces us to examine why women were not in agreement over McCain's pick for his running mate. We could simply dismiss this case because of Palin's weak performance or because of the nature of partisan politics, but this would leave untouched a rich opportunity to evaluate the complex interplay between gender, ideology, and representation. For decades, both conservative and feminist women's organizations have engaged as gender-conscious actors. Generally, feminist groups have been the ones urging for more women in politics as a means to getting women's interests represented. Palin's run, however, highlighted ideological divisions among women and showcased the role that conservative women's organizations play in making conservative politics meaningful for women. As these organizations counter the left, and feminist groups in particular, they demonstrate the centrality of women to conservative movement politics. Groups like CWA, IWF, and NeW position women in leadership roles and have them make conservative claims when speaking to lawmakers, the media, and the public.[52] This allows conservatives to argue that feminists do not necessarily speak for all women and that conservative politics can be welcoming to women. Over time, this may encourage the Republican Party to nominate even more women to elective office. And with a growing conservative women's movement, it may also mean that more women will view these candidates as people who can represent them.

Palin's nomination gave conservative and feminist organizations an opportunity to construct their own identities and articulate for whom they speak. In this way, the process of seeking and claiming representation produced outcomes beyond public policies. For example, Palin's nomination forced feminist groups to get specific. As I argued earlier, this is not necessarily detrimental. To the extent that activists can clarify their goals and even generate coalitions based on issues, not merely identity, they may have more success in achieving their goals.

That Palin's nomination sparked a public conflict among ideologically distinct women's organizations points to the need for understanding representation in more dynamic ways. Palin's case demonstrates that representative claims have political effects and consequences that require careful strategizing on the part of identity-based organizations. If we merely focus on whether a candidate for elective office supports feminist issues, for example, we miss the bigger picture about what is at stake in debates over representation in other contexts and among a variety of political actors.

Appendix: Description of National Women's Organizations

Organization	Year founded	Issue priorities
Feminist Majority Foundation (feminist)	1987	Global feminism; women in sports; women's health; violence against women; reproductive rights; arts and entertainment
National Organization for Women (feminist)	1966	Reproductive rights; violence against women; constitutional equality; ending racism; lesbian rights; economic justice
National Women's Political Caucus (feminist)	1971	Reproductive rights; electing pro-choice women to office; recruiting, training, and financially supporting women's bids for office
Business and Professional Women's Foundation (feminist)	1919	Workplace equity issues such as equal pay, work-life balance, family leave, health care
Concerned Women for America (conservative)	1979	Religious liberty; national sovereignty; anti-abortion; opposition to gay rights; opposition to pornography; education
Clare Boothe Luce Policy Institute (conservative)	1993	Providing leadership training and mentoring to conservative university women; promoting conservative curriculum on college campuses; school choice

Organization	Year founded	Issue priorities
Independent Women's Forum (conservative)	1992	Women in Iraq; women and work; national security; health/science; education; international women's rights; violence against women
National Federation of Republican Women (conservative)	1938	Recruiting, training, and working to elect Republican candidates, especially Republican women
Network of enlightened Women (conservative)	2004	Fostering education and leadership skills of conservative university women; promoting conservative values in higher education

NOTES

1. See, for example, Debra Dodson, *The Impact of Women in Congress* (Oxford: Oxford University Press, 2006); Michele Swers, *The Difference Women Make: The Policy Impact of Women in Congress* (Chicago: University of Chicago Press, 2002); Debra Dodson, Susan J. Carroll, and Ruth Mandel, *The Impact of Women in Public Office* (New Brunswick: Center for American Women and Politics, 1991); Sue Thomas, *How Women Legislate* (New York: Oxford University Press, 1994).

2. Thomas, *How Women Legislate;* Dodson, Carroll, and Mandel, *Impact of Women in Public Office.*

3. Dodson, Carroll, and Mandel, *Impact of Women in Congress;* Susan J. Carroll, "Representing Women: Congresswomen's Perceptions of Their Representational Roles," in *Women Transforming Congress,* ed. Cindy Simon Rosenthal (Norman: University of Oklahoma Press, 2002), 50–68.

4. Michele Swers, "Are Congresswomen More Likely to Vote for Women's Issue Bills Than Their Male Colleagues?" *Legislative Studies Quarterly* 23, no. 3 (1998): 445.

5. Hanna Fenichel Pitkin, *The Concept of Representation* (Berkeley: University of California Press, 1967), 61.

6. Ibid., 118.

7. Ibid.

8. Diana Fuss, *Essentially Speaking* (New York: Routledge, 1989), 2.

9. Jane Mansbridge, "Should Blacks Represent Blacks and Women Represent Women? A Contingent 'Yes,'" *Journal of Politics* 61, no. 3 (1999): 628–57; Will Kymlicka, *Multicultural Citizenship: A Liberal Theory of Minority Rights* (New York: Oxford University Press, 1995); Anne Phillips, *The Politics of Presence* (Oxford: Oxford University Press, 1995).

10. Mansbridge, "Should Blacks Represent Blacks and Women Represent Women?" 650.

11. Karen Celis et al., "Rethinking Women's Substantive Representation," *Representation* 44, no. 2 (2008): 99.

12. Michael Saward, "The Representative Claim," *Contemporary Political Theory* 5 (2006): 298. Emphasis in original.

13. Ronnee Schreiber, *Righting Feminism: Conservative Women and American Politics* (New York: Oxford University Press, 2008); Shane Phelan, "(Be)Coming Out: Lesbian Identity and Politics," *Signs: Journal of Women in Culture and Society* 18, no. 4 (1993): 765–90; Fuss, *Essentially Speaking.*

14. Phelan, "(Be)Coming Out: Lesbian Identity and Politics."

15. Schreiber, *Righting Feminism.*

16. Ibid.

17. Ronnee Schreiber, "Conservative Women as Leaders of Organizations," in *Gender and Women's Leadership,* ed. Karen O'Connor (Newbury Park: Sage, 2010).

18. NFRW press release, November 24, 2008.

19. Michelle Bernard, "Sarah Palin: An Everywoman Qualified by What She's Done," *Townhall,* September 4, 2008, http://www.townhall.com.

20. Janice Shaw Crouse, "Sarah Palin Will Make History," Concerned Women for America, August 29, 2008, http://www.cwfa.org.

21. Charlotte Allen, "It Takes a Feminist," Independent Women's Voice, October 27, 2008, http://www.iwvoice.org.

22. Carrie Lukas, "Is Sarah Palin a Feminist?" Independent Women's Forum, September 26, 2008, http://www.iwf.org.

23. Michelle Bernard, "The Sarah Palin Effect: Shattering America's Political Glass Ceiling," Independent Women's Forum, November 10, 2008, http://www.iwf.org/news.

24. Janice Shaw Crouse, "Stop Bullying Sarah," Concerned Women for America, September 12, 2008, http://www.cwalac.org/articles.

25. Karin Agness, "Sarah Palin: A Liberated Woman," *Townhall,* September 7, 2008, http://www.townhall.com.

26. Lukas, "Is Sarah Palin a Feminist?"

27. Letter dated December 4, 2008.

28. Bernard, "The Sarah Palin Effect."

29. Letter dated December 4, 2008. Emphasis in original.

30. Linda Hirshman, "Homeward Bound," *American Prospect,* November 25, 2005, http://www.prospect.org.

31. Janice Shaw Crouse, "Bless Her Heart: Poor Sarah Palin," Concerned Women for America, October 1, 2008, http://www.cwfa.org.

32. Michelle Easton, "Sarah Palin, Multitasker," *Washington Times,* October 28, 2008, http://www.washingtontimes.com.

33. John P. Bartkowski, *Remaking the Godly Marriage: Gender Negotiation in Evangelical Families* (New Brunswick: Rutgers University Press, 2001); Sally Gallagher and Christian Smith, "Symbolic Traditionalism and Pragmatic Egalitarianism," *Gender and Society,* 13, no. 2 (1999): 211–33.

34. Schreiber, *Righting Feminism.*

35. Michelle Malkin, "Send a Message to Sarah Palin," *Michelle Malkin* (blog), November 6, 2008, http://michellemalkin.com.

36. See, for example, Kathleen Parker, "Palin Problem," *National Review,* September 26, 2008, http://article.nationalreview.com; Laura Schlessinger, "Sarah Palin and Motherhood," *The Dr. Laura Blog,* September 2, 2008, http://www.drlaurablog.com.

37. Mansbridge, "Should Blacks Represent Blacks and Women Represent Women?"

38. Mission statement, National Organization for Women, http://www.nowpacs.org.

39. Ibid. Emphasis added.

40. "Not Every Woman Supports Women's Rights," National Organization for Women, August 29, 2008, http://www.now.org.

41. Schreiber, *Righting Feminism.*

42. "Not Every Woman Supports Women's Rights."

43. For example, the last time NOW endorsed a candidate for president was when Democrat Walter Mondale ran in 1984 with Geraldine Ferraro as his running mate.

44. "Feminist Majority PAC Endorses Barack Obama," Feminist Majority, September 16, 2008, http://www.feministmajoritypac.org.

45. "Women's Groups Endorse Barack Obama Despite Sarah Palin Being on Republican Ticket," *Chicago Sun Times,* September 16, 2008.

46. "Business and Professional Women PAC Endorses Barack Obama for President. Points to Strong Support for Working Women and Their Families," Business and Professional Women's Foundation, September 8, 2008, http://www.bpwusa.org.

47. "The National Women's Political Caucus Will Not Endorse Governor Palin," National Women's Political Caucus of Washington, August 30, 2008, http://www.wpcnet.org.

48. "Our Original Call to Action," *Women Against Sarah Palin* (blog), September 6, 2008, http://www.womenagainstsarahpalin.blogspot.com.

49. Ibid.

50. "National Women's Political Caucus Will Not Endorse Governor Palin."

51. "Have Conservatives Discovered Sexism?" National Organization for Women, September 5, 2008, http://www.now.org.

52. Schreiber, *Righting Feminism*.

SELECTED BIBLIOGRAPHY

Bacchetta, Paola. *Gender in the Hindu Nation: RSS Women as Ideologues.* New Delhi: Women Unlimited, 2004.

Bacchetta, Paola, and Margaret Power, eds. *Right-Wing Women: From Conservatives to Extremists Around the World.* New York: Routledge, 2002.

Benowitz, June Melby. *Days of Discontent: American Women and Right-Wing Politics, 1933–1945.* DeKalb: Northern Illinois University Press, 2002.

Blee, Kathleen M. *Inside Organized Racism: Women in the Hate Movement.* Berkeley: University of California Press, 2002.

———, ed. *No Middle Ground: Women and Radical Protest.* New York: New York University Press, 1997.

———. *Women of the Klan: Racism and Gender in the 1920s.* Berkeley: University of California Press, 1991.

Critchlow, Donald T. *Phyllis Schlafly and Grassroots Conservatism: A Woman's Crusade.* Princeton: Princeton University Press, 2005.

de Grazia, Victoria. *How Fascism Ruled Women: Italy, 1922–1945.* Berkeley: University of California Press, 1992.

Deutsch, Sandra McGee. *Counterrevolution in Argentina, 1900–1932: The Argentine Patriotic League.* Lincoln: University of Nebraska Press, 1986.

———. *Las derechas: The Extreme Right in Argentina, Brazil, and Chile, 1890–1939.* Stanford: Stanford University Press, 1999.

Durham, Martin. *Women and Fascism.* London: Routledge, 1998.

Ferber, Abby L., ed. *Home-Grown Hate: Gender and Organized Racism.* New York: Routledge, 2004.

González, Victoria, and Karen Kampwirth, eds. *Radical Women in Latin America: Left and Right.* University Park: Pennsylvania State University Press, 2001.

Gottlieb, Julie V. *Feminine Fascism: Women in Britain's Fascist Movement, 1923–1945.* London: I. B. Tauris, 2000.

———, ed. "Right-Wing Women in Women's History: A Global Perspective." *Journal of Women's History* 16, no. 3 (2004): 106–86.

Herzog, Dagmar, ed. *Sexuality and German Fascism.* New York: Berghahn Books, 2005.

Jeansonne, Glen. *Women of the Far Right: The Mothers' Movement and World War II.* Chicago: University of Chicago Press, 1996.

Jetter, Alexis, Annelise Orleck, and Diana Taylor, eds. *The Politics of Motherhood: Activist Voices from Left to Right.* Hanover: University Press of New England, 1997.

Koonz, Claudia. *Mothers in the Fatherland: Women, the Family, and Nazi Politics.* New York: St. Martin's Press, 1987.

Marshall, Susan E. *Splintered Sisterhood: Gender and Class in the Campaign Against Woman Suffrage.* Madison: University of Wisconsin Press, 1997.

McGirr, Lisa. 2001. *Suburban Warriors: The Origins of the New American Right.* Princeton: Princeton University Press, 2001.

Mosse, George L. *Nationalism and Sexuality: Middle-Class Morality and Sexual Norms in Modern Europe.* Madison: University of Wisconsin Press, 1985.

Nickerson, Michelle. *Mothers of Conservatism: Women and the Postwar Right.* Princeton: Princeton University Press, 2011.

Nielsen, Kim E. *Un-American Womanhood: Antiradicalism, Antifeminism, and the First Red Scare.* Columbus: Ohio State University Press, 2001.

Ofer, Inbal. *Señoritas in Blue: The Making of a Female Political Elite in Franco's Spain; The National Leadership of the Sección Femenina de la Falange (1936–1977).* Sussex: Sussex Academic Press, 2009.

Passmore, Kevin, ed. *Women, Gender, and Fascism in Europe, 1919–1945.* New Brunswick: Rutgers University Press, 2003.

Power, Margaret. *Right-Wing Women in Chile: Feminine Power and the Struggle Against Allende, 1964–1973.* University Park: Pennsylvania State University Press, 2002.

Sarkar, Tanika, and Urvashi Butalia, eds. *Women and the Hindu Right: A Collection of Essays.* New Delhi: Kali for Women, 1995.

Schreiber, Ronnee. *Righting Feminism: Conservative Women and American Politics.* New York: Oxford University Press, 2008.

Vandana, Joshi. *Gender and Power in the Third Reich: Female Denouncers and the Gestapo, 1933–45.* New York: Palgrave Macmillan, 2003.

Nancy Aguirre received a Master of Arts degree in Latin American Studies from the University of Chicago in 2007. Currently, she is a doctoral candidate in the Borderlands History program at the University of Texas at El Paso. Her research interests center on Porfirista exiles and the interactions between culture and media.

Kathleen M. Blee is Distinguished Professor of Sociology at the University of Pittsburgh. Her books include *Democracy in the Making* (2012); *Inside Organized Racism: Women in the Hate Movement* (2002); *The Road to Poverty* (2000, with Dwight Billings); *Women of the Klan: Racism and Gender in the 1920s* (1991); and two edited volumes, *Feminism and Anti-Racism: International Struggles for Justice* (2001, with France Winddance Twine) and *No Middle Ground: Women and Radical Protest* (1998).

Karla J. Cunningham, Ph.D., is a political scientist with the Rand Corporation. She has a diverse policy-relevant background in academia, defense intelligence, law enforcement, and the nonprofit sector. She has published extensively on women and political change in Muslim countries, as well as on political violence and stability.

Kirsten Delegard is an independent historian and research consultant in Minneapolis. She is the author of *Battling Miss Bolshevik: The Origins of Female Conservatism in the United States* (2011), co-editor with Nancy Hewitt of *Women, Families, and Communities* (2008), and the visual editor for *North Country: The Making of Minnesota* (2010). She is currently working on projects illuminating the history of race and power in the northern borderlands of the United States.

Sandra McGee Deutsch is Professor of History at the University of Texas at El Paso. Her books include *Counterrevolution in Argentina, 1900–1932: The Argentine Patriotic League* (1986); *The Argentine Right* (1993, co-edited with Ronald H. Dolkart); *Las derechas: The Extreme Right in Argentina, Brazil, and Chile, 1890–1939* (1999); and *Crossing Borders, Claiming a Nation: A History of*

Argentine Jewish Women, 1880–1955 (2010). Currently, she is working on Argentine antifascist women.

Kathleen M. Fallon is Associate Professor of Sociology at McGill University. Her interests lie in political sociology, international development, and gender studies. Specifically, she focuses on women's social movements, women's political rights, and democracy within sub-Saharan Africa, as well as other developing countries. She has done field research in Ghana, examining how democratization influenced women's rights and the emergence of the women's movement. Additionally, through comparative analyses and using qualitative and quantitative methods, she has explored how types of democratic transitions influence women's political representation.

Kate Hallgren is earning her Ph.D. at the Graduate Center, City University of New York. Her dissertation, "Mothers Raise the Army: Women's Activism, Popular Culture, and the Legacy of America's Great War, 1914–1941," discusses the roots of patriotic motherhood, its uses by diverse groups of women, and its impact on the politics of the interwar years.

Randolph Hollingsworth, Ph.D., researches the history of women in the southern United States and conservative ideology, often peering through a lens of feminist critical theory. With the advent of social technologies and in her role as Assistant Provost at the University of Kentucky, Hollingsworth is an emerging ethnohistorian interested in open knowledge initiatives.

Jill A. Irvine is Presidential Professor and Director of Women's and Gender Studies at the University of Oklahoma. She is the author of *The Croat Question: Partisan Politics in the Formation of the Yugoslav Socialist State* (1993) and co-editor of *State-Society Relations in Yugoslavia, 1945–1992* (1997) and *Natalija: Life in the Balkan Powder Keg, 1880–1956* (2008). She has written numerous articles, book chapters, and government reports about gender, war, and democratic transformations in the Balkans.

Vandana Joshi obtained her doctorate from Technical University, Berlin, in 2003. She is the author of *Gender and Power in the Third Reich: Female Denouncers and the Gestapo, 1933–45* (2003), which won her a Fraenkel Prize in Contemporary History, and is currently editing a multivolume series, Themes in Modern European History, 1789–1945. She teaches in Sri Vekateswara College, University of Delhi. Her areas of interest are comparative histories of war, genocide, gender, and sexuality.

Carol S. Lilly is Professor of History and Director of International Studies at the University of Nebraska–Kearney. Dr. Lilly received her Ph.D. from Yale University. She is the author of *Power and Persuasion: Ideology and Rhetoric in*

Communist Yugoslavia, 1945–1952 (2001) and co-author of *Natalija: Life in the Balkan Powder Keg, 1880–1956* (2008). She has also published several articles and book chapters on topics related to women's roles in the former Yugoslavia.

Annette Linden is a social psychologist and holds a Ph.D. in social sciences. Her dissertation (2009) is based on the systematic analysis of life course interviews that she held between 1996 and 2000 with activists of the extreme right in the Netherlands. The Ph.D. research project has produced a comprehensive grasp of processes and motives for long-term active involvement in an extreme right-wing movement.

Julie Moreau is a Ph.D. candidate in political science at McGill University. Her research interests include sexual citizenship, feminism, social movements, and democratization in Latin America and Africa. She is currently completing her fieldwork with LGBT organizations in Argentina, Uruguay, and South Africa.

Margaret Power is Professor of Latin American History at the Illinois Institute of Technology. She is the author of *Right-Wing Women in Chile: Feminine Power and the Struggle Against Allende, 1964–1973* (2002) and co-editor of *Right-Wing Women: From Conservatives to Extremists Around the World* (2002) and *New Perspectives on the Transnational Right* (2010). Her current research examines the anticolonial Nationalist Party of Puerto Rico from the 1920s to the 1950s.

Mariela Rubinzal is completing her doctorate at the Universidad Nacional de La Plata, Argentina. She has published several articles in Argentina and abroad on her main research topic: right-wing nationalism and the "social question" in the interwar period in Argentina. She has also researched and published on topics related to the study of memory and the recent past, and she participates in research groups focused on the world of work.

Daniella Sarnoff is a program director at the Social Science Research Council and an independent historian. Sarnoff has taught at Xavier University, Fordham University, and New York University and published on women, gender, and French fascism in the interwar years.

Ronnee Schreiber is Associate Professor of Political Science at San Diego State University. Her research interests are in the area of women and American political institutions. In 2008 Schreiber published *Righting Feminism: Conservative Women and American Politics* with Oxford University Press. Her other publications have appeared in *Political Communication, Journal of Urban Affairs, Sex Roles, Politics and Gender,* and several edited volumes. Her new research examines conservative women and the political construction of motherhood.

Meera Sehgal teaches sociology and women's and gender studies at Carleton College. Her research interests are in the areas of social movements, gender, globalization, militarism, transnational feminisms, and India. Based on ethnographic methods, her research examines the mobilization of women in the right-wing Hindu nationalist movement in India. Her more recent research focuses on a South Asian transnational feminist network and its consciousness-raising work in India, Pakistan, Nepal, Bangladesh, and Sri Lanka.

Louise Vincent is Associate Professor in the Department of Political and International Studies at Rhodes University. Her research deals with the politics of the body, by which she means ways in which social and political power relations can be understood to be written on the bodies of citizens. For the past five years, this interest has expressed itself in a variety of projects in which she attempts to read South Africa's democratic transition through a corporeal lens.

Veronica A. Wilson received her Ph.D. in U.S. and women's history from Rutgers University (2002). She is Associate Professor of History at the University of Pittsburgh at Johnstown, where she teaches courses on twentieth-century U.S. political, social, and gender history. She has published several articles on Cold War spies, political radicals, and FBI informants and is preparing book manuscripts about the gendered nature of Cold War espionage scandals and women radicals in the Great Plains.